The Millennium Cookbook

The future shines with

Beta Sigma Phi

EDITORIAL STAFF

Managing Editor	Mary Cummings
Executive Editor	Anita McKay
Editorial Manager	Georgia Brazil
Editor	Jan Keeling
Associate Editors	Kelly Cunningham, Ginger Dawson Elizabeth Miller, Mary Wilson
Typographers	Jessie Anglin, Sara Anglin
Project Coordinator	Tanis Westbrook
Award Selection Judge	Charlene Sproles
Art Director	Steve Newman
Illustrator	Barbara Ball
Test Kitchen	Charlene Sproles
Essayist	Mary Buckner

© Favorite Recipes® Press, A Division of Heritage House, Inc. 2000
  P.O. Box 305141, Nashville, Tennessee 37230

ISBN: 0-87197-484-3

Manufactured in the United States of America
First Printing 2000

Recipe for Cover photograph is on page 188.

Contents

Marilyn and Bill Ross

Dear Friends in Beta Sigma Phi,

We have had the privilege of enjoying home cooking from Saint John's, Newfoundland, to San Diego, California. From Whitehorse, Yukon Territory, to Ocala, Florida. From Johnson County, Kansas, to Perth, Australia. And there is one truth that you should accept, and that is the best cooks in all the world are you Beta Sigma Phi cooks. This selection of your recipes is testimony to that truth.

This year we were at a Louisiana convention in Lafayette, chaired by Gail Domingue, and it was a very good one. Rose DeRouen, Linda Trahan, and Paulette Counce invited us for dinner after the convention. Rose fixed broccoli for me Cajun-style (page 172), and she has a picture of *me* (Bill Ross) enjoying broccoli. I must confess to you that it was absolutely delicious. You can understand that I am only supposed to eat the maximum of 1200 calories a day and as little fat and sugar as possible. Down there on the Bayou, I used up a year's supply in that dish of broccoli. Was it worth it? You bet!

Please join us in dedicating this cookbook to you who have made hospitality an art form. This is the first book of your new millennium, and I hope it is the best one.

The first cookbook was published in your silver anniversary year. It was a success, and each succeeding book has been a success. Whenever we think of your cookbooks, we think of the contributions they have made to all of the great service projects that you enjoy. We think how they have helped little boys and girls to a better life. How they have served every age group and every aspect of Beta Sigma Phi life. They have helped make every event, and every moment, better.

With every good wish to each and every one of you for the best that life can give, we remain

Gratefully, your friends,

Marilyn & Bill

Marilyn and Bill Ross

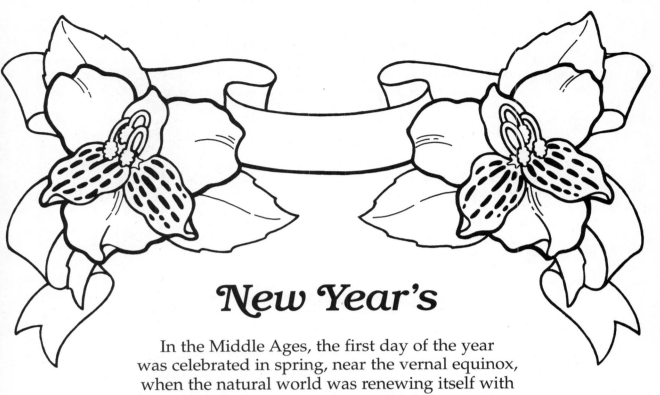

New Year's

In the Middle Ages, the first day of the year
was celebrated in spring, near the vernal equinox,
when the natural world was renewing itself with
flowers and green shoots. Europeans called it
Annunciation Day and held a religious feast
honoring the angel's first visit to the Virgin Mary.
Since that time, popes, kings, and legislators
have made changes in our calendar, so now we
celebrate New Year's Day in the middle of winter.
For us, this holiday means good food, toasting, and
personal resolutions. It's a time for fresh starts and
futuristic thinking. This first chapter of
The Millennium Cookbook holds a treasury of fresh
new recipes to start your year off with flair.

DIRTY SANTA GAME

*T*his game will be loads of fun as well as a way to handle those gifts that just don't have a place in your life. The gifts should be rewrapped, and the group composed of good friends who like to have fun. Your Beta Sigma Phi chapter, bridge club, or other group can play as individuals or couples.

For individual play, write numbers on small pieces of paper that can be placed in a bowl for easy drawing. If bridge club partners are playing the game, start with the couple who has the lowest score and progress to the highest.

The person or couple to choose the first gift gets to open it for all to see. The next person has the choice of selecting an unopened gift or taking the gift that has just been unwrapped. By the time the evening is over, the highest scoring couple or the person with the highest number has the choice of all the gifts. Items may be taken from the same person several times or the same item may travel from person to person. This is a great way to dispose of unwanted gifts and increase the possibility that the gifts will find welcome homes.

Judith A. Goodyear
McAlester, Oklahoma

SPECTACULAR ICE BOWLS

*T*hese easy-to-make creations will be fabulous additions to any buffet table. Use them as centerpieces, serving bowls, or wherever your imagination leads. Mound boiled shrimp in an ice bowl decorated with dill sprigs and add cocktail sauce in a smaller ice bowl decorated with lime slices, or a flowered ice bowl for scoops of ice cream or sherbet.

Select two glass or stainless bowls that can nest with a space between of 1/2 to 1 inch. Place the smaller bowl inside the larger and tape securely with the tops flush. Insert flowers, herb sprigs, fruit slices, or other decorative material between the bowls; use long skewers to help move things around if necessary.

Add the water carefully to avoid disarranging the decorations; the water should fill the space between the bowls to about 1/2 inch from the top. Place in the freezer for at least 24 hours.

Let the bowls stand at room temperature for 10 to 20 minutes or until the bowls separate easily and the ice bowl can be inverted onto a tray. Return to the freezer until just before serving time, turn the bowl right side up, fill, and accept the compliments.

Jill Sellers, Beta Beta Chi
Cedar Hill, Texas

NUMBER THE BALLS

*M*ake your New Year's buffet combine refreshments and decorations. Select four of your favorite cheese ball recipes. I like to use one that is fruit-flavored, one that is a meat, another that is seafood, and the fourth, vegetable-flavored. Shape each into one of the numerals of the New Year; try to make each numeral about 6 inches tall. Arrange the numerals on a large tray and mound assorted crackers and vegetable and fruit dippers around the cheese balls. Make the cheese balls in advance and refrigerate until just before arranging on the serving tray.

Dorothy Malo, Laureate Phi
San Diego, California

MEMORIES

*Y*our family, Beta Sigma Phi chapter, neighborhood, or other close groups can relive those precious good times any time of the year, but New Year's is especially appropriate. When inviting participants, ask them to bring photos taken during activities of the previous year. Place the photos in a large bowl. Provide a large piece of poster board with the date at the top. Have each guest draw a photo, affix it to the poster board, and add a short narrative memory as a caption. After enjoying the memories, be sure to put the board away carefully so that it can be displayed in succeeding years. These "living history" boards will become a priceless tradition.

Karen Moss, Alpha Kappa Nu
Ft. Worth, Texas

HOLIDAY CREAM CHEESE LOG

Form the cheese log on an attractive serving plate before covering it with the nut coating and you'll be able to serve it right out of the refrigerator.

**8 ounces cream cheese,
    softened**
**1 teaspoon garlic salt,
    or 1 garlic clove,
    minced**
**1/4 cup (1/2 stick) butter,
    melted**

**1/3 cup packed brown
    sugar**
**9 or 10 drops of
    Worcestershire sauce**
**1/4 to 1/2 cup chopped
    almonds or pecans**

Beat the cream cheese and garlic salt in a bowl until blended. Shape the cream cheese mixture into a log on a plate. Mix the butter, brown sugar, Worcestershire sauce and chopped nuts in a bowl. Pour the butter mixture evenly over the cream cheese log. Chill, covered, for at least 1 hour, until ready to serve. Serve with crackers. Yield: 8 servings.

Edna Weber, Preceptor Beta Beta
Kelowna, British Columbia, Canada

ZESTY BEEF CHEESE BALL

1 (2-ounce) jar extra-
  lean dried beef
1 (3-ounce) can sliced
  mushrooms
1 bunch green onions,
  cut in 2-inch pieces
24 ounces cream cheese,
  softened
1 (4-ounce) can chopped
  black olives
1/2 teaspoon salt
1/2 teaspoon cayenne
  pepper
1/2 teaspoon MSG
1 cup chopped pecans or
  walnuts

Combine the beef, mushrooms and green onions in a food processor container fitted with a steel blade; process until finely chopped. Beat the cream cheese in a mixing bowl until light and fluffy. Add the beef mixture and olives to the cream cheese and mix well. Stir in the salt, cayenne pepper and MSG and mix well. Shape into a large ball or two smaller balls. Roll in chopped nuts until all sides of ball are covered. Chill, covered, until ready to serve. Serve with crackers. Yield: 24 servings.

Rochelle Judice, Xi Beta Omega
New Iberia, Louisiana

FETA AND GARLIC PATÉ

This paté makes a terrific sandwich spread and is wonderful on crackers, bread, bagels, or pita crisps. To make pita crisps, split pita breads in half, brush with flavored oil, and sprinkle with salt. Stack pitas and cut into quarters. Arrange in a single layer on a baking sheet. Bake at 400 degrees for 10 minutes.

2 garlic cloves
4 anchovy fillets, or 1
  teaspoon anchovy
  paste
1/4 cup (1/2 stick) butter,
  softened
8 ounces cream cheese,
  softened
6 ounces feta cheese
1/4 cup sour cream
1 tablespoon chopped
  fresh chives or green
  onions
Dash of Tabasco sauce
Pinch of freshly ground
  pepper

Finely chop the garlic cloves and anchovy fillets in a food processor by pulsing 4 or 5 times. Add the butter, cream cheese, feta cheese, sour cream, chives, Tabasco and pepper; process until smooth and creamy. Yield: 2 cups.

Rita Irwin, Theta Psi
Uxbridge, Ontario, Canada

Shelly Madrid, Beta Epsilon, Roswell, New Mexico, makes Confetti Vegetable Dip a day before serving by mixing 16 ounces cream cheese, 1 cup sour cream, a jar of bacon bits, small cans of chopped black olives and chopped green chiles, chopped bell pepper and red onion, and 2 tablespoons lemon juice.

TUNA PATÉ

16 ounces cream cheese,
  softened
2 (6-ounce) cans flaked
  tuna
1/4 cup mayonnaise
1/4 cup finely chopped
  onion
1/4 cup finely chopped
  celery
Salt and pepper to taste
1 cup shredded Cheddar
  cheese

Combine the cream cheese, tuna and mayonnaise in a food processor container and process until smooth. Add the onion, celery, salt and pepper and pulse 5 or 6 times until blended. Wrap in plastic wrap and chill until serving time. Roll in Cheddar cheese and serve with crackers. Yield: 16 to 20 servings.

Judy Burkett, Xi Alpha Omicron
Nacogdoches, Texas

ARTICHOKE DIP

Artichoke Dip is especially appealing when served in a quiche dish, and it makes a great accompaniment for other finger foods.

2 (14-ounce) cans
  artichoke hearts (not
  marinated), drained,
  chopped
2 (4-ounce) cans
  chopped green chiles,
  drained
2 cups Hellman's
  mayonnaise
2 cups freshly grated
  Parmesan cheese
1 (2-ounce) jar pimentos
1 cup shredded
  Monterey Jack cheese
Cayenne pepper or
  paprika
Tortilla chips

Combine the artichokes, chiles, mayonnaise, Parmesan cheese and pimentos in a large bowl and mix well. Spoon the artichoke mixture into a 9-inch round baking dish. Sprinkle with the Monterey Jack cheese and cayenne pepper. Bake at 350 degrees for 30 minutes or until bubbly and edges are light brown. Serve with tortilla chips.
Yield: 10 to 12 servings.

Anita Foster, Xi Kappa Omega
Pickerington, Ohio

Beer Dip is a specialty of Melodie Huffman, Vincinnes, Indiana. She combines 16 ounces softened cream cheese and a 1-ounce envelope of ranch dressing mix, blends well, then stirs in 2 cups shredded Cheddar cheese and 1/3 cup of an extra-stout beer. She suggests St. James Gate Dullin. The mixture will be mushy after mixing but just right after refrigerating, covered, overnight. Serve with pretzels for dipping.

TACO BEAN DIP

Serve this awesome bean dip with tortilla chips or corn chip scoops. The recipe serves a whole party, and the dip warms up beautifully the following day.

1 pound lean ground beef	**8 ounces cream cheese, softened**
1 envelope taco seasoning mix	**1 (8-ounce) jar picante sauce**
1 (16-ounce) can refried beans	**Hot red pepper sauce to taste**
1 (10-ounce) can tomatoes with green chiles	**Dash of garlic salt**
	Dash of Nature's Seasoning
1 (32-ounce) brick Velveeta cheese, cubed	

Brown the ground beef in a skillet according to directions on envelope of taco seasoning. Combine the ground beef mixture, refried beans, tomatoes with green chiles, Velveeta cheese, cream cheese, picante sauce, hot red pepper sauce, garlic salt and Nature's Seasoning in a deep saucepan over low to medium heat. Cook until cheese is melted, stirring occasionally. Serve with chips. Yield: 40 servings.

Tonja Harrison, Rho
St. John, Kansas

CONFETTI DIP

Confetti Dip tastes great the day after it is made. It also works well when made with roasted garlic mayonnaise.

8 cups shredded Cheddar cheese	**2 or 3 small fresh jalapeños, chopped**
1 (11-ounce) can white shoepeg corn, drained	**1 red bell pepper, chopped**
1 bunch green onions, chopped	**1/2 cup mayonnaise**

Combine the cheese, shoepeg corn, green onions, jalapeños and bell pepper in a large bowl and mix well. Stir in the mayonnaise. Chill, covered, until serving time. Serve with corn chip scoops. Yield: 4 cups.

Natalie Dominguez, Xi Beta Theta
Tucumcari, New Mexico

Mildred Sharp, Kappa Master, McClave, Colorado, makes Cocktail Barbecued Hot Dogs by cutting all-beef hot dogs in 1 1/2-inch pieces, combining with 1 cup each rum, ketchup, and brown sugar in a slow cooker, and cooking on Low for 2 hours.

CHILE CORN DIP

2 cups shredded Cheddar cheese	**1 (4-ounce) can chopped green chiles**
1 cup mayonnaise	**3 to 4 green onions, chopped**
1/2 cup sour cream	
1 (11-ounce) can shoepeg corn, drained	

Combine the cheese, mayonnaise, sour cream, shoepeg corn, green chiles and green onions in a large bowl and mix well. Chill, covered, for at least 2 hours before serving. Serve with crackers or sturdy chips. Yield: 3 cups.

Mary S. Wartelle, Xi Phi Iota
Apple Valley, California

CRAB MEAT DIP

3 ounces cream cheese, softened	**Salt and pepper to taste**
1/2 cup mayonnaise	**6 drops of Tabasco sauce**
2/3 (10-ounce) can tomato soup	**2 teaspoons sugar**
	2 (4-ounce) cans crab meat, drained, flaked
1 garlic clove, minced	

Combine the cream cheese and mayonnaise in a medium bowl and mix well. Stir in the soup. Add the garlic, salt, pepper, Tabasco and sugar and mix well. Fold in the crab meat. Chill, covered, for at least 2 hours until serving time. Serve with chips, crackers or vegetable sticks. Yield: 3 cups.

Virginia Fast, Kappa Master
Knoxville, Iowa

CRAB ARTICHOKE DIP

This dip is especially tasty when served with white Zinfandel.

1 (8-ounce) package imitation crab meat, chopped	**1 cup mayonnaise**
	1/4 cup finely chopped onion
1 (14-ounce) can artichoke hearts, drained, chopped	**8 ounces low-fat cream cheese, softened**
3/4 cup shredded mozzarella cheese	**Fresh bagels, chopped into bite-size pieces**

Combine the crab meat, artichoke hearts, mozzarella cheese and mayonnaise in a medium bowl and mix well. Stir in the onion and cream cheese. Place in a 9-inch pie plate or baking dish and bake at 350 degrees for 18 to 20 minutes or until hot and bubbly. Serve warm with the bagel pieces. Yield: 4 cups.

Holly Crowell, Zeta Kappa
Red Oak, Iowa

PESTO FETA DIP

This very garlicky dip was featured at our first meeting this year, and was enjoyed so much that everyone received the recipe.

1 garlic bulb
1 large garlic clove
5 ounces feta cheese
6 large leaves fresh basil
1 tablespoon lemon
   juice
2 tablespoons extra-
   virgin olive oil
¼ cup pine nuts
   (optional)

Remove the papery skin from the garlic bulb and bake, uncovered, at 350 degrees in a small baking dish for 1 hour. Let cool. Remove any residual skin. Combine the baked garlic, raw garlic clove, feta cheese and basil in a food processor container and process until smooth. Add the lemon juice and olive oil and process for 1 minute longer. Add the pine nuts and process until blended but pine nut pieces remain. Serve with crackers or pita bread. Yield: 1 cup.

Ellen Drudge, Theta Psi
Uxbridge, Ontario, Canada

PEPPERONI PLEASER

How many recipes can be said to have won a "Whose Wife Is the Best Cook Award"? This one can!

2 cups shredded
   mozzarella cheese
2 cups shredded Cheddar
   cheese
1½ cups mayonnaise
1 (4-ounce) can chopped
   green chiles, drained
1 medium onion,
   chopped
1½ ounces sliced
   pepperoni
1 (4-ounce) can sliced
   black olives, drained

Combine the mozzarella cheese, Cheddar cheese, mayonnaise, green chiles and onion in a bowl and mix well. Turn the cheese mixture into a shallow baking dish or pie plate. Arrange the pepperoni slices and olives over the top. Bake, uncovered, at 325 degrees for 25 minutes or until steaming hot and pepperoni is desired crispness. Serve with rye chips or crackers. Yield: 16 servings.

Julie Bisbee, Iota Theta
Pella, Iowa

Joan Diane Pringle, Preceptor Epsilon Theta, Pinellas Park, Florida, makes a Liverwurst Spread for crackers or tea sandwiches by mixing a pound of liverwurst, ¼ cup pickle relish, 1 tablespoon mustard, and ¼ cup mayonnaise in a food processor.

PIZZA DIP

The attractive layered appetizer looks like a pizza.

8 ounces cream cheese,
   softened
1 (8-ounce) jar Crosse
   and Blackwell
   cocktail sauce
2 large onions, chopped
2 large green bell
   peppers, chopped
1 tomato, peeled,
   chopped
1 (4-ounce) can chopped
   black olives, drained
2 (3-ounce) cans
   chopped mushrooms,
   drained
3 cups shredded
   mozzarella cheese

Spread the cream cheese evenly over a 10-inch flat plate. Layer the cocktail sauce, onions, bell peppers, tomato, olives, mushrooms and mozzarella cheese over the cream cheese. Use crackers to scoop from the edges of the dip, or spread the dip on the crackers. Yield: 12 to 16 servings.

Ruthie Fortune, Laureate Delta Omicron
Pace, Florida

SALSA REUBEN DIP

8 ounces cream cheese,
   softened
1 cup sour cream
1 cup thick and chunky
   salsa
4 ounces corned beef,
   finely chopped
3 ounces Swiss cheese,
   shredded
½ cup sauerkraut,
   drained, squeezed dry
1 to 2 garlic cloves,
   minced
Salt and pepper to taste
Fresh cilantro, chopped

Combine the cream cheese, sour cream and salsa in a large mixing bowl and beat at low speed until well blended. Add the corned beef, Swiss cheese, sauerkraut, garlic, salt and pepper and mix well. Spoon the cream cheese mixture into a greased 9- to 10-inch pie pan or quiche dish. Bake at 350 degrees for 20 to 30 minutes or until bubbly and heated through. Sprinkle with the cilantro for the last few minutes of baking time. Serve with party rye bread, tortilla chips or fresh vegetables for dipping. Yield: 3 cups.

Jan Irwin, Preceptor Delta Alpha
Cherokee, Iowa

Rita Korbal, Xi Alpha Lambda, Sioux Falls, South Dakota, combines 8 ounces cream cheese, 1 cup sour cream, 1½ cups shredded mozzarella cheese, a package of corned beef (chopped), and a 14-ounce can of sauerkraut in a slow cooker, cooking for 2 to 3 hours. Serve Hot Reuben Dip on rye bread or crackers.

REUBEN DIP

2 (12-ounce) packages
   corned beef, chopped
2 cups shredded Swiss
   cheese
1 (14-ounce) can
   sauerkraut, drained
1 cup mayonnaise
1 teaspoon dry mustard
Loaves of party rye
   bread

Combine the corned beef, cheese, sauerkraut, mayonnaise and mustard in a large bowl and mix well. Turn the mixture into a 2-quart baking dish. Bake, uncovered, at 350 degrees for 30 minutes or until hot and bubbly. Serve with bread slices for dipping. Yield: 20 to 25 servings.

Molly A. Patterson, Preceptor Beta Xi
Seminole, Oklahoma

SHRIMP DIP

Shrimp Dip tastes even better when made a day ahead so flavors may marry.

8 ounces cream cheese,
   softened
1 cup sour cream
2 envelopes Italian
   salad dressing mix
2 (4-ounce) cans tiny
   shrimp, drained
2 teaspoons lemon juice
1 large green bell pepper,
   finely chopped

Place the cream cheese in a medium bowl. Beat in the sour cream slowly until blended. Add the dressing mix, shrimp, lemon juice and bell pepper and mix well. Chill, covered, until serving time. Serve with chips or crackers. Yield: 3 cups.

Tiffany Stirling
Pinedale, Arizona

ARTICHOKE BALLS

1 (14-ounce) can
   artichoke hearts,
   rinsed, drained
1 cup seasoned dry
   bread crumbs
2 tablespoons lemon
   juice
2 eggs, beaten
4 garlic cloves, crushed
4 to 5 tablespoons
   grated Parmesan
   cheese

Mash the artichoke hearts in a medium bowl with a fork. Add the bread crumbs, lemon juice, eggs, garlic and 2 tablespoons of the cheese and mix well. Chill, covered, for at least 4 hours. Preheat the oven to 400 degrees. Shape the artichoke mixture into small balls and roll in the remaining 2 to 3 tablespoons cheese. Arrange on a baking sheet and bake for 10 minutes or until light golden brown. Yield: 6 to 8 servings.

Shannon Simmons, Alpha Rho Epsilon
Sugar Land, Texas

OLIVE BALLS

1 cup shredded Cheddar
   cheese
1/4 cup (1/2 stick) butter
   or margarine,
   softened
1/4 teaspoon
   Worcestershire sauce
1 cup baking mix
1 (5-ounce) jar pimento-
   stuffed olives,
   drained

Preheat the oven to 400 degrees. Combine the cheese, butter and Worcestershire sauce in a medium bowl and mix well. Add the baking mix, stirring until a soft dough forms (use hands if necessary). Pat the olives dry with paper towels. Enclose each olive in 1 teaspoon of dough. Arrange about 1 inch apart on an ungreased baking sheet. Bake for 10 minutes or until golden. Yield: 40 pieces.

Beth Johnson, Lambda Upsilon
Pleasant Hill, Missouri

CHEESY GRAPES

This appetizer is sensational when served with apples, pears, crackers, and champagne.

8 ounces cream cheese,
   softened
2 to 3 teaspoons bleu
   cheese
1 tablespoon milk
1 pound seedless red or
   green grapes
1 1/4 cups coarsely
   chopped pecans or
   walnuts

Combine the cream cheese, bleu cheese and milk in a medium bowl and beat until smooth. Rinse the grapes and pat dry. Add the grapes to the cheese mixture, stirring gently by hand until coated. Roll the coated grapes in the nuts. Arrange on a waxed-paper-lined plate or tray. Chill, covered, until serving time. Yield: 24 to 30 servings.

Marsha Swanson, Xi Eta Pi
West Bend, Iowa

MARINATED MUSHROOMS

1 pound nickel- to
   quarter-size
   mushrooms, cleaned
3/4 cup vegetable oil
1/3 cup red wine vinegar
2 tablespoons lemon
   juice
3 teaspoons chopped
   chives
1 teaspoon tarragon
1 teaspoon salt
1/2 teaspoon sugar
1 small garlic clove,
   minced or pressed

Combine the ingredients in a medium bowl. Chill, covered, for several hours; stir occasionally. Drain. Serve with toothpicks. Yield: 8 to 16 servings.

Alta K. Anderson, Laureate Beta Phi
Seattle, Washington

MEXICAN DEVILED EGGS

Serve these man-pleasing deviled eggs with barbecue, cold tins, or just about any meal.

8 hard-cooked eggs
1/2 cup shredded Cheddar cheese
1/4 cup mayonnaise
1/4 cup salsa
2 tablespoons chopped green onions
1 tablespoon sour cream
Salt to taste

Halve the eggs lengthwise; remove the yolks to a small bowl and arrange the whites, hollow side up, on a plate. Add the cheese, mayonnaise, salsa, green onions, sour cream and salt to the yolks and mash well. Fill the whites evenly with the yolk mixture. Serve immediately or chill until ready to serve. Yield: 16 servings.

Geraldine Maxwell, Laureate Delta Tau
Amarillo, Texas

RAMAKI

1 pound sliced bacon
2 (8-ounce) cans whole water chestnuts, drained
1/4 cup sugar
12 ounces ketchup
1/2 cup packed brown sugar

Cut the bacon slices crosswise in thirds. Roll the water chestnuts in sugar to coat. Wrap a bacon strip around each water chestnut and secure with a toothpick. Arrange in a shallow baking pan. Bake at 350 degrees for 20 minutes or until bacon is crisp. Pour off some of the drippings. Mix the ketchup and brown sugar in a small bowl. Pour the ketchup mixture evenly over the wrapped water chestnuts and bake for 15 minutes longer. Yield: 10 to 20 servings.

Carleen Fry, Alpha Tau
Columbus, Indiana

BEEF AND BACON ROLL-UPS

My husband's boss said he would give him a raise if he prepared this again for one of our parties!

1 pound sliced bacon, halved lengthwise
2 pounds smoked cocktail franks
1 pound light brown sugar

Wrap a half slice of bacon around each cocktail frank and secure with a toothpick. Layer the wrapped franks and brown sugar 1/2 at a time in a slow cooker. Cook on Low for 3 to 4 hours, stirring occasionally. Yield: 30 to 40 servings.

Linda McConnell, Preceptor Iota Sigma
Carrollton, Texas

SWEET-AND-SOUR MEATBALLS

2 pounds lean ground beef
1/3 cup parsley flakes
2 tablespoons soy sauce
1/2 teaspoon garlic powder
2 eggs
1 1/4 teaspoons pepper
1/3 cup ketchup
2 teaspoons onion salt
1 cup dry rolled oats
1 tablespoon lemon juice
1 (16-ounce) can jellied cranberry sauce
1 (12-ounce) bottle chili sauce
2 tablespoons brown sugar

Combine the ground beef, parsley flakes, soy sauce, garlic powder, eggs, pepper, ketchup, onion salt and rolled oats in a large bowl and mix well. Shape into 1-inch balls. Arrange in a single layer on baking sheets. Bake at 350 degrees for 20 to 30 minutes or until cooked through. Combine the lemon juice, cranberry sauce, chili sauce and brown sugar in a large saucepan. Cook over medium heat until heated through, stirring occasionally. Stir in the meatballs. Simmer for at least 1/2 hour and up to 2 hours. Yield: 40 servings.

Barb Roberts, Preceptor Alpha
Astoria, Oregon

SWEET-AND-SOUR SWEDISH MEATBALLS

5 slices firm white bread
2/3 cup milk
3 pounds lean ground beef
1 envelope dry onion soup mix
3/4 teaspoon pepper
2 eggs
1/2 teaspoon oregano
1 (15-ounce) can sliced pineapple, drained, 1/4 cup juice reserved
3/4 cup sweet pickles, drained, sliced, 1/4 cup juice reserved
1/2 cup vinegar
2/3 cup sugar
2 level tablespoons cornstarch
2/3 teaspoon ground cloves
1/2 teaspoon salt
1 (4-ounce) jar pimentos, drained

Crumble the bread into a large bowl and stir in the milk to moisten. Add the ground beef, soup mix, pepper, eggs and oregano and mix well. Shape into 1/2-inch balls. Arrange in a large baking pan. Bake at 400 degrees for 20 to 25 minutes or until cooked through. Combine the reserved pineapple juice, reserved pickle juice, vinegar, sugar, cornstarch, cloves and salt in a medium saucepan over low heat. Cook for 3 minutes or until thickened, stirring constantly. Stir in the pineapple, pickles and pimentos. Pour the pineapple sauce over the cooked meatballs and serve hot. Yield: 90 to 100 meatballs.

Jayne A. Hornsby, Xi Alpha Xi
Hueytown, Alabama

SWEET-AND-SOUR CHICKEN WINGS

3 pounds chicken wings
1 teaspoon salt
Vegetable oil for deep-
frying
1 cup cornstarch
6 eggs, beaten
1/4 cup soy sauce
1/2 cup vinegar
3 tablespoons ketchup
1/2 cup sugar
1/2 cup red currant jelly
2 tablespoons lemon
juice
1/2 teaspoon salt

Disjoint the wings and discard the tips. Rinse and pat dry. Sprinkle with the 1 teaspoon salt. Heat the oil to 375 degrees. Roll the wing pieces in cornstarch to coat; dip in eggs. Deep-fry for 3 to 4 minutes or until golden. Drain on a paper towel. Arrange in a shallow baking dish. Combine the soy sauce, vinegar, ketchup, sugar, currant jelly, lemon juice and the 1/2 teaspoon salt in a saucepan over medium-high heat. Bring to a boil, stirring constantly. Reduce heat and simmer for 10 minutes. Pour the sauce over the chicken. Bake at 350 degrees for 30 minutes or until hot and bubbly. Yield: 20 to 30 servings.

Susan Calcutt, Mu Zeta
Tillsonburg, Ontario, Canada

BROILED MUSSELS AND CLAMS

2 dozen mussels, cleaned
2 dozen littleneck clams,
cleaned
3 tablespoons finely
chopped flat parsley
1 teaspoon finely
chopped garlic
1/3 cup olive oil
1/2 cup unflavored bread
crumbs
1 very ripe fresh plum
tomato, cut into
strips (may
substitute canned)

Place the mussels and clams in separate covered kettles over high heat. Heat until they open. Remove from heat. Detach mussels and clams from shells and rinse with own juice to remove all traces of sand. Mix the parsley, garlic, olive oil and bread crumbs in a large bowl. Let stand for 20 minutes. Wash the mussel and clam shells and arrange in a shallow baking dish. Preheat the broiler for 5 minutes. Fill each shell with the correct mollusk and top with a tomato strip. Broil for 3 to 5 minutes or until lightly browned. Serve with lemon wedges. Yield: 20 to 30 servings.

Margaret Colognesi, Gamma Nu
Sturbridge, Massachusetts

Ann Ramroth, Laureate Gamma Nu, Winter Park, Florida, beats 1 egg with 1 1/2 sticks softened butter and a 6-ounce jar Old English cheese spread, spreads on bread slices, cuts each slice into 4 sticks and bakes at 350 degrees for 10 minutes. Serve these Hot Cheese Sticks as an appetizer or with Italian dishes.

❖ SEAFOOD NACHOS

1 tablespoon butter
1 pound shrimp, cooked,
peeled, deveined
1/2 pound cooked crab
meat, flaked
1/2 pound cooked
whitefish (cod),
flaked
1 (14-ounce) bag tortilla
chips
1 (15-ounce) jar nacho
cheese sauce
2 cups shredded
mozzarella cheese
2 cups shredded Cheddar
cheese
1 (2-ounce) can sliced
black olives, drained
3 cups chopped lettuce
1 cup diced tomatoes
1 (15-ounce) jar salsa
8 ounces sour cream

Melt the butter in a large skillet over medium heat. Add the shrimp, crab meat and fish and sauté for 3 to 5 minutes. Spread the tortilla chips evenly over a large pizza pan. Microwave the nacho cheese sauce in a microwave-safe container on Medium for 1 minute or until thinned. Layer half the cheese sauce, the seafood mixture, mozzarella cheese, Cheddar cheese and olives over the tortilla chips. Bake at 350 degrees for 12 to 15 minutes or until cheeses are melted. Sprinkle with lettuce and tomatoes. Serve with salsa and sour cream for dipping.
Yield: 6 to 10 servings.

Julie Schlup, Pi Tau
California, Missouri

FIESTA ROLL-UPS

8 ounces cream cheese,
softened
1/2 cup picante sauce
1 green onion, chopped
6 (8-inch) flour tortillas
1 cup shredded spinach
3 thin slices turkey
lunch meat
6 thin slices American
cheese
1/4 cup chopped pimentos

Place the cream cheese in a large bowl and stir until smooth. Stir in the picante sauce and green onion. Spread about 1/4 cup of the cream cheese mixture over each tortilla. Layer 1/6 of the spinach, 1/2 slice of lunch meat and 1 slice of cheese over the cream cheese on each tortilla. Sprinkle with pimentos. Roll tightly as for a jelly roll. Arrange the rolls seam side down in a shallow baking dish. Chill, covered, for 8 to 12 hours. Cut each roll into 6 slices and secure with toothpicks. Serve with additional picante sauce.
Yield: 36 servings.

Patricia Ann Yewell, Preceptor Beta Mu
Carterville, Illinois

HAM AND CHEESE STRUDEL

1/2 pound sliced ham
16 ounces cream cheese, softened
1/3 cup chopped walnuts or pecans
3 tablespoons horseradish, or to taste

2/3 cup well-drained crushed pineapple
Pinch of salt
1 tablespoon Parmesan cheese
1/2 batch croissant dough, or purchased croissant dough

Chop all but 2 slices of the ham. Combine the chopped ham, cream cheese, walnuts, horseradish, pineapple, salt and Parmesan cheese in a medium bowl and mix well. Roll dough into two 8×15-inch rectangles on greased baking sheets. Place ham slice lengthwise in the center of each dough rectangle. Spread half the cream cheese mixture down the center of each ham slice. Cut each side into 1/2-inch diagonal strips. Fold strips alternately over the filling to resemble a braid. Bake at 340 degrees for 25 to 30 minutes or until dough begins to brown. Cool, slice and serve. Yield: 24 servings.

Peg McVitty, Laureate Beta Mu
Forest, Ohio

MEAT AND CHEESE ROLLS

Frozen puff pastry sheet, thawed
1/4 to 1/2 pound thinly sliced turkey
1/4 to 1/2 pound thinly sliced ham

2 ounces pepperoni, sliced
1 cup shredded mozzarella cheese
1 egg white, lightly beaten

Roll the pastry sheet into a 12-inch square. Layer the turkey, ham and pepperoni slices over the pastry, to within 1/2 inch of the edge. Sprinkle the cheese over the pepperoni. Brush 1/2 egg white over the 1/2-inch pastry edges. Roll the pastry tightly as for a jelly roll and brush with remaining egg white. Bake at 425 degrees for 20 minutes or until golden brown. Cool and slice. Yield: 12 servings.

Barbie Schneider, Xi Gamma Eta
Paris, Tennessee

CHOCOLATE-COVERED MUNCHIES

25 whole graham crackers, broken into bite-size pieces
3 cups salted peanuts
2 1/2 cups raisins
1 pound confectioners' sugar

2 cups semisweet chocolate chips
1 (18-ounce) jar crunchy peanut butter

Combine the graham cracker pieces, peanuts and raisins in a large bowl. Place half the confectioners' sugar in each of two 1-gallon sealable plastic bags. Combine the chocolate chips and peanut butter in a heavy saucepan over low heat. Heat until melted, stirring constantly. Pour the chocolate mixture over the graham crackers and stir until well coated. Quickly place half the chocolate mixture in each bag with the confectioners' sugar. Seal bags and shake well. Store in an airtight container in the refrigerator. Yield: 13 cups.

Jeri Patterson, Omicron Master
Maryville, Missouri

BRANDY OR VODKA SLUSH

This delicious party beverage is strong on taste, but not too strong on the alcohol.

1 (12-ounce) can frozen orange juice, thawed
1 (6-ounce) can frozen lemonade, thawed
1 1/2 to 2 cups brandy or vodka

1 cup sugar
Water
Sour mix, lemon-lime soda, cola or other mixer

Combine the orange juice, lemonade, brandy and sugar in an ice cream freezer container. Add water to the fill line. Freeze using manufacturer's directions. When ready to serve, use an ice cream scoop to scoop into glasses and add mixer of choice. Yield: 20 to 30 servings.

Patricia A. Astle, Preceptor Chi
Baraboo, Wisconsin

CHEESEBURGER CHOWDER

This quick, tasty chowder is great when having family or friends in for a casual dinner. It may be served alone or over rice or pasta.

1/2 pound ground beef
1/2 cup chopped onion
4 tablespoons chopped green bell pepper
1 tablespoon Worcestershire sauce

2 (10-ounce) cans Cheddar cheese soup
2 soup cans milk

Brown the ground beef with the onion and bell pepper in a skillet until onions are translucent, stirring until ground beef is crumbly; drain. Combine the ground beef mixture, Worcestershire sauce, soup and milk and bring to a simmer. Simmer for 5 minutes. Yield: 6 to 8 servings.

Kay Karlin, Mu Theta
Salina, Kansas

CHICKEN FLORENTINE SOUP

2 pounds chicken pieces
1 large onion, chopped
4 tablespoons butter
4 to 5 tablespoons flour
3 cups milk
2 (10-ounce) packages
  frozen chopped
  spinach

1 cup chopped fresh
  mushrooms, or
1 (4-ounce) can sliced
  mushrooms
2 (6-ounce) boxes long
  grain wild rice

Place the chicken in a kettle, cover with water and bring to a boil; reduce heat. Simmer for 45 minutes or until chicken is cooked through. Reserve 4 cups of the chicken broth. Remove skin and bones and chop chicken. Sauté the onion in butter in a large kettle over medium-low heat until tender. Whisk in the flour and cook for 1 minute, stirring constantly. Remove from heat. Mix the milk with the warm reserved chicken broth in a large bowl (heat in the microwave if broth has cooled). Slowly add the milk mixture to the onion mixture, stirring until blended. Stir in the spinach, mushrooms and rice with seasoning packets. Return to the stovetop. Simmer for about 30 minutes or until rice is tender, stirring frequently. Yield: 8 large servings.

Ellen R. Althaus Day, Gamma Pi
Wellsville, New York

CRAB BISQUE

1 (10-ounce) can cream
  of asparagus soup
1 (10-ounce) can cream
  of mushroom soup
1 (6-ounce) can crab
  meat

1 (13-ounce) can
  evaporated milk, or
  1¹/₂ cups half-and-half
¹/₄ cup sherry
Salt and pepper to taste
Paprika

Blend the soups, crab meat, evaporated milk, sherry, salt and pepper in a large saucepan. Cook over low heat until heated through, stirring frequently. Serve in individual bowls with a sprinkle of paprika over each serving. Yield: 4 to 6 servings.

Betsy Fisher, Laureate Omicron
Nashville, Tennessee

Jacqui Cosper, Omicron Mu, Ft. Stockton, Texas, makes Easy Cheesy Potato Soup by cooking 6 to 8 peeled chopped potatoes in water to cover, adding 8 ounces cream cheese, 8 ounces Velveeta cheese, a 4-ounce can of chopped green chiles, a beef bouillon cube, garlic salt and pepper to taste, and some chopped green onions. Bring to the boiling point. Delicious with grilled cheese sandwiches.

FRENCH ONION SOUP

1¹/₂ pounds yellow
  onions (4 medium),
  peeled, halved
  lengthwise
4 tablespoons butter
4 (10-ounce) cans
  condensed beef broth
¹/₂ cup dry white wine or
  water

1 cup water
¹/₂ teaspoon celery salt
¹/₄ teaspoon garlic
  powder
8 slices French bread,
  toasted
8 slices Gruyère or
  Swiss cheese

Thinly slice the onion halves by hand or in a food processor fitted with a slicing disk. Place the onions and butter in a microwave-safe dish. Microwave, covered, on High for 16 minutes or until onions are tender and transparent, stirring once. Stir in the beef broth, wine, water, celery salt and garlic powder. Microwave, covered, for 10 minutes or until soup is steaming hot. Serve in individual bowls, each serving topped with toast and cheese. Yield: 8 servings.

Nivia M. Wilson
Galveston, Texas

SPICY LENTIL SOUP

This satisfying soup is a wonderful protein dish.

2 teaspoons olive oil
2 onions, chopped
3 cloves garlic, finely
  chopped
2 teaspoons cumin
¹/₂ teaspoon paprika
¹/₂ teaspoon cayenne
  pepper
2 tablespoons flour

7 cups low-fat chicken
  broth
1¹/₂ cups dry red lentils,
  rinsed
2 tablespoons tomato
  paste
1 bay leaf
1 (13-ounce) can
  evaporated milk

Heat the oil in a large heavy saucepan or Dutch oven over medium-high heat. Add the onions and garlic and cook until softened, stirring constantly. Stir in the cumin, paprika and cayenne pepper and cook for 1 minute, stirring constantly. Stir in the flour. Stir in the chicken broth, lentils, tomato paste and bay leaf. Cover and bring to a boil, stirring occasionally. Reduce heat and simmer for 25 to 30 minutes or until lentils are tender. Discard the bay leaf. Pour half the lentil mixture into a blender or food processor container and process until smooth. Return processed mixture to the saucepan. Stir in the evaporated milk. Simmer for 5 minutes or until soup is steaming hot. Add salt and pepper to taste. Serve garnished with cilantro. Yield: 8 servings.

Mary D. Cooley, Xi Master
Langley, British Columbia, Canada

CRAB ASPIC

The friend who gave me this recipe served it often at dinner parties . . . in the 1940s.

1 envelope unflavored gelatin	Pinch of cayenne pepper
1/4 cup cold water	1/2 cup whipping cream, whipped
1 1/4 cups tomato juice	1 1/2 cups flaked cooked crab meat
3 tablespoons mild vinegar	1/2 cup chopped celery
1/2 teaspoon salt	1/4 cup chopped green bell pepper
4 tablespoons ketchup	
1 tablespoon onion juice	

Soften the gelatin in the cold water in a medium bowl. Combine the tomato juice, vinegar, salt, ketchup, onion juice and cayenne pepper in a saucepan over medium heat. Cook just until heated through, stirring constantly. Add the tomato juice mixture to the gelatin and stir until well blended. Let cool until syrupy. Add the whipped cream, crab meat, celery and bell pepper, folding gently until evenly distributed. Chill and serve. Yield: 8 servings.

Alta Mae Seiler, Alpha Iota Master
Chico, California

❖ CHATEAUBRIAND WITH COGNAC SAUCE

Our sorority chapter held a special fund-raiser, an auction of "social occasions," one offered by each member. For our social occasion, my husband and I entertained three sorority sisters and their husbands at a candlelight dinner party to celebrate the Millennium New Year's Eve. (Our guests were the three couples who bid on our "Millennium New Year's Eve Party.") It was a memorable evening of fabulous food, wine, and friendship, and it added over $500 to our chapter treasury. The menu for this celebration was designed around a spectacular Chateaubriand.

2 (2 1/2-pound) beef tenderloins	2 tablespoons Cognac
5 garlic cloves, slivered	2 tablespoons Dijon mustard
3 tablespoons olive oil	1/2 cup butter, softened
4 shallots, minced	3 tablespoons chopped parsley
2 tablespoons butter	Salt and pepper to taste
2 cups beef stock	

Cut deep slits in the tenderloins and insert garlic slivers in the slits. Heat the olive oil in a large heavy skillet over medium heat. Brown the tenderloins on all sides in the oil. Remove the meat to a rack in a roasting pan. Roast at 450 degrees for about 40 minutes or to 150 degrees on a meat thermometer for medium-rare or until done to taste. Sauté the shallots in the 2 tablespoons butter in a skillet over medium-low heat until softened. Stir in the stock and cook over medium heat until reduced by half. Add the Cognac and bring to a boil. Boil for one minute; reduce heat to low. Whisk in the mustard, then the 1/2 cup butter. Heat just until the butter is melted. Stir in the parsley and season to taste. Carve the tenderloins into 1/2-inch slices. Serve with the Cognac sauce, your choice of vegetables and an excellent red wine. Yield: Serves 12.

Bunny Baker, Iota Master
Calgary, Alberta, Canada

MARINATED PEPPER-CRUSTED TENDERLOIN

Serve with a salad and garlic mashed potatoes for a delectable gourmet meal.

1 cup port	4 garlic cloves, crushed
1 cup soy sauce	1 (5- to 6-pound) beef tenderloin, trimmed
1/2 cup olive oil	2 tablespoons coarsely ground pepper
1 1/2 teaspoons pepper	
1 teaspoon dried thyme	
1/2 teaspoon Tabasco sauce	

Combine the port, soy sauce, olive oil, the 1 1/2 teaspoons pepper, thyme, Tabasco sauce and garlic in a bowl and mix well. Place the beef in a large shallow baking dish. Pour the port mixture over the beef. Marinate, tightly covered, in the refrigerator for 8 to 12 hours, turning occasionally. Drain the marinade into a saucepan over medium-high heat and bring to a boil. Boil for 3 minutes. Remove from heat. Rub the beef with the 2 tablespoons coarsely ground pepper and place on a rack in a roasting pan. Roast at 425 degrees for 45 to 60 minutes or to 140 degrees on a meat thermometer for medium-rare, 150 degrees for medium, brushing frequently with the marinade. Yield: 6 to 8 servings.

Lyn Roetzel, Preceptor Rho
Sioux Falls, South Dakota

For a super-easy fresh bread try Beer Biscuits from Donna Marie Stiffler, Xi Epsilon Iota, Acworth, Georgia. She mixes 4 cups reduced-fat biscuit mix with 1/4 cup sugar and a 12-ounce can of lite beer, drops dough by tablespoonfuls onto a greased baking sheet, and bakes at 400 degrees until light brown.

SPICY BEEF CHILI

This sensational chili is for cookouts on the dock when the fish and crabs aren't biting, and for friends and family in my home when the weather is too cold for us to be outside. Serve with saltines, oyster crackers, or garlic toast. You may top with shredded cheese and chopped onions, or serve over cooked rice if desired. If anyone wants the chili extra hot, serve with additional Tabasco sauce.

3 pounds lean ground beef	2 soup cans water
2 large onions, chopped	1 tablespoon Worcestershire sauce
1 to 2 tablespoons minced garlic	1 tablespoon seasoned salt
2 (28-ounce) cans crushed tomatoes	1 tablespoon pepper
2 (15-ounce) cans garlic-and-herb tomato sauce	2 tablespoons chili powder
2 (10-ounce) cans tomato soup	1 tablespoon Tabasco sauce
1 tablespoon Kitchen Bouquet	Salt to taste
	2 or 3 (16-ounce) cans kidney beans

Brown the ground beef, 1/2 at a time, in a skillet, stirring until crumbly. Remove the beef to a large kettle. Sauté the onions in the beef drippings left in the skillet for 3 to 5 minutes. Stir in the garlic. Mix the onion mixture, tomatoes, tomato sauce, soup, Kitchen Bouquet, water, Worcestershire sauce, seasoned salt, pepper, chili powder and Tabasco sauce in a bowl. Pour into the kettle with the beef. Simmer, uncovered, for 1 to 2 hours, stirring frequently with a pancake turner to prevent sticking. Adjust the seasonings, adding salt if needed. Stir in the beans and simmer, uncovered, for 1 hour longer. Add more water while simmering if thicker than desired. Yield: 12 to 15 servings.

Louise S. Culbreth, Xi Gamma Psi
Saint Marys, Georgia

HAM AND SWISS DIJON LOAF

If you don't have time to make the dough for this savory loaf from scratch, you can use frozen bread dough.

4 cups flour	1 1/2 cups chopped cooked ham
2 tablespoons sugar	
1/2 teaspoon salt	1 cup shredded Swiss cheese
2 envelopes fast-rising yeast	1/2 cup chopped dill pickle
1 cup water	1 egg, beaten
1/4 cup Dijon mustard	
2 tablespoons margarine	

Combine 3 cups of the flour, sugar, salt and yeast in a large bowl. Combine the water, mustard and margarine in a small saucepan over medium heat and heat to 125 to 130 degrees, stirring occasionally. Stir the mustard mixture into the flour mixture. Add enough of the remaining flour to make a soft dough, stirring in 1/4 cup at a time. Knead for 4 minutes on a lightly floured service. Roll into a 12- to 14-inch circle on a greased baking sheet. Sprinkle the ham, cheese and pickle down the center third of the dough. Make cuts from filling to dough edges at 1-inch intervals along both sides of filling. Bring strips from opposite sides of filling together, twist and place ends at an angle across filling. Cover loosely with a tea towel or plastic wrap. Let the dough rise in a warm place for 15 minutes. Brush loaf with egg. Bake at 375 degrees for 25 minutes. Serve warm. Refrigerate leftovers. Reheat to serve. Yield: 1 loaf.

Cheryl Archer, Preceptor Alpha Eta
Calgary, Alberta, Canada

SWEET-AND-SOUR PORK

1 1/2 pounds pork (chop, tenderloin or roast), cut into 1/2-inch chunks	2 large ripe tomatoes, cut into wedges
6 tablespoons soy sauce	1 (12-ounce) can juice-pack pineapple chunks
Cornstarch	1 (6-ounce) package instant fried rice
Vegetable oil for deep-frying	1 (4-ounce) can sliced mushrooms, drained
1 (24-ounce) jar sweet-and-sour sauce	
2 green bell peppers, cut into wedges	

Place the pork in a medium bowl. Stir in the soy sauce and marinate in the refrigerator, covered, for 1 hour. Dredge the pork pieces in the cornstarch. Shake off loose cornstarch. Deep-fry at 375 degrees, a few pieces at a time, for 5 to 8 minutes or until golden brown; drain. Combine the sweet-and-sour sauce and pork in a saucepan over medium heat and cook until heated through, stirring occasionally. Combine the bell peppers, tomatoes and undrained pineapple in another saucepan over very low heat. Simmer for 10 minutes, stirring occasionally. Prepare the fried rice using package directions. Stir the mushrooms into the fried rice. Place a serving of rice on each plate, spoon the pork mixture over the rice and spoon the pineapple mixture over the pork. Yield: 6 to 8 servings.

Cindy Bingheim, Xi Gamma Omega
Gardner, Illinois

CHAMPAGNE TENDERLOIN

Serve this dish with sliced baked potatoes topped with cheese and sour cream . . . and with candlelight, and soft music.

2 pork tenderloins
1/4 cup soy sauce
2 tablespoons brown sugar
3 garlic cloves, crushed
1/4 cup Jack Daniel's whiskey
1/3 cup sour cream

1/3 cup mayonnaise-type salad dressing
1 tablespoon honey mustard
1 tablespoon finely chopped green onion
1 1/2 teaspoons vinegar

Place the pork in a nonmetallic pan. Combine the soy sauce, brown sugar, garlic and whiskey in a small bowl and mix well. Pour the whiskey mixture over the pork. Marinate, covered, for 3 hours at room temperature, stirring occasionally. Remove the pork from the marinade. Pour the marinade into a small saucepan over medium-high heat. Bring to a boil. Boil for 3 to 4 minutes. Arrange the pork in a shallow 9×13-inch glass baking dish. Bake at 425 degrees for 30 minutes or until cooked through, basting several times with the marinade. Combine the sour cream, mayonnaise-type salad dressing, honey mustard, green onion and vinegar in a small bowl and mix well. Remove pork from oven, slice thinly and cover with mustard sauce to serve. Yield: 4 servings.

Carol H. Goll, Beta Zeta Mu
Mabank, Texas

BREAKFAST CASSEROLE

For an irresistible breakfast, serve this sausage casserole with biscuits and jelly.

1 (32-ounce) bag frozen hash brown potatoes
1/2 cup (1 stick) margarine, melted
2 pounds sausage, browned, crumbled, drained

1 dozen eggs, scrambled
1 cup shredded Cheddar or Swiss cheese

Layer the potatoes in a 9×13-inch baking dish; drizzle with margarine. Layer the sausage and scrambled eggs over the potatoes. Sprinkle with the cheese. Cover tightly with foil and bake at 350 degrees for 45 minutes. Remove the foil and bake for 15 minutes longer. Serve immediately. Yield: 8 servings.

Janet Smith, Alpha Xi
Hazard, Kentucky

GREEN CHILE STEW

2 tablespoons olive oil
2 pounds boneless pork, cut into 1/2-inch cubes
1/2 cup chopped onion
1 garlic clove, minced
1/4 cup flour
2 (7-ounce) cans green chiles, drained, chopped

2 cups chopped peeled fresh tomatoes
1 fresh jalapeño pepper, chopped
1 teaspoon salt
1/2 teaspoon pepper
1/2 teaspoon sugar
1 cup chicken or beef broth

Heat the olive oil in a 4-quart Dutch oven. Brown the pork in the hot oil. Stir in the onion and garlic. Add the flour and cook over medium heat for 1 to 2 minutes, stirring constantly. Add the green chiles, tomatoes, jalapeño pepper, salt, pepper and sugar and mix well. Add the broth; reduce heat. Simmer, covered, for 1 to 1 1/2 hours or until meat is tender and cooked through. Serve with flour tortillas.
Yield: 6 to 8 servings.

Suzanne J. Seger, Alpha Tau
Columbus, Indiana

STROMBOLI

Hungry teenagers love it! Try Stromboli with assorted fresh vegetables and chocolate brownie pudding with vanilla ice cream.

1 (1-pound) loaf frozen bread dough
3 tablespoons mustard
12 slices American cheese
4 ounces provolone cheese, shredded
4 ounces mozzarella cheese, shredded
1/2 pound Italian sausage, browned, crumbled, drained

1/2 pound pepperoni, sliced
1 large tomato, chopped
1 small onion, thinly sliced
1 teaspoon oregano
1/2 teaspoon pepper
1/2 teaspoon garlic powder
1/2 cup grated Parmesan cheese
2 tablespoons olive oil

Let bread dough thaw and rise according to package directions. Roll 1/2 inch thick into a 12×15-inch rectangle. Spread the mustard evenly over the dough. Layer the American cheese, provolone cheese, mozzarella cheese, sausage, pepperoni, tomato and onion over the mustard. Sprinkle with oregano, pepper, garlic powder and Parmesan cheese. Drizzle with olive oil. Roll as for a jelly roll and seal the edges. Rub the roll with olive oil and prick all over with a fork. Place on a greased baking sheet. Bake at 400 degrees for 25 to 30 minutes. Yield: 12 servings.

Judy Hayen, Xi Eta Pi
Mallard, Iowa

CAJUN CHICKEN

1 tablespoon flour	1½ pounds boneless
1 teaspoon poultry	skinless chicken
seasoning	breasts, cut into
¾ teaspoon garlic salt	½-inch strips
½ teaspoon paprika	2 tablespoons butter
¼ teaspoon black	Italian parsley and chile
pepper	peppers (optional)
⅛ to ¼ teaspoon	
cayenne pepper	

Combine the flour, poultry seasoning, garlic salt, paprika, black pepper and cayenne pepper in a large resealable plastic bag. Add the chicken to the mixture, ½ at a time, and shake to coat. Cook the chicken in the butter in a large skillet over medium heat for 8 to 10 minutes or until juices run clear. Garnish with parsley and peppers. Yield: 4 to 6 servings.

Rena Heinz, Preceptor Iota Omicron
San Angelo, Texas

OVEN-FRIED CHICKEN

20 chicken breasts,	1 cup pancake mix
halved	Salt to taste
½ cup peanut oil	1 tablespoon paprika

Preheat the oven to 450 degrees. Pour the peanut oil evenly over the bottom of a large disposable oven-proof foil roasting pan, making sure the bottom is completely covered with oil. Place the pancake mix, salt and paprika in a quart-size brown paper bag. Hold the bag closed and shake to mix. Pat chicken breasts very dry. Shake the chicken pieces in the paper bag, several at a time, until completely coated. Place the chicken in the oiled roasting pan. Bake for ½ hour. Turn each piece for even crisping; reduce heat to 350 degrees. Bake for 30 minutes longer or until chicken is cooked through and skin is crisp. Remove from the pan immediately. Serve hot or cold. Yield: 40 servings.

Elizabeth C. Lund
Chestnut Ridge, New York

Joyce A. Keller, Preceptor Epsilon Theta, Pinellas Park, Florida, makes Chicken and Sauerkraut special by lining a baking dish with rinsed, drained sauerkraut, arranging 6 to 8 skinned chicken thighs on the sauerkraut, and pouring 2 cups of Russian dressing over the top. After baking at 350 degrees for 45 minutes, add Swiss cheese slices and bake for 15 minutes longer.

ARABIAN LAMB

8 ounces mixed dried	2 tablespoons flour
fruit (apricots,	4 tablespoons butter
prunes, pears, apples,	2 tablespoons
peaches), chopped	vegetable oil
Juice and zest of	¼ teaspoon each ground
1 lemon	ginger, nutmeg,
1½ cups boiling water	cumin, cinnamon and
2 pounds lamb, cut in	turmeric
2-inch cubes	½ cup sour cream
Salt and pepper	

Place the dried fruit in a bowl. Sprinkle with the lemon juice and zest. Pour the boiling water over the fruit mixture. Let stand for at least 10 minutes. Season the lamb with salt and pepper and dredge in the flour. Brown on all sides in the butter and oil in a heavy skillet. Sprinkle the ginger, nutmeg, cumin, cinnamon and turmeric over the lamb and stir well. Place the lamb mixture in a slow cooker and add the fruit mixture. Cook on High for 30 minutes. Turn heat to Low and cook for 6 to 7 hours. Stir in the sour cream just before serving. Serve with rice or noodles. Yield: 6 to 8 servings.

Sybil V. Evans, Preceptor Gamma Pi
Issaquah, Washington

VENISON SCHNITZEL

My husband is an enthusiastic deer hunter, and this is one of our favorite dishes. We have served it to friends who didn't know at first that they were not eating beefsteak.

4 to 6 venison loin	1½ cups dry bread
steaks	crumbs
½ cup flour	2 to 4 tablespoons
½ teaspoon garlic salt	vegetable oil
or seasoned salt	1½ cups chicken broth
½ teaspoon pepper	2 teaspoons flour
2 eggs, beaten	1 cup sour cream
4 teaspoons milk	½ teaspoon dillweed
1 teaspoon paprika	

Pound the steaks into ¼-inch thickness. Coat with a mixture of the ½ cup flour, garlic salt and pepper. Mix the eggs and milk together in a shallow bowl. Dip the coated steaks in the egg mixture; dredge in a mixture of the paprika and bread crumbs. Cook in oil in a large skillet over medium heat for 4 to 5 minutes per side or until done to taste. Remove to a warm platter. Add the chicken broth to the juices in the skillet, stirring to deglaze. Stir in the 2 teaspoons flour, sour cream and dillweed. Cook over medium-low heat until thickened, stirring constantly; do not boil. Serve over the steaks. Yield: 4 to 6 servings.

Margaret M. Baker, Alpha Omega
Indian Head, Maryland

CREAMED LOBSTER WITH BRIE

Crab meat may be substituted for the lobster and champagne for the white wine. Serve with a nice green salad and crusty French bread.

2 (10-ounce) packages frozen pastry shells (12 shells), thawed	1¼ cups half-and-half
2 tablespoons butter	½ cup dry white wine
1 small red onion, finely chopped	6 ounces Brie cheese, rind removed, cut up
1 garlic clove, minced	½ pound cooked fresh or frozen lobster, cut into chunks (1½ cups)
2 tablespoons flour	
⅛ teaspoon ground red pepper	

Bake pastry shells using package directions. Melt the butter in a medium saucepan. Add the onion and garlic and cook over medium heat for 5 minutes or until tender, stirring constantly. Stir in the flour, red pepper, half-and-half and wine; the mixture may appear curdled but it will smooth as it cooks. Cook for 5 to 10 minutes or until thickened and bubbly, stirring constantly. After it thickens, cook for 1 minute longer, stirring. Stir in the Brie and heat until melted, stirring. Stir in the lobster and heat through. Spoon the lobster mixture into the baked pastry shells. Garnish with peppercorns, capers, figs or almonds as desired. Yield: 12 servings.

Judith A. Murrill, Preceptor Sigma
Corvallis, Montana

❖ QUESADILLA PIE

1 (10-ounce) package frozen chopped spinach, cooked, drained, cooled	1 cup mild salsa
2 cups cottage cheese	½ cup corn kernels
1 egg	2 tablespoons chopped fresh coriander
¼ cup shredded Monterey Jack or Cheddar cheese	2 garlic cloves, minced
¼ teaspoon pepper	10 large flour tortillas
1 (19-ounce) can kidney beans, drained, rinsed	1 large tomato, sliced
	½ cup shredded Monterey Jack or Cheddar cheese
	1 tablespoon chopped fresh coriander

Place the spinach in a large bowl. Process the cottage cheese in a food processor or blender until smooth. Add the egg, the ¼ cup Monterey Jack cheese and pepper and mix by pulsing 4 or 5 times. Add the cheese mixture to the spinach and mix well. Mash the beans in a medium bowl. Stir in the salsa, corn and the 2 tablespoons coriander. Stir the garlic into the cheese mixture. Place 1 tortilla on a baking sheet. Spread ½ cup of the cheese mixture evenly over the tortilla. Place another tortilla over the cheese mixture. Spread ½ cup of the bean mixture evenly over the tortilla. Repeat the layers 3 times. Add a tortilla, spread with the remaining cheese mixture and top with another tortilla. Arrange the tomato slices over the tortilla. Sprinkle with the ½ cup Monterey Jack cheese and the 1 tablespoon coriander. Bake at 350 degrees for 30 minutes. Broil for 2 to 3 minutes to brown. Yield: 8 servings.

Vera Abbott, Xi Eta Kappa
Cloyne, Ontario, Canada

HOT FRUIT SALAD

This is a great dish for any special holiday brunch or dinner. It is wonderful served with any kind of meat—beef, pork, chicken, ham, or turkey. It smells so good when it is baking, and it tastes even better.

⅓ cup brandy	1 (28-ounce) can sliced peaches, drained
1 (20-ounce) can pineapple chunks, drained, juice reserved	2 apples, peeled, cut in chunks
1 (8-ounce) jar maraschino cherries, drained, juice reserved	2 or 3 bananas, sliced
	2 large oranges, cut up
	1½ tablespoons butter or margarine
6 tablespoons sugar	⅛ to ¼ teaspoon nutmeg
2 tablespoons cornstarch	⅛ to ¼ teaspoon cinnamon

Combine the brandy with enough pineapple juice and cherry juice to make 1½ cups liquid. Mix the sugar and cornstarch together and stir into the brandy liquid. Combine the pineapple, cherries, peaches, apples, bananas and oranges in a large baking dish. Pour the brandy mixture over the fruit. Dot with butter and sprinkle with nutmeg and cinnamon. Bake, uncovered, at 400 degrees for 45 minutes, stirring occasionally. Yield: 12 to 15 servings.

Adele Eggers, Laureate Alpha Lambda
Grants Pass, Oregon

PLIEBOLLEN

My husband is Dutch, and we often enjoy this traditional Dutch New Year's Eve treat.

1 envelope dry yeast
1 cup lukewarm milk
2¼ cups flour
2 teaspoons salt
1 egg, lightly beaten
1½ cups mixed currants
  and raisins
1 green apple, chopped
Vegetable oil for deep-
  frying
Confectioners' sugar

Combine the yeast and ¼ cup of the milk in a small bowl, stirring until dissolved. Combine the flour, salt, egg and remaining ¾ cup milk in a large bowl and mix well. Stir in the yeast mixture. Add the currants, raisins and apple and stir well. Let stand, covered with a tea towel, in a warm place until doubled in bulk. Heat the oil in a deep fryer. Punch down the dough and shape into balls. Deep-fry a few at a time for 8 to 10 minutes or until golden brown; drain on a paper towel. Sprinkle with confectioners' sugar. Yield: about 20 balls.

Caroline Driesson, Preceptor Omicron Alpha
Dana Point, California

DATE NUT COOKIES

Even people who don't care for dates seem to find these cookies delicious. They may be served at room temperature but are also wonderful when served frozen.

1 (14-ounce) can
  sweetened condensed
  milk
8 ounces dates, finely
  chopped
½ cup finely chopped
  walnuts or
  pecans
1 (12-ounce) package
  butter crackers
3 ounces cream cheese
2 cups confectioners'
  sugar
1 teaspoon vanilla
  extract
½ to 1 tablespoon milk

Combine the condensed milk and dates in a 1-quart glass bowl. Microwave on High for 5½ to 6 minutes or until mixture is very thick, stirring twice. Stir in the nuts. Spoon about 1 teaspoon of the date mixture onto a butter cracker; top with another cracker to make a sandwich. Make sandwiches with remaining date mixture and crackers. Place the cream cheese in a 1-quart glass bowl and microwave on High for ½ to 1 minute or until softened. Add the confectioners' sugar and vanilla and stir until smooth. Stir in enough milk to make of spreading consistency. Spread over each cookie. Store in an airtight container or freeze. Yield: 5 dozen cookies.

Carol Siekmeier, Xi Upsilon
Onalaska, Wisconsin

UPSIDE-DOWN APPLE PECAN PIE

1 cup chopped pecans
½ cup firmly packed
  brown sugar
⅓ cup melted margarine
1 (2-crust) package
  pastry mix
6 cups sliced peeled
  apples
¼ cup sugar
2 tablespoons flour
½ teaspoon cinnamon
⅛ teaspoon nutmeg

Preheat the oven to 450 degrees. Combine the pecans, brown sugar and margarine in a small bowl and mix well. Spread the mixture in the bottom of a 9-inch metal pie pan. Prepare the pastry using package directions. Roll the dough into two 12-inch circles. Fit one of the circles over the pecan mixture in the pie pan. Combine the apples, sugar, flour, cinnamon and nutmeg in a large bowl and mix well. Spoon the apple mixture into the pastry-lined pan. Top with the remaining pastry, fluting edge and cutting vents. Bake for 8 minutes. Reduce heat to 350 degrees and bake for 20 to 25 minutes or until golden. Cool upright for 5 minutes. Invert onto a serving plate and remove pie pan. Let cool for 1 hour before serving. Yield: 6 to 8 servings.

Tina Yosick, Preceptor Alpha Eta
Overland Park, Kansas

SAWDUST PIE

1½ cups coarsely
  chopped pecans
1½ cups graham cracker
  crumbs
1½ cups large-flake
  coconut
1½ cups sugar
7 or 8 egg whites, lightly
  beaten
1 unbaked pie shell
Caramel sauce

Combine the pecans, graham cracker crumbs, coconut and sugar in a large bowl and mix well. Fold in the egg whites until evenly distributed. Batter will be stiff. Pour into a deep-dish pie pan lined with an unbaked pie shell. Bake at 350 degrees for 40 minutes or until knife inserted in center comes out clean. Remove from oven. Pour caramel sauce over the pie, or drizzle the sauce over each piece before serving. May serve with whipped cream around the edges or vanilla ice cream on the side. Yield: 6 to 8 servings.

Barbara J. Taylor, Xi Upsilon
Strafford, Missouri

Jan Breakbill, Laureate Beta, Bradenton, Florida, makes Party Bananas by cutting bananas into 1½-inch pieces, dipping in orange juice, rolling in confectioners' sugar, and coating with toasted coconut. Color the coconut if you wish.

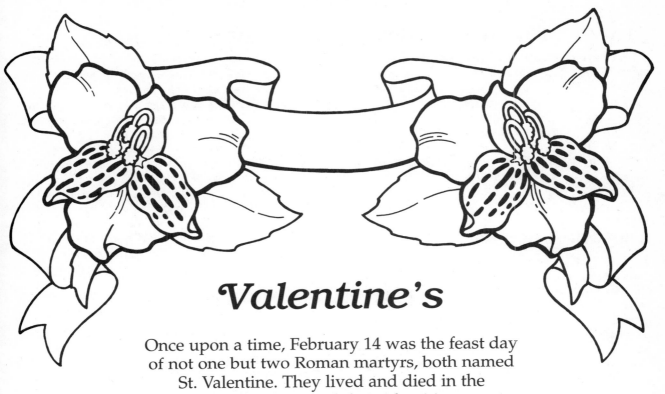

Valentine's

Once upon a time, February 14 was the feast day
of not one but two Roman martyrs, both named
St. Valentine. They lived and died in the
third century A.D., and their identities were
intermingled, so now we remember only one
St. Valentine, the patron saint of lovers.
On Valentine's Day, we celebrate love and
romance by exchanging flowers, cards, and gifts
to express affection. What better way to show
your heartfelt fondness for friends and loved ones
than by serving up a romantic symphony of
tasty temptations. Each one of the recipes in this
section is a work of pure poetry.

WRAPPED WITH LOVE

Secret sisters, moms, and daughters will appreciate the beauty of any gift that shows this much caring. Select a valentine tray of any size that will hold an assortment of small gift items. Make a bed of pink, red, or white metallic bag stuffing and arrange the items in the stuffing. Place the entire tray on a large piece of pink, red, or white lace, gather the lace on top, and secure with a beautiful fluffy bow. Add a Victorian valentine and deliver your picture-perfect gift.

Darla M. Timmons, Preceptor Delta
Bozeman, Montana

A SPOONFUL OF LOVE

Unforgettable place settings, trays, or party favors are easy and inexpensive. White plastic spoons with smooth handles are the base. Use a permanent marker to write or print "a spoonful of love" on the handles. Place three milk chocolate kisses in the bowl of each spoon and wrap with plastic wrap. Add a bow to secure the plastic wrap and flare the edge of the plastic. These appear even more festive if you can find kisses wrapped in valentine-colored foil or use colored plastic wrap.

Joyce Symank, Laureate Eta Alpha
Valley Mills, Texas

VALENTINE STORIES

What could be more appropriate than sharing valentine stories with your friends, and what could be a better setting than a couples party? Make it a brunch or lunch for a more casual affair, or an evening party with a romantic glow.

Decorate for either occasion using large hearts cut from red, white, or pink construction paper, balloons (heart-shaped, if you can find them), and crepe paper streamers in the same colors. For favors or place-cards, fill clear plastic bags (some have red hearts) with assorted valentine candies, tie with a red ribbon, and attach children's valentines. A bouquet of pink and white tulips in a lovely vase makes a simple but effective centerpiece.

If it is an evening occasion, achieve that romantic glow with candles on the table and the addition of strings of tiny white Christmas tree lights.

In such a setting, who can resist recapturing and sharing the story of how they met, fell in love, were proposed to, and married? Don't be surprised if the tales range from romantic to tear jerkers to giggly.

June Clark, Alpha Delta Phi
Deepwater, Missouri

MINIBASKET VALENTINES

Easy to make, inexpensive, and a joy to give or receive, minibaskets can be used for placecards or favors, or massed as a table centerpiece. Our chapter makes an annual project of preparing the minibaskets to take to one school and one adult handicapped activity center. The smiles we get are a real joy.

Collect the lids from nontoxic bottles or spray cans. The red, white, and pink ones from hair spray, fabric softener, or shave cream are appropriate for Valentine's Day.(You may wish to collect green ones for St. Patrick's or add blue ones for Independence Day.) Wash the lids well, in the dishwasher if possible. Add handles of pipecleaners hot-glued to the inside of the lids. Decorate the outside with stickers or painted hearts, tie ribbons to the handles, and fill with holiday treats.

Faye Williams, Zeta Xi
Kennett, Missouri

FRAGRANT FAVORS

Make favors to take home using a small glass rose-bowl with a slight rim. Fill with shredded plastic foam and wedge a circle of wet floral foam into the top. Wrap a length of tulle about 12 inches long around the top and secure with an elastic band; flute the tulle as desired. Glue a stout wooden pick to the bottom of a pretty glass votive candle holder and insert it into the center of the foam. Use four to six flowers and appropriate greenery for each bowl. (Fresh or silk flowers with short stems work best.) Arrange the flowers and greenery around the candle holder by securing them in the floral foam, and add a scented votive candle.

Pat Grelowski, Preceptor Xi
Lloydminster, Alberta, Canada

TROPICAL ESCAPE

Plan and execute a "Winter Blah Buster" just when you think spring will never come. Decorate with a yellow paper moon, cardboard palm trees, Hawaiian print tablecloths, leis, shells, coral, and whatever else will set the mood. Provide sun lamps, Hawaiian music, grass mats, and tropical snacks of fruit, nuts, wine, cheese, etc. Send out tropical-themed invitations and enjoy.

I planned a "just-for-two blah-buster" by sending my husband an invitation, renting a room in a nearby hotel, and having all the decorations, music, and atmosphere in place when he arrived. We had a blast!

Jude Gonzalez, Preceptor Zeta
Sterling, Illinois

FESTIVE SHRIMP AND CHEESE SPREAD

This recipe makes a generous amount and may be halved if desired.

2/3 cup small curd
  cottage cheese
16 ounces cream cheese,
  softened
3 tablespoons minced
  roasted red
  bell pepper
1 tablespoon minced
  garlic

1 teaspoon Dijon
  mustard
Dash of paprika
Salt and coarsely
  ground pepper
  to taste
8 ounces tiny shrimp,
  cooked

Combine the cottage cheese and cream cheese in a large bowl and beat until fluffy. Combine the roasted bell pepper, garlic, mustard, paprika, salt and pepper in a small bowl and blend well. Fold the garlic mixture and shrimp into the cheese mixture until evenly distributed. Chill, covered, for 8 to 12 hours. Serve with assorted crackers. Yield: 3 cups.

Betty Carmichael, Phi Master
Sun City West, Arizona

VALENTINE PIZZA DIP

This hors d'oeuvre was a hit at our Valentine's Day Couples' Night Out party. A heart-shaped serving dish makes it extra special.

16 ounces cream cheese,
  softened
1 to 2 tablespoons milk
1 (12-ounce) bottle chili
  sauce
1/2 to 3/4 cup thinly sliced
  red onion
1/2 to 3/4 cup thinly sliced
  green bell pepper

1/2 to 3/4 cup sliced
  mushrooms
1/2 cup sliced black
  olives
2 cups shredded
  mozzarella cheese

Combine the cream cheese and milk in a bowl and beat until of spreading consistency. Spread in a heart-shaped or 12-inch-round serving dish. Spread the chili sauce over the cream cheese layer to within 1/2 inch of the edge. Layer the onion, bell pepper, mushrooms, olives and mozzarella cheese over the chili sauce. Serve with corn chips or taco chips. Yield: 8 servings.

Barbara M. Allen, Laureate Alpha
Brewer, Maine

VALENTINE SANDWICH CAKE

This fun "cake" looks as if it tastes sweet, but it is really a sandwich!

2 (6-ounce) cans tuna,
  drained
Mayonnaise
Celery
Pickle relish
1 loaf firm white bread
1 (14-ounce) tub
  pimento cheese

16 ounces cream cheese,
  softened
Red food coloring
1 red bell pepper
10 green olives

Combine the tuna, mayonnaise, celery and pickle relish in desired amounts in a bowl and mix well. Arrange 6 bread slices on a baking sheet, edges touching. Spread the tuna mixture evenly over the bread slices. Cover with 6 more bread slices to form the sandwich. Spread a thin layer of mayonnaise over the top bread slices. Layer the pimento cheese evenly over the mayonnaise. Cover with 6 more bread slices. Spread another thin layer of mayonnaise over the bread. Blend the cream cheese and red food coloring until desired shade of pink. Frost the sandwich with the cream cheese mixture as for a sheet cake. Cut the bell pepper in slices to make heart shapes and arrange over the top. Make rosettes of the olives to garnish. Yield: 12 to 15 servings.

De Ann Wilson, Beta Zeta Zeta
Odessa, Texas

ORIENTAL SPLIT PEA SOUP

If you're tired of the "same old stuff" for a cold, snowy day, try this recipe served with crusty bread, tossed salad, chow mein noodles, and fortune cookies.

1 pound split peas
2 ham hocks
1 small onion
2 ribs celery
2 large carrots
1 bay leaf

2 (3-ounce) packages
  chicken flavor ramen
  noodles
Shredded Cheddar cheese
Soy sauce to taste
  (optional)

Cook the split peas with the ham hocks, onion, celery, carrots and bay leaf for 50 to 55 minutes using the directions on the split peas package. Add the ramen noodles with their flavor packets. Cook for 10 minutes longer, adding sufficient water to cover ingredients and stirring frequently to prevent sticking. Discard the bay leaf. Sprinkle cheese over each serving. Serve with soy sauce. Yield: 8 to 10 servings.

Sherry Kester
Romney, West Virginia

RED HOT SALAD

A hit at our Valentine's Day party. Serve with little meat sandwiches of your choice.

1/3 cup red hot cinnamon candies	6 ounces cream cheese, softened
1 cup boiling water	1/2 cup finely chopped celery
1 (3-ounce) package lemon gelatin	1/2 cup finely chopped walnuts or pecans
2 tablespoons sugar	1/3 cup mayonnaise
1 cup applesauce	

Dissolve the candies in the water in a medium bowl. Add the gelatin, sugar and applesauce and mix well. Pour into an 8-inch-square dish. Chill, covered, until set. Combine the cream cheese, celery, nuts and mayonnaise in a bowl and stir vigorously until light and well blended. Spread evenly over the gelatin. Yield: 8 servings.

Maxine Houser, Preceptor Eta Omicron
West Sacramento, California

RED HOT APPLESAUCE SALAD

4 cups water	4 cups applesauce
9 ounces red hot cinnamon candies	8 ounces whipped topping
2 (6-ounce) packages cherry gelatin	

Combine the water and candies in a saucepan. Heat over low heat until candies are completely dissolved, stirring constantly. Bring to a boil. Remove immediately from heat. Add the gelatin, stirring until completely dissolved. Stir in the applesauce. Pour into a 9×13-inch baking dish or a mold. Chill, covered, for 6 to 8 hours or until firm. Top with whipped topping just before serving. Yield: 24 servings.

Erika Hollis, Chi Theta
Paris, Illinois

RASPBERRY SALAD

1 (3-ounce) package raspberry gelatin	3 ounces cream cheese, softened
1 (12-ounce) package frozen unsweetened raspberries	1 (8-ounce) can crushed pineapple

Pour the dry raspberry gelatin into a medium bowl. Thaw and drain the raspberries, reserving the liquid. Combine the reserved raspberry liquid with enough water or juice to make 2 cups. Bring the liquid to a boil in a saucepan over medium-high heat; remove from heat. Pour over the gelatin and stir to dissolve. Stir in the raspberries and the cream cheese. Add the crushed pineapple and mix well. Pour into a serving dish. Chill, covered, for at least 2 hours. Yield: 6 to 8 servings.

Olive Graham, Laureate Gamma Kappa
Columbia, Missouri

FROZEN CHERRY SALAD

1 (21-ounce) can cherry pie filling	1 cup miniature marshmallows, halved
1 (15-ounce) can crushed pineapple	16 ounces whipped topping
1 (14-ounce) can sweetened condensed milk	

Combine the pie filling, pineapple and condensed milk in a medium bowl and mix well. Fold in the marshmallows and whipped topping. Pour into an 8-cup mold. Freeze for at least 3 hours. Remove from freezer 30 minutes before serving. Yield: 16 servings.

Patricia Lou Magerkurth, Laureae Eta Gamma
Granite Shoals, Texas

FRESH FRUIT SALAD

8 ounces berry-flavored Neufchâtel cheese, softened	1/2 cup whipping cream, whipped
2 tablespoons fresh lemon juice	2 quarts fresh fruit, cut into bite-size pieces
1 teaspoon grated lemon zest	1/2 cup chopped pecans or walnuts

Beat the cheese, lemon juice and zest in a mixing bowl at medium speed until soft and creamy. Fold in the whipped cream. Chill until serving time. Place the fruit in a large glass serving bowl. Spread the cream cheese mixture over the fruit and sprinkle with the nuts. Yield: 10 servings.

Juanita Corkwell, Laureate Chi
Ellenton, Florida

STRAWBERRY PRETZEL DESSERT SALAD

3/4 cup (1 1/2 sticks) butter	2 (3-ounce) packages strawberry gelatin
2 cups crushed pretzels	2 cups boiling water
1 cup sugar	2 (10-ounce) packages frozen sliced strawberries
8 ounces cream cheese, softened	
8 ounces whipped topping	

Preheat the oven to 400 degrees. Place the butter in a microwave-safe dish. Microwave on Medium until butter is melted. Stir in the pretzels and half the sugar. Press into a 9×13-inch baking pan sprayed with nonstick cooking spray. Bake for 8 minutes. Let cool. Combine the cream cheese, the remaining sugar and whipped topping in a mixing bowl. Beat at high speed until smooth. Spread over the cooled pretzel crust. Dissolve the gelatin in the boiling water in a medium bowl. Stir in the strawberries. Let stand for 10 minutes. Pour over the cream cheese mixture. Chill, covered, for at least 2 hours. Yield: 24 servings.

Helen Dietrich, Phi Master
Cincinnati, Ohio

HONEY-GLAZED CITRUS SALAD

4 cups torn lettuce
1/2 cup thinly sliced
 red onion
1/4 cup chopped fresh
 parsley
2 oranges, peeled,
 sectioned, drained
2 grapefruit, peeled,
 sectioned, drained

1 pint strawberries,
 halved
2 tablespoons
 vegetable oil
2 tablespoons cider
 vinegar
2 tablespoons honey

Place the lettuce, onion, parsley, oranges, grapefruit and strawberries in a large bowl. Toss to combine. Combine the oil, vinegar and honey in a smaller bowl and whisk to blend. Pour over the lettuce mixture just before serving. Toss and serve.
Yield: 6 servings.

Carol Kubit, Xi Theta Chi
Brookpark, Ohio

GRAPE CHICKEN SALAD

2 1/2 pounds boneless
 skinless chicken
 breasts
2 1/2 cups seedless red
 grapes, halved
2 1/2 cups salted cashew
 halves
3 ribs celery, sliced

1 (15-ounce) can
 mandarin oranges,
 drained (optional)
1 cup mayonnaise
3/4 cup sour cream
1 tablespoon tarragon
 vinegar
Lettuce leaves (optional)

Simmer the chicken in water to cover in a large saucepan over medium heat for 20 minutes or until cooked through. Drain and chop the chicken. Combine the chicken, grapes, cashews, celery and mandarin oranges in a large bowl and mix gently. Combine the mayonnaise, sour cream and vinegar in a small bowl and blend well. Pour over the chicken mixture. Toss to coat. Chill, covered, for at least 1 hour. Serve in a lettuce-lined serving dish.
Yield: 12 servings.

Vicki Cavins, Xi Zeta Nu
Batesville, Indiana

ELEGANT BEEF WELLINGTON

Serve with garlic mashed potatoes and sugar snap peas for a romantic evening.

4 (4-ounce) beef
 tenderloin steaks
1 1/2 teaspoons garlic salt
1/8 teaspoon pepper
2 tablespoons butter,
 melted
8 ounces mushrooms,
 finely chopped

1/4 cup chopped onion
2 tablespoons minced
 fresh parsley
1/4 cup dry sherry
4 frozen puff pastry
 shells, thawed
1 egg, lightly beaten
Mushroom Sauce

Season the steaks with garlic salt and pepper. Cook steaks in butter in a large skillet over medium heat, 2 to 4 minutes on each side. Remove from skillet; drain on paper towels. Place on a platter. Chill, covered, in the refrigerator. Add the mushrooms, onion, parsley and sherry to the drippings in the skillet. Sauté until onion is tender and liquid evaporates. Spread the mushroom mixture evenly over the steaks. Roll out the pastry shells to 6-inch squares on a lightly floured surface. Place steaks, mushroom side down, over the pastry squares. Brush edges of pastry with part of the egg. Fold the pastry to enclose the steaks, pinching ends to seal. Arrange wrapped steaks seam side down in a 10×15-inch baking pan. Brush with the remaining egg. Bake at 425 degrees for 15 to 20 minutes or until golden brown. Serve with Mushroom Sauce. Yield: 2 to 4 servings.

MUSHROOM SAUCE

1/3 cup chopped onion
6 fresh mushrooms,
 sliced
2 tablespoons butter,
 melted
2 tablespoons flour
1 (10-ounce) can beef
 broth

1/2 cup Burgundy or
 other dry wine
1/4 teaspoon
 Worcestershire sauce
1/4 teaspoon salt
Dash of pepper
1 bay leaf

Sauté the onion and mushrooms in the butter in a skillet over medium-low heat until vegetables are tender. Add the flour and stir until smooth. Cook for 1 minute, stirring constantly. Stir in the broth and wine gradually. Cook over medium heat until mixture is thickened and bubbly, stirring constantly. Stir in the Worcestershire sauce, salt, pepper and bay leaf. Reduce heat to low. Simmer for 10 minutes. Discard bay leaf.

Pam Edwards, Preceptor Eta
Mobile, Alabama

❖ PORK TENDERLOIN WITH CRANBERRY CREAM SAUCE

Serve with boiled parsleyed new potatoes, turnip casserole, and peas or green beans. Enjoy the meal and accept the compliments!

1 pound pork tenderloin	1/2 cup whipping cream
3 tablespoons vegetable oil	1/2 (16-ounce) can whole cranberry sauce
Salt and pepper to taste	1 1/2 cups veal stock or canned chicken broth
6 tablespoons madeira or dry sherry	2 tablespoons butter
Juice of 1/2 lemon	Orange slices

Slice the pork into sixteen 1/4-inch slices. Flatten the slices between sheets of waxed paper. Heat the oil in a large heavy skillet over medium heat. Brown the pork on both sides in the hot oil, adding salt and pepper. Remove the pork from the skillet and place in a 6×9-inch baking dish or casserole. Add the madeira and lemon juice to the drippings in the skillet and deglaze by heating and stirring. Stir in the cream. Cook the liquid over medium-high heat until thickened, stirring constantly. Stir in the cranberries, stock and butter. Cook over medium-high heat until further reduced and thickened, stirring constantly. Pour over the pork. Heat in the oven at 325 degrees for 20 to 30 minutes. Garnish with orange slices. Yield: 4 servings.

*Marilyn Dubuc, Alpha Master
Laval, Quebec, Canada*

GRILLED PORK

You can use hotter peppers in this lovely Valentine's Day dish, but your kisses will be fewer!

2 to 4 medallions of pork tenderloin	2 tablespoons vegetable oil
2 teaspoons kosher salt	2 tablespoons vinegar
1 tablespoon soy sauce	Salt and pepper to taste
1 teaspoon whiskey	1/2 cup Dijon mustard
1 teaspoon cornstarch	1/2 cup molasses
1 small head cabbage, shredded	1/2 cup balsamic vinegar
2 red bell peppers, shredded	1 tablespoon chili powder

Pound the pork into 1/2-inch thickness and place in a glass dish. Combine the kosher salt, soy sauce, whiskey and cornstarch in a small bowl and blend well. Pour over the pork and turn until coated. Marinate, covered, in the refrigerator for 1 to 2 hours. Grill over hot coals for 15 minutes or until cooked through, turning and basting frequently with the reserved marinade. Combine the cabbage, bell peppers, oil, vinegar, salt, pepper and mustard in a medium bowl and mix well. Chill, covered, until ready to serve. Combine the molasses, balsamic vinegar and chili powder in a small bowl and blend well. Layer the cabbage mixture and grilled pork in a large serving dish and drizzle with the molasses mixture. Yield: 2 to 4 servings.

*Helene Buchan, Laureate Gamma Nu
Bellevue, Washington*

HEART-SHAPED HAM LOAVES

1 pound ground ham	1 teaspoon mustard
1/2 pound ground fresh pork	2 tablespoons cornstarch
1 1/2 cups soft bread crumbs	1/2 cup sugar
1 egg, beaten	1 (15-ounce) can pitted sour cherries
1/4 cup packed dark brown sugar	

Combine the ham, pork, bread crumbs and egg in a large bowl and mix well. Press the ham mixture into heart-shaped muffin cups. Blend together the brown sugar and mustard and spread over the filled muffin cups. Bake at 350 degrees for 45 minutes or until cooked through. Combine the cornstarch, sugar and cherries in a saucepan over low heat. Cook until thick and clear, stirring constantly. Spoon over the ham loaves at serving time. Yield: 6 servings.

*Julia Gibson, Preceptor Chi
Tallahassee, Florida*

STUFFED PARSLEY CHICKEN

1/4 cup chopped parsley	1 (3-pound) whole chicken
1 tablespoon chopped chives	1 onion, sliced
1 tablespoon finely chopped mushrooms	1 rib celery, sliced
2 tablespoons chopped cooked ham	1 carrot, sliced
1 garlic clove, minced	Giblets (excluding liver)
2 tablespoons butter, softened	1 cup chicken broth
	2 tablespoons chopped parsley

Combine the parsley, chives, mushrooms, ham, garlic and butter in a small bowl and mix well. Using your fingers, carefully loosen the skin from the chicken breast meat, starting at the neck and working to the drumstick. Spoon the ham mixture into the opening between the skin and meat. Press the skin back in place. Sprinkle salt and pepper inside the chicken and truss. Oil a small roasting pan with 1 tablespoon vegetable oil. Place the onion, celery, carrot and giblets in the pan. Place the chicken over the vegetables. Brush lightly with oil. Cover loosely with foil and roast for 45 minutes. Remove the foil and roast at 325 degrees for 45 minutes longer or until golden. Remove from oven. Remove chicken from pan to an ovenproof serving plate and return to oven to keep warm. Discard the giblets. Remove the vegetables to a blender container. Add the chicken broth and process until smooth. Drain all but 1 tablespoon drippings from the pan. Stir in the vegetable mixture. Cook over medium heat until very hot, stirring constantly. Stir in the parsley. Serve as gravy with the chicken. Yield: 2 to 4 servings.

Elaine Goring, Xi Beta Tau
London, Ontario, Canada

EASY SICILIAN CHICKEN

1 (3- to 3¹/2-pound)	*¹/2 to 1 teaspoon oregano*
chicken, cut in pieces	*¹/4 to ¹/2 cup grated*
5 potatoes, peeled,	*Parmesan cheese*
quartered	*3 tablespoons olive oil*
4 garlic cloves, peeled	*Salt and pepper to taste*

Rinse the chicken and place in a large lidded electric skillet with the potatoes and garlic. Sprinkle with the oregano and Parmesan cheese. Drizzle with the olive oil. Cover the skillet. Bake at 350 degrees for 1 hour and 15 minutes or until potatoes are brown and crusty. Yield: 6 servings.

Linda Beck, Xi Beta Alpha
Washington, Pennsylvania

TARRAGON CHICKEN

This might become your special Valentine's Day dinner every year. The flavor can be varied by varying the vegetables, liqueur, and herb.

4 fresh asparagus	*¹/4-inch-thick slice*
spears, trimmed	*yellow bell pepper*
2 boneless skinless	*2 cups chicken broth*
chicken breasts	*¹/2 cup orange juice*
2 teaspoons fresh	*1 tablespoon balsamic*
tarragon, or ¹/2	*vinegar*
teaspoon dried	*¹/4 cup heavy cream*
Salt and pepper to taste	*3 tablespoons Grand*
¹/4-inch-thick slice red	*Marnier (orange*
bell pepper	*liqueur)*

Place the asparagus and a small amount of water in a microwave-safe dish. Microwave, loosely covered, on High for 1 minute. Rinse in cold water and drain. Rinse the chicken and pat dry. Lay a 12-inch-square piece of plastic wrap on the work surface; spray with nonstick cooking spray. Place the chicken breast smooth side down on the plastic wrap. Spray the breast with nonstick cooking spray. Place another piece of plastic wrap over the chicken. Pound into ¹/4-inch thickness. Remove the top plastic wrap. Sprinkle chicken with tarragon, salt and pepper. Lay 2 asparagus spears and one each of the bell pepper strips in the center of the chicken. Roll up tightly as for a jelly roll, making sure chicken surrounds vegetables completely. Enclose chicken roll in the plastic wrap, twist the ends of the wrap and tie securely with string. Repeat procedure for other chicken breast. Heat the broth in a medium saucepan. Add the wrapped chicken rolls and bring to a simmer. Simmer for 20 minutes, turning chicken occasionally. Remove the chicken to a warming plate. Add the orange juice, vinegar and a pinch of tarragon to the saucepan liquid. Bring to a boil. Cook over high heat until reduced by half, stirring occasionally. Stir in the cream and Grand Marnier. Cook over medium-high heat until slightly thickened, stirring frequently. Spoon the cream sauce over a serving plate. Remove the plastic wrap from the chicken. Slice chicken on slight diagonal. Fan out into medallions and arrange over the sauce. Yield: 2 to 4 servings.

Sarina Koch, Eta Chi
Port Alberni, British Columbia, Canada

CHICKEN WITH MUSHROOM SAUCE

Delicious served with mashed potatoes, a fresh green salad, and your choice of vegetable.

Skinless boneless	*1 soup can milk*
chicken breasts	*1¹/2 teaspoons sage*
Salt and pepper to taste	*1¹/2 teaspoons rosemary*
Flour for coating	*2 tablespoons chopped*
chicken	*parsley*
2 (10-ounce) cans	*1¹/2 teaspoons thyme*
mushroom soup	

Season the chicken with salt and pepper. Coat with the flour. Brown in hot oil in an electric skillet. Combine the soup, milk, sage, rosemary, parsley and thyme in a medium bowl and mix well. Pour the soup mixture over the browned chicken in the electric skillet. Cook, covered, at 350 degrees for 1 hour, reducing temperature if necessary.
Yield: 2 to 6 servings.

Marge M. Trujillo, Laureate Xi
Socorro, New Mexico

CHICKEN BREASTS PARMESAN

4 chicken breasts
1/2 cup pancake mix
1/4 teaspoon salt
Dash of pepper
1 (10-ounce) can cream
    of mushroom soup
1/3 cup milk
1/2 envelope dry onion
    soup mix
1/2 cup grated Parmesan
    cheese
1 tablespoon dried
    parsley flakes

Coat the chicken with a mixture of the pancake mix, salt and pepper. Arrange the chicken in an 8×8-inch baking dish. Blend the soup, milk and onion soup mix in a small bowl until smooth. Pour the soup mixture over the chicken. Bake, tightly covered, at 375 degrees for 1 hour. Remove the cover. Sprinkle chicken with Parmesan cheese. Bake, uncovered, for 15 minutes longer. Sprinkle with parsley and serve. Yield: 4 servings.

Dollie Lowery, Preceptor Alpha Sigma
Albuquerque, New Mexico

CHICKEN STROGANOFF

4 slices bacon, crisp-
    cooked, crumbled
1 pound boneless
    skinless chicken
    breasts
1 small onion, chopped
1 (4-ounce) can sliced
    mushrooms, drained
1 1/2 cups chicken broth
1 garlic clove, minced
1/2 teaspoon salt
1/8 teaspoon paprika
Pepper to taste
2 tablespoons flour
1 cup sour cream
Hot cooked noodles

Drain the bacon, and return 2 tablespoons drippings to the skillet. Cut the chicken breasts into 1/4-inch strips. Cook the chicken, onion and mushrooms in the reserved bacon drippings in the skillet over medium heat for 10 minutes or until chicken is cooked through. Stir in the chicken broth, garlic, salt, paprika, pepper and bacon. Simmer, covered, for 10 minutes. Blend the flour and sour cream until smooth; add to the chicken mixture. Bring to a boil; reduce heat. Cook and stir for 2 minutes or until thickened. Serve over noodles. Sprinkle with more paprika if desired. Yield: 4 servings.

Darlene Fier, Laureate Gamma Alpha
Dewitt, Iowa

Wanda Gish, Laureate Alpha Rho, Marshall, Michigan, makes Raspberry Jam by processing 5 cups chopped green tomatoes until pulpy in a blender, mixing with 5 cups sugar in a saucepan and boiling for 5 minutes. Dissolve three 3-ounce packages raspberry gelatin in the hot mixture and seal in hot sterilized jelly jars.

PARMESAN CHICKEN ALFREDO

8 boneless skinless
    chicken breasts
2 cups buttermilk
3 cups dry bread crumbs
1 cup grated Parmesan
    cheese
1 teaspoon minced
    garlic
1 tablespoon Italian
    seasoning
1 teaspoon seasoned
    salt
1 teaspoon paprika
Alfredo Sauce

Soak the chicken breasts in the buttermilk in a large bowl for at least 15 minutes. Remove chicken from buttermilk 1 piece at a time and coat with a mixture of the bread crumbs, cheese, garlic, Italian seasoning, seasoned salt and paprika. Arrange on a greased baking pan. Bake, covered, at 400 degrees for 30 minutes. Bake, uncovered, for 15 minutes longer. Serve with Alfredo Sauce. Yield: 6 to 8 servings.

ALFREDO SAUCE

1/2 cup (1 stick) butter
1/2 cup heavy cream
3/4 cup grated Parmesan
    cheese
2 tablespoons chopped
    parsley

Melt the butter in a small saucepan over medium heat. Stir in the cream and bring to a simmer. Add the cheese and parsley and stir until smooth. Yield: 1 1/2 cups.

Melody Lade, Xi Epsilon Kappa
Rusk, Texas

CHICKEN PASTA IN CREAM SAUCE

Dine on this scrumptious dish accompanied by a bottle of red wine, crusty garlic bread, and that special someone! The freshly grated Parmesan or asiago cheese makes the pasta irresistible.

3 boneless skinless
    chicken breasts,
    cubed
1 cup Italian-seasoned
    bread crumbs
3 garlic cloves, minced
2 tablespoons olive oil
1 cup chopped green
    onions
1/4 pound prosciutto,
    diced
2 cups heavy cream
1 (8-ounce) can tiny
    peas
1 pound bow tie pasta,
    cooked, drained
1 cup shredded
    mozzarella cheese
Freshly grated
    Parmesan or asiago
    cheese

Roll the chicken in the bread crumbs to coat. Sauté the chicken and garlic in olive oil in a skillet over medium heat until chicken is half cooked. Stir in the green onions and prosciutto. Sauté until chicken is cooked through. Reduce heat. Add the cream and peas and heat until mixture starts to thicken, stirring constantly. Remove from heat and pour over the pasta. Sprinkle with the mozzarella cheese. Serve with Parmesan cheese. Yield: 6 servings.

Sherolyn Johnson, Theta Kappa
Bentonville, Arkansas

SALMON WITH DILL SAUCE

This simple-to-prepare dish is good for the man or woman who wants to impress his or her "valentine." Serve with spinach and mandarin salad, sautéed asparagus, hot French bread, and raspberry iced tea.

1 (10-ounce) can chicken broth	1/2 cup sour cream
1/2 cup dry white wine	1/2 cup chopped seeded cucumber
1/2 cup chopped red onion	2 tablespoons mayonnaise
2 (3/4-inch-thick) salmon steaks	1/4 teaspoon dillweed
	2 cups cooked rice

Combine the broth, wine and onion in a skillet. Bring to a boil; reduce heat. Add the salmon. Simmer, covered, for 10 minutes. Remove 2 tablespoons of the liquid from the skillet and combine with the sour cream, cucumber, mayonnaise and dillweed, stirring until well mixed. Serve the salmon and rice accompanied by the sour cream sauce in a gravy boat or small bowl. Yield: 2 servings.

Mary McAlvain, Laureate Delta Mu
Wichita Falls, Texas

BUTTERFLY SHRIMP PARMESAN

I received this heart-healthy recipe over the Internet on a "food chatline." I discovered the contributor lived only 15 miles from my home, and she and I became great friends.

1 1/2 pounds large shrimp with tails, peeled	1/2 cup thinly sliced green onions
1 cup shredded low-fat Parmesan cheese	1 tablespoon minced garlic
1/4 cup Italian-seasoned dry bread crumbs	1/8 teaspoon crushed red pepper flakes, or to taste
2 tablespoons unsalted butter or butter substitute	1/3 cup minced fresh parsley
3/4 cup chopped red bell pepper	6 tablespoons 1% milk

Butterfly each shrimp by cutting it almost all the way through along its outer curved edge and opening like a book. Remove the dark vein. Place the cheese and bread crumbs in a small bowl and toss to combine.

Melt the butter in a large nonstick skillet over medium-high heat. Add the bell pepper, onions, garlic, red pepper flakes and shrimp and sauté for 5 minutes or until shrimp turns pink to opaque. Stir in the parsley. Bring the milk to a boil in a small saucepan. Stir into the shrimp mixture. Add the cheese mixture and cook until cheese is melted, stirring constantly. Serve immediately. Yield: 4 servings.

Dolores E. Dee, Xi Alpha Delta
Bethel, Connecticut

DEEP-FRIED DANISH CAMEMBERT

Camembert cheese, fresh or canned, chilled	2 eggs, lightly beaten
Flour for coating	1 cup fine bread crumbs
	Vegetable oil for frying

Make sure the cheese is cold. Leave whole or cut into small wedges. Roll in flour until lightly coated. Dip in eggs, then roll in bread crumbs to coat. Chill, covered, until ready to deep-fry. Fry the cheese in 1 1/2 inches very hot vegetable oil until golden. Drain briefly on paper towels. Yield: 2 servings.

Beth Dillistone, Laureate Alpha
Nanaimo, British Columbia, Canada

ASPARAGUS SMITANE

1 pound asparagus, trimmed, pared	1 1/4 cups sour cream
1 tablespoon butter	2 tablespoons crisp-cooked crumbled bacon
2 tablespoons grated onion	1/4 cup freshly grated Parmesan cheese
1/2 cup white wine	

Stand the asparagus in boiling salted water in a saucepan. Cook for about 15 minutes, making sure tips remain above water. Drain and keep hot. Heat the butter in a small saucepan over medium-low heat. Cook the onion in the butter until tender, stirring occasionally. Add the wine; simmer until all liquid evaporates. Stir in the sour cream. Bring to a boil; reduce heat. Simmer for 3 minutes. Arrange the asparagus on a serving platter. Smother with the wine sauce. Sprinkle with bacon and cheese. Serve immediately. Yield: 4 servings.

Debi Creighton, Preceptor Xi Eta
Weldon, California

Dee Thorn, Xi Nu, Las Vegas, Nevada, mixes a can of undrained 4-bean salad with a can of drained whole kernel corn and 1/2 cup chopped red bell pepper and heats to make a Winter Salad.

STRAWBERRY ALMOND KNOTS

My daughter has always loved strawberries, and every Valentine's Day I make this treat for her. It is a delight to see her face light up when she sees it.

3 ounces cream cheese, softened	2 tablespoons slivered almonds
1/4 cup frozen strawberries in syrup, thawed	2 (8-count) packages crescent dinner rolls
1 teaspoon almond extract	1/2 cup confectioners' sugar
1 teaspoon strawberry extract	

Combine the cream cheese, half the strawberries, almond extract and strawberry extract in a small bowl and mix well. Fold the slivered almonds gently into the cream cheese mixture. Separate the crescent dough into 8 rectangles; press perforations firmly to seal. Spread about 2 teaspoons of the cream cheese mixture evenly over each rectangle. Roll as for a jelly roll. Stretch each dough roll slightly and tie into a loose knot. Arrange on an ungreased cookie sheet. Bake at 375 degrees for 15 to 20 minutes or until golden. Remove to a serving plate. Combine the confectioners' sugar and the remaining strawberries. Drizzle over the knots. Sprinkle with slivered almonds. Yield: 8 servings.

Susan Osterberg, Xi Alpha Sigma
Clovis, New Mexico

STRAWBERRY NUT BREAD

A great recipe for when strawberries are in season. Serve at socials and also as a breakfast bread.

3 cups flour	1 1/4 cups vegetable oil
1 teaspoon baking soda	2 cups sliced strawberries, fresh or frozen
1 teaspoon salt	
1 teaspoon cinnamon	
2 cups sugar	1 cup chopped pecans or walnuts
4 eggs, beaten	

Combine the flour, baking soda, salt, cinnamon and sugar in a bowl and stir to blend. Add the eggs and oil and stir just until dry ingredients are moistened. Fold in the strawberries and pecans. Spoon into 2 greased 5×9-inch loaf pans. Bake at 350 degrees for 60 to 70 minutes or until a tester inserted in the center comes out clean. Yield: 38 half-slice servings.

Bonnie Sandlin, Alpha Theta Master
Lakeland, Florida

CHERRY STREUSEL COFFEE CAKE

Be sure to have copies of the recipe ready to hand out when you serve this cake!

2 1/4 cups flour	1 tablespoon lemon juice
3/4 cup sugar	
2/3 cup butter, softened	1 egg
1/2 teaspoon baking powder	1 teaspoon almond extract
1/2 teaspoon baking soda	1 (21-ounce) can cherry pie filling
3/4 cup evaporated milk	1/3 cup sliced almonds

Combine the flour and sugar in a large bowl. Cut in the butter until crumbly. Remove 1/2 cup of the flour mixture and set aside. Stir the baking powder and baking soda into the remaining flour mixture. Combine the evaporated milk and lemon juice and stir well; let stand for 5 minutes until thickened. Add the egg and almond extract and beat until well mixed. Add to the flour mixture and stir just until moistened. Spread 2/3 of the batter over the bottom and about 1 inch up the side of a greased 9-inch springform pan. Fill with the pie filling. Drop small spoonfuls of the remaining 1/3 of the batter over the pie filling. Stir the almonds into the set aside flour mixture and sprinkle evenly over the dessert. Bake at 350 degrees for 50 to 55 minutes or until golden. Yield: 8 to 10 servings.

Ev Mcleod, Xi Zeta
Yorkton, Saskatchewan, Canada

STRAWBERRY CREAM MUFFINS

Serve with fresh fruit and coffee for a great breakfast.

4 cups flour	4 eggs, lightly beaten
2 cups sugar	2 cups sour cream
2 teaspoons baking powder	1 cup vegetable oil
1 teaspoon baking soda	1 teaspoon vanilla extract
1 teaspoon salt	
3 cups strawberries, coarsely chopped	

Combine the flour, sugar, baking powder, baking soda and salt in a large bowl and mix well. Add the strawberries and toss gently. Combine the eggs, sour cream, oil and vanilla in a medium bowl and mix well. Add the egg mixture to the flour mixture, stirring just until moistened. Fill greased or paper-lined muffin cups 2/3 full. Bake at 400 degrees for 20 to 25 minutes or until muffins test done. Yield: 24 muffins.

Sylvia A. Swanson, Xi Alpha Xi
Burnsville, Minnesota

FOURTEEN-LAYER CHOCOLATE CAKE

A friend who says he always wants the icing to be as thick as the cake adores this cake! It looks especially attractive when sliced very thin.

1/2 cup (1 stick) margarine, room temperature	1 1/2 cups sifted flour
	1 1/2 cups sifted self-rising flour
1/2 cup (1 stick) butter, room temperature	1 cup milk
	1 teaspoon vanilla extract
2 cups sugar	Cocoa Frosting
4 eggs, room temperature	

Preheat the oven to 350 degrees. Cream the margarine, butter and sugar in a mixing bowl at high speed until light and fluffy. Add the eggs 1 at a time, mixing well after each addition. Add the flours alternately with the milk, mixing well after each addition. Stir in the vanilla. Prepare 8-inch cake pans with non-stick cooking spray and a light dusting of flour. Measure 1/4 cup batter into each cake pan. Layers will be very thin. Bake for about 8 minutes or until cake tests done. Remove layer from each pan to make room for the next one. Spread the Cocoa Frosting between the layers and over the top and side of the cooled cake. Yield: 16 to 20 servings.

COCOA FROSTING

2 cups sugar	1/2 cup evaporated milk
4 tablespoons baking cocoa	1 tablespoon vanilla extract
1/2 cup (1 stick) margarine	

Combine the sugar, cocoa, margarine, evaporated milk and vanilla in a saucepan over medium-high heat. Bring to a boil. Boil for 2 minutes; remove from heat.

Yvonne Johnson
Brantley, Alabama

MOUNDS BAR CAKE

1 (2-layer) butter fudge cake mix	1 (14-ounce) package flaked coconut
1 (4-ounce) package instant chocolate pudding	1 cup evaporated milk
	1 1/2 cups sugar
1 cup milk	1/2 cup (1 stick) margarine
1 cup sugar	2 cups semisweet chocolate chips
1 (10-ounce) package large marshmallows	1 1/2 cups chopped pecans

Prepare the cake mix using the package directions, stirring in the dry pudding mix before baking. Bake in a greased and floured 9×13-inch baking pan at 350 degrees for 30 minutes or until cake tests done. Remove from oven. Do not remove from baking pan. Combine the milk and the 1 cup sugar in a medium saucepan over medium-high heat. Bring to a boil. Remove from heat. Add the marshmallows and stir until melted. Stir in the coconut. Pour evenly over the cake. Combine the evaporated milk, the 1 1/2 cups sugar and margarine in a medium saucepan over medium-high heat. Bring to a boil; remove from heat. Add the chocolate chips, stirring until melted. Stir in the pecans. Spread over the marshmallow layer. Yield: 15 to 24 servings.

Brenda Barrett, Preceptor Omicron Eta
Navasota, Texas

CHOCOLATE CHERRY ANGEL CAKE

1 large angel food cake	8 ounces whipped topping
1 (21-ounce) can cherry pie filling	2 tablespoons grated semisweet chocolate
2 tablespoons baking cocoa	

Slice off the top 1/2 inch of the cake carefully with a long serrated knife. Cut down into the cake almost to the bottom, marking lines for leaving a 1/2-inch shell. Scoop out the center with a curved knife or spoon, being careful to leave a 1/2-inch-thick base. Save the scooped-out cake pieces for another use. Place the cake on a serving plate. Spoon the pie filling evenly into the cavity of the cake. Combine the cocoa and whipped topping in a medium bowl, folding until well blended. Spoon 1/2 cup of the cocoa mixture over the cut surface of the top cake slice. Replace the cake slice on the cake. Frost side and top of cake with remaining cocoa mixture. Sprinkle top with grated chocolate. Chill, covered, for 1 hour or until serving time. Yield: 8 to 12 servings.

Susan MacLeod, Xi Omega Nu
Rosenberg, Texas

Marilyn Van Vleit, Xi Delta Eta, Salem, Oregon, prepares and bakes a white cake mix in 2 round layers, splits the layers horitzontally, and spreads fudge topping and raspberry preserves over alternate layers while stacking on a parchment-lined baking sheet. She beats 3 egg whites until soft peaks form, adds a 7-ounce jar of marshmallow cream, beating until stiff, frosts the cake, and bakes at 475 degrees for 3 minutes. Do not chill, but serve the Meringue Torte the same day.

CHOCOLATE CHERRY CAKE

1 (2-layer) package
    chocolate cake mix
2 eggs, beaten
1 teaspoon almond
    extract
1 (21-ounce) can cherry
    pie filling
1 cup chocolate chips

1/4 cup (1/2 stick) butter
    or margarine
1/4 cup sugar
1/4 cup milk
1 cup whipped cream
1 (4-ounce) jar
    maraschino cherries

Combine the cake mix, eggs, almond extract and cherry pie filling in a large bowl and mix by hand. Pour into a greased and floured 9×13-inch glass baking pan. Bake at 350 degrees for 35 to 40 minutes or until cake tests done. Combine the chocolate chips, butter, sugar and milk in a small saucepan. Heat over medium heat until chocolate chips melt and mixture is smooth and hot, stirring constantly. Do not boil. Pour over the warm cake. Top each serving with 1 tablespoon whipped cream and a cherry.
Yield: 24 servings.

Patricia A. Siron, Laureate Gamma Mu
Mexico, Missouri

CHERRY FUDGE CAKE

1 (18-ounce) package
    chocolate fudge cake
    mix
1 cup fudge ice cream
    topping
2 (21-ounce) cans cherry
    pie filling

8 ounces whipped
    topping
1/2 cup maraschino
    cherries
Chocolate curls
    (optional)

Prepare and bake the cake mix using the package directions for a 9×13-inch cake pan. Remove from oven. Pour the fudge topping over the cake immediately and spread evenly. Cool. Spread the cherry pie filling over the fudge layer. Spread the whipped topping over the pie filling. Garnish with maraschino cherries and chocolate curls. Chill, covered, until ready to serve. Yield: 24 servings.

Sue Stinar, Gamma Upsilon
Bagley, Minnesota

Charlotte Hall, Xi Alpha Psi, Lenoir City, Tennessee, makes a heart-healthy Strawberry Dream Trifle using sugar-free strawberry gelatin dissolved in boiling water according to package directions and substituting lemon-lime soda for cold water. She layers cubed angel food cake, partially set gelatin, sliced fresh strawberries, and light whipping topping in a glass bowl.

RED VELVET CAKE

My husband and I were married on Valentine's Day in 1941, and I always baked this cake for our anniversary. My husband died in 1994. I still occasionally bake this cake on that special day.

1/2 cup (1 stick) butter,
    softened
1 1/2 cups sugar
2 eggs
1 ounce red food
    coloring
2 tablespoons cocoa

2 1/4 cups sifted flour
1 teaspoon salt
1 cup buttermilk
1 teaspoon vanilla
    extract
1 tablespoon vinegar
1 teaspoon baking soda

Beat the butter, sugar and eggs in a bowl until smooth. Make a paste of the food coloring and cocoa; stir into the egg mixture. Sift together the flour and salt. Add the sifted dry ingredients and buttermilk alternately, mixing well after each addition. Stir in the vanilla. Hold the vinegar in a spoon over the batter and add the baking soda. The mixture will foam over into the bowl. Blend into the batter. Pour batter into two 9-inch heart-shaped pans. Bake at 350 degrees for 30 to 35 minutes or until cake tests done. Cool in the pans for 10 minutes. Remove to a wire rack to cool completely. Slice each layer in half horizontally (I use a string and pull it through the center). Use a buttercream frosting between the layers. Frost the top and sides with a divinity icing.
Yield: 8 to 12 servings.

Sammie Glenn, Preceptor Beta Mu
Carterville, Illinois

CHOCOLATE CHIP CAKE

This is a favorite of mine, an easy-cake recipe to make when you really don't have much time.

1 (2-layer) yellow
    cake mix
1 (4-ounce) package
    chocolate instant
    pudding mix
3 eggs

1 cup sour cream
3/4 cup water
3/4 cup vegetable oil
1 cup milk chocolate
    chips

Combine the cake mix, pudding mix, eggs, sour cream, water and oil in a large bowl and mix well. Stir in the chocolate chips. Pour into a greased and floured bundt pan. Bake at 350 degrees for 35 to 40 minutes or until cake tests done. Cool in the pan for 10 minutes. Invert onto a serving plate to cool completely. Sprinkle with confectioners' sugar when cool.
Yield: 16 servings.

Barbara Appleton, Xi Gamma Beta
Paris, Arkansas

STRAWBERRY HEART CAKE

1 (2-layer) white cake
    mix
1 (3-ounce) package
    strawberry gelatin
3 tablespoons flour
1/3 cup vegetable oil
4 eggs
1 (10-ounce) package
    frozen sweetened
    strawberries, thawed

1/2 cup cold water
1/2 cup (1 stick) butter or
    margarine, softened
5 to 5 1/2 cups
    confectioners' sugar
Red hot cinnamon
    candies (optional)

Combine the cake mix, gelatin and flour in a mixing bowl. Beat in the oil and eggs. Drain the strawberries, reserving 1/2 cup of the liquid. Add the strawberries and cold water to the batter and mix well. Pour the batter into two waxed paper-lined 8-inch baking pans, one square and one round. Bake the square cake at 350 degrees for 30 to 35 minutes, the round one for 35 to 40 minutes, or until cakes test done. Cool in the pans for 10 minutes. Remove to a wire rack to cool completely. Combine the butter and strawberry liquid in a mixing bowl and blend well. Add the confectioners' sugar gradually. Beat for 2 minutes or until light and fluffy. Place the square cake layer diagonally on a large covered board. Cut the round cake layer in half and frost the cut sides with the strawberry frosting. Place the frosted sides against the top two sides of the square cake layer, forming a heart. Frost sides and top of cake. Decorate with red hot candies. Yield: 12 to 16 servings.

Beverly Raze, Preceptor Alpha Nu
Ontario, Oregon

VALENTINE RASPBERRY CAKE

Strawberries or other berries may be substituted for the raspberries.

1 (10-ounce) package
    frozen raspberries,
    thawed
2 tablespoons rum
1 1/2 tablespoons
    cornstarch
2 cups whipping cream
1 teaspoon vanilla
    extract

1/4 cup confectioners'
    sugar
1 frozen pound cake,
    thawed
Fresh raspberries to
    garnish

Place the raspberries in a medium bowl. Pour the rum over the raspberries. Let stand, covered, for 2 hours. Drain, reserving the liquid. Combine the reserved liquid and the cornstarch in a saucepan over medium heat. Cook until thickened, stirring constantly. Remove from heat. Cool to lukewarm. Stir in the raspberries. Combine the whipping cream, vanilla and confectioners' sugar in a mixing bowl. Beat at high speed until stiff peaks form. Split the cake horizontally and place the bottom layer on a serving plate. Spread half the raspberry mixture over the cake bottom and spread enough whipped cream to cover the raspberries. Place the top layer over the bottom layer and repeat the raspberry and whipped cream layers. Frost the sides of the cake with whipped cream. Garnish with fresh raspberries. Chill, covered, until serving time.
Yield: 6 to 8 servings.

Linda A. Hume, Xi Eta Lambda
Napa, California

FRESH TOMATO CAKE

1 cup packed dark
    brown sugar
1 cup (2 sticks) butter,
    softened
2 eggs
3 cups flour
2 teaspoons baking
    powder
1 teaspoon baking
    soda
1 teaspoon nutmeg
1 teaspoon salt

2 cups chopped peeled
    seeded ripe tomatoes
1/2 cup pecans or
    walnuts, chopped
1/2 cup dates, chopped
1/2 cup raisins, chopped
8 ounces cream cheese,
    softened
2 teaspoons vanilla
    extract
1 pound confectioners'
    sugar

Cream the brown sugar and half the butter in a mixing bowl until light and fluffy. Beat in the eggs. Sift the flour, baking powder, baking soda, nutmeg and salt into the bowl and mix well. Stir in the tomatoes, nuts, dates and raisins. Pour into a greased and floured 9×13-inch baking pan. Bake at 350 degrees for 35 minutes or until cake tests done. Cool on a wire rack. Combine the remaining butter, cream cheese and vanilla in a mixing bowl and mix well. Beat in the confectioners' sugar gradually to make of spreading consistency. Frost the cooled cake. Valentine decorations, preferably the edible kind, may be arranged over the frosted cake.
Yield: 15 to 20 servings.

Pat McKelvy, Theta Sigma
Brackettville, Texas

Sharon M. Scott, Preceptor Alpha, Missoula, Montana, makes Sweetheart Chocolate Fondue for two by melting 1 cup chocolate chips with 1/4 cup light cream, a tablespoon of orange, cherry, coffee, or hazelnut liqueur, and 1/2 teaspoon vanilla. Dip fresh fruit or pound cake pieces and roll in almonds or coconut.

LINCOLN POUND CAKE

1 1/2 cups (3 sticks) butter, softened	1 teaspoon lemon juice
3 cups sugar	5 eggs
1 teaspoon vanilla extract	3 cups flour
	1 cup evaporated milk

Combine the butter, sugar, vanilla and lemon juice in a large bowl and beat until smooth and creamy. Add the eggs 1 at a time, mixing well after each addition. Add the flour to the egg mixture alternately with the evaporated milk, mixing well after each addition. Pour into a greased and floured bundt pan or a 10-inch tube pan. Bake at 350 degrees for 1 3/4 hours. Cool in the pan before inverting on a serving plate. Yield: 12 to 16 servings.

Bethene Boardman, Xi Mu Epsilon
Princeton, Illinois

EIGHT-MINUTE CHOCOLATE FROSTING

For Valentine's day, use strawberry jam as the filling between the layers of a 2-layer cake. Sprinkle the frosted cake with nuts or red sugar in a heart design.

2 egg whites	1/3 cup water
1 1/2 cups sugar	1 teaspoon vanilla extract
1/4 teaspoon cream of tartar	

Combine the egg whites, sugar, cream of tartar and water in the top of a double boiler. Beat with an electric mixer at high speed for 1 minute. Place over boiling water. Beat at high speed for 7 minutes or until stiff peaks form. Remove from heat. Stir in the vanilla. Beat at high speed for 2 minutes or until thickened. Spread over a cooled cake. Yield: fills and frosts 2 (8- or 9-inch) layers or 1 (9×13-inch cake).

Beverly Relvas, Xi Chi Eta
Modesto, California

CHOCOLATE PEANUT SWEETIES

1 cup peanut butter	1 1/2 cups milk chocolate chips
1/2 cup (1 stick) butter, softened	1 tablespoon vegetable oil
3 cups confectioners' sugar	
5 dozen miniature pretzels	

Combine the peanut butter and butter in a mixing bowl and beat until smooth. Add the confectioners' sugar and beat until light and fluffy. Shape into 1-inch balls. Press each ball on a single pretzel. Place

on waxed paper-lined baking sheets. Chill, covered, for about 1 hour or until peanut butter mixture is firm. Combine the chocolate chips and oil in a heavy saucepan or microwave-safe bowl and heat or microwave until chocolate is melted. Stir to blend. Dip the peanut butter portion of each confection—not the pretzel—into the chocolate mixture. Return to the baking sheet, pretzel side down. Chill, covered, for at least 30 minutes before serving. Store in the refrigerator. Yield: 5 dozen.

Beth Richter, Xi Delta
Greeley, Colorado

RED HOT CINNAMON CANDY

This confection is a big hit with the kids. Someone in my family often makes it for Valentine's Day, Christmas, and even our big Fourth of July party.

2 cups water	1 1/2 teaspoons oil of cinnamon
1 1/2 cups light corn syrup	
4 cups sugar	
1 1/2 teaspoons red food coloring	

Place the water, corn syrup and sugar in a large saucepan over high heat. Do not stir before or during cooking. Cook rapidly to 300 to 310 degrees on a candy thermometer. Remove from heat. Add the food coloring and oil of cinnamon and stir well. Pour evenly over a buttered baking sheet. Let stand until cool and clear red. Break into small pieces. Store in an airtight container. Yield: about 4 dozen pieces.

Tammie Dickerson, Xi Gamma Phi
Belton, Missouri

COOKIES AND CREAM CHEESECAKE BONBONS

24 chocolate sandwich cookies	1 pound confectioners' sugar
8 ounces cream cheese, softened	Fresh raspberries and raspberry leaves (optional)
1 cup nonfat dry milk powder	
1 teaspoon vanilla extract	

Place 12 cookies in a food processor container and process to make fine crumbs. Pour the crumbs onto a waxed paper-lined baking sheet. Coarsely chop the remaining 12 cookies. Combine the cream cheese, dry milk powder and vanilla in a mixing bowl and beat at medium speed until smooth. Add the confectioners' sugar, 1 cup at a time, mixing at low speed after each addition. Stir in the coarsely chopped cookies.

Chill, covered, for 2 hours or until firm. Shape about 1 rounded tablespoonful of dough into a 1¼-inch ball, rolling mixture between palms. Roll in cookie crumbs and place on waxed paper. Repeat with remaining dough. Garnish with raspberries and leaves if desired. Store in an airtight container in the refrigerator. Yield: 3 dozen.

Linda Poe, Beta Psi
Connell, Washington

PRALINE TRUFFLE CUPS

6 ounces vanilla-flavored candy coating	⅓ cup heavy cream
	¼ cup finely ground pecans
6 ounces semisweet baking chocolate, cut into pieces	1 tablespoon praline liqueur or maple syrup
2 tablespoons butter or margarine, cut up	

Melt the candy coating in a heavy 2-quart saucepan over low heat, stirring constantly. Remove from heat. Spread 1 teaspoon coating over the bottom and up the side of each of 24 tiny paper candy cups. Let stand for 1 hour or until hardened. Melt the chocolate in a heavy 2-quart saucepan over low heat, stirring constantly. Remove from heat. Add the butter, cream, pecans and liqueur and mix well. Chill for about 35 minutes, stirring frequently, until thickened and mixture mounds when dropped from a spoon. Spoon the chocolate mixture into a decorator tube fitted with a star tip. Pipe into rosettes in the candy-coated paper cups. Chill for about 30 minutes or until chocolate is firm. Peel the paper from the cups before serving. For **Cherry Truffle Cups,** omit the pecans, substitute 2 tablespoons cherry liqueur for the praline liqueur, and place a candied cherry half in each cup before filling. For **Crème de Menthe Truffle Cups,** substitute ¼ cup finely ground almonds for the pecans and 2 tablespoons crème de menthe for the praline liqueur. To make **Raspberry Truffle Cups,** omit the pecans, substitute 2 tablespoons raspberry liqueur for the praline liqueur, and place a fresh raspberry in each cup before filling. Yield: 2 dozen.

Donna Aven, Preceptor Alpha Alpha
Pearl River, New York

Dawn R. Ashenfelter, Xi Gamma Omega, Mesa, Arizona, makes Unbelievable Dessert by layering ½ cup melted butter, a 24-ounce jar of applesauce, a yellow or white cake mix, a 14-ounce package of red hots, and a can of root beer in a slow-cooker and cooking on High for 6 hours. Serve with whipped cream.

ONE-BOWL BROWNIES

1 cup vegetable oil	4 eggs
⅜ cup baking cocoa	1½ cups flour
2 cups sugar	1 teaspoon baking powder
2 tablespoons white corn syrup	1 teaspoon salt
1 teaspoon vanilla extract	1 cup chopped walnuts or pecans

Combine the oil, cocoa, sugar, corn syrup, vanilla, eggs, flour, baking powder, salt and nuts in a large bowl and mix well by hand. Do not overmix. Pour the cocoa mixture into a 9×13-inch baking pan sprayed with nonstick cooking spray. Bake at 350 degrees for 30 minutes or until of desired doneness. Do not overbake. Yield: 24 brownies.

Janelle Lewis, Laureate Zeta Eta
Bryan, Texas

STRAWBERRY BAVARIAN PIE

2 pints fresh strawberries	½ cup cold water
¾ cup sugar	2 teaspoons lemon juice
1 envelope unflavored gelatin	1 cup whipping cream
	Almond Crumb Pie Shell

Thinly slice 1½ pints of the strawberries, reserving the remainder for garnish. Combine the sliced strawberries and sugar in a large bowl and mix well. Let stand until sugar dissolves. Soften the gelatin in the water. Place in a saucepan over low heat and stir until gelatin dissolves. Stir the gelatin mixture and lemon juice into the sugared strawberries. Beat the whipping cream in a chilled mixing bowl until stiff peaks form. Fold the whipped cream into the strawberry mixture. Chill, covered, for 45 minutes or until mixture mounds when dropped from a spoon. Pour into the Almond Crumb Pie Shell. Chill, covered, until set, about 4 hours. Garnish with remaining strawberries. Yield: 6 to 8 servings.

ALMOND CRUMB PIE SHELL

1 cup graham cracker crumbs	6 tablespoons butter or margarine, melted
½ cup finely chopped pecans or almonds	2 tablespoons sugar

Preheat the oven to 375 degrees. Combine the crumbs, nuts, butter and sugar in a small bowl and mix well. Press the mixture over the bottom and up the side of a 9-inch pie plate sprayed with nonstick cooking spray. Bake for 8 minutes.

Mary Lou Reilly, Preceptor Alpha Nu
Plover, Wisconsin

KAHLUA PIE

16 ounces cream cheese,
  softened
1 cup heavy cream
1 (6-ounce) package
  instant chocolate
  pudding mix

¾ cup Kahlúa
1 prepared chocolate
  graham cracker pie
  crust
16 ounces whipped
  topping

Beat the cream cheese in a bowl until smooth. Add the cream and mix well. Stir in the dry pudding mix and Kahlúa and beat until stiff. Pour into the pie crust. Chill, covered, for at least 1 hour before serving. Keeps well for at least 2 days. Cover with whipped topping before serving. Yield: 6 servings.

Margaret M. Haugland, Xi Beta Gamma
Benton City, Washington

❖ HOT FUDGE TARTS

Be sure to use real chocolate chips for these delectable tarts, and be creative with the centers. Lots of other candies will work as well as those that are listed.

⅔ cup semisweet
  chocolate chips
½ cup (1 stick) butter,
  softened
¾ cup sugar
2 eggs
1 teaspoon vanilla
  extract
½ cup flour
Miniature
  marshmallows

Maraschino cherries
Chocolate kisses
Mint chocolate patties,
  quartered
1 cup semisweet
  chocolate chips
1 (14-ounce) can
  sweetened condensed
  milk

Preheat the oven to 375 degrees. Combine the ⅔ cup chocolate chips and butter in a 1-quart saucepan over low heat. Cook for 5 to 7 minutes or until chocolate is melted and mixture is smooth, stirring occasionally. Pour into a medium bowl. Cool for 5 minutes. Stir the sugar, eggs and vanilla into the chocolate mixture. Add the flour gradually, stirring until smooth. Line miniature muffin cups with paper liners. Spoon about 2 teaspoons batter into each liner, filling about ⅓ full. Bake for 12 to 14 minutes or until toothpick inserted in center comes out clean. Remove from oven. Immediately press desired filling into center of each tart (marshmallows, 3 per tart; cherries, 1 per tart; chocolate kisses, 1 upside down in the tart; mint chocolate patties, ¼ per tart). Return to oven and bake for 2 minutes longer. Let cool for 5 minutes. Combine 1 cup chocolate chips and condensed milk in a 1-quart saucepan over medium-low heat. Cook for 2 to 3 minutes or until chocolate is melted and mixture is smooth, stirring constantly. Drop 1 tea-spoon of the chocolate mixture over each tart. Chill for 1 hour to set the glaze. Store at room temperature in an airtight container. Yield: 30 tarts.

Tammy Sheehan, Delta
Urbandale, Iowa

LUSCIOUS CHERRY CHEESECAKE

1 cup coarse graham
  cracker crumbs
3 tablespoons sugar
3 tablespoons melted
  butter or margarine
9 ounces light cream
  cheese, softened
1 cup sugar

3 tablespoons flour
2 tablespoons water
1 teaspoon almond
  extract
3 eggs,
1 egg white
1 (21-ounce) can light
  cherry pie filling

Preheat the oven to 325 degrees. Combine the graham cracker crumbs, the 3 tablespoons sugar and butter in a small bowl and mix well. Press into a 9-inch springform pan sprayed with nonstick cooking spray. Bake for 10 minutes. Remove from oven. Turn heat to 450 degrees. Combine the cream cheese, the 1 cup sugar, flour, water and almond extract in a mixing bowl and blend well. Add 3 of the eggs, 1 at a time, mixing well after each addition. Beat in the egg white. Pour the mixture evenly over the crust. Smooth if necessary. Bake for 10 minutes. With cheesecake still in the oven, reduce heat to 250 degrees. Bake for 30 minutes longer or until center is slightly firm. Remove to a wire rack to cool completely. Loosen the cooled cake from the side of the pan before releasing ring. Place on a serving plate. Spread the cherry pie filling gently over the top; some will drop down side onto serving plate. Keep leftovers in the refrigerator and cut with a warm knife to serve. Yield: 12 servings.

Janice Cordina, Xi Delta Upsilon
Parker, Colorado

EIGHT-MINUTE CHEESECAKE

8 ounces cream cheese,
  softened
⅓ cup sugar
1 cup sour cream
2 teaspoons vanilla
  extract
16 ounces whipped
  topping

1 prepared graham
  cracker pie shell
Fresh fruit
  (strawberries, kiwi
  fruit, raspberries)

Place the cream cheese in a large mixing bowl and beat until smooth. Beat in the sugar gradually. Blend in the sour cream and vanilla. Fold the whipped topping into the cream cheese mixture gently until well blended. Spoon into the pie shell. Chill, covered, for 2 to 4 hours or until set. Garnish with a single fruit or a combination of fruits. Keep leftovers in the refrigerator. Yield: 6 servings.

Kathy Poulter, Beta Tau
Goderich, Ontario, Canada

STRAWBERRY CHEESECAKE

1 (6-ounce) package
   zwieback
1/2 cup sugar
1/2 teaspoon cinnamon
1/2 cup (1 stick)
   margarine, melted
24 ounces cream cheese,
   softened
1 1/2 cups sugar

4 eggs
1 teaspoon vanilla
   extract
1 pint fresh strawberries
1 (10-ounce) package
   frozen sweetened
   strawberries, thawed
1 tablespoon cornstarch

Crush the zwieback into crumbs. Combine the zwieback crumbs, the 1/2 cup sugar, cinnamon and margarine in a bowl and mix well. Press into a 10-inch springform pan sprayed with nonstick cooking spray. Combine the cream cheese, the 1 1/2 cups sugar, eggs and vanilla in a mixing bowl and beat until smooth. Pour over the zwieback crust. Bake at 375 degrees for 40 minutes or until lightly browned. Arrange the fresh strawberries over the top of the cake, points up. Combine the frozen strawberries and cornstarch in a saucepan over medium heat. Cook until thickened, stirring constantly. Remove from heat and let cool. Pour over the fresh strawberries on the cake. Yield: 12 servings.

Dorothy Wegner
San Marcos, Texas

SWEETHEART STRAWBERRY CHIFFON CHEESECAKE

15 whole graham
   crackers, crushed into
   crumbs
1/2 cup (1 stick)
   margarine, melted
2 tablespoons
   confectioners' sugar
1 (3-ounce) package
   strawberry gelatin
1 cup hot water
1 cup thawed frozen
   strawberries or fresh
   strawberries

8 ounces cream cheese,
   softened
1 1/2 cups sugar
1 (12-ounce) can
   evaporated milk,
   chilled
2 teaspoons vanilla
   extract

Preheat the oven to 350 degrees. Combine the cracker crumbs, margarine and confectioners' sugar in a bowl and mix well. Reserve about 1/2 cup of the mix-ture. Press the remainder over the bottom and about 1 inch up the side of a 10-inch springform pan sprayed with nonstick cooking spray. Bake for 10 minutes. Combine the gelatin, hot water and straw-berries in a bowl and mix well. Chill, covered, in the refrigerator until almost set. Combine the cream cheese and sugar in a bowl and beat until smooth. Place the chilled evaporated milk in a large deep mixing bowl and beat at high speed until very thick. Blend in the cream cheese mixture, then the gelatin mixture, then the vanilla. Pour into the prepared pan. Sprinkle with the reserved crumb mixture and/or decorate with sliced strawberries. Chill, covered, for 2 or 3 hours. Remove from the springform pan before serving or slicing. Yield: 12 servings.

Marilyn Becker, Preceptor Pi
Polson, Montana

❖ STRAWBERRY TRUFFLE CHEESECAKE

1 1/2 cups crushed
   chocolate sandwich
   cookies
2 tablespoons melted
   butter
24 ounces cream cheese,
   softened
1 1/2 cups sugar
3 large eggs
1 cup sour cream

1 teaspoon vanilla
2 cups semisweet
   chocolate chips
8 ounces cream cheese,
   softened
1/2 cup strawberry
   preserves
1/2 cup heavy cream
1 pint strawberries,
   quartered

Combine the crushed cookies and butter in a small bowl and mix well. Press into a 9-inch springform pan sprayed with nonstick cooking spray. Combine 24 ounces cream cheese and sugar in a large bowl and beat until smooth. Add the eggs 1 at a time, mix-ing well after each addition. Blend in the sour cream and vanilla. Pour the cream cheese mixture over the cookie crust. Melt 1 cup of the chocolate chips in a saucepan over low heat, stirring constantly. Combine the melted chips with 8 ounces cream cheese in a bowl and mix well. Drop by rounded tablespoonfuls over the sour cream mixture. Do not swirl. Bake at 325 degrees for 1 hour and 15 minutes. Cool on a wire rack. Spread the preserves evenly over the top. Combine the remaining 1 cup chocolate chips and cream in a saucepan over low heat and cook until the chips are melted and the mixture is smooth, stirring constantly. Pour over the layer of preserves. Arrange the cut strawberries over the top chocolate layer. Chill, covered, for at least 2 hours before serving. Yield: 12 servings.

Patricia Duke, Xi Lambda
Baton Rouge, Louisiana

TRUE LOVE CHEESECAKE

1 cup graham cracker
    crumbs
3 tablespoons sugar
1 teaspoon
    cinnamon
1/4 cup (1/2 stick) butter,
    melted
2 tablespoons finely
    chopped pecans
24 ounces cream cheese,
    softened
3/4 cup sugar
3 eggs

3/4 teaspoon vanilla
    extract
2 1/2 cups chopped peeled
    apples
1 tablespoon lemon juice
1/4 cup sugar
1/4 cup caramel topping
Sweetened whipped
    cream
2 tablespoons caramel
    topping
2 tablespoons chopped
    pecans

Preheat the oven to 350 degrees. Combine the graham cracker crumbs, the 3 tablespoons sugar, half the cinnamon, the butter and the 2 tablespoons finely chopped pecans in a bowl and mix well. Press over the bottom and a little up the side of a greased 9-inch springform pan. Bake for 10 minutes; cool. Combine the cream cheese and the 3/4 cup sugar in a mixing bowl and beat until smooth. Add the eggs, beating at low speed until smooth. Stir in the vanilla. Pour the cream cheese mixture over the graham cracker crust. Place the apples, lemon juice, the 1/4 cup sugar and the remaining 1/2 teaspoon cinnamon in a large bowl. Toss to combine. Spread the apple mixture over the cream cheese layer. Bake for 55 to 60 minutes or until center is almost set. Cool in the pan on a wire rack for 10 minutes. Run a knife carefully around the edge to loosen the cake from the side of the pan. Drizzle with the 1/4 cup caramel topping. Let cool for at least 1 hour. Chill, covered, for 8 to 12 hours. Remove sides of pan. Garnish with whipped cream, drizzle with the 2 tablespoons caramel topping and sprinkle with the 2 tablespoons chopped pecans just before serving. Store leftover cheesecake in refrigerator. Yield: 12 servings.

Alice Barry, Preceptor Delta Eta
Arlington, Texas

CHERRY DELIGHT

My doctor's strong recommendation that I restrict red meat in my diet led me to search for other ways of getting protein. This simple and delicious dessert stands on its own.

1 1/2 (16-ounce) packages
    graham crackers
1/4 cup (1/2 stick)
    margarine, melted
8 ounces cream cheese,
    softened

1 (10-ounce) package
    firm tofu
8 ounces whipped
    topping
1 (21-ounce) can cherry
    pie filling

Crush or roll the graham crackers into crumbs. Combine the crumbs and margarine in a small bowl and mix well. Press into the bottom of a 9×13-inch baking pan sprayed with nonstick cooking spray. Combine the cream cheese and tofu in a blender container and process until smooth. Pour into a large bowl. Fold in the whipped topping. Stir in the pie filling. Pour into the prepared pan. Chill, covered, until set. Cut into squares and serve. Yield: 16 servings.

Patricia M. Haston, Laureate Phi
Higginsville, Missouri

PEACH MELBA SQUARES

1/2 cup butter, melted
2 cups vanilla wafer
    crumbs (about 60
    wafers)
1/2 cup chopped pecans,
    toasted
1 (3-ounce) package
    peach-flavored
    gelatin
1/2 cup boiling water
1 (14-ounce) can
    sweetened condensed
    milk

1/4 cup lemon juice from
    concentrate
1 (29-ounce) can sliced
    peaches, drained
2 cups whipping cream,
    whipped
1 (10-ounce) package
    frozen raspberries in
    syrup, drained
1 tablespoon cornstarch

Combine the butter, crumbs and pecans in a bowl and mix well. Pat evenly over the bottom of a greased 7×12-inch baking dish. Dissolve the gelatin in the boiling water in a large bowl. Stir in the condensed milk and lemon juice and mix well. Reserve 12 to 15 peach slices for garnish; chop the remaining slices. Fold the chopped peaches and whipped cream into the gelatin mixture. Pour into the prepared baking dish. Chill, covered, for 4 hours or until set. Combine the raspberries and cornstarch in a small saucepan over medium heat. Cook until clear and slightly thickened, stirring constantly. Cut the chilled peach dessert into squares. Garnish with the reserved peach slices and drizzle with the raspberry sauce. Yield: 12 to 15 servings.

Patricia Reece, Omicron Beta
Ripon, California

LaRhue D. Hansen, Laureate Beta Zeta, Sedalia, Missouri, makes Change of Pace Chess Squares by using strawberry or lemon cake mix mixed with 1 egg and 1/4 cup melted butter for the crust and 2 eggs, 8 ounces cream cheese and 4 cups confectioners' sugar for the top layer. Bake at 350 degrees for 40 to 45 minutes.

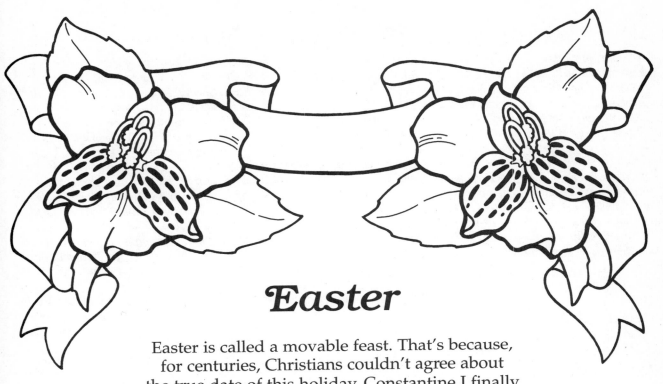

Easter

Easter is called a movable feast. That's because, for centuries, Christians couldn't agree about the true date of this holiday. Constantine I finally settled matters—in the West at least. In 325 A.D., his Council of Nicaea decided on the first Sunday after the full moon following the vernal equinox. Complicated, but it seems to work.

The name Easter probably derives from "Eastre," an Anglo-Saxon goddess of spring and fertility. Rabbits and eggs, both fertility symbols, come to us from that early tradition. Early Anglo-Saxons painted eggs with bright colors to represent spring sunlight. One of their favorite traditions seems to have been Easter egg–rolling contests. Don't you just love those? In this chapter, you'll find some very fertile ideas for your own Easter celebration.

MOSAIC EASTER EGGS

*P*ierce both ends of each egg with a large needle that has been heated over a flame. Make each hole about the size of a pea, place a straw over one of the holes, and blow the contents out of the other hole into a bowl. (The contents can be saved and used later in cooking.) Select an assortment of lightweight colored paper and make a multitude of punches with a paper punch. Use tweezers to dip the punched-out shapes in white glue and place them on the eggshells in desired patterns. Be sure to press the paper shapes firmly over the shell to remove air bubbles. Let the decorated shells dry completely. Although the decorated eggs can be coated with shellac, it is not really necessary as they tend to become very hard over the years and hold up very well.

Kathleen Radcliffe, Laureate Beta
Lancaster, Pennsylvania

THE PERFECT PET

*U*se a very clean container with a lid. Select a small plant and rinse the roots until they are very clean. Place several marbles in the bottom of the container and fill with dechlorinated water to about 1 inch from the top. Place a beta fish in the container. Punch a hole in the lid and thread the plant roots through. Place the lid on the container and place a few marbles on the lid.

If giving as a gift, provide the following "Care for Your Perfect Pet" instructions:

The water should be replenished once a month, or whenever it starts to reduce. Only use dechlorinated water, especially when changing it entirely. Leave some air space between the lid and the water level.

After one to two months you may need to cut back the roots. Take off the marbles, lift out the plant and lid together, and rinse under running water. Cut any long or dark roots and replace the lid and plant on the container. Replace the marbles.

Keep the container away from direct cold or heat. Pet stores sell a pellet food called beta bits that will keep your fish healthy and colorful.

This is a gift for all ages, and especially good for people in nursing homes.

Kathy Verchick, Omega Lambda
Lake City, Florida

Jennifer Dickeson, Iota, Lewiston, Idaho, makes Pretzel Kisses in holiday colors by arranging mini-pretzels on a lightly greased baking sheet, adding an unwrapped milk chocolate kiss to each pretzel, baking at 275 degrees for 2 to 3 minutes, pressing the melted chocolate over the pretzels and topping each with "M&M's". Use pastels for Easter treats.

EASTER PARADE

*I*ssue invitations which instruct guests to make and wear an Easter bonnet. Decorate the room with appropriate Easter/spring colors and items. Set the tables with pastel tablecloths and napkins, put small candy-filled Easter baskets at each place, and add a blooming plant as a centerpiece. Make name tags in advance with a letter of the alphabet added to each. The centerpiece plants and other Easter-related gifts should then be labeled with letters for door prize drawings.

After a light, spring-fresh lunch of chicken salad, miniature muffins, and assorted fruit, it will be time for the Easter Parade. Each guest is given the opportunity to parade, displaying and describing her bonnet. After the parade, serve dessert and vote for the prize-winning bonnets—the largest, funniest, most beautiful, most original, etc.

A few years ago our chapter invited the local newspaper to our Easter Parade and they had so much fun that there was a full 3-page spread in the Sunday paper with lots of pictures.

Ann-Joy Hardy, Xi Zeta Iota
Winter Haven, Florida

NARCISSUS CUPS

*W*e prepared these as decorations and favors for a senior citizens' dinner. Use medium-size votive cups, half-filling the cups with artificial potting soil pellets. Place a single narcissus bulb about a half-inch deep in the soil and top with a clump of moss. Water lightly and watch it grow. The only trick is picking the right time to start the bulbs.

Ona L. Mackey, Xi Beta
Sulphur, Oklahoma

DINOSAUR TREASURE EGGS

*T*his is great for birthday parties or Easter basket surprises. Make a mixture of 1 cup flour, 1 cup used coffee grounds, 1/2 cup salt, 1/2 cup fine sand from the craft department, and powdered tempera paint in the color you desire. Add a small amount of water and mix until the material is the consistency of dough. Divide and form into portions the size and shape of an egg. Insert small plastic dinosaurs or other toys into the eggs and reshape. Let stand to air-dry for 2 to 3 days, turning occasionally for even drying, or place in a 150- to 200-degree oven for 20 minutes and let cool. The little ones will enjoy breaking open an egg to find a surprise.

Rhonda Snyder, Xi Zeta Omega
Lewis, Kansas

BROWN BAG EASTER BONNETS

*F*ill a brown paper bag for each guest with an assortment of decorating materials such as ribbon, artificial flowers, lace, buttons, small stuffed toys, paper plates, foil, and plastic wrap. Be sure that there is an ample supply of sticky tape, staplers, and scissors. Give your guests their bags, start the time clock for whatever time you choose, and finish with the parade of completed (or semi-completed) bonnets. Choose a winner.

Dorothy Bilton
Oshawa, Ontario, Canada

BUNNY CAKE

*T*urning a plain cake into a birthday or Easter bunny spectacular is easier than you think. Prepare and bake a yellow cake mix according to the package directions for two 9-inch round layers. Assemble the cake with currant jelly between the layers and frost the top and side with a favorite white frosting tinted pink. Now prepare marshmallow bunnies as follows:

Dilute a drop or two of red food coloring with a drop or two of water and use a toothpick to draw eyes, a nose, and a mouth on 18 to 20 large marshmallows. Draw 3 buttons on each of 10 additional marshmallows and set aside to dry. Cut 5 marshmallows into halves and cut each half lengthwise into halves. Use toothpicks to assemble the bunnies: Skewer a body with buttons and a head with a face together. Run two toothpicks diagonally through each body so that the ends protrude and the short marshmallow strips can be skewered on for arms and the longer strips attached for legs.

Cut ears from white paper about 1½ inches long and ⅝ inch wide in the middle. Shade the centers of the ears with a red pencil and fold lengthwise. Use scissors to make two slits in each bunny head to insert the ears. Position the finished bunnies around the outside of the cake and add small pink gumdrops where the hands meet. If the cake is a birthday cake, make additional bunny faces for the top to serve as candle holders.

Ethel Goble, Pi Master
Brighton, Illinois

Rich Olive Spread is a specialty of Barbara Giaiomini, Preceptor Eta, Lebanon, New Hampshire. She combines chopped black olives, chopped green olives, 3 cloves of freshly chopped garlic, chopped red onion and basil, and olive oil to taste. After chilling for 1 hour and mixing well, she serves with crackers or nacho rounds.

HAWAIIAN FRUIT DIP

My daughter always thought this was the best dip for fruit. When she was six, she would eat it with a spoon. Now she's thirty, and she still likes to eat it with a spoon!

1 (4-ounce) package instant vanilla pudding mix	**1 (8-ounce) can juice-pack crushed pineapple**
1¼ cups cold milk	**⅓ cup shredded coconut**
½ cup sour cream	

Combine the pudding mix and milk in a medium bowl and blend well. Blend in the sour cream. Stir in the pineapple and coconut. Chill, covered, for 30 minutes to 1 hour or until set and cold. Serve with assorted fresh fruit dippers. Yield: 2¾ cups.

Sandi Davison, Laureate Gamma Upsilon
Kansas City, Missouri

ASPARAGUS ROLL-UPS

Great as an appetizer or a side dish.

16 fresh asparagus spears	**2 tablespoons minced chives**
16 sliced sandwich bread, crusts trimmed	**¼ cup (½ stick) butter or margarine, melted**
8 ounces cream cheese, softened	**3 tablespoons grated Parmesan cheese**
4 slices bacon, crisp-cooked, crumbled	

Preheat the oven to 400 degrees. Place the asparagus and a small amount of water in a skillet over medium heat. Cook for 6 to 8 minutes or until tender; drain. Flatten the bread with a rolling pin. Combine the cream cheese, bacon and chives in a small bowl and mix well. Spread 1 tablespoon of the bacon mixture over each bread slice. Top with 1 asparagus spear. Roll up tightly; place seam side down on a greased baking sheet. Brush with butter and sprinkle with Parmesan cheese. Cut each roll-up in half. Bake for 10 to 12 minutes or until lightly browned.
Yield: 32 appetizers.

Barbara Osborn, Xi Sigma
Holtville, California

Berny Suchan, Xi Zeta, Yorktown, Saskatchewan, Canada, makes Mushroom Cheese Hors d'Oeuvres by arranging stemless mushroom caps on a baking sheet, placing a cube of mozzarella cheese in each, sprinkling with crumbled crisp-cooked bacon, and baking at 350 degrees for 15 minutes.

CARROT ORANGE BISQUE

Delicious when served with ham, turkey, or pork roast. My family likes it served as a first course "to tempt the Easter Bunny." May substitute turkey or vegetable broth for the chicken broth. May prepare ahead through the purée step, then chill or freeze until ready to resume recipe.

2 large onions, chopped	1/4 teaspoon nutmeg
1/4 cup (1/2 stick) butter	1 tablespoon grated
1 tablespoon cumin	orange zest
1 teaspoon dried	1 1/2 pounds carrots,
tarragon, or 1	shredded or thinly
tablespoon fresh	sliced
1/3 teaspoon dried	2 cups chicken broth
thyme, or 1 teaspoon	1/2 cup white rice,
fresh	uncooked
1 tablespoon honey or	1/2 cup heavy cream
sugar	1/2 cup sour cream
2 teaspoons salt	2 cups fresh orange juice
1 teaspoon pepper	

Sauté the onions in the butter in a 4- or 5-quart saucepan over medium heat until translucent. Stir in the cumin, tarragon, thyme, honey, salt, pepper, nutmeg, orange zest and carrots. Cook over medium heat for 5 minutes, stirring frequently. Stir in the broth; bring to a boil. Stir in the rice; reduce heat. Simmer, tightly covered, over low heat for about 30 minutes. Remove from heat. Let stand until cool. Purée in small batches in a blender until smooth. Bring to a simmer in a saucepan over medium heat. Stir in the cream and sour cream and cook until heated through. Just before serving, stir in the orange juice. Garnish with fresh herbs and/or sour cream. Leftovers may be lightly reheated, but do not boil. Yield: 10 to 12 servings.

Jeanne A. McKinnie, Xi Beta Phi
Nine Mile Falls, Washington

For Fresh as Spring Peach Punch, Susan Parsley, Xi Eta Delta, Savannah, Georgia, combines peach nectar, peach schnapps, and champagne. Add an ice ring of peach nectar, peach slices, and fresh mint leaves.

Hazel Ivey, Beta Epsilon Omicron, Brackettville, Texas, makes Champagne Punch by mixing equal parts pink lemonade and cranberry juice, and twice as much champagne or ginger ale.

GARDEN CHEESE SOUP

Once we were struck by a snowstorm that prevented my brother from returning home with his hockey team. He called to ask if they could stay with us. I opened the freezer—by the time the team arrived, I was able to serve them nice hot soup and rolls.

1 cup sliced celery	Frozen chopped broccoli,
1 cup chopped onion	cauliflower and
2 tablespoons butter or	carrots to make
margarine	2 cups
2/3 cup flour	1 cup frozen hash brown
4 cups water	potatoes
6 chicken bouillon	3 cups milk
cubes	2 1/2 cups shredded
1/4 teaspoon pepper	Cheddar cheese

Sauté the celery and onion in butter in a large kettle or Dutch oven over medium heat until tender. Combine the flour and water in a medium bowl and stir until smooth. Add the flour mixture gradually to the celery mixture. Stir in the bouillon cubes, pepper and vegetables. Bring to a boil; reduce heat. Simmer, covered, for 15 minutes. Stir in the milk and cheese. Cook over medium heat until heated through and cheese is melted, stirring constantly; do not boil. Garnish as desired. Keep leftovers in refrigerator. Yield: 8 to 12 servings.

Gloria Upham, Beta Master
Truro, Nova Scotia, Canada

NACHO POTATO SOUP

Recipe may be easily doubled.

1 (5-ounce) package au	2 cups water
gratin potatoes	2 cups milk
1 (11-ounce) can whole	2 cups chopped
kernel corn, drained	American cheese
1 (10-ounce) can diced	Dash of hot pepper
tomatoes, drained	sauce (optional)
1 (4-ounce) can green	Minced fresh parsley
chiles	(optional)

Combine the potatoes, corn, tomatoes, green chiles and water in a 3-quart saucepan and mix well. Bring to a boil; reduce heat. Simmer, covered, for 15 to 18 minutes or until potatoes are tender. Add the milk, cheese and hot pepper sauce. Cook until cheese is melted, stirring constantly. Garnish with parsley. Yield: 6 to 8 servings (2 quarts).

Diane L. Pruett, Preceptor Alpha Upsilon
Tamaqua, Pennsylvania

✤ CHILLED SWEET PEPPER SOUP

I am known as "not a very good cook," but when I serve this soup, my friends say, "You made this?" and people who don't know me well say, "You lied! You're a great cook!" Serve with fresh tomato sandwiches on really good bread, a fresh fruit salad, and brewed iced tea. The addition of the sour cream is optional, but it adds a refreshing tang to the sweet soup.

1 tablespoon butter or margarine	Dash of ground red pepper
2 medium carrots, chopped	Dash of nutmeg
1 large onion, chopped	3 ounces cream cheese, cubed, softened
1 1/4 cups chicken broth	1/2 cup milk or light cream
1 yellow bell pepper, chopped	Sour cream (optional)
1/2 teaspoon salt	

Melt the butter in a saucepan over medium heat. Stir in the carrots and onion. Cook for about 10 minutes or until tender, stirring occasionally. Stir in the chicken broth and bell pepper. Bring to a boil over medium-high heat; reduce heat. Simmer, covered, for 15 minutes or until pepper is tender. Remove from heat; cool slightly. Stir in the salt, red pepper, nutmeg and cream cheese. Remove half the mixture to a blender container and process until smooth. Pour into a large bowl. Repeat with remaining cheese mixture. Chill, covered, for at least 4 hours. Stir in the milk just before serving. Thin the sour cream with a little milk and drizzle over the soup. Ladle into individual bowls. Yield: 4 servings.

*Margaret (Megan) Bryant, Phi Omega
Albany, Oregon*

TAFFY APPLE SALAD

Serve a large bowl of this wonderful salad with poultry or pork.

1 (20-ounce) can juice-pack crushed pineapple	1 1/2 teaspoons apple cider vinegar
2 cups miniature marshmallows	8 ounces whipped topping
2 tablespoons flour	5 medium apples, cut up
1/2 cup sugar	10 ounces Spanish peanuts
1 egg, beaten	

Drain the pineapple and reserve the juice. Combine the marshmallows and pineapple in a small bowl and mix well. Combine the reserved pineapple juice, flour, sugar, egg and vinegar in a saucepan over low heat. Cook until thickened, stirring constantly. Chill

the pineapple mixture and the vinegar mixture in separate bowls, covered, for 8 to 12 hours. Combine the two mixtures and the apples in a large bowl and mix well. Garnish with the peanuts.
Yield: 12 to 14 servings.

*Jo Ann Clements, Preceptor Alpha Rho
Albuquerque, New Mexico*

GREEN AND GOLD SALAD

I received this recipe in 1973 on a trip to Alaska! It has been my daughter's favorite salad ever since. Serve with ham, baked potatoes, and dinner rolls.

1 (3-ounce) package lime gelatin	1 1/2 cups shredded Cheddar cheese
1/2 cup boiling water	8 ounces whipped topping
1 (15-ounce) can crushed pineapple	
1 tablespoon lemon juice	

Dissolve the gelatin in the boiling water. Stir in the undrained pineapple and lemon juice. Chill, covered, until slightly thickened. Fold in the cheese and whipped topping. Pour into a 5-cup ring mold sprayed with nonstick cooking spray. Chill, covered, until serving time. Yield: 8 servings.

*Janette Spencer, Laureate Upsilon
El Dorado, Arkansas*

PEANUT PEA SALAD

Great with ham at Easter time or for any buffet. I use petite frozen peas.

3 1/2 cups frozen peas, thawed, drained	1 cup red-skinned peanuts
1 large onion, chopped	Paprika Salad Dressing
1 cup chopped celery	

Combine the peas, onion, celery and peanuts in a glass bowl. Add the Paprika Salad Dressing at least 1 hour before serving. Toss to combine. Chill, covered, until serving time. Yield: 10 to 12 servings.

PAPRIKA SALAD DRESSING

2/3 cup olive oil	2 tablespoons sugar
3 tablespoons vinegar	1/2 teaspoon paprika
1/2 teaspoon salt	1/2 teaspoon pepper

Place the oil, vinegar, salt, sugar, paprika and pepper in a lidded jar and shake well to combine. Feel free to adjust amounts of ingredients to your taste.

*Dottie Kollar, Gamma Zeta
Vallejo, California*

CREAMY APRICOT SALAD

Serve with ham, mashed potatoes, and corn.

2 (3-ounce) packages apricot gelatin	1 cup sugar
1 (15-ounce) can crushed pineapple	1 (8-ounce) jar junior baby food apricots
1 cup cold water	12 ounces whipped topping
8 ounces cream cheese, softened	

Combine the gelatin and undrained pineapple in a saucepan over medium heat. Heat until gelatin is dissolved, stirring frequently. Remove from heat; stir in the cold water. Combine the cream cheese, sugar and apricots in a mixing bowl and beat at medium speed until creamy. Add the gelatin mixture. Fold in the whipped topping. Spread in a 9×13-inch glass dish. Chill, covered, until serving time. Yield: 12 servings.

Carolyn Carlson, Kappa Beta
Dowagiac, Michigan

SUNNY SPRING TOSSED SALAD

1/2 cup sunflower seeds	1/2 teaspoon salt
1/2 cup slivered almonds	1/2 teaspoon dry mustard
2 tablespoons butter or margarine	4 cups torn leaf lettuce
1/3 cup vegetable oil	1 (11-ounce) can mandarin oranges, drained
3 tablespoons apple cider vinegar	1 ripe avocado, peeled, diced
1 tablespoon lemon juice	1 or 2 green onions, chopped
2 teaspoons sugar	

Sauté the sunflower seeds and almonds in butter in a small skillet over medium heat until lightly toasted and fragrant. Let stand until cool. Place the oil, vinegar, lemon juice, sugar, salt and mustard in a lidded jar and shake well to combine. Place the lettuce, oranges, avocado, green onions and almond mixture in a large bowl. Toss to combine. Drizzle with the vinegar mixture. Serve immediately. Yield: 6 to 8 servings.

Juanita Fleming, Preceptor Beta Mu
Prineville, Oregon

Try Chili Dressing for spinach salad, made by Sandra Thrasher, Preceptor Beta Mu, Prineville, Oregon. Blend 1 cup mayonnaise with 1/4 cup chili sauce, the juice of 1 lemon, and minced green onion to taste. Cut spinach leaves into strips, moisten lightly with salad oil and lemon juice, and chill before adding the dressing.

❖ CURRIED GRAPE AND SHRIMP SALAD

1 pound shrimp, cooked, sliced	2 tablespoons chopped green bell pepper
2 cups seedless green grapes	1/8 teaspoon ginger
2 cups cashews	1 tablespoon lemon juice
1/2 cup sour cream	1/2 teaspoon salt
1/2 cup mayonnaise	1/2 teaspoon curry powder
2 tablespoons minced onion	

Place the shrimp, grapes and cashews in a bowl and toss to combine. Combine the sour cream, mayonnaise, onion, bell pepper, ginger, lemon juice, salt and curry powder in a small bowl and mix well. Pour over the shrimp mixture and mix well. Chill, covered, for 2 to 3 hours before serving over lettuce leaves. Yield: 6 to 8 servings.

Jean Schauer, Beta Gamma
Klamath Falls, Oregon

HONEY BAKED HAM

The "close-fitting kettle" in this recipe means the smallest kettle into which you can fit the ham. The initial simmering is done to remove the too-salty taste and add a delicate flavor.

1 (13- to 15-pound) smoked cooked ham	1/3 cup real maple syrup
2 to 3 bottles gingerale	1 1/4 cups chicken stock
3 cups dry white wine	2 tablespoons Dijon mustard
5 tablespoons Dijon mustard	3 tablespoons real maple syrup
1/3 cup honey	2 teaspoons cornstarch

Remove and discard the ham's rind. Score the ham with diagonal cross-cuts. Place in a close-fitting kettle and cover with gingerale. Bring to a boil; reduce heat. Simmer, uncovered, for 20 to 30 minutes; drain. Remove the ham to a roasting pan. Pour the wine over the ham. Cover with foil and bake at 350 degrees for 1 hour. Brush with a mixture of the 5 tablespoons mustard, the honey and the 1/3 cup maple syrup, using all of the mixture. Bake, uncovered, for 1 1/2 hours longer or to 140 degrees on a meat thermometer. Baste occasionally after the glaze has set—about 45 minutes. If glaze gets too dark before temperature reaches 140 degrees, tent the ham with foil. Remove the ham to a serving plate and cover loosely with foil to keep warm. Skim the fat from the drippings. Add 1 cup of the chicken stock, the 2 tablespoons mustard and the 3 tablespoons maple syrup to the drippings in the pan; bring to a boil.

Dissolve the cornstarch in the remaining ¼ cup chicken stock and whisk into the sauce to thicken. The sauce should be a rich dark color; strain it and pour into a gravy boat. Yield: 20 to 24 servings.

Denise Gerling, Laureate Delta Gamma
Bolton, Ontario, Canada

FRUITED BAKED HAM

1 cup pineapple or orange juice	1 (5- to 6-pound) cooked ham
¾ cup packed light brown sugar	Whole cloves
2 teaspoons dry mustard	½ cup raisins
½ teaspoon each ground cloves and ginger	1 tablespoon cornstarch
⅛ teaspoon nutmeg	1 tablespoon cold water
¼ cup rum	Green and red seedless grapes

Combine the pineapple juice, brown sugar, mustard, ground cloves, ginger and nutmeg in a saucepan over medium-high heat; bring to a boil. Remove from heat. Stir in the rum. Pierce the ham several times with a fork. Place it in a large oven bag or double plastic bags. Pour the rum mixture over the ham. Tie the bag tightly and chill for 8 to 12 hours. Turn the ham. Continue marinating for at least 3 days, turning daily. Preheat the oven to 325 degrees when ready to cook. Remove the ham from the bag, reserving the marinade. Place the ham on a rack in a roasting pan. Roast, covered, to 135 degrees on a meat thermometer, usually 1 hour, or 22 to 25 minutes per pound. Remove from oven. Score top in diamond shapes and stud the corners of each diamond with whole cloves. Increase the oven temperature to 425 degrees. Bake for ½ hour, basting frequently with the marinade. Remove from oven. Plump the raisins in hot water and drain. Remove the ham to a serving platter and remove the rack from the pan. Dissolve the cornstarch in 1 tablespoon cold water or marinade. Add the raisins and cornstarch to the pan juices. Cook over medium heat until clear and thickened, stirring constantly. Serve with the ham. Garnish the ham platter with seedless grape clusters. Yield: 6 to 8 servings.

Jo Anne Arnold, Laureate Alpha Nu
Satellite Beach, Florida

Kandi Buck, Gamma Theta, Rapid City, South Dakota, prepares Mustard Delight to serve with ham by mixing 1 cup sugar, 1 tablespoon flour, 1 tablespoon dry mustard, ¼ teaspoon salt, 2 well-beaten eggs, ½ cup vinegar, ¼ cup water, and 2 tablespoons butter and cooking over medium heat until thickened, stirring constantly.

HOLIDAY HAM WITH RAISIN SAUCE

1 (8- to 10-pound) butt end of cooked ham	1 bay leaf
2 garlic cloves, peeled	1 medium onion, quartered
10 to 12 peppercorns	Raisin Sauce

Place the ham in a large kettle, wide part down. Cover with water. Add the garlic, peppercorns, bay leaf and onion. Bring to a boil; reduce heat. Simmer over low heat for 3 hours. Remove ham to a serving platter. Serve with Raisin Sauce. Yield: 12 to 20 servings.

RAISIN SAUCE

6 tablespoons raisins	Few grains of salt
2 cups cold water	Paprika to taste
2 tablespoons butter, melted	5 tablespoons marmalade
2 tablespoons cornstarch or flour	1½ tablespoons lemon juice

Place the raisins and cold water in a saucepan over medium-high heat. Bring slowly to a boil; reduce heat. Simmer for 15 minutes. Mix the butter, cornstarch, salt and paprika in a small bowl. Stir into the raisin liquid over medium-high heat. Simmer for 5 minutes, stirring constantly. Remove from heat. Stir in the marmalade and lemon juice.

Carol Ann Schaefer, Preceptor Alpha Alpha
Pearl River, New York

BAKED EGG SURPRISE

A welcome change from scrambled eggs! This brunch dish can be prepared the night before and served the next morning, perhaps after Easter sunrise services.

4 tablespoons butter	1 cup shredded sharp Cheddar cheese
4 tablespoons flour	3 English muffins, halved, toasted
1½ cups milk	
2 ripe tomatoes, sliced	
10 hard-cooked eggs, sliced	

Preheat the oven to 350 degrees. Melt the butter in a saucepan over medium heat. Add the flour and stir well. Whisk in the milk and cook over medium heat until medium thick, stirring constantly with the wire whisk to avoid lumps. Remove from heat. Layer half the tomatoes, half the eggs and half the white sauce in a buttered casserole. Repeat the layers. Sprinkle the cheese over the top. Bake for 10 minutes or until cheese is slightly brown. Serve over English muffins. Yield: 6 servings.

Anne Kittrell, Laureate Zeta
Orange Beach, Alabama

BREAKFAST BUNDLES

These delectable bundles can be made ahead of time and refrigerated for 48 hours or frozen for 1 month. Serve with fresh fruit.

2 tablespoons butter	2 teaspoons minced
2 tablespoons flour	fresh chives or green
1 cup milk	onion tops
1/2 cup shredded Cheddar	1/2 teaspoon thyme
cheese	8 sheets phyllo dough,
1/4 teaspoon salt	thawed
1/4 teaspoon pepper	1/4 cup (1/2 stick) butter,
6 eggs, lightly beaten	melted
1 cup chopped smoked	3 tablespoons grated
ham	Parmesan cheese
2 tablespoons minced	
fresh parsley	

Preheat the oven to 375 degrees. Melt the 2 tablespoons butter in a saucepan over medium heat. Whisk in the flour. Whisk in the milk. Cook for 5 minutes or until thickened, stirring constantly. Stir in the Cheddar cheese, salt and half the pepper. Cook until cheese is melted, stirring constantly. Remove from heat. Combine the eggs, ham, parsley, chives, thyme, a pinch more salt and the remaining pepper in a nonstick skillet over medium heat. Cook until eggs are scrambled but still moist, stirring. Stir into the cheese mixture. Let stand until cool. Brush 1 sheet of phyllo lightly with melted butter. Fold in half lengthwise; brush with butter. Spoon 1/2 cup of the egg mixture over the dough near an end. Sprinkle with 1 teaspoon Parmesan cheese. Roll gently, tucking in the sides. Arrange on a baking sheet and bake for 10 minutes or until golden. Yield: 8 servings.

Paula Morse, Xi Kappa
Kingston, Nova Scotia, Canada

BRUNCH ENCHILADAS

Serve with a spring garden salad.

2 cups chopped cooked	1 tablespoon flour
ham	2 cups half-and-half
1/2 cup chopped green	6 eggs, beaten
onions	1/4 teaspoons salt
10 (8-inch) flour	(optional)
tortillas	
2 cups shredded Cheddar	
cheese	

Combine the ham and onions in a bowl and mix well. Spoon 1/3 cup of the ham mixture down the center of each tortilla. Top each with 2 tablespoons of cheese. Roll up, tucking in ends, and place seam side down in a buttered 9×13-inch baking dish. Combine the flour, half-and-half, eggs and salt in a bowl, beating until smooth. Pour over the tortillas. Chill, covered, for 8 to 12 hours. Remove from refrigerator 30 minutes before baking. Bake, covered, at 350 degrees for 25 minutes. Bake, uncovered, for 10 minutes longer. Sprinkle with the remaining cheese. Bake for 3 minutes longer. Let stand for 10 minutes before serving. Yield: 10 servings.

Faye A. Magers, Laureate Beta Upsilon
Chester, Illinois

CHEDDAR APPLE BREAKFAST LASAGNA

1 cup sour cream	2 1/2 cups shredded
1/3 cup packed brown	Cheddar cheese
sugar	1 (21-ounce) can apple
2 (9-ounce) packages	pie filling
frozen French toast	1 cup granola with
8 ounces sliced cooked	raisins
ham	

Blend the sour cream and brown sugar in a bowl. Prepare the French toast using the package directions. Place 6 slices in a buttered 9×13-inch baking pan. Layer the ham, 2 cups of the cheese and the remaining 6 slices toast over the first layer. Spread the pie filling evenly over the top. Sprinkle with granola. Bake at 350 degrees for 25 minutes. Sprinkle with the remaining 1/2 cup cheese and bake until cheese is melted. Serve with the sour cream mixture. Yield: 15 servings.

Marylou Burns, Laureate Alpha Pi
Rockford, Illinois

LEG OF LAMB

This is the easiest leg of lamb ever!

1 leg of lamb	1 teaspoon sugar
1 brewed cup of coffee,	2 teaspoons milk
regular or	
decaffeinated	

Bake the lamb in a roasting pan at 325 degrees for 30 to 35 minutes per pound. Make a cup of coffee 1/2 hour before baking time is over. Add the sugar and milk to the coffee. Pour the coffee mixture over the lamb. Remove the lamb from the pan at the end of baking time. Make gravy in the pan with flour, salt, pepper and the drippings.
Yield: 6 to 8 servings.

Nancy Schroder, Preceptor Epsilon Sigma
Fremont, California

GRAND LAMB CASSEROLE

1 (1-pound) breast of lamb	1 cup chopped carrots
1/2 cup sliced onions	2 cups canned tomatoes
1 tablespoon butter or margarine	11/2 teaspoons salt
1 cup boiling water	1/4 teaspoon pepper
1 cup chopped peeled potatoes	3 tablespoons quick-cooking tapioca
	6 to 8 unbaked biscuits

Cut the lamb into small pieces. Brown the lamb with the onions in the butter in a heavy skillet over medium-high heat. Add the boiling water. Place in a 10-inch-square casserole sprayed with nonstick cooking spray. Bake, covered, at 350 degrees for 1 hour or until meat is tender. Add the potatoes, carrots, tomatoes, salt and pepper. Bake, covered, for 30 minutes longer or until vegetables are tender. Sprinkle the tapioca over the lamb mixture and mix thoroughly. Arrange the biscuits over the lamb mixture. Bake, uncovered, for 12 to 15 minutes longer or until biscuits are brown. Yield: 6 servings.

Ruby G. Hartje, Xi Gamma Nu
Anna, Illinois

SLOW-COOKER CHICKEN AND STUFFING

21/2 cups chicken broth	1 teaspoon poultry seasoning
1 cup (2 sticks) butter, melted	1 teaspoon salt
1/2 cup chopped onion	1/2 teaspoon pepper
1/2 cup chopped celery	12 cups day-old bread cubes
1 (4-ounce) can mushroom pieces, drained	2 eggs, beaten
	1 cup undiluted cream of chicken soup
11/2 teaspoons rubbed sage	6 cups chopped cooked chicken

Combine the chicken broth, butter, onion, celery, mushrooms, sage, poultry seasoning, salt, pepper and bread cubes in a saucepan over medium heat. Bring to a simmer. Simmer for 10 minutes. Remove the bread with a slotted spoon to a large bowl. Combine the eggs and soup in a bowl and mix well. Add the egg mixture to the broth mixture in the saucepan and stir until smooth. Pour the egg mixture over the bread cubes and toss to combine. Place the bread mixture in a slow cooker. Add the chicken. Cook on Low for 41/2 to 5 hours or until chicken is tender. Yield: 14 to 16 servings.

Donna Utecht, Alpha Nu
Norfolk, Nebraska

❖ POLLO RELLENO

6 skinless boneless chicken breasts	2 ounces Monterey Jack cheese
1/2 cup cornmeal	2 tablespoons snipped cilantro or parsley
1/2 envelope taco seasoning mix (2 tablespoons)	1/4 teaspoon red pepper
1 egg, beaten	1 (8-ounce) bottle green or red taco sauce
1 (4-ounce) can whole green chiles, rinsed, seeded	1/4 cup shredded Cheddar or Monterey Jack cheese

Rinse the chicken and pat dry. Pound 1/8 inch thick between sheets of plastic wrap. Combine the cornmeal and taco seasoning in a bowl and mix well. Place the egg in a shallow bowl. Cut the chiles in half lengthwise. Cut the 2 ounces Monterey Jack cheese into six 41/2-inch strips. Place a chile strip on each chicken piece near its edge. Place a cheese strip over each chile strip. Sprinkle with cilantro and red pepper. Roll to enclose the filling. Dip each chicken roll in the egg, then roll in the cornmeal mixture. Place seam side down in a shallow baking pan. Bake, uncovered, at 375 degrees for 25 to 30 minutes or until chicken is cooked through. Heat the taco sauce. Remove chicken from oven and sprinkle with the Cheddar cheese. Garnish with tomatoes and serve with the taco sauce. Yield: 6 servings.

Ruth Drummond, Xi Master
Pueblo, Colorado

LINGUINI AND RED CLAM SAUCE

2 garlic cloves, chopped	1 (28-ounce) can diced tomatoes, slightly drained
2 medium onions, chopped	
1/4 cup (1/2 stick) butter	4 (7-ounce) cans chopped or whole baby clams
1/4 cup olive oil	
2 tablespoons chopped parsley	1 pound linguini, cooked, drained
1 (15-ounce) can tomato sauce	

Sauté the garlic and onions in the butter and olive oil in a large saucepan over medium-low heat, cooking until onions are tender. Stir in the parsley, tomato sauce and tomatoes. Simmer, covered, for about 25 minutes. Stir in the clams. Cook for 5 minutes longer. Pour over the linguini and garnish with chopped parsley. Serve immediately, with Parmesan cheese. Yield: 5 to 6 servings.

Judy Stauch, Laureate Theta Delta
Simi Valley, California

PAELLA

1 pound fresh deveined peeled shrimp	1/2 cup sliced pepperoni
2 garlic cloves, crushed	1 (10-ounce) package frozen green peas and pearl onions, thawed
2 tablespoons butter or margarine	1/4 teaspoon cayenne pepper
1 tablespoon cornstarch	
1 1/4 cups chicken broth	1 1/2 cups instant rice, uncooked
1 (14-ounce) can stewed tomatoes, undrained	1/8 teaspoon saffron

Sauté the shrimp and garlic in butter in a skillet over medium heat for about 2 minutes or until shrimp are pink. Add the cornstarch and cook for 1 minute, stirring. Stir in the chicken broth, tomatoes, pepperoni, peas and onions and cayenne pepper. Bring to a boil, stirring occasionally. Stir in the rice and saffron. Remove from heat and cover. Let stand for 5 minutes. Fluff with a fork. Yield: 4 servings.

Cindy Gardner, Preceptor Epsilon
Pearl, Mississippi

SALMON PATTIES

A great dish for Lent!

1 (15-ounce) can pink salmon, drained	1/4 cup milk
	Italian-seasoned bread crumbs
1 (6-ounce) can chunky crab meat, drained	
1 teaspoon dill	1 teaspoon Old Bay seasoning (optional)
egg	

Combine the salmon, crab meat and dill in a medium bowl. Blend the egg and milk. Add the egg mixture to the salmon mixture and mix well. Add enough bread crumbs to allow mixture to be shaped into patties. Shape 4 patties and place them in a large skillet sprayed with nonstick cooking spray. Cook over medium heat for about 5 minutes on each side or until hot in the center and golden brown. Yield: 4 servings.

Jennifer Voight, Nu Beta
Troy, Michigan

ASPARAGUS CASSEROLE

2 (15-ounce) cans asparagus	1 small can slivered almonds, toasted
6 hard-cooked eggs, sliced	1/2 cup shredded Cheddar cheese
2 (10-ounce) cans cream of mushroom soup	8 saltine crackers, crumbled
1 (4-ounce) jar chopped pimentos	2 tablespoons butter

Layer the asparagus, eggs, soup, pimentos and almonds in a buttered 9×12-inch baking dish. Sprinkle with the cheese and cracker crumbs. Dot with butter. Bake at 350 degrees for 30 minutes or until hot and bubbly. Yield: 8 to 10 servings.

Betty H. Combs, Alpha Xi
Hazard, Kentucky

MARINATED BRUSSELS SPROUTS

2 (10-ounce) packages frozen brussels sprouts, thawed	1 (16-ounce) bottle Italian dressing
Red or white onions to taste, chopped	

Boil the brussels sprouts in water to cover in a saucepan over medium-high heat for 5 minutes. Let stand until cool. Add the onions and mix well. Stir in the dressing, adding 2 additional tablespoons vinegar if desired. Pour the brussels sprouts mixture into a bowl. Toss to coat well. Let stand, covered, at room temperature for 12 hours. Chill and serve. Yield: 12 servings.

Lynn Koch, Preceptor Chi
Omaha, Nebraska

SWEET-AND-SOUR BRUSSELS SPROUTS

My sons-in-law love this dish. One of them said his mother simply opened a can of vegetables and put them in a pot—he'd never had spiced-up vegetables until he married my daughter!

1 pound sliced bacon, chopped	1 teaspoon salt
	1/2 teaspoon dry mustard
1 medium onion, chopped	1/4 teaspoon pepper
1/3 cup cider vinegar	2 (10-ounce) packages frozen brussels sprouts
3 tablespoons sugar	

Cook the bacon in a saucepan over medium-low heat for about 10 minutes or until brown and crisp. Remove the bacon with a slotted spoon. Sauté the onion in the bacon drippings until tender. Stir in the vinegar, sugar, salt, mustard and pepper. Cook the brussels sprouts using the package directions; drain. Place in a serving dish. Pour the vinegar mixture over the brussels sprouts. Sprinkle with the bacon. Serve immediately. Yield: 6 to 8 servings.

Winnie S. Hall, Laureate Lambda
Annapolis, Maryland

CARROT BAKE

3 pounds baby carrots,
  cooked
8 eggs
1¹/2 cups sugar
¹/2 cup plus 1 tablespoon
  flour
3 teaspoons baking
  powder
3 teaspoons vanilla
  extract
1 cup (2 sticks) butter,
  melted

1 tablespoon cinnamon
1¹/2 cups crushed
  cornflakes
¹/2 cup (1 stick) butter,
  melted
¹/4 cup plus
  3 tablespoons brown
  sugar
¹/2 cup chopped pecans
  or walnuts

Place the carrots in a food processor container and process until smooth. Beat the eggs well in a large bowl with a wire whisk. Add the sugar, flour, baking powder, vanilla, the 1 cup butter, cinnamon and carrots; mix well. Pour into a 9×13-inch baking dish. Combine the cornflakes, the ¹/2 cup butter, brown sugar and nuts in a small bowl and mix well. Sprinkle evenly over the carrot mixture. Bake, uncovered, at 350 degrees for 1¹/4 hours. Yield: 20 servings.

Dorothy Byers, Laureate Alpha Iota
Weirton, West Virginia

CORN PUDDING

1 (17-ounce) can cream-
  style corn
3 eggs, slightly beaten
3 tablespoons sugar
3 tablespoons flour
1 (4-ounce) jar chopped
  pimentos

1 small green bell
  pepper, chopped
1 cup milk
Butter
Salt to taste
Chopped onion

Combine the corn, eggs, sugar, flour, pimentos, bell pepper and milk in a large bowl and mix well. Stir in butter, salt and onion. Bake, uncovered, at 350 degrees for 1 hour. Yield: 6 to 8 servings.

Betty J. Bowers, Beta Omicron Master
Fort Worth, Texas

CRUNCHY POTATO CASSEROLE

1 (32-ounce) package
  frozen hash brown
  potatoes, thawed
¹/2 cup (1 stick) butter,
  melted
1 teaspoon salt
¹/4 teaspoon pepper
¹/2 cup chopped onion

1 cup undiluted cream of
  celery soup
2 cups sour cream
2¹/2 cups shredded
  Cheddar cheese
2 cups cornflakes
¹/4 cup (¹/2 stick) butter,
  melted

Combine the potatoes, the ¹/2 cup butter, salt, pepper, onion, soup, sour cream and cheese in a large bowl. Pour into a 9×13-inch baking dish. Sprinkle with the cornflakes and drizzle with the ¹/4 cup butter. Bake, uncovered, at 350 degrees for 45 minutes. Serve with baked ham or chicken. Yield: 12 servings.

Victoria Tornetto, Laureate Gamma Eta
St. Louis, Missouri

EVERYBODY'S FAVORITE SPINACH

All members of our family, even those who don't usually eat spinach, like this dish. I usually double the recipe.

2 (10-ounce) packages
  frozen chopped
  spinach
¹/2 (10-ounce) can cream
  of mushroom soup
¹/2 cup mayonnaise

¹/2 cup shredded sharp
  Cheddar cheese
2 tablespoons grated
  onion
Cheese crackers, crushed

Cook the spinach using the package directions; drain. Place in a shallow baking dish. Combine the soup, mayonnaise, cheese and onion in a small bowl and mix well. Pour over the spinach. Sprinkle with the crushed crackers. Bake for 20 minutes.
Yield: 4 servings.

Margie Shanafelt, Nu Master
Centralia, Illinois

CORN STUFFING

This stuffing is great with roast beef or pork, chicken, or turkey.

¹/2 cup chopped celery
  with leaves
1 small onion
1 (17-ounce) can cream-
  style corn
¹/4 cup water
¹/8 teaspoon pepper
1 teaspoon poultry
  seasoning

1 (8-ounce) package
  herb-seasoned
  stuffing mix
2 eggs, slightly beaten
¹/4 cup (¹/2 stick)
  margarine, melted

Combine the celery, onion, corn, water, pepper, poultry seasoning, stuffing mix and eggs in a large bowl and mix well. Shape into 7 or 8 balls. Place in a slow cooker. Pour margarine over the stuffing. Cook on Low for 3 to 4 hours. Yield: 6 to 8 servings.

Jane O'Mara, Nu Omega
Burlington, Kansas

CHEESY PINEAPPLE CASSEROLE

Serve very hot to accompany ham.

2 (15-ounce) cans
pineapple chunks,
drained
1 cup sugar
5 tablespoons flour
1½ cups shredded
mozzarella cheese

1½ cups shredded
Cheddar cheese
¾ cup crushed butter
crackers
½ cup (1 stick) butter,
melted

Place the pineapple in a 4-quart baking dish. Sprinkle with a mixture of the sugar and flour. Combine the cheeses and layer over the sugar layer. Sprinkle with the cracker crumbs. Drizzle the butter over the top. Bake, uncovered, at 350 degrees for 30 minutes. Yield: 6 to 8 servings.

Barbara H. Jones, Iota
Hoover, Alabama

BAKED PINEAPPLE

½ cup (1 stick) butter or
margarine, softened
1 cup sugar
4 large eggs

1 (16-ounce) can crushed
pineapple
5 slices bread, cubed

Cream the butter and sugar in a bowl until light and fluffy. Add the eggs 1 at a time, mixing well after each addition. Stir in the undrained pineapple. Fold in the bread. Pour into a buttered 1½-quart baking dish. Bake, uncovered, at 350 degrees for 1 hour. Yield: 8 servings.

Millie Steeber, Upsilon Master
Aurora, Colorado

EASTER BUNNY BREAD

1 pound frozen bread
dough, thawed
1 large egg, beaten

Assorted jelly beans

Cut the dough into 6 equal pieces. Shape 2 pieces into large flat ovals to make 2 bunny bodies. Shape 2 pieces into balls for bunny heads. Cut each remaining piece into 6 smaller pieces. Shape 4 of the small pieces into ovals for feet, 4 into balls for front paws, and the remaining 4 into 2-inch-long ear shapes. Place the bodies on a large buttered baking sheet, spacing well apart. Attach the heads, feet, paws and ears. Brush with beaten egg. Bake at 375 degrees for 20 minutes. Cool on wire racks. Decorate with jelly-beans while still warm. Tie ribbons around the necks if desired. Yield: 2 bunnies.

Mary Ann Williams, Chi Iota
Summerfield, Illinois

NUTTY ORANGE COFFEE CAKE

¾ cup sugar
½ cup chopped pecans
2 teaspoons grated
orange zest
4 ounces reduced-fat
cream cheese,
softened
2 (8-count) cans
refrigerator
buttermilk biscuits

½ cup (1 stick) butter or
margarine, melted
1 cup sifted
confectioners' sugar
2 tablespoons fresh
orange juice

Combine the sugar, pecans and orange zest in a small bowl and mix well. Place about ¾ teaspoon cream cheese in the center of each biscuit. Fold the biscuit in half over the cheese, pressing edges to seal. Dip each biscuit in the butter; dredge in the pecan mixture. Place the biscuits curved side down in a single layer in the curves of a lightly buttered 12-cup bundt pan, spacing evenly. Place any remaining biscuits around the center of the pan, filling in spaces if necessary. Drizzle any remaining butter over the biscuits and sprinkle with any remaining sugar. Bake at 350 degrees for 40 minutes or until cake tests done. Combine the confectioners' sugar and orange juice in a small bowl and stir until smooth to make the glaze. Remove the cake from the oven and invert immediately onto a serving plate. Drizzle with the glaze. Yield: 16 servings.

Christine Mitchell, Preceptor Eta
Mobile, Alabama

CRESCENT ROLLS

1 cup milk
1 cup shortening
1 cake yeast
¼ cup warm water
1 tablespoon sugar
1 teaspoon salt

2 eggs, beaten
½ cup sugar
4½ cups flour
1 teaspoon baking
powder

Scald the milk. Stir in the shortening. Let stand until cool. Dissolve the yeast in the warm water; stir in the 1 tablespoon sugar and salt. Beat the eggs with the ½ cup sugar in a small bowl until well mixed. Combine the shortening mixture, yeast mixture and egg mixture in a large bowl. Stir in the flour and baking powder to make a smooth dough. Chill, covered, for 8 to 12 hours, or for up to 3 days. When ready to bake, allow dough to come to room temperature. Divide into 4 portions. Roll one quarter at a time into a circle, as thin as is practical. Brush melted butter over the circle and cut it into pie-shaped wedges. Roll up each wedge from large end to small, making a classic crescent shape. Arrange on baking sheets and let rise, covered, for 2 to 3 hours or until very light and doubled in size. Preheat the oven to 400 degrees. Bake for about 10 minutes or until nicely browned. Serve at once. Yield: 10 to 15 rolls.

Milly Lewis, Laureate Eta
Klamath Falls, Oregon

"CRAISY" CHOCOLATE MUFFINS

2 cups flour	*³/4 cup craisins (dried*
¹/4 cup sugar	*cranberries)*
¹/4 cup firmly packed	*2 cups milk chocolate*
brown sugar	*chips*
2 teaspoons baking	*³/4 cup milk*
powder	*¹/3 cup vegetable oil*
¹/2 teaspoon salt	*1 egg*

Combine the flour, sugars, baking powder and salt in a large bowl and mix well. Stir in the craisins and 1³/4 cups of the chocolate chips. Combine the milk, oil and egg in a small bowl and mix well. Add to the dry ingredients, stirring just until moistened. Spoon into 12 buttered muffin cups. Sprinkle with the remaining chocolate chips. Bake at 375 degrees for 18 to 21 minutes or until golden. Cool in the pans for 5 minutes before serving. Yield: 1 dozen.

Kari Holland, Kappa Tau
Edmond, Oklahoma

FAT-FREE CARROT MUFFINS

2¹/4 cups flour	*8 ounces nonfat yogurt*
¹/2 cup sugar	*2 egg whites*
1 teaspoon cinnamon	*¹/2 cup applesauce*
1 teaspoon salt	*¹/2 cup raisins*
1 teaspoon baking	*¹/3 cup packed brown*
powder	*sugar*
¹/4 teaspoon ginger	*1 teaspoon vanilla*
1¹/2 cups finely shredded	*extract*
carrots	

Combine the flour, sugar, cinnamon, salt, baking powder and ginger in a bowl and mix well. Combine the carrots, yogurt, egg whites, applesauce, raisins, brown sugar and vanilla in a large bowl and mix well. Add the dry ingredients to the carrot mixture and stir just until moistened. Spoon into 18 muffin tins sprayed with nonstick cooking spray. Bake at 350 degrees for 25 minutes or until lightly browned. Cool in the pans. Sprinkle with confectioners' sugar if desired. Yield: 1¹/2 dozen.

Waneta Housh, Laureate Nu
Mesa, Arizona

PRETZELS

Serve with mustard or pizza sauce and a favorite drink.

4 cups flour	*1 egg, beaten*
1 tablespoon sugar	*Pickling salt*
1¹/2 cups warm water	

Combine the flour, sugar and water in a bowl. Knead on a floured surface for about 1 minute. Pinch off small balls of dough and roll each into a 6-inch-long cylinder. Shape by crossing over ends. Place on a buttered baking sheet. Brush with egg and sprinkle with salt. Bake at 425 degrees for about 25 to 30 minutes or until golden brown. Yield: about 2 dozen.

Claudia M. Long, Kappa Kappa
Meriden, Kansas

SWEET SCONES

I remember eating these with homemade preserves while sipping freshly brewed tea from real china at Grandma's house.

1 egg, separated	*1 cup lard*
3 cups flour	*¹/2 teaspoon baking soda*
4 teaspoons baking	*1¹/4 cups buttermilk*
powder	*¹/2 cup raisins or*
1 cup sugar	*currants*
2 teaspoons salt	

Beat the egg white in a medium bowl until stiff peaks form. Mix the yolk with 1 teaspoon water and set aside. Place the flour, baking powder, sugar, salt and currants in a bowl. Cut in the lard until crumbly. Mix the baking soda and buttermilk together; add to the buttermilk mixture and mix well. Stir in the raisins. Roll the dough into a ³/4-inch-thick rectangle. Cut into approximately 24 squares. Arrange on an ungreased baking sheet. Brush dough with yolk mixture. Bake at 425 degrees for 15 minutes or until golden. Yield: 1 dozen.

Donna Krueger
Owensound, Ontario, Canada

Helen E. Calkins, Preceptor Mu Nu, Santa Rosa, California, makes Anytime Very Crisp Waffles by combining 2 cups buttermilk baking mix, ¹/2 cup vegetable oil, 1 egg, and a 10-ounce bottle of club soda and mixing well with a wire whisk. Bake all the batter according to waffle iron instructions and freeze any leftovers for another time.

GRANDMA'S WAFFLES

My grandmother learned this recipe from her mother when she was a little girl. At that time they made waffles in a waffle iron over a gas burner. She taught my mother how to make them and my mother in turn gave me the recipe, along with a waffle iron.

1½ cups sifted flour	2 eggs, separated
½ teaspoon salt	1 cup milk
2 teaspoons baking powder	4 tablespoons melted shortening

Sift the flour, salt and baking powder together. Beat the egg yolks in a mixing bowl. Stir in the milk and shortening. Add the flour mixture and beat until smooth. Beat the egg whites until stiff peaks form; fold into the flour mixture. Bake in a hot waffle iron until golden brown. Yield: 4 large waffles.

Paula Frank, Alpha Chi
Little Rock, Arkansas

APRICOT NECTAR CAKE

1 (2-layer) package yellow cake mix	¾ cup apricot nectar
¾ cup vegetable oil	4 eggs
3 tablespoons lemon extract	Juice of 3 lemons
	2 cups confectioners' sugar

Combine the cake mix, oil, lemon extract, nectar and eggs in a mixing bowl. Beat at high speed for 6 minutes. Spoon into a buttered 10-inch tube pan. Bake at 350 degrees for 55 minutes. Pour a mixture of the lemon juice and confectioners' sugar over the warm cake. Yield: 16 servings.

Maxine McGuire, Laureate Theta
Knoxville, Tennessee

GRAND MARNIER CAKE

We served this impressive dessert at a sixtieth birth-day party with a single sparkle candle on the cake.

1 (2-layer) chocolate cake mix	1 envelope unflavored gelatin
½ cup Grand Marnier	Coarsely grated zest of 2 oranges
1 (6-ounce) can frozen orange juice concentrate	2 cups whipping cream
¾ cup sugar	¾ cup confectioners' sugar

Prepare the cake mix in 2 layer pans using package directions. Cool for 1 hour before assembly. Slice each layer in half horizontally to make 4 layers. Place each layer cut side up on waxed paper and sprinkle with 1 tablespoon of the Grand Marnier. Combine the orange juice, sugar and gelatin in a saucepan over medium heat to make the filling. Cook for about 5 minutes or until the sugar and gelatin are dissolved, stirring constantly. Remove from heat. Stir in the orange zest and 3 tablespoons of the Grand Marnier. Press a sheet of waxed paper over the surface of the filling. Chill for 20 minutes or until no longer warm. Beat the cream in a mixing bowl until soft peaks form. Add the confectioners' sugar gradually, beating until stiff peaks form. Fold in 1 tablespoon Grand Marnier. Spread ¼ cup of the orange juice filling between the layers. Spread the whipped cream over the top and side of the cake. Chill, covered, for at least 4 hours before serving. Yield: 8 to 10 servings.

Norma Shore, Laureate Beta Gamma
Lively, Ontario, Canada

LIGHT CHOCOLATE CUPCAKES

Serve as a special treat with ice cream.

4 ounces unsweetened chocolate	1¾ cups sugar
1 cup (2 sticks) margarine	1 cup flour
	4 large eggs
¼ teaspoon butter flavoring	1 teaspoon vanilla extract
1½ cups broken pecans or walnuts	

Melt the chocolate and margarine in a heavy saucepan over low heat. Add the butter flavoring and nuts; stir to coat. Remove from heat. Combine the sugar, flour, eggs and vanilla in a bowl and mix just until blended; do not beat. Stir in the chocolate mixture carefully; do not beat. Fill 18 paper-lined muffin cups ⅔ full. Bake at 325 degrees for about 30 to 35 minutes or until a wooden pick inserted in the center comes out clean. Yield: 1½ dozen.

Linda Smith Dawson, Preceptor Beta Delta
Kinston, North Carolina

HAWAIIAN PARTY CAKE

1 (2-layer) yellow cake mix	Whipped topping
	½ cup chopped pecans or walnuts
1 (15-ounce) can crushed pineapple	½ cup toasted coconut
1 cup sugar	
1 small box butter pecan or vanilla instant pudding mix	

Prepare and bake the cake mix in a 9×13-inch cake pan using the package directions. Combine the undrained pineapple and sugar in a heavy saucepan over medium-high heat and bring to a boil. Boil for 5 to 10 minutes or until slightly syrupy. Pour over the hot cake when it is removed from the oven. Cool in the pan on a wire rack. Prepare the pudding mix using the package directions. Pour over the cooled cake. Spread whipped topping over the pudding. Sprinkle the nuts and coconut over the whipped topping. Chill, covered, until ready to serve. Yield: 15 servings.

Anita E. Anderson, Beta Beta
DeWitt, Iowa

WHIPPED CREAM POUND CAKE

1 cup (2 sticks) butter, softened
3 cups sugar
6 eggs
1 teaspoon lemon extract
1 teaspoon vanilla extract
1/2 teaspoon salt
3 cups flour
2 cups heavy cream

Cream the butter and sugar in a mixing bowl until light and fluffy. Add the eggs 1 at a time, mixing well after each addition. Add the lemon extract, vanilla and salt; mix well. Add the flour a little at a time alternately with the cream, starting and ending with the flour. Pour into a greased and floured 10-inch tube pan and place in a cold oven. Turn the oven temperature to 325 degrees. Bake for 1 1/2 hours. Invert on a funnel to cool completely. Loosen the cake from the side of the pan. Invert onto a cake plate. Yield: 16 servings.

Catherine Aycock, Laureate Tau
Gainesville, Georgia

PEANUT BUTTER EGGS

3 cups (6 sticks) butter
3 pounds confectioners' sugar, sifted
18 ounces marshmallow creme
1 tablespoon vanilla extract
2 (18-ounce) jars smooth peanut butter, warmed
16 ounces chocolate chips
1 tablespoon shortening

Melt the butter in the top of a double boiler over boiling water. Add the confectioners' sugar slowly, stirring until smooth. Add the marshmallow creme 1/3 at a time, stirring until smooth. Stir in the vanilla. Stir in the peanut butter. Remove from heat. Cool the mixture until it can be shaped. Shape the peanut butter mixture into egg shapes. Place on waxed paper in the refrigerator. Chill, covered, for 8 to 12 hours. Melt the chocolate chips and shortening to make the chocolate coating (enough for 25 to 30 eggs). Dip the chilled eggs in the chocolate coating and return to the refrigerator for about 10 minutes or until coating is set. Yield: 80 eggs.

Lori Matsudaira, Gamma Mu
Lusby, Maryland

MARSHMALLOWS

Most people don't realize you can make marshmallows, but they are fun to make. You may add food coloring while beating the sugar mixture. They may be rolled in toasted or plain coconut or finely chopped nuts, or dipped in melted almond bark.

2 cups sugar
3/4 cup boiling water
2 envelopes unflavored gelatin
1/2 cup cold water
1 teaspoon vanilla extract
1/2 teaspoon salt
Confectioners' sugar

Cook the sugar and the 3/4 cup boiling water in a saucepan over medium heat for 10 minutes or until the mixture spins a thread from the spoon. Dissolve the gelatin in the 1/2 cup cold water. Add to the hot syrup, stirring until dissolved. Remove from heat. Let stand until cool. Add the vanilla and salt. Beat until very stiff. Place in an 8-inch-square baking dish. Let stand until set. Cut into squares and roll in confectioners' sugar. Yield: 3 dozen.

Bonnie Chrastil, Laureate Gamma
Chadron, Nebraska

FRUITY BISCOTTI

Egg substitute to equal 4 eggs
1/2 cup sugar
1/4 cup nonfat dry milk powder
1/2 cup vegetable oil
2 1/4 cups flour
2 teaspoons baking powder
1 teaspoon vanilla extract
1 tablespoon grated orange zest
1 cup chopped walnuts
1/4 cup dried cherries, chopped
1/4 cup dried apricots, chopped

Combine the egg substitute, sugar, milk powder, oil, flour, baking powder, vanilla, orange zest, walnuts, cherries and apricots in a medium bowl and mix well. Divide the dough into 2 equal portions. Shape each portion into a log. The mixture will be sticky; use extra flour on hands while shaping. Place on a baking sheet. Bake at 360 degrees for 25 minutes. Remove from oven and slice into 1-inch slices. Return to oven to bake for 7 to 9 minutes on each side. Cool on a wire rack. Yield: 2 dozen.

Teddy Bei, Preceptor Eta Mu
Port Charlotte, Florida

MOUNTAIN MIST BREAD PUDDING

We were served this pudding on board a small Alaskan cruise ship. The chef shared the recipe. It's even better the next day (if there are any leftovers!). I prefer using challah for the bread.

4 tablespoons butter, softened	1½ teaspoons vanilla extract
12 thick slices bread	½ cup flaked coconut
4 cups milk	½ cup graham cracker crumbs
4 eggs	
3 egg yolks	¼ cup cinnamon
⅔ cup sugar	½ cup brown sugar
2 teaspoons lemon juice	

Butter the bread slices on both sides. Combine the milk, eggs, egg yolks, sugar, lemon juice and vanilla in a bowl and mix well. Place a layer of bread slices in an 11×13-inch baking dish; be sure the entire surface is covered, with no spaces between slices. Combine the coconut, cracker crumbs, cinnamon and brown sugar in a bowl and mix well. Layer half the crumb mixture, the remaining bread and the remaining crumb mixture over the bread layer. Pour the milk mixture slowly over the top, allowing the bread to absorb the liquid. Place the baking dish in a larger baking pan. Add water to the larger pan to a depth of 1 inch. Bake in the center of the oven at 350 degrees for 45 minutes or until set. Cool on a wire rack. Yield: 15 to 20 servings.

Keran Lang, Preceptor Iota Eta
Yuba City, California

LEMON CHARLOTTE

1 envelope unflavored gelatin	Grated zest of 1 lemon
¼ cup cold water	26 to 28 ladyfingers
⅔ cup sugar	½ cup lemon schnapps or rum
¼ cup lemon juice	
4 eggs, separated	1 cup whipping cream

Soften the gelatin in the water. Combine the sugar, lemon juice and egg yolks in a double boiler. Cook over simmering water until thick enough to coat a spoon, stirring constantly; do not boil. Remove from heat. Add the gelatin mixture, stirring until gelatin is dissolved. Stir in the lemon zest. Let stand until cool. Line the bottom of a buttered 3×5×9-inch loaf pan with waxed paper. Cut 22 to 24 ladyfingers to 3 inches long. Pour the schnapps in a shallow pie plate. Dip the ladyfingers in the schnapps and stand them vertically, cut side up, around the edge of the loaf pan. Beat the egg whites in a bowl until stiff but not dry. Beat the cream in a separate bowl until stiff peaks form. Fold the lemon mixture, egg whites and whipped cream together gently. Pour into the prepared loaf pan, smoothing the top. Cut enough of the remaining ladyfingers to fit over the top of the filling. Dip in the schnapps and layer over the filling. Chill, covered, for 8 to 12 hours. Run a knife around the edge of the pan before serving. Invert onto a serving plate. Remove the waxed paper. Top with more whipped cream and shreds of lemon zest. Slice crosswise to serve. Yield: 10 to 12 servings.

Vicki McAvoy, Xi Alpha Omega
Mt. Pleasant, South Carolina

LEMON MERINGUE DESSERT

4 egg whites	1 cup whipping cream, whipped
½ teaspoon cream of tartar	½ teaspoon salt
1 cup sugar	Lemon Filling

Preheat the oven to 275 degrees. Beat the egg whites until foamy. Add the cream of tartar and beat until stiff, dry peaks form. Add the sugar, 2 teaspoons at a time, beating well after each addition. Continue beating until sharp peaks form. Line 2 well-buttered 8-inch cake pans with manila paper. Butter the paper. Spread the meringue in the pans. Bake for 10 minutes. Cool slightly. Remove from pans. Layer 1 meringue, half the Lemon Filling and half the whipped cream on a serving plate. Repeat the layers. Chill for 2 to 3 hours before serving. Yield: 12 servings.

LEMON FILLING

4 egg yolks	⅓ cup lemon juice
¼ teaspoon salt	3 teaspoons grated lemon zest
½ cup sugar	

Beat the egg yolks lightly in the top of a double boiler. Add the salt and sugar and mix well. Stir in the lemon juice. Cook over boiling water for about 10 minutes or until thick, stirring constantly. Remove from heat. Stir in the lemon zest. Let stand until cool.

Doris White
Memphis, Missouri

Deborah Kearney, Xi Eta Zeta, Brights Grove, Ontario, Canada, makes Peachy Tofu Pudding by processing 10 ounces silken tofu, 14 ounces canned peaches, 2 tablespoons sugar, and a small package of vanilla instant pudding mix until smooth and folding in 2 cups whipped topping. Garnish with peach slices.

Summer Holidays

Honor, Freedom, Work—
stirring themes to celebrate in summer!
The first Memorial Day in 1868 honored our Civil War
dead with parades, flags, and speeches. Confederate
Memorial Day is still observed in April by Alabama,
Mississippi, Florida, and Georgia.
Independence Day, the Fourth of July, was first
observed in Philadelphia on July 8, 1776. The Declaration
of Independence was read aloud, city bells rang, bands
played, and politicians made speeches. Did you know that
Independence Day was not a legal holiday until 1941?
Labor Day originated in 1882 when the Knights of Labor
paraded through New York City. Congress made
the holiday official in 1894 with more speeches! As we
know, speeches go best with lots of great food. Here are
some truly inspirational ideas for summer celebrating.

DECORATE! DECORATE! DECORATE!

No matter what the holiday or special day may be, always decorate! It will really help your family and friends enjoy the occasion more. A meal alone, no matter how good, is soon forgotten. With decorations, however, the occasion becomes a memory and a tradition that your children will pass on to their children. I am so sorry that I didn't start sooner. Now I make every occasion extra-special with decorations.

Marybeth Buchanan, Laureate Alpha Beta
Yuma, Arizona

ANYTIME PINATAS

Children and grownups alike love piñatas. No matter what the holiday or occasion, there is a suitable shape. Fill with candies, small toys, and other gifts. Hang the piñata from a tree or in a location with plenty of room for swinging the broomstick, and watch the fun!

Georgeana Rainwater, Preceptor Gamma Gamma
Broken Arrow, Oklahoma

FRIENDS ARE THE FLOWERS

This is a great way to show prospective members the Beta Sigma Phi message as a part of Rush with this theme: Friends are the Flowers in the Garden of Life. Prepare place cards or name tags, attaching a packet of flower seeds to each. Use flowered paper plates, napkins, and cups. Use fresh flowers or blooming potted plants for the centerpiece, table decorations, and game or door prizes. Make up games that have flower themes, such as a quiz about flowers.

Carol Brownlow, Preceptor Alpha Delta
Prescott, Arizona

ANY HOLIDAY SPECIAL POPPERS

Our chapter has made a tradition of this holiday service project. We make these treats for any holiday to take to nursing homes, senior citizen luncheons, and private homes. Save the cardboard rolls from paper towels and toilet paper. Cut the longer rolls into shorter lengths. Cut holiday print dinner-size napkins in half and roll the paper tubes in the napkins. Fill the tubes with animal crackers, hard candies, or other small treats. Tie the ends with ribbon or, for those who have a difficult time untying the ribbons, just tuck the fabric into the tubes.

Suzanne Mock, Laureate Pi
Hampden, Maine

HOBO BASH

This party is fun anytime, but especially for a couples rush party. Send out invitations on torn pieces of brown paper bag enclosed in miniature hobo pouches. This is the invitation that we send:

It's a HOBO gathering not to be missed,
as hobos we are dressed.
Fancy attire is not required;
old hats, old coats, old boots are best.
Under the towering oak trees
a campfire we will make,
and in the Mross back forty
of dinner we'll partake.
At 6:00 we will gather
to serve the hobo meal.
The date is _____ ,
It's free—what a deal!

We provide logs to sit on, an open campfire, tables made from large cardboard boxes covered with newpapers, and brown paper bags as placemats. Tin cans with dead flowers for centerpieces and candle lanterns complete the decor. Tableware consists of metal pie tins and utensils wrapped in a bandana napkin hobo pouch. Be sure that your menu includes s'mores prepared over the campfire. Entertainment can include best costume contest, guessing the number of dried beans in a jar, etc., with the prizes being cans of pork and beans.

Ginny Mross, Alpha Chi Chi
Pleasanton, Texas

A FISHY CENTERPIECE

Use a small fish bowl filled with distilled water. Partially fill the bowl with colored marbles. Add several glass floating fish, place the bowl on a glass plate, and scatter sea shells on the plate around the bowl. I used this centerpiece at a special fishermen's breakfast and the guys loved it.

Kay Ponstein, Xi Beta Epsilon
Ghent, Minnesota

HOMEMADE FOOD GIFTS

Homemade goodies are a welcome gift any time of the year. Make that gift even more special with a little extra. Prepare a gift basket containing individually wrapped cookies, candies, or your own specialty. Add small packages of certain ingredients used to make them, along with a copy of each recipe. To be sure that these delicacies are served in their prime, include any storage or serving instructions.

Roxanna E. Cooper, Xi Beta Mu
Elkins, West Virginia

SUNFLOWER CAKE

What better symbol of summertime fun than a sunflower cake? Prepare and bake a yellow cake mix according to the package directions for two 9-inch round pans. Place one of the layers on a large round tray and arrange twinkies around the cake to form the petals. Add enough yellow food coloring to your favorite homemade or canned white frosting to make the bright yellow of sunflower petals. Frost the cake and twinkies. Arrange chocolate chips in the center of the cake to emulate sunflower seeds. This is especially spectacular if the chocolate chips are carefully spiraled from the center as the seeds are naturally. Use the other cake layer for another sunflower, or eat as desired.

Bev Schelling, Delta Zeta
Atlantic, Iowa

ROSE LIGHTS

Make unique candle favors or decorations for any occasion. Use small clay flowerpots—the 1½-inch size is best. Fill the pots with florist moss and secure with glue. Insert artificial rose leaves into the moss and bend them over the side of the pot. Select artificial roses in a color the enhances your color scheme, and secure in the center of the moss. Slide a clear votive cup into the center of the rose and glue a few of the petals to the cup. Add a votive candle in a coordinating color to the cup.

Kathy Embree, Preceptor Alpha Tau
Blue Springs, Missouri

VELVET TOUCH KEEPSAKE GIFT WRAPPING

Make a sturdy box into a keepsake of any occasion. Use a paper bag to prepare a pattern for the box by wrapping the box top and bottom separately, then removing the paper, adding a small measure for wrapping over the edges of the box to attach on the inside. Cut away any overlapping paper to avoid extra material at the corners. Use black velvet for a beautiful elegant box. Cut the velvet using the prepared paper pattern and attach to the box with a craft glue suitable for fabric. Wrap both the top and bottom of the box and set aside to dry completely. Cut a foam ball into halves and attach to the top of the box. Insert a large bow into the foam and add your choice of artificial flowers to the ball. Yellow roses are gorgeous. Add a gift to the box if you wish but the box itself is a beautiful keepsake.

Alice Cote-Tetreault, Gamma Kappa
Moosup, Connecticut

QUICK TABLE DECORATIONS

Save those seasonal and holiday greeting cards. By the time all the chapter members have contributed their collections, you should have a good supply for any occasion. Select a suitable tablecloth color for the holiday: white is good anytime, add red and blue for patriotic, green for Christmas or St. Patricks, red for Valentines, gold, tan, and brown for fall events, etc. Scatter the cards over the table, and secure with double-stick tape if necessary. Be sure to remove any personal notes that you don't wish to share—reading the cards is part of the fun.

Lilly Ann McKinney, Xi Alpha Alpha
Opelousas, Louisana

BEST-DRESSED BANANA SUMMER SOCIAL

Invitations to the social should instruct each guest to bring a banana in costume. I have seen bananas dressed as Elvis, Eve, country bumpkins, skiers, and many other imaginative guises. After judging the bananas for the "best-dressed" prize, use the bananas for banana splits. Keep the fun going by making your own hand-cranked ice cream in assorted flavors and furnishing toppings, whipped cream, cherries, and nuts.

Dot Schoenfeldt
West Linn, Oregon

SPICY SHRIMP COCKTAIL

1 (7-ounce) package Italian salad dressing mix	1 cup finely chopped onion
1 pound small shrimp, cooked, shelled, deveined	1 large ripe tomato, chopped
1 bunch cilantro, stems removed	2 ripe avocados, chopped
	4 chiles serrano, finely chopped (optional)

Prepare the salad dressing in a cruet or other container with a tight-fitting lid, using the package directions. Combine the shrimp, cilantro, onion, tomato, avocados and chiles in a bowl and mix well. Shake the salad dressing. Add it gradually to the shrimp mixture, tossing to combine. Serve in cocktail cups with crackers. Yield: 4 servings.

Mandy Pena, Laureate Alpha Nu
McAllen, Texas

SHRIMP LIVORNESE

Shrimp Livornese is a "signature dish" at my favorite Italian restaurant, where I have been eating for almost 40 years. The recipe serves one as an appetizer and may be doubled to serve as an entrée. Serve with toast points when used as an appetizer, a crisp green salad when used as an entrée.

1 garlic clove, finely chopped	3 ounces heavy cream
4 pats of butter	1/2 ounce dry sherry
5 large shrimp, peeled, deveined	

Sauté the garlic in the butter in a medium sauté pan over medium heat for 1 or 2 minutes. Stir in the shrimp and sauté for 2 minutes. Stir in the cream and simmer for 3 minutes. Add the sherry, stirring gently. Serve immediately. Yield: 1 appetizer.

Barbara Champion, Xi Beta Omega
Overland Park, Kansas

MARINATED SHRIMP

Here is another shrimp dish that may be served as an appetizer or an entrée. The shrimp should be no smaller than the size that comes with 24 in a pound.

2 tablespoons apple cider vinegar	1 tablespoon minced fresh parsley
2 tablespoons lemon juice	1/4 teaspoon paprika
1/4 cup vegetable oil	1 teaspoon salt
1 small onion, minced	1/8 teaspoon pepper
2 garlic cloves, minced	1 pound shrimp, cooked, peeled, deveined
3 tablespoons horseradish	

Combine the vinegar, lemon juice, oil, onion, garlic, horseradish, parsley, paprika, salt and pepper in a bowl and mix well. Add the shrimp, stirring to coat well. Marinate, covered, in the refrigerator for at least 4 hours, stirring occasionally. Serve with cocktail picks or forks. Yield: 2 to 4 servings.

Linda Lewis, Alpha Alpha Chi
Ft. Myers, Florida

For Pimento Cheese Deluxe, Katherine Taylor, Laureate Eta Beta, Hilltop Lakes, Texas, combines 2 cups shredded Cheddar or longhorn cheese, 2 cups shredded Monterey Jack cheese, 1 cup shredded Swiss cheese, 8 ounces cottage cheese, a 2-ounce jar of chopped pimentos, garlic powder to taste, and enough mayonnaise to make the desired consistency.

❖ MINTED ICED TEA

This very refreshing beverage got me through the morning sickness of three pregnancies—without the bourbon, of course! Be sure to use regular tea, not flavored or herbal.

2 quarts water	8 to 16 fresh mint leaves
4 regular or decaffeinated tea bags	1 (2-liter) bottle gingerale
1 cup sugar	Bourbon (optional)
Juice of 2 lemons, rinds reserved	

Bring the water to a boil in a 2- to 3-quart saucepan over high heat. Remove from heat. Add the tea bags and steep, covered, for 10 minutes. Discard the tea bags. Pour the tea into a gallon pitcher. Stir in the sugar to dissolve. Fill the pitcher with ice and stir well. Stir in the lemon juice. Add the rinds. Bruise the mint leaves on a cutting board with the bottom of a glass or the handle of a knife; stir into the tea and mix well. Pour equal amounts of tea and gingerale in a glass of ice. Add a splash of bourbon.
Yield: 8 to 10 servings.

Cheryl Midkiff, Zeta Zeta
Farmington, New Mexico

TEA PUNCH

3 rounded tablespoons instant unsweetened tea	1 (6-ounce) can frozen lemonade, thawed
3 envelopes artificial sweetener (optional)	2 rounded tablespoons frozen orange juice, thawed
4 cups water	32 ounces gingerale

Combine the tea, sweetener, water, lemonade, orange juice and gingerale in a large pitcher and mix well. Yield: 8 to 10 servings.

Beverly Cover, Preceptor Alpha Rho
Albuquerque, New Mexico

FISH CHOWDER

2 tablespoons margarine	1 teaspoon salt, or to taste
1 medium onion, chopped	1/8 teaspoon pepper, or to taste
1/2 cup chopped celery	1 pound fish fillets
2 cups hot water	2 cups milk
2 cups diced potatoes	
1/2 cup sliced carrots	

Melt the margarine in a 2-quart saucepan over medium heat. Add the onion and celery. Cook until vegetables are tender, stirring occasionally. Add the hot water, potatoes, carrots, salt and pepper. Simmer, covered, for 10 to 15 minutes, stirring occasionally.

Add the fish. Cook, covered, for 10 minutes or until fish is cooked through. Turn the heat down to low. Add the milk and reheat; do not boil. Yield: 6 servings.

Catherine Foote, Xi Delta
Halifax, Nova Scotia, Canada

CLAM CHOWDER WITH DUMPLINGS

Serve with hush puppies and iced tea.

1 thick slice salt pork, cut into small pieces	3 cups fresh minced clams or canned clams
2¹/₂ pounds potatoes, peeled, diced	3 quarts water
1 onion, chopped	2¹/₂ teaspoons salt
	Corn Bread Dumplings

Fry the salt pork in a large Dutch oven over medium heat for 5 to 10 minutes or until brown and crisp. Add the potatoes, onion, clams, water and salt and mix well. Bring to a boil; reduce heat. Simmer, covered, for 1¹/₂ to 2 hours or until potatoes are tender. Add the Corn Bread Dumplings to the chowder for the last 10 to 12 minutes of cooking time.

CORN BREAD DUMPLINGS

¹/₂ cup flour	1 teaspoon salt
2 cups cornmeal	Warm water

Combine the flour, cornmeal and salt in a bowl. Stir in enough warm water to make a mixture that is easy to handle and pat into a dumpling. Shape into dumplings. Yield: 6 servings.

Suzy Bare, Xi Delta Sigma
Havelock, North Carolina

FRESH APPLE SALAD

1 (20-ounce) can juice-pack pineapple chunks	1 tablespoon lemon juice
2 tablespoons cornstarch	1 cup mayonnaise
2 tablespoons water	1 to 2 teaspoons poppy seeds
¹/₄ cup (¹/₂ stick) butter	4 to 6 cups chopped unpeeled red apples
¹/₄ cup sugar	2 cups seedless green grapes

Drain the pineapple, reserving the juice. Dissolve the cornstarch in the water. Combine the pineapple juice, butter, sugar and lemon juice in a saucepan over medium heat. Bring to a boil. Stir in the cornstarch mixture. Cook until thickened, stirring constantly. Remove from heat. Cool completely. Stir in the mayonnaise and poppy seeds. Pour the poppy seed mixture over the pineapple chunks, apples and grapes in a large bowl and mix well. Chill, covered, until ready to serve. Yield: 10 to 12 servings.

Roberta Lalim, Zeta Master
Tioga, North Dakota

LAYERED GELATIN SALAD

1 (3-ounce) package strawberry gelatin	2 (3-ounce) packages lemon gelatin
1 (10-ounce) package frozen strawberries	1 (3-ounce) packages black raspberry gelatin
1 cup milk	1 (16- to 20-ounce) can blueberries, undrained
1 cup sour cream	

Dissolve the strawberry gelatin in 1 cup boiling water. Add the strawberries, stirring until thawed. Pour into a 9×13-inch dish. Chill until set. Mix together the milk and sour cream. Dissolve both packages lemon gelatin in 1 cup boiling water. Stir in the sour cream mixture. Pour over the strawberry gelatin layer. Chill until set. Dissolve the black raspberry gelatin in 1 cup boiling water. Stir in the blueberries. Pour over the lemon gelatin layer. Chill until set. Yield: 12 to 16 servings.

Judy Wood, Xi Beta Zeta
Milwaukee, Wisconsin

RED, WHITE AND BLUE SALAD

2 (3-ounce) packages raspberry gelatin	8 ounces cream cheese, softened
3 cups hot water	¹/₂ cup pecans, chopped
1 enveloped unflavored gelatin	1 teaspoon vanilla extract
¹/₂ cup cold water	1 (16-ounce) can blueberries
1 cup evaporated milk	
1 cup sugar	

Dissolve 1 package raspberry gelatin in 2 cups hot water. Pour into a 9×13-inch dish. Let stand until firm. Dissolve the plain gelatin in the cold water. Combine the evaporated milk and sugar in a saucepan over medium-low heat; do not boil. Add the cream cheese, pecans and 1 package raspberry gelatin, stirring until blended. Stir in the vanilla. Remove from heat. Let cool completely. Pour over the raspberry gelatin layer. Chill until set. Dissolve the remaining package raspberry gelatin in the remaining 1 cup hot water. Stir in the undrained blueberries. Pour over the cream cheese layer. Chill until firmly set. Yield: 16 servings.

JoAnna Beckman, Eta Eta
Susanville, California

CHERRY COLA SALAD

For Canada Day, spread or pipe whipped cream around the edges of the 9×13-inch pan, making a maple leaf shape on the center of the gelatin's surface.

3/4 cup water
3/4 cup sugar
1 (21-ounce) can cherry
   pie filling
1 (6-ounce) package
   cherry gelatin
1 tablespoon lemon
   juice

1 (14-ounce) can juice-
   pack crushed
   pineapple
1 cup cola beverage
1/2 cup chopped pecans
   or walnuts (optional)

Combine the water and sugar in a medium saucepan over medium-high heat. Bring to a boil. Stir in the pie filling. Bring to a boil. Remove from heat. Place the gelatin in a medium bowl. Add the pie filling mixture. Stir in the lemon juice, undrained pineapple, cola and nuts. Pour into a 5-cup mold or a 9×13-inch glass pan. Chill, covered, until set. Cut into squares. Garnish with whipped cream if desired.
Yield: 10 to 12 servings.

Dianne Cushing, Laureate Theta
Greenwood Kings County, Nova Scotia, Canada

CORNED BEEF SALAD

1 (3-ounce) package
   lemon gelatin
1/2 cup vegetable juice
   cocktail
3/4 cup mayonnaise
1 (12-ounce) can corned
   beef, shredded

1 cup chopped celery
1 small onion, chopped
2 hard-cooked eggs,
   finely chopped
2 tablespoons pickle
   relish

Dissolve the gelatin in 1/2 cup boiling water in a large bowl. Stir in the vegetable juice. Let cool completely. Stir in the mayonnaise, corned beef, celery, onion, eggs and pickle relish. Pour into a 5-cup mold. Chill, covered, until set. Yield: 8 servings.

Rita Collins, Laureate Tau
Gainesville, Georgia

Mildred Burns, Alpha Master, Alamosa, Colorado, makes Full-Meal Checkerboard Sandwiches by layering ham and cheese slices alternately in a 9×13-inch dish for about 1/3 of the depth, adding a layer of potato salad, and adding layers of ham and cheese in reverse order. After chilling, covered, for 2 hours, she secures quartered hard-cooked eggs on top using toothpicks and cuts into squares.

LOW-CALORIE CRAB SALAD

I make this tasty, easy dish often when we go camping in Florida. Serve any time the weather is warm.

4 cups shredded Boston
   or romaine lettuce
2 (6-ounce) cans crab
   meat, rinsed, drained
2 hard-cooked eggs,
   chopped
1/2 cup low-fat
   mayonnaise
1/4 cup chile sauce

3 tablespoons chopped
   green bell pepper
1 tablespoon lemon
   juice
1/4 teaspoon
   Worcestershire sauce
1/4 teaspoon Tabasco
   sauce
2 tomatoes, quartered

Arrange the lettuce in large individual salad bowls. Arrange the crab meat over the lettuce. Sprinkle with the eggs. Combine the mayonnaise, chile sauce, bell pepper, lemon juice, Worcestershire and Tabasco in a small bowl and whisk to blend. Spoon over the salads. Garnish with the tomatoes. Yield: 4 servings.

Jackie Vanderspoel, Beta Beta
Fort Myers Beach, Florida

CHICKEN MACARONI SALAD

1 pound chicken breast,
   cooked, shredded
1 1/2 cups mayonnaise-
   type salad dressing
1 1/2 cups mayonnaise
1/2 cup shredded carrots
1 tablespoon sweet
   pickle relish
1 (8-ounce) can
   pineapple tidbits,
   drained

1/4 cup chopped onion
1/2 cup chopped celery
2 tablespoons sugar
1 cup shredded sharp
   Cheddar cheese
1/2 teaspoon pepper
Dash of salt
1 pound macaroni,
   cooked, drained

Place the chicken, salad dressing, mayonnaise, carrots, relish, pineapple, onion, celery, sugar and cheese in a large bowl 1 ingredient at a time, mixing well after each addition. Stir in the pepper and salt. Add the macaroni and mix well. Chill, covered, until serving time. Yield: 10 to 15 servings.

Elaine Canono-Lynott, Rho Beta
Goodland, Kansas

Beverly Keathley, Xi Tau Sigma, Dallas, Texas, makes a Unique Summer Salad by cutting cantaloupe and avocado into bite-sized pieces, adding cherry tomato halves, and sprinkling with fresh lemon juice. Mix gently several times while chilling for several hours.

❖ NORTH SHORE CHICKEN SALAD

2 large garlic cloves,
   minced
1 tablespoon Dijon
   mustard
1/2 teaspoon salt
1/4 teaspoon sugar
1/4 teaspoon freshly
   ground pepper
1/4 cup rice wine vinegar
1/3 cup vegetable oil
4 cups warm cooked
   wild rice (cooked in
   chicken broth)

Juice of 1/2 lemon
1 whole chicken breast,
   cooked, chopped
3 green onions including
   tops, sliced
1/2 red bell pepper,
   chopped
2 ounces fresh pea pods,
   cut in 1-inch pieces
1 or 2 ripe avocados, cut
   into bite-size pieces
1 cup pecan halves,
   toasted

Combine the garlic, mustard, salt, sugar, pepper, vinegar and oil in a food processor container and process until smooth. Place the rice and lemon juice in a medium bowl and toss to combine. Let cool. Add the chicken, onions, bell pepper, pea pods and garlic mixture. Toss to combine. Chill, covered, for 2 to 4 hours. Add the avocados and pecans and toss gently just before serving. Serve in a salad bowl lined with lettuce leaves. Yield: 6 servings.

Kari Holland, Kappa Tau
Edmond, Oklahoma

GRILLED CHICKEN PASTA SALAD

This quick, easy salad is great whether served cold in the summer or warm in the winter.

1 pound bow tie pasta,
   cooked, drained
1 (12-ounce) jar
   marinated artichoke
   hearts
1 (7-ounce) jar roasted
   red peppers, drained,
   sliced
1/3 cup sliced black
   olives
1 (28-ounce) jar chunky
   spaghetti sauce

1/2 cup olive oil
2 tablespoons wine
   vinegar
2 tablespoons minced
   fresh parsley
1/2 teaspoon salt
1 pound boneless
   skinless chicken
   breasts
1 tablespoon toasted
   pine nuts (optional)

Combine the pasta, artichokes, roasted peppers, olives, spaghetti sauce, olive oil, vinegar, parsley and salt in a large bowl. Chill, covered. Broil or grill the chicken until cooked through. Thinly slice and serve over the pasta salad. Garnish with the pine nuts. Yield: 6 to 8 servings.

Alexis Bullard, Epsilon Nu
Birmingham, Alabama

RICE AND CHICKEN SALAD

A nice light luncheon meal when served on a bed of lettuce with fruit and rolls on the side.

2 cups chopped cooked
   chicken breast
2 tablespoons butter or
   margarine
1 cup cooked rice
   (cooked in chicken
   broth)
1 cup chopped celery
1 (8-ounce) can chopped
   water chestnuts

2 tablespoons minced
   onion
1 cup mayonnaise
2 tablespoons lemon
   juice
Salt to taste
1/8 teaspoon pepper

Sauté the chicken in the butter in a skillet over medium heat until heated through. Place the rice in a large bowl. Add the chicken, celery, water chestnuts and onion and mix well. Combine the mayonnaise, lemon juice, salt and pepper in a. separate bowl and mix well. Stir into the rice mixture. Chill, covered, for 1 hour before serving. Yield: 6 servings.

Anita Thrash, Iota
Clarkston, Washington

MINTED PASTA AND FRUIT SALAD

10 ounces rotini
4 fresh pears, diced
2 teaspoons fresh lemon
   juice
2 cups halved seedless
   red grapes
1 (11-ounce) can
   mandarin oranges,
   drained
4 ounces feta cheese,
   crumbled
1 teaspoon oregano
2 tablespoons chopped
   fresh mint

1 tablespoon white wine
   vinegar
3 tablespoons orange
   juice
2 tablespoons vegetable
   oil
1/2 teaspoon freshly
   ground pepper
1/2 head romaine lettuce,
   torn into bite-size
   pieces

Cook the pasta using the package directions; drain and cool. Place the pears and lemon juice in a large bowl and toss to combine. Add the grapes, oranges, cheese, oregano, mint and pasta and mix gently. Combine the vinegar, orange juice, oil and pepper in a small bowl and whisk well. Add to the pasta mixture. Toss lightly before serving. Spoon the salad over the romaine on a large serving platter. Serve cold or at room temperature. Yield: 8 servings.

Marie Bray, Laureate Gamma Nu
Orlando, Florida

VEGETARIAN MACARONI SALAD

1 (16-ounce) can kidney
  beans
White vinegar
1 (8-ounce) can peas,
  drained
1 (8-ounce) can diced
  carrots, drained
1 (16-ounce) can green
  beans, drained
1 (2-ounce) jar chopped
  pimentos, drained
1/2 cup chopped green
  bell pepper

1 medium onion,
  chopped
1 cup diced celery
9 ounces macaroni,
  cooked, drained
2 cups mayonnaise-type
  salad dressing
2 cups heavy cream
3/4 cup sugar
1 teaspoon dry mustard

Place the kidney beans in a small bowl with enough white vinegar to cover. Let stand for 1 hour; drain. Combine the marinated beans, peas, carrots, green beans, pimentos, bell pepper, onion and celery in a large bowl and mix well. Stir in the macaroni. Combine the salad dressing, cream, sugar and mustard in a small bowl and stir until smooth. Pour over the macaroni mixture and mix well. Chill, covered, until serving time. Yield: 15 to 20 servings.

Joellen Skonseng, Alpha
Fargo, North Dakota

CHEESY PASTA SALAD

This easy pasta salad is refreshing on a hot summer day like the Fourth of July. Serve with grilled hamburgers or hot dogs.

1 pound rotini, cooked,
  drained
1 cup mayonnaise-type
  salad dressing
1 cup chopped cucumber
1 cup chopped red bell
  pepper

8 ounces Cheddar
  cheese, diced
1/2 teaspoon salt
1/2 teaspoon pepper

Combine the rotini, salad dressing, cucumber, bell pepper, cheese, salt and pepper in a large bowl and mix well. Chill, covered, until serving time. Yield: about 20 servings.

Macaela Hild, Rho Kappa
Wichita, Kansas

Mary Lee Kellner, Preceptor Alpha, Evans Mills, New York, makes A Honey of a Dressing by blending 1 cup salad oil with 1/2 cup honey, 1/3 cup ketchup, 1/2 cup vinegar, 3/4 teaspoon Worcestershire sauce and 1/2 teaspoon salt. It is wonderful with fruit, greens and other vegetables.

❖ SUMMER BARLEY SALAD

1/4 cup pearl barley,
  rinsed
1/4 cup olive oil
3 tablespoons fresh
  lemon juice
4 ripe Roma tomatoes
1 cup cooked corn
  kernels

1 cup (1/2-inch-diced)
  peeled cucumber
1/2 cup minced red onion
1/2 cup chopped parsley
1/2 cup chopped mint
  leaves
Salt and pepper to taste

Place the barley with 8 cups salted water in a saucepan over high heat. Bring to a boil; reduce heat. Simmer over medium heat for 45 minutes or until tender; drain well. Remove to a large bowl. Toss the warm barley with the olive oil and lemon juice. Cool to room temperature. Dice the tomatoes in 1/2-inch pieces. Add the tomatoes, corn, cucumber, onion, parsley, mint, salt and pepper and toss to combine. Yield: 8 servings.

Barbara J. Wiscarson, Preceptor Beta Lambda
Cottage Grove, Oregon

❖ CHILI CORN BREAD SALAD

1 (8-ounce) package corn
  bread mix
1 (4-ounce) can chopped
  chiles, undrained
1/8 teaspoon cumin
1/8 teaspoon oregano
Pinch of rubbed sage
1 cup mayonnaise
1 cup sour cream
1 envelope ranch salad
  dressing mix
2 (15-ounce) cans pinto
  beans, rinsed, drained

2 (15-ounce) cans whole
  kernel corn, drained
3 medium tomatoes,
  chopped
1 cup chopped green bell
  pepper
1 cup chopped green
  onions
10 slices bacon, crisp-
  cooked, crumbled
2 cups shredded Cheddar
  cheese

Prepare the corn bread batter using the directions on the package. Stir in the chiles, cumin, oregano and sage. Spread in a buttered 8-inch-square baking pan. Bake at 400 degrees for 20 to 25 minutes or until edges begin to brown. Let stand until cool. Combine the mayonnaise, sour cream and dressing mix in a small bowl and mix well. Crumble half the corn bread into a 9×13-inch baking pan. Layer half the bell pepper, half the beans, half the mayonnaise mixture, half the corn, half the tomatoes, half the green onions, half the bacon and half the cheese over the corn bread. Repeat the layers; dish will be very full. Chill, covered, for 2 hours before serving. Yield: 12 servings.

Dorothy Sparks, Xi Alpha Omicron
Nacogdoches, Texas

ARTICHOKE CONFETTI SALAD

Serve with rolls and barbecue.

1 envelope Italian salad
  dressing mix
8 ounces tri-color rotini,
  cooked, drained
1 to 1½ cups shredded
  mozzarella cheese
1 purple onion, shredded
10 ounces fresh spinach

½ cup pine nuts
1 (3-ounce) package
  sliced salami,
  chopped
1 cup green olives, sliced
2 (14-ounce) cans
  artichoke hearts
½ teaspoon oregano

Prepare the salad dressing using the directions on the package. Combine the rotini, cheese, onion, spinach, pine nuts, salami, olives, artichokes and oregano in a large bowl. Pour the dressing over the rotini mixture and stir well. Chill, covered, until serving time. Yield: 6 to 8 servings.

Jerry La Londe, Preceptor Beta Rho
Spokane, Washington

ZESTY ARTICHOKE SALAD

1 head iceberg lettuce
½ bunch romaine
½ to ¾ cup chopped red
  or white onion
1 (6-ounce) jar
  artichokes

½ to ¾ cup grated
  Parmesan cheese
2 cups shredded
  mozzarella cheese
½ to ¾ cup Italian
  dressing

Tear or cut up the iceberg and romaine lettuce into a large bowl. Scatter the onion over the lettuce. Add the undrained artichokes; use a knife and fork to cut up the artichokes in the bowl. Sprinkle with the Parmesan cheese, then with the mozzarella cheese. Toss to mix well. Add Italian dressing. Toss and serve. Yield: 6 to 8 servings.

Carla Trower, Preceptor Epsilon Xi
Jefferson City, Missouri

CAULIFLOWER AND BROCCOLI SALAD

1 pound sliced bacon,
  crisp-cooked,
  crumbled
1 head broccoli,
  trimmed, chopped
1 head cauliflower,
  trimmed, chopped

1 medium Vidalia onion,
  chopped
2 cups shredded Cheddar
  cheese
1 (8-ounce) jar coleslaw
  dressing

Drain the bacon on paper towels. Combine the broccoli, cauliflower, onion, cheese and dressing in a large bowl and mix well. Chill, covered, for 8 to 12 hours, stirring occasionally. Yield: 8 to 10 servings.

Ginny Clarke, Xi Beta Kappa
Independence, Missouri

LAYERED CAULIFLOWER SALAD

1 pound sliced bacon,
  crisp-cooked,
  crumbled
1 head lettuce,
  shredded
1 head cauliflower,
  finely chopped

2 cups mayonnaise-type
  salad dressing
1 medium Vidalia onion,
  chopped
¾ cup grated Parmesan
  cheese
½ cup sugar

Drain the bacon on paper towels. Layer the lettuce, cauliflower, bacon, salad dressing, onion, cheese and sugar in a large salad bowl. Chill, covered, for 8 to 12 hours. Mix well and serve. Yield: 16 to 18 servings.

Marie Trepinski, Xi Theta Mu
Port Charlotte, Florida

CORN, BEAN AND PEA SALAD

1 (16-ounce) can French-
  style green beans
1 (16-ounce) can tiny
  peas
1 (16-ounce) can white
  shoepeg corn
1 (2-ounce) jar chopped
  pimentos

½ cup chopped green
  bell pepper
½ cup minced onion
½ cup cider vinegar
½ cup vegetable oil
½ cup sugar
1 teaspoon salt
½ teaspoon pepper

Drain all the canned vegetables. Combine the first 6 ingredients in a large glass bowl. Whisk the vinegar, oil, sugar, salt and pepper in a small bowl. Pour the dressing over the vegetables and mix well. Chill, covered, for 8 to 12 hours. Yield: 15 to 20 servings.

Lorraine Coble, Laureate Gamma Zeta
Rialto, California

LAYERED VEGETABLE SALAD

1 head lettuce, torn into
  bite-size pieces
½ cup chopped onion
½ cup chopped celery
1 (15-ounce) can sliced
  water chestnuts,
  drained
1 (10-ounce) package
  frozen green peas

1½ cups mayonnaise
1 tablespoon sugar
2 large tomatoes, sliced
4 hard-cooked eggs,
  sliced
6 slices bacon, crisp-
  cooked, crumbled
½ cup shredded Cheddar
  or Swiss cheese

Layer the lettuce, a mixture of the onion and celery, the water chestnuts, peas and mayonnaise evenly in a large glass salad bowl. Sprinkle with the sugar. Chill, covered, for 8 to 12 hours. Layer the tomatoes, eggs and bacon over the mayonnaise at serving time. Top with the cheese. Yield: 4 to 6 servings.

Lettie Loveleen Turner, Preceptor Zeta Tau
Orange Park, Florida

ORIENTAL SALAD

Serve with rice and grilled fish or chicken.

1 cup sugar
1 cup water, room
temperature
1 cup peanut oil
1 cup white vinegar
1 (8-ounce) can water
chestnuts, rinsed,
drained
1 medium carrot, peeled
1 rib celery
2 (15-ounce) cans white
corn, drained
1 (15-ounce) can sweet
peas, drained

1 (2-ounce) jar
pimentos, drained,
chopped
1 (15-ounce) can bean
sprouts, drained
1 cup sliced fresh
mushrooms
1/2 cup finely chopped
green onions
1/2 cup finely diced green
bell pepper
Salt and pepper to taste
Crisp lettuce leaves

Dissolve the sugar in the water in a large glass bowl. Stir in the oil and vinegar. Slice the water chestnuts, cutting out any discolored areas. Slice the carrot into 1/4-inch slices. Slice the celery diagonally into 1/4-inch slices. Whisk the vinegar mixture until well blended. Add the water chestnuts, carrot, celery, corn, peas, pimentos, bean sprouts, mushrooms, green onions and bell pepper; stir well to coat all vegetables. Chill, covered, for 8 to 12 hours. Drain as much of the marinade as possible before serving. Add the salt and pepper. Toss well. Serve over lettuce leaves. Yield: 8 to 10 servings.

Rochelle Kornegay, Xi Alpha Xi
Hueytown, Alabama

COOL POTATO SALAD

Vidalia onions keep the "cool" taste in this surprisingly light potato salad. The cucumbers and onions stay unbelievably crisp, even through a couple of days as refrigerated leftovers.

5 or 6 small "pickling"
cucumbers
1 large Vidalia onion,
peeled, julienned
1/3 cup salt

3 pounds russet
potatoes, pared,
cooked, chopped
1/3 cup fat-free Italian
dressing

Pare the cucumbers or wash them well. Slice them thinly, about 6 slices per inch. Make several layers of cucumbers and onions in a bowl, generously salting each layer. Chill, covered, for up to 24 hours. Rinse well a couple of times with cool water. Dry with paper towels. Place the cucumber mixture, potatoes and dressing in a large bowl and mix well. Chill, covered, until ready to serve. Yield: 10 to 12 servings.

Mary Jo Hogan, Xi Delta Iota
Canton, Georgia

SAUERKRAUT SALAD

2 cups sugar
1/2 cup white vinegar
1 (27-ounce) can
sauerkraut, rinsed,
drained

1 cup chopped onion
1 cup chopped green bell
pepper
1 cup chopped celery
1 (2-ounce) jar pimentos

Heat the sugar and vinegar in a small saucepan over medium heat until sugar is dissolved, stirring frequently. Combine the sauerkraut, onion, bell pepper, celery and pimentos in a large bowl and mix well. Pour the vinegar mixture over the vegetables and mix well. Chill, covered, for 8 to 12 hours. Yield: 10 to 12 servings.

Patricia Hall, Xi Delta Omega
Bartow, Florida

CREAMY COLESLAW

1 teaspoon salt
2/3 cup sugar
1/3 cup white vinegar

1 head of cabbage,
thinly shredded
1 cup heavy cream

Combine the salt, sugar and vinegar in a large bowl and mix well. Add the cabbage and mix gently. Gently fold in the cream. Yield: 8 to 10 servings.

Mona Mae Russo, Laureate Epsilon Phi
Pittsburgh, Pennsylvania

RED AND GREEN SLAW

1 (1 1/2-pound) savoy
cabbage, thinly
shredded
1/2 cup thinly shredded
red cabbage
1/2 cup thinly sliced
green onions

1/2 cup chopped parsley
1 tablespoon sugar
1 1/2 teaspoons salt
1/2 teaspoon celery seed
1/3 cup white vinegar
1/4 cup vegetable or
olive oil

Combine the cabbages, green onions and parsley in a large bowl. Shake the sugar, salt, celery seed, vinegar and oil in a covered jar until sugar dissolves. Add the dressing to the slaw at the table or the cabbage will go limp. If not eating it all at one time, serve the slaw in small salad bowls and add dressing individually. Yield: 6 to 8 servings.

Jackie Boos, Preceptor Alpha Eta
Overland Park, Kansas

Betty Milam, Preceptor Gamma, Germantown, Tennessee, cooks a pound of broken spaghetti, rinses and drains well, and adds a cup of Italian salad dressing, a can of diced tomatoes, and 1/4 cup Salad Supreme seasoning. Marinate in the refrigerator for several hours and enjoy Easy Spaghetti Salad.

NUTTY COLESLAW

1 (3-ounce) package
beef-flavored ramen
noodles, crumbled
1/2 cup chopped green
onions
1 cup sunflower seeds
1 (2-ounce) package
toasted almonds

1 (10-ounce) package
coleslaw
1/3 cup olive oil
1/3 cup sugar
1/3 cup apple cider
vinegar

Set aside the flavor packet from the ramen noodles. Place the noodles, green onions, sunflower seeds, almonds and coleslaw in a large bowl and toss to combine. Shake the oil, sugar, vinegar and flavor packet in a covered jar until well blended. Add to the coleslaw mixture. Toss and serve. Yield: 8 servings.

Grace M. Viator, Laureate Epsilon Rho
Nederland, Texas

BLUEBERRY SPINACH SALAD

This great summer salad looks very festive, especially when the table decor is red, white, and blue. Serve with grilled meat and crusty bread for a light, delicious meal that requires very little last-minute preparation.

12 ounces fresh baby
spinach, washed,
stems removed, dried
1 cup fresh blueberries,
washed
3/4 cup pecan or walnut
halves, toasted
1 cup crumbled bleu
cheese

1/2 cup vegetable oil
3 tablespoons blueberry
vinegar
1 teaspoon Dijon
mustard
1 teaspoon sugar
1/8 teaspoon white
pepper
Salt to taste

Place the spinach, blueberries and nuts in a large salad bowl and toss to combine. Sprinkle the bleu cheese over the top. Chill, covered, until ready to serve. Shake the oil, vinegar, mustard, sugar, white pepper and salt in a covered jar until well blended. Add enough of the dressing to the salad to coat all ingredients when tossed. Toss and serve.
Yield: 6 to 8 servings.

Catherine M. Cash, Xi Gamma Zeta
Tucson, Arizona

Jan Prickel, Theta Nu, Batesville, Indiana, prepares Fresh Fruit Kabobs using skewers of bite-size fruit served with a dip made of 1 cup unsweetened applesauce, 1 cup low-fat vanilla yogurt, 1 teaspoon cinnamon, and 1/4 teaspoon nutmeg.

SPINACH AND STRAWBERRY SALAD

2 bunches spinach,
washed, trimmed,
dried
2 pints strawberries,
sliced
1/2 cup sugar
2 tablespoons sesame
seeds
1 tablespoon poppy
seeds

1 1/2 teaspoons minced
onion
1/4 teaspoon
Worcestershire sauce
1/4 teaspoon paprika
1/2 cup vegetable oil
1/4 cup vinegar

Cut or tear the spinach into bite-size pieces. Place spinach and strawberries in a large bowl and toss to combine. Shake the sugar, sesame seeds, poppy seeds, onion, Worcestershire sauce, paprika, oil and vinegar in a covered jar until well blended. Pour over the strawberry mixture. Toss and serve.
Yield: 8 to 12 servings.

Jill Wagner, Sigma Mu
Golconda, Illinois

BARBECUED BEEF BRISKET

Serve with baked beans, herbed potatoes, coleslaw, potato salad, and hard rolls.

1 (5-pound) beef brisket
1 teaspoon garlic
powder
1 teaspoon onion
powder
1 teaspoon celery
powder

3 tablespoons liquid
smoke
1 tablespoon
Worcestershire sauce
1 cup barbecue sauce,
any brand

Trim the fat from the brisket. Rub the brisket on all sides with the garlic, onion and celery powders. Sprinkle with the liquid smoke. Wrap tightly in foil. Chill for 12 to 24 hours, or freeze until ready to cook. Preheat the oven to 300 degrees. Open the foil and sprinkle the brisket with the Worcestershire sauce. Rewrap and place in a 9×13-inch baking pan. Bake for 5 hours, adding water occasionally if brisket appears to be drying out. Remove the brisket to a serving platter. Cut into thin slices on the diagonal. Blend the drippings with the barbecue sauce. Pour over the brisket. Yield: 12 to more than 20 servings.

Ella S. Mantei, Laureate Alpha
Albuquerque, New Mexico

Norma Smith, Alpha Delta Upsilon, Shell Knob, Missouri, makes Tipsy Meatballs by simmering browned meatballs in a sauce of 1 cup ketchup, 1 cup beer, 1/4 cup sugar, and 4 teaspoons each vinegar and Worcestershire sauce for 4 hours.

SAVORY BARBECUED BEEF BRISKET

Serve with baked potato wedges or fries.

1 (7- to 8-pound) beef brisket	3 tablespoons soy sauce
2 cups ketchup	1 teaspoon celery salt
3/4 cup lemon juice	7 or 8 garlic cloves, crushed
1 cup packed brown sugar	2 cups white wine
3 tablespoons Dijon mustard	

Trim the fat from brisket and pierce all over with a fork. Place in a large roasting pan. Combine the ketchup, lemon juice, brown sugar, mustard, soy sauce, celery salt, garlic and wine in a bowl and blend well. Pour over the brisket. Bake, covered with foil, at 325 degrees for 5 hours. Remove the foil. Reduce oven temperature to 350 degrees and bake for 1 hour longer. Remove the brisket to a serving platter and slice. Skim the fat from the juices. Serve the juices on the side. Yield: 10 servings.

Meredith McMindes, Sigma Eta
Chesterfield, Missouri

EASY BARBECUED BRISKET

2 tablespoons liquid smoke	2 tablespoons freshly ground pepper
2 tablespoons salt	1 1/2 tablespoons onion salt
2 tablespoons celery seed	1 (9- to 10-pound) brisket, untrimmed
1 1/2 tablespoons garlic salt	1 (18-ounce) jar spicy barbecue sauce
2 tablespoons Worcestershire sauce	

Combine the liquid smoke, salt, celery seed, garlic salt, Worcestershire sauce, pepper and onion salt in a small bowl and mix well to form a paste. Trim the large pieces of fat from the brisket. Spread the paste over the surface of the brisket and place in a large sealable plastic bag. Marinate, sealed, in the refrigerator for 8 to 12 hours. Remove the brisket to a 10×13-inch baking pan. Bake, covered, at 250 degrees for 5 hours or until beef is tender. Remove the brisket from the pan and let cool. Reduce oven temperature to 350 degrees. Slice the brisket. Drain the liquid from the pan and discard. Return the brisket to the pan. Pour the barbecue sauce over and between the brisket slices. Bake, uncovered, for 1 hour longer. Yield: 12 to 14 servings.

Pamela J. Chauvin, Laureate Beta
Lafayette, Louisiana

BEER BAKED BEEF

1 (3- to 4-pound) beef brisket	1 garlic clove
1/4 cup chili sauce	1 (12-ounce) can beer
2 tablespoons brown sugar	1 onion, sliced

Season the brisket with salt and pepper. Place in a 9×13-inch baking dish. Combine the chili sauce, brown sugar, garlic and beer in a bowl and blend well. Pour over the brisket. Cover with onion slices. Bake, covered, at 350 degrees for 3 1/2 hours or until beef is tender. Bake, uncovered, for 30 minutes longer, basting occasionally with the juices. Serve with the juices, accompanied by rolls, mustard, mayonnaise and horseradish. Yield: 8 to 10 servings.

Janet Shark, Preceptor Theta
Buhl, Idaho

❖ SPAGHETTI ROAST

4 tablespoons olive oil	2 tablespoons Tabasco sauce
4 (15-ounce) cans tomato sauce	4 garlic cloves, chopped
4 (4-ounce) cans mushrooms	2 cups red wine
4 tablespoons Worcestershire sauce	Flour
4 teaspoons A.1. steak sauce	1 (4- to 6-pound) rump roast
	1 pound spaghetti

Combine the olive oil, tomato sauce, mushrooms, Worcestershire, steak sauce, Tabasco, garlic and wine in a bowl and blend well. Rub the roast with salt and pepper. Roll the roast in flour, coating well. Brown in hot oil in a 6-quart roasting pan or Dutch oven. Pour the Tabasco mixture over the roast. Bake, covered, at 200 degrees for 5 hours or until roast is tender. Cook the spaghetti in boiling water in a saucepan for half the amount of time specified on the package directions; drain well. Remove the roast to a serving platter. Add the spaghetti to the sauce in the roasting pan and cook over medium heat until spaghetti is tender. Slice the roast and serve with the spaghetti. Yield: 8 to 10 servings.

Linda Bartee
Vacaville, California

Ida "Dolly" Trombetti, Laureate Gamma Upsilon, Columbus, Ohio, combines 3 pounds uncooked beef chunks with 1 can each cream of mushroom, cream of chicken, and cream of celery soups in a slow cooker, mixes well, cooks on Low for 7 to 8 hours, and serves over rice or noodles for Super Easy Stew.

BARBECUED MEATBALLS

1½ pounds lean ground
   beef
1 (5-ounce) can
   evaporated milk
¾ cup quick-cooking
   oats
1 medium onion,
   chopped
1 medium green bell
   pepper, chopped

Salt and pepper to taste
1 cup ketchup
½ cup water
1 tablespoon vinegar
1 tablespoon sugar
1 tablespoon
   Worcestershire sauce

Combine the ground beef, evaporated milk, oats, half the onion, half the bell pepper, salt and pepper in a bowl and mix well. Shape into 1-inch balls and place in a 9×13-inch baking dish. Combine the ketchup, water, vinegar, sugar, Worcestershire sauce, the remaining onion and the remaining bell pepper in a saucepan over medium heat. Heat for 5 to 10 minutes or until the sugar is dissolved, stirring frequently. Pour over the meatballs. Bake, uncovered, at 350 degrees for 45 minutes or until meat is cooked through. Yield: 20 to 25 servings.

Mary Prehm, Xi Gamma Eta
Paris, Tennessee

SUMMER BURGERS

1 cup sour cream
1 egg
4 slices fresh bread, torn
   in pieces
1 onion, chopped
1½ teaspoons salt

½ teaspoon pepper
3 tablespoons
   Worcestershire sauce
3 pounds lean ground
   beef
12 thin slices bacon

Combine the sour cream, egg, bread, onion, salt, pepper and Worcestershire sauce in a bowl and mix well. Add the ground beef and mix well. Shape into patties. Wrap each patty with a slice of bacon; secure with a toothpick. Grill over medium-high heat for 10 minutes. Turn the patties and grill over lower heat for 5 to 10 minutes longer, or until of the desired degree of doneness. Yield: 12 servings.

Rosie Marcotte, Alpha Omega
Nebraska City, Nebraska

Phyllis Carver, Alpha Theta Master, Lakeland, Florida, makes Super Sloppy Joes by browning and draining 2 pounds ground beef with a chopped onion, adding 2 cans chicken gumbo soup, ½ soup can water, a small jar of spaghetti sauce, and 2 teaspoons Worcestershire sauce, simmering for 30 to 40 minutes and serving on buns.

❖ SPICY MEAT LOAF

2 pounds lean ground
   beef
2 cups picante sauce
1½ cups rolled oats
1 envelope taco
   seasoning mix
½ teaspoon garlic
   powder

1 cup shredded Cheddar
   cheese
1 (4-ounce) can sliced
   black olives, drained
1 (4-ounce) can chopped
   green chiles

Combine the ground beef, ½ cup of the picante sauce, the oats, taco seasoning and garlic powder and mix well. Shape into a loaf and place in a 9×13-inch baking pan or a 5×9-inch loaf pan. Combine the remaining 1½ cups picante sauce, the cheese, olives and chiles and mix well. Pour the olive mixture over the loaf. Bake at 375 degrees for 30 to 35 minutes or until center is no longer pink. Yield: 10 servings.

Kathy Sanchez, Xi Apha Gamma Sigma
Burleson, Texas

HOT DOG CHILI

This chili is great when served with hot dogs or spooned over nacho chips. Notice that the ground beef is not browned before cooking with the other ingredients.

1 pound lean ground
   beef
1 medium onion,
   chopped
1 (6-ounce) can tomato
   paste
3 cans water

½ cup ketchup
1 teaspoon white or
   dark vinegar
½ teaspoon chili
   powder
1 teaspoon salt

Combine the ground beef, onion, tomato paste, 1 can of water, the ketchup and vinegar in a large kettle over medium heat and mix well; reduce heat. Cook over low heat for 1½ hours, stirring occasionally and adding the remaining cans of water as necessary. Yield: 6 to 8 servings.

Sandy Casdorph, Preceptor Alpha Nu
Elkview, West Virginia

Gloria Dimmick, Xi Gamma Iota, Orlando, Florida, makes Seniors' and Kids' Favorite Casserole by browning and draining a pound of ground beef with a small chopped onion, adding a large can of spaghetti and a large can of mixed vegetables, and baking in a casserole at 325 degrees for 30 minutes. A cup of cheese may be mixed in or sprinkled on top.

HEARTY SPAGHETTI SAUCE

Delicious over spaghetti or veal Parmesan and rice.

1½ pounds lean ground beef	1½ teaspoons poultry seasoning
1 (48-ounce) can tomato juice	1½ teaspoons nutmeg
1 (12-ounce) can tomato paste	1½ teaspoons thyme
1 (10-ounce) can tomato soup	1½ teaspoons oregano
	1 tablespoon sugar
	¼ cup grated Parmesan cheese
1½ teaspoons sage	¼ cup chopped parsley

Brown the ground beef in a skillet, stirring until crumbly; drain well. Stir in the tomato juice, tomato paste and tomato soup. Add the sage, poultry seasoning, nutmeg, thyme, oregano, sugar, cheese and parsley and stir well. Bring to a boil; reduce heat. Simmer, covered, for 1 to 1½ hours, stirring frequently. Serve over cooked spaghetti.
Yield: 12 to 15 servings.

Sandra Jeanne Beaven, Laureate Delta Delta
West Hill, Ontario, Canada

BEEF AND BOW TIES

1 pound lean ground beef	1½ cups uncooked bow tie pasta
3 garlic cloves, crushed	2 tablespoons sliced fresh basil
2 cups chopped fresh tomatoes	3 tablespoons grated Parmesan cheese
¾ teaspoon salt	
¼ teaspoon pepper	

Brown the ground beef with the garlic in a large non-stick skillet over medium heat for 8 to 10 minutes or until beef is no longer pink, stirring it into ¾-inch crumbles; drain well. Stir in the tomatoes, salt and pepper. Cook over medium heat for 5 minutes, stirring occasionally. Cook the pasta using the package directions; drain. Toss the beef mixture with the hot pasta and the basil in a large bowl. Sprinkle with the cheese and serve. Yield: 4 servings.

Jane Hajdukiewicz, Eta Master
Tallahassee, Florida

GRILLED SWEET-AND-SOUR PORK

1 cup packed brown sugar	¼ teaspoon pepper
¾ cup teriyaki sauce	⅛ teaspoon garlic powder
¾ cup dry red wine	1 (4- to 5-pound) boneless loin roast, rolled and tied
¾ cup chili sauce	
½ teaspoon ground cloves	

Combine the brown sugar, teriyaki sauce, wine, chili sauce, cloves, pepper and garlic powder in a large glass dish and whisk well. Add the pork. Marinate, covered, in the refrigerator for 8 to 12 hours, turning occasionally. Drain the pork, reserving the marinade. Grill over hot coals for 2 to 2½ hours or to 165 degrees on a meat thermometer, turning and basting frequently with the reserved marinade. Let stand for 10 to 15 minutes before carving.
Yield: 10 to 12 servings.

Gail Scott, Mu Tau
Cambridge, Iowa

TOURTIERE

1 pound lean ground pork	1 teaspoon salt
1 cup water	⅛ teaspoon sage
½ cup chopped onion	Dash of black pepper
½ cup dry bread crumbs	Dash of ground nutmeg
	1 (2-crust) pie pastry

Brown the ground pork in a skillet, stirring until crumbly; drain. Stir in the water, onion, brad crumbs, salt, sage, pepper and nutmeg. Simmer, covered, for 20 minutes or until onion is tender, stirring frequently. Line a 9-inch pie plate with 1 pastry layer. Pour the pork mixture into the shell. Top with the remaining pastry, fluting edge and cutting vents. Brush with beaten egg if desired. Bake at 400 degrees for about 30 minutes or until golden brown.
Yield: 8 servings.

Lillian Laing, Preceptor Epsilon Delta
Garden Grove, California

BARBECUED PORK CHOPS

Serve with scalloped corn and a fruit salad.

½ cup water	1 slice fresh lemon, or 1 teaspoon bottled lemon juice
¼ cup cider vinegar	
2 tablespoons sugar	
1 tablespoon mustard	1 medium onion, sliced
1½ teaspoons salt (or less)	½ cup ketchup or tomato sauce
½ teaspoon black pepper	2 tablespoons Worcestershire sauce
¼ teaspoon cayenne pepper	1 teaspoon liquid smoke
	6 pork chops

Combine the water, vinegar, sugar, mustard, salt, black pepper, cayenne pepper, lemon and onion in a saucepan over medium heat. Cook for 20 minutes, stirring occasionally. Stir in the ketchup, Worcestershire sauce and liquid smoke and bring to a boil. Remove from heat. Trim the fat from the pork chops and arrange them in a single layer in a large baking pan. Pour the vinegar sauce over the pork. Bake, uncovered, at 350 degrees for 1 hour and 25 minutes, turning once. Yield: 6 servings.

Rosalie Minor, Preceptor Delta Chi
Liberty, Missouri

STUFFED PORK CHOPS

1 cup coarsely chopped red bell pepper (1 medium)	*¹⁄₂ teaspoon cumin*
	¹⁄₄ teaspoon salt
¹⁄₂ cup thinly sliced red onion, separated into rings	*¹⁄₄ teaspoon coarsely ground pepper*
	2 tablespoons cider vinegar
¹⁄₄ cup chopped fresh cilantro or parsley	*2 tablespoons vegetable oil*
1 (10-ounce) package frozen whole kernel corn, thawed, drained	*6 (1-inch-thick) pork chops*

Prepare the grill; heat until coals are ash white. Combine the bell pepper, onion, cilantro, corn, cumin, salt, pepper, vinegar and oil in a medium bowl and mix well to make the corn relish. Split each pork chop from an outer edge toward the bone, making a pocket. Place about 2 tablespoons corn relish in each pocket. Grill for 20 minutes or until cooked through, turning occasionally. Serve the remaining corn relish over the pork chops. Yield: 6 servings.

Joan Robbins, Laureate Beta
East Greenwich, Rhode Island

BARBECUED SPARERIBS

1 tablespoon sugar	*1 tablespoon plus 1 teaspoon Worcestershire sauce*
2 teaspoons each salt, pepper and paprika	
3 pounds pork spareribs	
1 cup ketchup	*1 teaspoon prepared mustard*
2 tablespoons light brown sugar	*1 teaspoon liquid smoke*
2 teaspoons minced garlic	*¹⁄₂ teaspoon hot pepper sauce*

Mix together the sugar, salt, pepper and paprika to make the spice rub mixture. Rub the ribs with the mixture. Place the ribs meaty side up on a rack in a large roasting pan. Cover with foil. Bake for 2¹⁄₂ to 3 hours or until meat is very tender. Combine the ketchup, brown sugar, garlic, Worcestershire sauce, mustard, liquid smoke and hot pepper sauce in a medium saucepan. Bring to a boil; reduce heat. Simmer, uncovered, for 25 to 30 minutes or until liquid thickens slightly and flavors develop, stirring occasionally. Brush the sauce over the baked ribs. Grill the ribs 4 to 6 inches from the heat source for 12

to 14 minutes or until lightly charred, basting once or twice with the sauce and turning 3 or 4 times to prevent burning. Cut into individual ribs and serve with any remaining sauce. Yield: 6 to 8 servings.

Judy Clark, Xi Phi Iota
Apple Valley, California

❖ SUPER STUFFED PIZZA

¹⁄₂ pound Italian sausage	*2 (17-ounce) frozen thin-crust cheese pizzas, thawed*
¹⁄₂ pound fresh mushrooms, sliced	*1 tablespoon olive oil*
1 small onion, chopped	*1 cup shredded mozzarella cheese*

Cook the sausage with the mushrooms and onion in a skillet over medium heat for 10 minutes or until sausage is browned and vegetables are tender, stirring frequently; drain. Lay a 2¹⁄₂-foot piece of foil over a 12- to 14-inch pizza pan. Place 1 pizza on the foil. Spread the sausage mixture over the pizza. Top with the other pizza, placing it cheese side down. Press the pizzas together. Bring the edges of the foil together and seal. Bake at 375 degrees for 20 to 25 minutes. Brush the pizza with olive oil. Layer the mozzarella cheese over the pizza. Bake, uncovered, for 15 to 20 minutes longer. Yield: 8 servings.

Judy Behnke, Xi Gamma Alpha
Norfolk, Nebraska

BARBECUE SAUCE FOR CHICKEN

The amount of sauce made by this recipe will barbecue about 6 chickens, but the recipe is easily halved. To make sure the chicken will get done on the grill without drying out, first stack the cleaned chicken parts in a large baking pan, cover with foil, and bake for 1¹⁄₄ hours at 300 degrees.

²⁄₃ cup chili powder	*2 tablespoons pepper*
¹⁄₄ cup hickory-smoked salt	*Juice of 12 lemons, or 1¹⁄₂ cups bottled lemon juice*
1 tablespoon garlic salt	
2 tablespoons paprika	*1 pound (4 sticks) margarine, melted*
2 tablespoons cumin	

Combine the chili powder, hickory-smoked salt, garlic salt, paprika, cumin and pepper in a bowl. Add ¹⁄₄ cup of the lemon juice and mix well. Whisk the remaining lemon juice and margarine together and stir into the chili powder mixture. Brush on a barbecuing chicken. Yield: 2 cups.

Ethel E. Manuel, Laureate Theta
Stone Mountain, Georgia

CHICKEN CORN FRITTERS

Serve with white gravy, ranch dressing, or ketchup for dipping.

1 (15-ounce) can whole
    kernel corn, drained
2 cups finely chopped
    cooked chicken
1 egg, lightly beaten
1/2 cup milk
2 tablespoons butter or
    margarine, melted

1/2 teaspoon salt
1/8 teaspoon pepper
1/8 teaspoon garlic salt
1 3/4 cups flour
1 teaspoon baking
    powder
Oil for deep-frying

Place the corn in a bowl. Crush lightly with a potato masher. Add the chicken, egg, milk, butter, salt, pepper and garlic salt. Add a mixture of the flour and baking powder to the corn mixture, stirring just until combined. Heat 2 inches of oil to 375 degrees. Drop the batter by 1/4 cups in the oil, 2 or 3 at a time. Fry 3 minutes on each side or until golden brown; drain well. Yield: 1 dozen.

Linda Mueller, Xi Mu Chi
Garden City, Missouri

BAKED REUBEN CHICKEN

This great potluck dish can be made ahead of time. Serve with coleslaw or a green salad.

8 boneless skinless
    chicken breasts
1/4 teaspoon salt
1/8 teaspoon pepper
2 cups sauerkraut,
    rinsed, drained

1 1/4 cups low-calorie
    Russian dressing
4 to 6 slices low-fat
    Swiss cheese
1 tablespoon chopped
    parsley

Place the chicken in a large nonstick baking pan. Sprinkle with the salt and pepper. Layer the sauerkraut over the chicken. Pour the dressing over the sauerkraut. Top with the cheese. Bake, covered, at 325 degrees for 1 hour or until fork can be inserted easily. Sprinkle with the parsley before serving. Yield: 4 large servings.

Laura Lee Wetzel, Alpha Master
Carson City, Nevada

Joan Webb, Laureate Epsilon Zeta, Vista, California, prepares Baked Herbed Chicken by arranging a cut-up chicken in a foil-lined baking dish and sprinkling with 1/2 teaspoon each oregano, rosemary, thyme, and seasoned salt. Bake at 450 degrees for 1 hour. Serve the chicken, throw away the foil, and enjoy an instant dinner and a clean pan. Delicious cold for picnics, too.

SPICY CHICKEN ENCHILADAS

1 (10-ounce) can cream
    of celery soup
1 (10-ounce) can cream
    of chicken soup
1 cup sour cream
1 (10-ounce) can
    tomatoes with green
    chiles
6 chicken breasts

1 (4-ounce) can chopped
    green chiles
1/2 cup chopped onion
2 tablespoons margarine
1 teaspoon chili powder
6 large or 10 small flour
    tortillas
2 cups shredded Cheddar
    cheese

Combine the soups and sour cream in a bowl and mix well. Drain the tomatoes with green chiles, reserving the juice. Cook the chicken in the reserved juice in a saucepan over medium-low heat for 20 minutes or until cooked through. Chop the chicken. Combine the chopped green chiles, onion, margarine, chili powder, 3 tablespoons of the soup mixture and the drained tomatoes with green chiles in a large saucepan over medium-low heat. Cook for 10 to 20 minutes or until onion is tender, stirring occasionally. Combine the chile mixture and chicken in a bowl and mix well. Fill the tortillas with the chicken mixture. Roll to enclose the filling. Arrange the enchiladas in a large baking pan. Spoon the remaining soup mixture over the enchiladas. Bake, covered, with foil, at 375 degrees for 15 minutes. Remove the foil. Layer the cheese over the top and bake for 5 to 10 minutes longer or until cheese is melted. Yield: 6 to 8 servings.

Sherry Siebert, Pi Sigma
Houston, Texas

HORN ISLAND CHICKEN

Our first sailing trip of the season, to Horn Island, is often made on Memorial Day. When we reach Horn Island and set up camp, we prepare this tasty dish over a very small Coleman gas stove. Shrimp or beef may be substituted for the chicken.

3 large onions, chopped
1/4 cup (1/2 stick) butter
8 ounces fresh
    mushrooms, sliced
Tony's Seasoning (or
    your favorite
    seasoning) to taste
1 (10-ounce) can golden
    mushroom soup

6 boneless skinless
    chicken breasts, cut
    into bite-size pieces
1 (8-ounce) can sliced
    water chestnuts
12 to 15 snow peas,
    trimmed

Sauté the onions in the butter in a 10-inch skillet until onions are translucent. Stir in the mushrooms and Tony's seasoning to taste. Lightly season the chicken and add to the onion mixture. Sauté over medium heat for 5 to 10 minutes or until chicken is cooked through. Stir in the golden mushroom soup. Cook, covered, over medium heat for 3 to 5 minutes or until mixture is bubbling. Stir in the water chestnuts and snow peas. Cook, covered, for 3 to 5 minutes longer. Yield: 6 servings.

Ginny Ingwersen, Iota Epsilon
Baton Rouge, Louisiana

SAUERKRAUT CHICKEN

It was a winter evening, we were very hungry, and we were all on the Atkins diet. This dish fit the diet requirements and made as feel as if we were eating something very special. Serve with a tossed green salad.

2 to 3 tablespoons vegetable oil	²⁄₃ cup sliced mushrooms
4 large chicken breasts	1 (16-ounce) can sauerkraut, drained, rinsed
Seasoned salt to taste	
¹⁄₄ teaspoon garlic powder	¹⁄₂ cup sour cream
¹⁄₄ cup grated Parmesan cheese	2 tablespoons water

Heat the oil over medium heat in an electric skillet or other large skillet. Sprinkle the chicken breasts with seasoned salt, garlic powder and cheese. Brown the chicken in the hot oil, turning frequently. Remove the chicken from the skillet. Brown the mushrooms in the hot oil. Return the chicken to the skillet. Squeeze the excess moisture from the sauerkraut. Spread over the chicken. Mix the sour cream and water together; spread over the sauerkraut. Simmer, covered, for 20 to 25 minutes or until chicken is cooked through. Yield: 4 servings.

Gael Berhow, Xi Alpha Eta
Coquille, Oregon

TEX-MEX TURKEY TENDERLOIN

This recipe is good for those on a low-sugar, low-carb diet. Serve with a green salad and fruit compote.

1 pound turkey tenderloin steaks, ¹⁄₂ inch thick	1 cup chopped zucchini
	¹⁄₄ cup sliced green onion
1 teaspoon cumin	1 (4-ounce) can chopped green chiles, drained
¹⁄₈ teaspoon salt	
¹⁄₈ teaspoon pepper	Fresh chile peppers (optional)
1 cup chopped tomato	

Rinse the turkey and pat dry. Sprinkle a mixture of the cumin, salt and pepper over both sides of the turkey steaks. Place the turkey in a large cold skillet sprayed with nonstick cooking spray. Cook over medium heat for 10 to 12 minutes or until tender. Remove the turkey to a serving platter. Cover with foil to keep warm. Combine the tomato, zucchini, green onion and chiles in the skillet over high heat. Stir-fry for 1 to 2 minutes. Remove from heat. Spoon the vegetables over the turkey and serve. Yield: 4 servings.

Betty Osterdock, Zeta Master
Mesa, Arizona

❖ POTATO-CRUSTED CRAB BURGERS

Guests are always delighted with this "fancy burger," a change of pace when you are used to ordinary burgers. Try serving with rémoulade, a spicy cold sauce you can make by mixing 1 cup mayonnaise, 2 teaspoons hot mustard, 1 tablespoon chopped sweet pickle, 1 tablespoon chopped fresh parsley, and 1 teaspoon tarragon.

2 tablespoons butter or margarine	2 cups fresh bread crumbs
1 each red and green bell pepper, chopped	3 large eggs
	¹⁄₄ cup Dijon mustard
1 purple onion, chopped	2 cups instant potato flakes
1 garlic clove, minced	
1 pound fresh crab meat, or 3 (4-ounce) cans crab meat, drained, flaked	Vegetable oil
	6 hard rolls, split

Melt the butter in a large skillet over medium heat. Add the bell peppers, onion and garlic. Sauté for 3 minutes or until tender. Combine the onion mixture, crab meat, bread crumbs, eggs and mustard in a bowl and mix well. Shape into 6 patties. Roll gently in the potato flakes, coating well (patties are fragile). Cook 2 at a time in hot oil in a skillet over medium-high heat for 2 minutes on each side or until golden; drain. Place on a baking sheet. Bake at 350 degrees for 15 minutes or until heated through. Serve each patty on a roll with lettuce, tomato and rémoulade. Yield: 6 servings.

Barbara Eadie, Xi Beta Lambda
Greencastle, Pennsylvania

Hyla Williams, Nu Beta, Bloomfield Hills, Michigan, marinates four 6- to 8-ounce salmon fillets in a mixture of ¹⁄₂ cup maple syrup, ¹⁄₄ cup orange juice, 1 teaspoon cayenne pepper, 1 teaspoon dillweed, 1 teaspoon orange zest, and salt and pepper to taste in the refrigerator for 1 to 6 hours. Grill over medium-high heat for 4 to 5 minutes per side. Super Salmon it is!

LEMON-LIME SALMON

6 tablespoons olive oil
1/4 cup orange juice
3 tablespoons lemon
  juice
1 tablespoon lime juice
2 tablespoons soy sauce
1/2 small red onion,
  thinly sliced
2 garlic cloves, minced

1/2 inch gingerroot,
  peeled, thinly sliced
Sprig of thyme
1 bay leaf
1 teaspoon peppercorns,
  crushed
4 (6- to 8-ounce) salmon
  fillets

Combine the first 11 ingredients and mix well to make the marinade. Pour into a resealable plastic bag. Place the salmon in the bag and seal, turning to coat. Let stand in the refrigerator for 30 to 60 minutes. Place on a grill over medium-hot coals. Grill for 5 to 7 minutes on each side or until desired degree of doneness. Yield: 4 servings.

Mary Ellen Cramer, Xi Zeta Psi
Stroudsburg, Pennsylvania

BAKED STEELHEAD

I often used this recipe to cook the fish my son caught while fishing the Wilson River. The recipe calls for baking in the oven, but it may also be cooked on a grill or by the stream over hot coals.

1 (8- to 10-pounce) fresh
  whole steelhead,
  cleaned
3/4 cup (1 1/2 sticks) butter
  or margarine, softened

1/2 teaspoon garlic salt
1/2 teaspoon pepper
1 lemon

Leave the tail on when cleaning the fish; the head may be left on if desired. Rub half the butter into the cavity of the fish. Sprinkle the cavity with salt and pepper. Squeeze the lemon into the cavity. Slice the lemon rind and place in the cavity. Close the cavity and rub the outside of the fish with the remaining butter. Wrap the whole fish in heavy-duty foil, closing well to seal in moisture and juices. Bake at 350 to 400 degrees for 20 to 25 minutes or until cooked through. Yield: 8 to 10 servings.

Maggie Sargeant, Preceptor Alpha Omega
Redmond, Oregon

Evelyn Austin, Beta Mu Master, Susanville, California, makes Parmesan Egg on Toast by buttering a slice of bread, pressing a depression in the center with a fork, breaking an egg carefully into the depression, sprinkling with salt, pepper and Parmesan cheese, and baking at 475 degrees for 5 to 6 minutes.

❖ ASPARAGUS PIE

1 cup flour
1 cup (2 sticks) butter,
  softened
1/8 teaspoon salt
1 egg
1 teaspoon lemon juice
4 eggs
1/2 teaspoon salt
1 cup half-and-half
1 cup milk

2 cups fresh asparagus
  pieces
1 medium onion
8 mushrooms, sliced
1 cup shredded
  Monterey Jack cheese
1 cup grated Parmesan
  cheese
1/8 teaspoon each pepper
  and nutmeg

Combine the flour, butter and 1/8 teaspoon salt in a food processor fitted with a steel blade and process until the mixture resembles coarse crumbs. Add 1 egg and lemon juice and process until the mixture forms a ball. Wrap in plastic wrap. Chill for 30 minutes. Roll into a 12-inch circle on a lightly floured surface. Fit into a 9-inch pie plate. Bake at 400 degrees for 12 to 14 minutes or until golden. Combine 4 eggs, 1/2 teaspoon salt, half-and-half and milk in a mixing bowl and beat until smooth. Sauté the asparagus, onion and mushrooms in a small amount of oil in a skillet over medium heat for 5 minutes. Place the mixture in the baked pie crust. Sprinkle with the Monterey Jack cheese. Pour the egg mixture over the vegetables. Sprinkle with the Parmesan cheese, pepper and nutmeg. Bake at 350 degrees for 45 to 50 minutes. Yield: 6 to 8 servings.

Janetta Kunkel, Laureate Eta
Warner Robins, Georgia

HERBED CHEESE CASSEROLE

This recipe serves one, but may be increased for a group. Fresh herbs in summer make it really special. Mix 2 of the 3 cheeses Cheddar, Swiss, and Monterey Jack for the "mixed shredded cheese."

1/4 cup mixed shredded
  cheese
1/4 cup ricotta cheese
2 eggs
1/4 cup light cream
1/4 teaspoon dillweed

1/4 teaspoon dried
  parsley
1/4 teaspoon of your
  favorite herb, such as
  chives, basil, thyme

Combine the mixed cheese, ricotta, eggs, cream, dillweed, parsley and selected herb in a medium bowl and mix well. Pour into a buttered single-serving baking dish. Bake at 400 degrees for 20 minutes. Yield: 1 serving.

Jean Saveraid, Xi Theta Zeta
Huxley, Iowa

ORIENTAL VEGETABLE PANCAKES

Serve with your choice of breakfast meats.

3 cups shredded cabbage	2 tablespoons soy sauce
1/2 cup finely chopped onion	2 teaspoons salt
1 teaspoon celery seed	1/4 teaspoon pepper
2 cups cooked brown rice	1 1/2 cups chicken broth
	1 tablespoon cornstarch
8 eggs, beaten	1 tablespoon soy sauce
	Vegetable oil

Combine the cabbage, onion, celery seed and rice in a bowl. Combine the eggs, 2 tablespoons soy sauce, salt and pepper in a separate bowl and beat until smooth. Fold the cabbage mixture into the egg mixture. Place the chicken broth, cornstarch and 1 tablespoon soy sauce in a saucepan over medium heat to make the sauce. Cook until thickened, whisking constantly. Keep warm. Pour 1/3-cup portions of the cabbage mixture over a hot, lightly oiled griddle. Brown on both sides. Serve the sauce in an insulated container, or use a table warmer. Yield: 6 pancakes.

Barb Roberts, Preceptor Alpha
Astoria, Oregon

VEGETABLE TORTELLINI

Tortellini is small ring-shaped pasta stuffed with meat or cheese. Serve as the main course with bread and a tossed salad, or as a side dish with beef or chicken.

6 cups very hot tap water	1/4 cup olive oil
3 teaspoons chicken bouillon granules	1 teaspoon minced garlic
12 ounces fresh cheese tortellini	1/4 cup grated Parmesan cheese
1 (16-ounce) package frozen mixed vegetables (broccoli, cauliflower, carrots)	Pepper to taste

Combine the water, bouillon and tortellini in a large saucepan. Cover and bring to a boil. Add the vegetables. Bring to a boil; reduce heat. Cook, uncovered, for 8 to 10 minutes or until vegetables are hot (but still crisp) and tortellini is tender. Remove from heat. Drain, reserving 1/2 cup liquid. Heat the olive oil and garlic in the saucepan over medium heat. Add the tortellini mixture and the reserved 1/2 cup liquid. Toss to combine. Remove from heat. Sprinkle each serving with Parmesan cheese and pepper. Yield: 4 servings.

Inga Horrigan, Preceptor Epsilon
Lawton, Oklahoma

ZUCCHINI PIE

1/4 cup (1/2 stick) margarine	1/4 teaspoon basil
	1/4 teaspoon oregano
4 cups chopped or sliced peeled zucchini	2 eggs, beaten
1 cup sliced onions	2 cups shredded mozzarella cheese
2 tablespoons parsley flakes	1 (4-count) package refrigerator crescent rolls
1/2 teaspoon salt	
1/4 teaspoon garlic powder	2 teaspoons prepared mustard

Melt the margarine in a large saucepan over medium-low heat. Add the zucchini and onions and cook for 5 to 10 minutes, stirring occasionally. Add the parsley, salt, garlic, basil and oregano and cook until onions are translucent. Add a mixture of the eggs and cheese and cook until cheese melts, stirring constantly. Unroll the refrigerator dough. Shape into a rectangle, pressing the perforations to seal. Fit into a 9-inch pie plate as if making a crust. Spread the mustard over the dough. Add the zucchini mixture and spread evenly. Bake at 350 degrees for 18 to 20 minutes or until crust is golden and filling is hot. Let stand for 10 minutes before slicing.
Yield: 4 to 6 servings.

Bonnie Pardiac, Psi Master
Campbell River, British Columbia, Canada

ZUCCHINI QUICHE

2 cups shredded zucchini	1 cup shredded Cheddar cheese
1 onion, chopped	
3 eggs	1 cup baking mix
1/2 cup vegetable oil	Pepper to taste

Spray a baking sheet that has raised sides with nonstick cooking spray. Combine the zucchini, onion, eggs, oil, cheese, baking mix and pepper in a large bowl and mix well. Pour in a thin layer in the prepared baking sheet. Bake at 350 degrees for 45 to 50 minutes. Let cool in the pan. Cut into bars and serve.
Yield: 15 servings.

Carol Riggins, Laureate Omega
Gary, West Virginia

Diana Allen, Preceptor Alpha Zeta, Arlington, Texas, makes Three-Flavor Baked Potatoes. Slice baking potatoes, sweet potatoes, and onions crosswise about 1/2 inch thick. Assemble individual foil packets about baking potato size by alternating potato, sweet potato, and onion slices, adding butter, salt, and 1 spring of fresh rosemary, sealing the foil and baking at 375 degrees for 1 hour or until tender.

ZESTY BAKED BEANS

1 pound ground beef	*2 tablespoons prepared*
5 slices bacon	*mustard*
1 large onion, chopped	*1 (30-ounce) can pork*
1/2 cup ketchup	*and beans*
1/2 cup packed brown	*1 (15-ounce) can lima*
sugar	*beans, drained*
1 tablespoon dry	*1 (15-ounce) can kidney*
mustard	*beans, drained*

Brown the ground beef with the bacon and onion in a skillet, stirring until the ground beef is crumbly; drain. Place the ground beef mixture in a large bowl. Add the ketchup, brown sugar and mustards and mix well. Stir in the pork and beans, lima beans and kidney beans. Pour into a 9×13-inch baking dish. Bake at 350 degrees for 30 minutes.
Yield: 12 servings.

Kathy Arana, Preceptor Theta
Twin Falls, Idaho

SAVORY BAKED BEANS

Serve with barbecued meat, corn on the cob, and a green salad.

4 slices bacon, crisp-	*1 tablespoon*
cooked, crumbled	*Worcestershire sauce*
1/2 cup chopped onion	*1 teaspoon prepared*
2 (16-ounce) cans pork	*mustard*
and beans	
2 tablespoons brown	
sugar	

Drain the bacon, leaving 2 tablespoons drippings in the skillet. Sauté the onion in the drippings over medium-low heat for 5 to 10 minutes or until tender. Combine the bacon and remaining ingredients in a large bowl and mix well. Pour into a 1 1/2-quart casserole. Top with additional bacon if desired. Bake, uncovered, at 325 degrees for 1 1/2 to 1 3/4 hours.
Yield: 8 to 12 servings.

Donna Sjogren, Preceptor Lambda
Ely, Nevada

BOURBON BAKED BEANS

4 (16-ounce) cans	*Dash of paprika*
Boston baked beans	*3 ounces bourbon*
1 tablespoon dry	*1/4 cup strong black*
mustard	*coffee*
1/4 teaspoon Tabasco	*1 tablespoon brown*
sauce	*sugar*

Combine the beans, mustard, Tabasco, paprika, bourbon and coffee in a large bowl and mix well. Pour into a large casserole or baking dish. Sprinkle with the brown sugar. Let stand for 1 hour. Bake, covered, at 375 degrees for 1 1/2 hours. Yield: 10 to 12 servings.

Nancy Blair, Preceptor Lambda
Ely, Nevada

HAWAIIAN BEANS

2 pounds lean ground	*1 large green bell pepper,*
beef	*chopped*
1 (20-ounce) can	*1 envelope dry onion*
pineapple chunks,	*soup mix*
drained	*1 (14-ounce) bottle*
2 (16-ounce) cans kidney	*ketchup*
beans	*1 1/2 cups water*
5 ribs celery, chopped	

Brown the ground beef in a skillet, stirring until crumbly; drain. Cut the pineapple chunks into small pieces. Combine the ground beef, kidney beans, celery, bell pepper, onion soup mix, ketchup, water and pineapple in a large kettle over medium-high heat. Bring to a boil; reduce heat. Simmer, uncovered, for 1 1/2 hours. Yield: 16 servings.

Pat Taylor, Laureate Eta
Bothell, Washington

BAKED JACK CORN

2 large eggs, beaten	*2 cups shredded Cheddar*
1 1/2 cups sour cream	*cheese*
2 (20-ounce) cans corn,	*1/2 cup bread crumbs*
drained	*1 (4-ounce) can chopped*
2 cups shredded	*green chiles*
Monterey Jack cheese	*Salt and pepper to taste*

Combine the eggs and sour cream in a large bowl and mix well. Stir in the corn, cheeses, bread crumbs, green chiles, salt and pepper. Pour the mixture into a buttered 9×13-inch baking pan. Bake at 350 degrees for 35 to 40 minutes or until a knife inserted near the center comes out clean. Sprinkle with additional Cheddar cheese and bake for 5 to 10 minutes longer. Let stand for 10 minutes before serving.
Yield: 6 to 8 servings.

Paige Rackers, Mu Zeta
Jefferson City, Missouri

Christy Bamman, Xi Mu Sigma, Blue Springs, Missouri, makes Grilled Vidalia Onions by peeling and coring the number of onions she needs, placing each on a square of foil, adding a beef bouillon cube and a pat of butter to the centers of each, wrapping tightly, and grilling over medium-hot coals for about 40 minutes.

BAKED ONION CASSEROLE

Great with steaks and other grilled meats.

6 medium onions, sliced
1/2 cup (1 stick) butter
1 cup milk
1 (10-ounce) can cream of chicken or mushroom soup

Salt and pepper to taste
3 cups shredded Swiss cheese
Slices of French bread
Dash of garlic powder (optional)

Sauté the onions in half the butter in a skillet for 5 to 10 minutes or until tender. Remove the onions to a 10×13-inch baking dish. Combine the milk, soup, salt and pepper in a bowl and mix well. Pour over the onions. Layer the cheese over the soup mixture. Melt the remaining butter. Dip the bread slices in the butter and arrange over the cheese layer. Bake at 350 degrees for 30 minutes or until bread is golden brown. Yield: 10 servings.

Betty Ducharme, Xi Master
Merritt Island, Florida

BUTTERMILK BATTERED ONION RINGS

Serve with salad, meat, and vegetables, or by themselves with plenty of ketchup.

Vegetable oil for deep-frying
2 large onions, sliced 1/2 inch thick

1 1/2 cups buttermilk
1 1/2 cups flour

Heat the oil in a deep-fryer to 375 degrees. Separate the onions into rings. Pour the buttermilk into a large shallow bowl. Place the flour in another shallow bowl. Dip each onion ring in buttermilk, then in flour, then in buttermilk and flour again. Deep-fry until golden brown. Drain on paper towels. Yield: 6 servings.

Doris J. Bain, Xi Epsilon
Chattanooga, Tennessee

FAMILY REUNION POTATOES

This recipe feeds a large crowd and goes with everything from hot dogs to steak.

2 (10-ounce) cans cream of potato soup
2 (10-ounce) cans low-fat cream of chicken soup
2 cups sour cream
4 cups shredded Cheddar cheese

1 teaspoon onion powder
1 1/2 teaspoons salt
1/2 teaspoon pepper
2 (32-ounce) bags frozen hash brown potatoes

Combine the soups, sour cream, 2 to 3 cups of the cheese, onion powder, salt and pepper in a large saucepan or Dutch oven over medium-low heat. Heat until the cheese is melted and the mixture is creamy, stirring frequently to prevent scorching. Remove from heat. Add the potatoes, stirring until well coated. Spread in a 9×13-inch baking dish that has been sprayed with nonstick cooking spray. Top with the remaining cheese. Bake at 400 degrees for 45 to 60 minutes or until hot and bubbly. Yield: 20 to 30 servings.

Lisa Norris, Lambda Upsilon
Pleasant Hill, Missouri

OATMEAL MUFFINS

3/4 cup whole wheat flour
3/4 cup white flour
1 cup dry rolled oats
1 tablespoon baking powder

3 tablespoons sugar
1/4 teaspoon salt
1 egg, beaten
1 cup low-fat milk
1/4 cup vegetable oil

Combine the flours, oats, baking powder, sugar and salt in a large bowl and mix well. Combine the egg, milk and oil in a separate bowl and mix well. Add the egg mixture to the dry ingredients and stir just until blended. Batter should be a little lumpy. Pour into 12 greased and floured muffin cups. Bake at 400 degrees for 15 to 20 minutes or until muffins spring back when touched. Yield: 1 dozen 3 1/2-inch muffins.

Allie Lusher, Alpha Master
Charlottetown, Prince Edward Island, Canada

VEGETABLE PULL-APARTS

1 medium red bell pepper, chopped
1 medium green bell pepper, chopped
1 medium onion, chopped
1 cup (2 sticks) butter

3 (5-count) cans large refrigerated biscuits
1/2 pound sliced bacon, crisp-cooked, crumbled
1/2 cup shredded Cheddar cheese

Sauté the bell peppers and onion in the butter in a large skillet for 5 to 10 minutes or until softened; remove from heat. Snip each biscuit into quarters. Combine the vegetable mixture, snipped biscuit dough, bacon and cheese in a large bowl and fold together gently with a rubber spatula. Pour into a greased and floured bundt pan. Bake at 350 degrees for 30 minutes. Invert onto a serving plate. Have guests pluck off pieces to serve themselves. Yield: 16 servings.

Louise I. Fleming, Laureate Alpha Lambda
Vienna, West Virginia

CHOCOLATE CAKE

This small, quick cake is easy to pack for a picnic. We always had it with ice cream on Independence Day.

1 cup sugar	¼ teaspoon salt
¼ cup shortening	1 egg
3 tablespoons baking cocoa	2 cups confectioners' sugar
1 cup buttermilk	3 to 4 tablespoons baking cocoa
1 teaspoon baking soda	Milk
1½ cups flour	
1 teaspoon vanilla extract	

Cream the sugar and shortening in a mixing bowl until light and fluffy. Add the 3 tablespoons baking cocoa and buttermilk and mix well. Add the flour, vanilla and salt; mix well. Beat in the egg. Pour the batter into a buttered 9×9-inch baking pan. Bake at 350 degrees for 30 minutes or until a wooden pick inserted in the center comes out clean. Remove from oven. Cool in the pan on a wire rack. Combine the confectioners' sugar and the 3 to 4 tablespoons baking cocoa in a bowl. Add enough milk to make of spreading consistency. Frost the cooled cake. Yield: 9 large servings.

LaRene T. Ayres, Laureate Alpha Alpha
Canton, Pennsylvania

PICNIC CAKE

1 cup water	½ teaspoon salt
1 cup (2 sticks) margarine	3 eggs
½ cup baking cocoa	¾ cup sour cream
2 cups sugar	Peanut Butter Chip
1¾ cups flour	Frosting and
1 teaspoon baking soda	Chocolate Glaze

Combine the water, margarine and baking cocoa in a saucepan over medium heat and bring to a boil. Boil for 1 minute; remove from heat. Combine the sugar, flour, baking soda and salt in a large mixing bowl. Add the eggs and sour cream and beat at medium speed until blended. Add the cocoa mixture and beat just until blended. Pour into a greased 10×15-inch jelly roll pan. Bake at 350 degrees for 25 to 30 minutes. Remove from oven and cool on a wire rack. Frost the cooled cake with Peanut Butter Chip Frosting. Drizzle Chocolate Glaze over the frosting. Yield: 12 to 15 servings.

PEANUT BUTTER CHIP FROSTING AND CHOCOLATE GLAZE

Be sure to use shortening for the glaze, not oil or margarine.

⅓ cup margarine	1 cup confectioners' sugar
⅓ cup milk	½ cup chocolate chips
10 ounces peanut butter chips	1 teaspoon shortening
1 teaspoon vanilla extract	

Combine the margarine, milk and peanut butter chips in a small saucepan. Heat over low heat for 5 to 10 minutes or until chips are melted and mixture is smooth, stirring constantly. Remove from heat. Stir in the vanilla and confectioners' sugar. Beat until smooth to make the frosting. Microwave the chocolate chips and shortening in a microwave-safe dish on High for 1 minute. Stir until smooth to make the glaze.

Sue A. Jedlicka, Xi Master
Beatrice, Nebraska

LEMON CORN CAKE

1 cup yellow cornmeal	2 teaspoons finely grated lemon zest
1 cup flour	1 tablespoon vegetable oil
½ cup sugar	1 egg yolk
1 tablespoon baking powder	⅔ cup milk
1 teaspoon salt	3 egg whites
6 ounces lemon yogurt	

Combine the cornmeal, flour, sugar, baking powder and salt in a large bowl. Combine the yogurt, lemon zest, oil, egg yolk and milk in another bowl and blend well. Add the yogurt mixture to the dry ingredients and stir just until moistened. Beat the egg whites in a mixing bowl until stiff peaks form. Fold into the cornmeal mixture. Pour into two 9-inch round cake pans sprayed with nonstick cooking spray. Bake at 400 degrees for 20 to 25 minutes or until a wooden pick inserted near the center comes out clean. Yield: 12 servings.

Lorraine Kirkpatrick, Preceptor Gamma Delta
Barstow, California

Laura Hannan, Xi Eta Theta, Wamego, Kansas, suggests making Ice Cream Cone Cupcakes by placing flat-bottom cones in muffin cups, filling ⅔ full with cake mix prepared using package directions, and baking at 350 degrees for 15 to 20 minutes. Cool, frost, and decorate as desired.

LEMON BERRY SHORTCAKE

3 teaspoons grated
   lemon zest
2 cups flour
1/3 cup sugar
1 tablespoon baking
   powder
1 teaspoon ground
   ginger
1/4 teaspoon salt

1/3 cup margarine
2/3 cup skim milk
8 ounces fat-free vanilla
   yogurt
3 cups blueberries,
   raspberries,
   blackberries or sliced
   strawberries
Confectioners' sugar

Preheat the oven to 375 degrees. Combine 2 teaspoons of the lemon zest, the flour, sugar, baking powder, ginger and salt in a large bowl. Cut in the margarine until crumbly. Stir in the milk. Knead gently 8 to 10 times on a floured surface. Roll the dough to 1/2-inch thickness. Cut with a star cookie cutter. Bake the stars on a greased baking sheet for 10 to 14 minutes or until golden. Blend the remaining lemon zest into the yogurt. At serving time, split each star horizontally. Spoon berries over the bottom half of the star. Spoon yogurt over the berries. Cover with the top half of the star. Sprinkle with powdered sugar. Yield: 8 servings.

Christi Bentley, Epsilon Xi
Marshall, Missouri

FRESH PEAR CAKE

3 cups flour
2 cups sugar
1 teaspoon baking soda
1 teaspoon cinnamon
1 1/4 cups vegetable oil
2 eggs, beaten

1 teaspoon vanilla
   extract
3 cups grated or chopped
   pears
1 cup pecans or walnuts

Sift the flour, sugar, baking soda and cinnamon into a bowl and mix well. Combine the oil, eggs, vanilla, pears and nuts in another bowl and mix well. Make a well in the sifted dry ingredients. Add the oil mixture all at once, stirring until well combined and moist. Pour into a 9×15-inch baking pan sprayed with nonstick cooking spray. Bake at 350 degrees for 45 minutes. Yield: 12 to 15 servings.

Frankie Wooster, Laureate Delta Mu
Wichita Falls, Texas

Mary Ann Engelmann, Psi Mu, Pembroke Pines, Florida, slices a pound cake into 3 layers, spreads 1 cup blueberry pie filling between 2 cake layers, adds a layer of strawberry pie filling and the remaining cake layer, and frosts with whipped topping to make Patriotic Pound Cake.

GINGERBREAD UPSIDE-DOWN CAKE

You may use fresh pears in season, substituting a heavy sugar-water syrup for the pear syrup. The recipe may be doubled and baked in a 9×13-inch baking pan to serve 12.

1/2 cup sugar
1 cup orange juice
2 teaspoons grated
   orange zest
1/4 cup flaked coconut
1 (15-ounce) can pear
   halves, drained,
     3/4 cup syrup reserved

1 (14-ounce) package
   gingerbread mix
1/4 teaspoon salt
1 tablespoon butter
2 tablespoons
   cornstarch

Combine the sugar, 1/4 cup of the orange juice, 1 teaspoon of the orange zest and the coconut in a bowl and mix well. Pour into a buttered 8-inch-square cake pan. Arrange the pears over the sugar mixture, cut side down. Prepare the gingerbread batter using the package directions. Pour evenly over the pears. Bake at 350 degrees for 30 to 35 minutes or until cake tests done. Combine the reserved pear syrup, 3/4 cup of the orange juice, the salt, butter and cornstarch in a small saucepan over low heat to make the orange sauce. Cook for 3 minutes or until thickened, stirring constantly. Remove from heat. Remove the cake from the oven and let cool in pan for 10 minutes. Invert on a serving plate. Serve with the orange sauce and/or whipped topping. Yield: 6 servings.

Sharon Hedden, Xi Beta
Harrah, Washington

SOUR CREAM POUND CAKE

You may wish to serve the cake with ice cream, chocolate sauce, fresh strawberries, or another favorite topping.

1 cup (2 sticks) butter or
   margarine, softened
3 cups sugar
6 eggs
1/4 teaspoon baking soda

1 teaspoon vanilla
   extract
3 cups flour
1 cup sour cream

Cream the butter and sugar in a mixing bowl until light and fluffy. Add the eggs 1 at a time, mixing well after each addition. Add the baking soda, vanilla and flour; mix well. Stir in the sour cream. Pour into a greased and floured 10-inch tube pan. Bake at 325 degrees for 1 1/2 hours or until cake tests done. Cool in the pan for 10 minutes. Invert onto a serving plate. Yield: 10 to 12 servings.

Sharon Ingram, Preceptor Epsilon Theta
St. Petersburg, Florida

APPLESAUCE BROWNIES

1/2 cup shortening	2 cups flour
1 1/2 cups sugar	1/2 teaspoon salt
1/2 teaspoon cinnamon	1 1/2 cups applesauce
2 tablespoons baking cocoa	2 tablespoons sugar
2 eggs	1/2 cup chopped pecans or walnuts
1 1/2 teaspoons baking soda	1 cup chocolate chips

Combine the shortening, 1 1/2 cups sugar, cinnamon, baking cocoa, eggs, baking soda, flour, salt and applesauce in a large mixing bowl and beat until well mixed. Pour into a greased 9×13-inch baking pan. Sprinkle a mixture of 2 tablespoons sugar, nuts and chocolate chips over the top. Bake at 350 degrees for 30 minutes. Cool and cut into bars. Yield: 3 dozen.

Mary Wycoff, Preceptor Alpha Eta
Merriam, Kansas

MARSHMALLOW BROWNIES

4 ounces unsweetened chocolate, melted	1 cup flour
1 cup (2 sticks) margarine, melted	2 cups miniature marshmallows
2 cups sugar	1 cup chopped walnuts or pecans
4 eggs	1 cup chocolate chips

Combine the unsweetened chocolate, margarine, sugar, eggs, flour, marshmallows, nuts and half the chocolate chips in a large bowl and mix well. Spread in a greased 9×13-inch baking dish. Bake at 350 degrees for 40 to 50 minutes or until brownies test done. Remove from oven. Sprinkle the remaining half of the chocolate chips over the warm brownies and swirl with a knife. Yield: 12 servings.

Debbie Helfrecht, Preceptor Gamma Theta
Pendleton, Oregon

CHERRY PINWHEEL COOKIES

2 (8-ounce) jars maraschino cherries, drained, 1 cup liquid reserved	2 teaspoons baking powder
	1/2 teaspoon salt
2 tablespoons cornstarch	1 cup sugar
1/4 teaspoon salt	1 cup (2 sticks) butter, softened
2 cups ground blanched almonds	2 eggs, beaten
3 cups sifted flour	1 teaspoon almond extract

Mince the cherries. Heat the reserved liquid with the cornstarch in a saucepan over low heat until thick-ened, stirring constantly. Remove from heat. Stir in 1/4 teaspoon salt, cherries and almonds. Let cool. Sift the flour, baking powder and 1/2 teaspoon salt together. Cream the sugar and butter in a mixing bowl until light and fluffy. Beat in the eggs and almond extract. Add the sifted dry ingredients; mix well. Chill the dough, wrapped in plastic wrap, for 45 minutes. Roll half the dough into an 8×12-inch rectangle on a lightly floured surface. Spread with half the cherry filling. Roll as for a jelly roll. Chill, wrapped in plastic wrap. Repeat for the other half of the dough. Slice the rolls 1/4 inch thick and arrange on buttered baking sheets. Bake at 375 degrees for 8 minutes or until desired degree of doneness. Yield: 6 dozen.

Debra Hinzman, Sigma
Rapid City, South Dakota

CRANBERRY ORANGE COOKIES

Frost these cookies with a mixture of 2 cups confectioners' sugar, 1/4 cup softened unsalted butter, 3 tablespoons orange juice concentrate, and 1/4 teaspoon vanilla extract.

1/4 cup unsalted butter, softened	1 1/2 cups flour
1/2 cup sugar	3/4 teaspoon baking powder
1/3 cup packed brown sugar	1/4 teaspoon baking soda
1 egg	1/4 teaspoon salt
1 teaspoon grated orange zest	1 1/2 cups halved fresh cranberries, or 1 cup dried
3 tablespoons orange juice concentrate	1/2 cup chopped pecans or walnuts

Line 2 cookie sheets with buttered parchment paper. Cream the butter and sugars in a large mixing bowl until light and fluffy. Beat in the egg. Add the orange zest and orange concentrate and beat until light. Add a mixture of flour, baking powder and baking soda; mix well. Stir in the cranberries and nuts. Drop by teaspoonfuls 2 inches apart onto the prepared cookie sheets. Bake at 375 degrees for 12 minutes or until light brown. Remove the cookies from the paper to cool. Yield: 3 dozen.

Peg Hattestad, Alpha Gamma
Marshall, Minnesota

Judy Morgan, Xi Gamma Upsilon, Vienna, West Virginia, brings 1 cup sugar and 1 cup light corn syrup to a boil, blends in 1 cup peanut butter, mixes in 6 to 8 cups cornflakes, presses into a buttered 9×13-inch pan, and cuts into squares to make Cornflake Treats.

UNBAKED PEANUT BUTTER BARS

2 cups butterscotch
  chips
1/2 cup peanut butter
1/2 cup (1 stick)
  margarine
1/2 teaspoon vanilla
  extract

1 (10-ounce) package
  miniature
  marshmallows
1/2 cup English walnuts
2/3 cup shredded coconut

Melt the butterscotch chips, peanut butter and margarine in a heavy saucepan over low heat, stirring until smooth. Remove from heat. Let cool. Stir in the vanilla, marshmallows, nuts and coconut. Spread evenly in a greased 9×13-inch baking dish. Chill, covered, until ready to serve. Cut into squares. Yield: 15 servings.

Bonnie J. Hula, Xi Omicron
Clarksville, Arkansas

WATERMELON COOKIES

This is a favorite dessert we serve at our cabin for our annual Labor Day party.

1 cup (2 sticks) butter or
  margarine, softened
1 cup sugar
1/2 teaspoon baking
  powder
1 egg

2 2/3 cup flour
Green and red food
  coloring
Miniature chocolate
  chips

Beat the butter in a large mixing bowl at medium speed for 30 seconds. Beat in the sugar and baking powder, then the egg. Beat in as much of the flour as is possible with the electric mixer; stir in the remaining flour by hand. Remove 3/4 cup of the dough to a small bowl. Add a few drops of green food coloring and mix well. Add a few drops of red food coloring to the remaining dough and mix well. Wrap each dough portion in plastic wrap and chill for 1 hour. Divide the green dough in half. Roll each half between sheets of waxed paper into a 5 1/2×8-inch rectangle. Place the rectangles on a baking sheet, still sandwiched between waxed paper sheets. Freeze for 15 to 20 minutes. Divide the red dough in half. Shape each half into an 8-inch log. Remove the green dough from the freezer. Remove the top sheet of waxed paper from one rectangle. Place one red dough log carefully on the rectangle. Let stand for about 5 minutes or until dough is easy to roll. Roll up as for a jelly roll from one of the wide ends, removing the bottom sheet of waxed paper as you roll. Pinch to seal. Repeat with the rest of the dough. Wrap the rolls in plastic wrap. To prevent the rolls from flattening as they chill, place each wrapped roll in a tall drinking glass and lay the glass on its side in the refrigerator. Chill for about 4 hours. Remove one roll from the refrigerator. Unwrap, and reshape if necessary. Cut into 3/8-inch slices. Cut cookies in half and arrange on a cookie sheet. Decorate with miniature chocolate chips to look like watermelon seeds. Bake at 375 degrees for 10 to 12 minutes or until edges are firm. Cool on the cookie sheet for 1 minute. Remove to a wire rack to cool completely. Repeat with the remaining dough. Yield: 100 cookies.

Linda Kelso, Xi Beta Delta
Maple Grove, Minnesota

ALL-AMERICAN APPLE PIE

Best served warm with cold milk or vanilla ice cream.

3 cups flour
1 1/2 teaspoons salt
1 1/4 cups shortening
1 egg, well beaten
1 tablespoon white
  vinegar
5 tablespoons water
1 1/2 cups sugar

3 tablespoons cornstarch
1/2 teaspoon ground
  cloves
2 teaspoons nutmeg
2 teaspoons cinnamon
1 teaspoon allspice
5 large apples, peeled,
  thinly sliced

Combine the flour and salt in a bowl. Cut in the shortening until crumbly. Combine the egg, vinegar and water and mix well. Add all at once to the flour mixture. Stir until dry ingredients are moistened. Roll into two 12-inch circles on a lightly floured pastry sheet or waxed paper. Combine the sugar, cornstarch, cloves, nutmeg, cinnamon and allspice in a small bowl and mix well. Fit 1 pastry into a 9-inch deep-dish pie plate. Sprinkle with a little less than half the sugar mixture. Add the apples. Sprinkle the remaining sugar mixture over the apples. Dot with butter. Top with the remaining pastry, sealing edge and cutting vents. Pat a little milk over the top and sprinkle with a little sugar. Bake at 450 degrees for 15 minutes. Reduce oven temperature to 350 degrees and bake for 45 minutes longer. Yield: 6 to 8 servings.

Cheryl Alexander, Zeta Nu
Westover, West Virginia

Billie Fitts, Xi Alpha Gamma Lambda, Palestine, Texas, makes Lemonade Pie by blending a 6-ounce can of frozen lemonade concentrate with 10 to 12 ounces whipped topping and a can of sweetened condensed milk and freezing in a graham cracker or vanilla wafer crust. Top with additional whipped topping when serving.

CRESCENT APPLE PIES

1 (8-count) can crescent rolls	1/2 cup (1 stick) butter or margarine
1 Granny Smith apple, peeled, cored	3/4 cup sugar
Dash of cinnamon	1 cup orange juice

Unroll crescent roll dough. Separate into 8 triangles. Cut the apple into 8 slices. Place 1 slice in the center of each dough triangle. Sprinkle a dash of cinnamon over each apple. Roll to enclose the apple. Arrange in a greased 9×13-inch baking pan. Combine the butter, sugar and orange juice in a heavy saucepan over medium-high heat. Bring to a boil. Remove from heat. Pour over the dough-wrapped apples. Bake at 350 degrees for 30 minutes. Serve with whipped topping and a cherry on top. Yield: 8 servings.

Dorothy G. Gellock, Delta Beta
Hoover, Alabama

DOUBLE-CRUST LEMON PIE

3 eggs	1/2 cup water
1 1/4 cups sugar	1 teaspoon grated lemon zest
2 tablespoons flour	1 (2-crust) pie pastry
1/8 teaspoon salt	1 lemon, peeled, thinly sliced
1/4 cup (1/2 stick) butter, softened	

Place the eggs in a large bowl, reserving 1 teaspoon egg white. Beat the eggs well. Add the sugar, flour, salt, butter, water and lemon zest and mix well. Pour into a pastry-lined pie plate. Arrange the lemon slices over the sugar mixture. Top with the remaining pastry, sealing edge and cutting vents. Brush with the reserved egg white and sprinkle with sugar. Bake at 400 degrees for 30 to 35 minutes or until golden brown. Serve warm. Yield: 6 to 8 servings.

Vicki Yeats, Alpha Psi
Sumner, Washington

APPLE DUMPLINGS

Most apple dumplings are made from whole apples. When made according to this recipe, every bite contains tender apple, juices, and crust. Serve warm with ice cream or milk.

2 cups water	1 1/2 cups sliced peeled apples
2 tablespoons butter or margarine	3/4 cup sugar
1 1/4 cups brown sugar	3/4 teaspoon cinnamon
1 1/2 teaspoons cinnamon	1 tablespoon butter, melted
1 (2-crust) pie pastry	

Combine the water, the 2 tablespoons butter, the brown sugar and cinnamon in a 5-quart Dutch oven over medium heat. Heat until the sugar dissolves, stirring constantly. Remove from heat. Prepare the pie pastry and roll into two 12-inch circles on a lightly floured surface. Combine the apples, sugar, cinnamon and melted butter in a bowl and mix well. Mound half the apple mixture in the center of each pastry. Bring up the edges to enclose the apple mixture, pinching to seal. Place the dumplings seam side down in the butter mixture in the Dutch oven. Bake, uncovered, at 350 degrees for 45 minutes or until golden brown. Yield: 8 to 10 servings.

Jean Taylor, Xi Delta Kappa
Hereford, Arizona

BANANA SPLIT DESSERT

1 (12-ounce) box vanilla wafers, crushed into fine crumbs	3 bananas, sliced
1/4 cup (1/2 stick) margarine, melted	1 (16-ounce) can crushed pineapple, drained
1 (6-ounce) package instant banana pudding	16 ounces whipped topping
1 (16-ounce) jar dry roasted peanuts, crushed	1 (6-ounce) jar maraschino cherries

Preheat the oven to 350 degrees. Mix the cookie crumbs and margarine together. Press into a 3-quart baking dish. Bake for 10 minutes. Let cool. Prepare the pudding using the package directions for a pie. Spread half the peanuts over the cooled cookie crust. Layer the pudding, bananas, pineapple and whipped topping over the peanuts. Sprinkle the remaining peanuts over the whipped topping. Top with cherries. Chill, covered, for 1 hour before serving. Yield: 8 servings.

Sue Wing, Preceptor Pi
Polson, Montana

BERRY CREAM CHEESE TRIFLE

3/4 cup confectioners' sugar	1 (10-ounce) angel food cake, torn in small pieces
1 teaspoon almond or vanilla extract	1 (21-ounce) can strawberry pie filling
6 ounces fat-free cream cheese, softened	1 (21-ounce) can blueberry pie filling
8 ounces fat-free whipped topping	

Combine the confectioners' sugar, almond extract and cream cheese in a mixing bowl and beat at low speed for 2 minutes. Add the whipped topping and beat at low speed for 1 minute. Fold in the cake pieces. Pour the strawberry filling into a deep glass bowl. Layer the cream cheese mixture over the filling, spreading to the edges. Layer the blueberry filling over the cream cheese mixture. Chill, covered, for at least 1 hour before serving. Yield: 12 servings.

Judy A. McQuaid, Preceptor Omega
Amherst, Ohio

BLUEBERRY DESSERT

11 whole graham crackers, crushed	8 ounces cream cheese, softened
1/4 cup sugar	1/2 cup sugar
1/4 cup (1/2 stick) butter, softened	1 (21-ounce) can blueberry pie filling
2 eggs	

Blend the graham crackers, 1/4 cup sugar and butter together. Press into a buttered 8×8-inch baking pan. Combine the eggs, cream cheese and the 1/2 cup sugar in a mixing bowl. Beat until creamy. Pour evenly over the graham cracker layer. Bake at 375 degrees for 15 to 20 minutes. Let cool. Layer the pie filling over the cooled cream cheese layer. Chill, covered, for 24 hours. Yield: 9 to 12 servings.

Betsy Scantlan, Beta Theta Xi
Richardson, Texas

OREO ICE CREAM DESSERT

1 (16-ounce) package chocolate sandwich cookies, crushed	1 (16-ounce) can chocolate syrup
1/2 cup (1 stick) butter, melted	1 (8-ounce) jar caramel syrup
1/2 gallon vanilla ice cream, softened	12 ounces whipped topping
	Almond slivers

Combine the crushed cookies and the butter in a bowl and mix well. Reserve 1 cup of the cookie mixture. Press the remaining mixture in a greased 9×13-inch baking dish. Spread the ice cream evenly over the cookie layer. Layer the chocolate syrup, caramel syrup, whipped topping and reserved 1 cup cookie mixture over the ice cream. Sprinkle with almond slivers. Freeze for 12 hours before cutting. Yield: 15 to 20 servings.

Brenda Graham, Alpha Beta Eta
Amarillo, Texas

HOMEMADE STRAWBERRY ICE CREAM

2 (3-ounce) packages strawberry gelatin	1 (13-ounce) can evaporated milk
2 cups boiling water	1 teaspoon vanilla extract
2 eggs	1 quart strawberries, mashed
1 1/2 cups sugar	
6 cups milk	

Dissolve the gelatin in the water; cool slightly. Beat the eggs in a mixing bowl at medium speed until frothy. Add the sugar gradually, beating until thick. Add the gelatin mixture, milk, evaporated milk and vanilla and mix well. Stir in the strawberries. Pour into an ice cream freezer container. Freeze using manufacturer's directions. Let stand for at least 1 hour before serving. Yield: about 1 gallon.

Helen Fort, Laureate Theta
Snellville, Georgia

LEMON LAYERED DESSERT

2 cups flour	1/2 cup confectioners' sugar
1 cup (2 sticks) butter, softened	16 ounces whipped topping
2 1/3 cups ground almonds	1 (6-ounce) package lemon pie filling mix
1/4 cup sugar	
8 ounces cream cheese, softened	

Combine the flour, butter, almonds and sugar in a bowl and mix until a ball forms. Press into a greased 9×12-inch baking pan. Bake at 350 degrees for about 30 minutes or until golden. Let cool. Beat the cream cheese, confectioners' sugar and half the whipped topping in a mixing bowl until light and fluffy. Spread over the cooled crust. Prepare the lemon pie filling using the package directions. Spread over the cream cheese layer. Chill for 1 hour or until cold. Spread the remaining whipped topping over the lemon layer. Sprinkle with slivered almonds if desired. Chill, covered, until serving time. Yield: 12 servings.

Rose Jackson, Lambda Delta
Amherstburg, Ontario, Canada

Jill Adams, Xi Alpha Delta, Murray, Kentucky, prepares a yummy Ice Cream Sandwich Dessert by fitting 7 or 8 ice cream sandwiches into a 9×13-inch dish, cutting around the edges if necessary. Cover with a generous layer of whipped topping and drizzle on the desired amount of chocolate syrup. Sprinkle with crushed Butterfinger candy bars and freeze until ready to serve.

PINEAPPLE DELIGHT

This easy-to-prepare dessert is ideal for an end-of-summer party.

2 envelopes unflavored gelatin	1½ teaspoons sugar
½ cup hot water	¼ teaspoon lemon juice
1 (20-ounce) can crushed pineapple	2 teaspoons vanilla extract
½ cup dry skim milk powder	½ teaspoon butter flavoring

Dissolve the gelatin in the hot water. Place the gelatin mixture and undrained pineapple in a blender container and process for 2 minutes. Add the milk powder, sugar, lemon juice, vanilla and butter flavoring and process for 3 minutes. Pour into a 5-cup mold. Chill, covered, for at least 1 hour before serving. Yield: 6 to 8 servings.

Rosemarie Keefe, Preceptor Beta Gamma
Albany, New York

STRAWBERRY PRETZEL DESSERT

1¼ cups crushed pretzels	2 tablespoons tequila
¼ cup sugar	2 tablespoons orange liqueur
½ cup (1 stick) butter, melted	1 (10-ounce) package frozen strawberries, thawed
1 (14-ounce) can sweetened condensed milk	Red food coloring
¼ cup lime juice	1 cup whipping cream, whipped

Combine the pretzels, sugar and butter in a bowl and mix well. Press into a buttered 10-inch springform pan. Chill until ready to use. Combine the condensed milk, lime juice, tequila and liqueur in a large mixing bowl. Beat until smooth. Fold in the strawberries and a few drops of red food coloring. Fold in the whipped cream. Pour the mixture into the pretzel crust and freeze. Thaw 10 to 15 minutes before serving. Yield: 10 to 12 servings.

Janice Mino, Xi Kappa
Austin, Minnesota

Judy Johnston, Beta Epsilon Tau, Houston, Texas, suggests a patriotic trifle she calls Glory, prepared in a large glass bowl. Cook a large package of banana pudding mix using package directions and pour the cooled pudding over angel food cake cubes in the bowl. Add a layer of strawberry pie filling, a layer of whipped topping, and sprinkle with fresh blueberries. Chill for 4 hours before serving.

PEACH KUCHEN

This is a dessert so refreshing and well liked that it can be served for any occasion, from a campfire to a formal dinner.

2 cups flour	4 cups sliced peaches, fresh or canned, drained
¼ teaspoon baking powder	1 cup sugar
2 tablespoons sugar	1 teaspoon cinnamon
½ teaspoon salt	2 egg yolks
½ cup (1 stick) butter or margarine, softened	1 cup heavy sweet cream or evaporated milk

Sift the flour, baking powder, 2 tablespoons sugar and salt into a bowl. Add the butter and mix until well combined. Pat into the bottom and halfway up the sides of a greased 9×13-inch baking pan. Layer the peaches over the flour mixture. Sprinkle a mixture of 1 cup sugar and cinnamon over the peaches. Bake at 375 degrees for 15 minutes. Blend the egg yolks and cream. Pour over the hot kuchen. Bake for 30 minutes longer. Yield: 12 servings.

Patricia Harding, Laureate Beta
Clarkston, Washington

HARVEST COBBLER

My mother often made this for a summer social to welcome peach harvesting season in California Central Valley.

2 cups sifted flour	1 cup sugar
½ teaspoon baking soda	2 tablespoons cornstarch
2 tablespoons shortening	¾ teaspoon cinnamon
¾ cup buttermilk	
2 pounds fresh peaches, sliced	

Sift the flour and baking soda into a bowl. Cut in the shortening until crumbly. Stir in the buttermilk. Knead lightly, about 5 strokes. Shape ¼ of the dough into a ball; shape the remaining dough into a larger ball. Roll the larger pastry into a circle on a lightly floured surface. Line a 2-quart casserole with the pastry circle. Combine the peaches, sugar, cornstarch and cinnamon in a bowl and mix well. Pour into the pastry-lined casserole. Roll the smaller pastry into a circle and place over the casserole, sealing edges and cutting vents. Bake at 350 degrees for 35 to 45 minutes or until golden brown and bubbly. Serve with whipped cream or vanilla ice cream. Yield: 10 to 12 servings.

Dorothy Bizzini, Laureate Delta Theta
Atwater, California

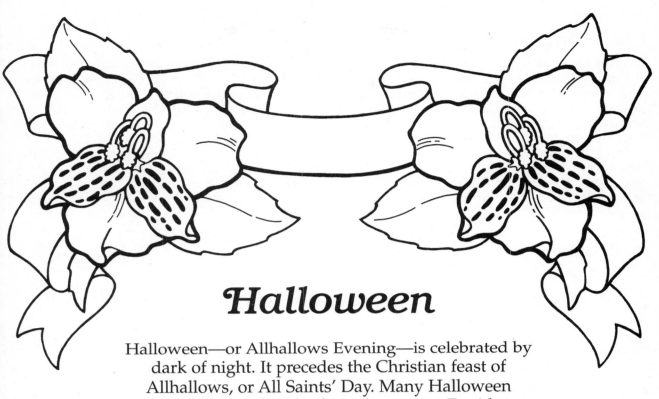

Halloween

Halloween—or Allhallows Evening—is celebrated by
dark of night. It precedes the Christian feast of
Allhallows, or All Saints' Day. Many Halloween
traditions come to us from the ancient Druids,
who believed that on a dark night late in the fall, Saman,
the lord of the dead, called forth hosts of evil spirits.
The Druids lit bonfires to ward off the demons.
Early Celts believed that dead spirits returned
to their earthly homes on that evening—for good or
evil purposes—i.e., tricks or treats. When the Romans
invaded Britain, they celebrated their festival at about
the same time. So, thanks to the Romans, we now
carve pumpkins and dunk for apples on Halloween.
Browse through this chapter for some new tricks,
clever treats, and frighteningly good Halloween ideas.

WHAT IS HE DOING?

Try this variation on charades. Think up various actions that can be written on slips of paper and performed by the person drawing the slip while the other guests guess. Have prizes for the best guesser as well as appropriate gag prizes for the actors. Such poses as milking a cow or starting a motorcycle may be more difficult to guess than you think.

I remember going trick or treating only once as a child. One lady opened her door and threw a pan of water that hit my mother. That is why there was only one to remember.

Carol Franssen, Tau
North Bend, Oregon

CHOCOLATE SPIDERS AND WEBS

Make edible creepies to top Halloween desserts or eat as candy. Prepare your patterns first:

Create a web pattern on a large piece of light-colored paper by drawing perpendicular lines and diagonals for a spoke-like design. Add several sets of connecting lines concentrically to complete the web design. Be sure that the lines are dark enough to show through a covering layer of waxed paper. You may wish to make several patterns in varying sizes.

Create a spider pattern by drawing a semi-circle about 1½ inches across on the paper. Draw a second semi-circle about ¼ inch inside the larger outline. These represent four spider legs. Duplicate the semi-circles in the opposite direction with the outer circles touching. Now you have eight legs. Draw an oval at the intersection of the circles that will represent the body and add a small circle for the head.

Melt a cup of milk chocolate chips over barely simmering water in a double boiler, stirring until smooth. Remove from the heat and let stand for about 10 minutes, or until cool but still melted. Place the pattern on a baking sheet or tray and cover with waxed paper. Fill a pastry bag or a plastic bag with the chocolate. If using a plastic bag, snip a tiny bit from one corner to form a tip. Pipe the chocolate into the desired shapes, following the patterns. Chill the shapes until firm. Peel the waxed paper away and store the shapes between layers of waxed paper in the refrigerator for up to 2 weeks. One cup of chocolate chips should make about two dozen spiders or one dozen webs. Add eyes to the spiders with white tube frosting.

Robin Hunter, Beta Beta
Sparks, Nevada

EASY ANYTHING COSTUME

This is the easy inexpensive answer to Halloween costuming for children or adults. I grew up in Alaska where my dad made me a fairy princess costume one year. This costume will cover as much clothing as you need to keep warm, or just shorts and t-shirt for warmer climates.

Measure the person's length from neck to ankle and double the measurement (this is the diameter). A few yards of clear plastic such as that used as painters' dropcloths will provide enough width. Now cut a hole in the center just big enough to slip over the head.

Spray the plastic with glue and sprinkle with glitter, sequins, or whatever material will create the costume look you want. Cut slits in the sides of the circle for arm holes. Add a belt and other accessories of your choice. This technique can create a princess, clown, ghoul, magician, or anything your imagination can devise.

Melanie Andrejczak, Alpha Iota Rho
Brenham, Texas

CREEPY BAKED APPLES

Make something delicious and appropriate for your Halloween supper. Core 6 apples to (but not through) the bottom. Arrange the apples in a baking pan and fill each opening with about 2 tablespoons of raspberry jelly. Bake the apples at 350 degrees for 25 minutes, adding additional jelly as it is absorbed. Arrange the baked apples on a platter covered with crushed chocolate wafer crumbs to look like dirt and insert a gummy worm in each apple opening.

Kathy Rand, Xi Alpha Pi
Madison, Wisconsin

JACK-O'-LANTERN FAVORS

Here is another recycling idea that is always a hit. Wash and dry fruit and vegetable cans. Be sure that there are no sharp edges. Spray the cans with bright orange paint and let dry completely. Paint jack-o'-lantern faces on the cans with acrylic paint. Punch holes on opposite sides of the face, twist wire around a pencil to make a handle, and secure the ends of the wire in the holes. Stuff the cans with green tissue paper and add the treats.

The same technique using white paint makes snowmen for a winter party. Add stocking caps made from discarded socks.

Leigh Ann Friedrich, Xi Mu Chi
Harrisonville, Missouri

HALLOWEEN DANCING GHOSTS

*D*ecorations *don't have to be expensive. These delightful ghosts require only imagination and recycling instincts (along with recycled materials). Tear some old white bed sheets into arm-length squares. One large sheet will make four ghosts. Cut black felt scraps into circles for eyes and glue them onto the squares, off-center, toward a corner.*

Wad grocery bags into a head-size ball, drape the sheet over it, and wrap string around the base of the ball. Adjust the fabric evenly. An arrangement of stakes, such as those salvaged from old political signs, can be pounded into the yard around a tree, down the sidewalk, or wherever you wish. Secure your ghosts to the stakes with large safety pins and watch your ghosts dance in the breeze. A host of ghosts dancing around a tree with the corners of the sheets pinned to each other as if holding hands is especially effective.

Alice Musson, Laureate Gamma
Edmonton, Alberta, Canada

TRICK OR TREAT FOOD TABLE

*U*se *your imagination to carry out the Halloween theme of your party. Start with a plain white or colored sheet on the buffet table and scatter fake cobwebs, spiders, hands, rats, or other creepy things on the sheet. Place the punchbowl in the center and fill with lime sherbet and lemon-lime soda; float some plastic eyes in the foam on top (be careful to keep little ones from choking on them).*

Make cupcakes tinted with green food coloring, frost, and decorate with shredded coconut. These can be labeled "monster heads." Here are some suggestions for labeling other food items: sausage pizza, "mummy skin;" spinach dip in a bread bowl, "Frankenstein brains;" candy corn and Spanish peanuts mixed, "vampire teeth and cavities;" popcorn sprinkled with cinnamon-sugar, "mini-bug brains." The food is only half the fun, so let your guests, children or adults, help name the dishes.

Maureen H. Trentadue, Zeta Iota
Ft. Wayne, Indiana

APPLE DIP

8 ounces cream cheese, softened	Chopped pecans or walnuts
8 ounces apple cinnamon cream cheese, softened	5 or 6 apples, cut into wedges
1/2 cup caramel dip for apples	Fruit Fresh or lemon juice

Blend the two cream cheeses together. Spread over a large dinner plate, leaving a 1-inch border. Spread the caramel dip evenly over the cream cheese layer. Sprinkle with nuts. Chill, covered, until serving time. Toss the apple wedges with Fruit Fresh. Arrange around the dip on the plate. Provide spreaders for applying the dip to the apples.
Yield: 10 to 12 servings.

Margaret Parker, Rho Master
Raton, New Mexico

THE GREAT PUMPKIN

Select three favorite cheeses for this delicious appetizer. For example, you may choose to use 1 cup Cheddar, 1 cup mozzarella, and 1 cup Swiss cheese.

1 small pumpkin	1 cup heavy cream
4 slices white bread, toasted	Nutmeg
3 cups shredded cheese, mix of 3 varieties	

Rinse the pumpkin. Cut off the top and reserve. Scoop out all pulp and seeds. Tear the bread into small pieces. Layer the bread and the 3 cheeses in the pumpkin. Pour in the cream. Sprinkle with nutmeg. Replace the top. Place pumpkin in an 8×8-inch baking dish. Bake at 350 degrees for 1 to 1 1/2 hours or until tender. Serve with breadsticks or crudités. Yield: more than 20 appetizer servings.

Janet M. Hamilton, Xi Zeta Epsilon
Kalamazoo, Michigan

PIGSKIN PUFFS

1 cup water	3/4 cup flour
1/2 cup (1 stick) margarine	1/2 cup cornmeal
1/4 teaspoon salt	4 eggs

Place the water and margarine in a saucepan over medium-high heat. Bring to a boil, stirring constantly. Stir the salt, flour and cornmeal into the rapidly boiling margarine mixture. Boil for 1 minute. Remove from heat. Let cool slightly. Add the eggs 1 at a time, beating well after each addition. Drop by tablespoons on a nonstick baking sheet. Bake at 400 degrees for 50 minutes or until golden brown. Let cool. Scoop out the centers of the puffs and fill with chili and beans, seasoned burger mix or cream cheese and honey. Yield: 6 to 8 servings.

Dorathea Renner
Smith, Nevada

WITCHES' SNACK MIX

I enjoy making this concoction with my five-year-old. We say the Halloween names as we make it, laughing the whole time.

1 cup Blood Drops (red hot cinnamon candies)
1 cup Owl Eyes (peanuts)
1 cup Cat Eyes ("M & M's" Peanut Chocolate Candies)
1 cup Chicken Toenails (candy corn)
1 cup Colored Flies ("M & M's" Plain Chocolate Candies)
1 cup Butterfly Wings (corn chips)
1 cup Earthworms (corn curls)
1 cup Cat Claws (sunflower seeds)
1 cup Ants (raisins)
1 cup Snake Eyes (chocolate chips)
1 cup Cobwebs (broken Triscuits)
1 cup Lizard Lips (shoestring potatoes)
1 cup Bat Bones (pretzels)

Stir all together and store in an airtight container. Yield: 13 cups.

Marilyn Dietze, Beta Sigma Phi
Nebraska City, Nebraska

HALLOWEEN PARTY MIX

This mix freezes well.

1 (11-ounce) package mini pretzels
1 (10-ounce) package mini peanut butter crackers
1 cup dry roasted peanuts
1 cup sugar
1/2 cup (1 stick) butter or margarine
1/2 cup light corn syrup
2 tablespoons vanilla extract
1 teaspoon baking soda
1 (10-ounce) package "M & M's" Chocolate Candies
1 (18-ounce) package candy corn

Combine the pretzels, crackers and peanuts in a large bowl. Combine the sugar, butter and corn syrup in a large saucepan over medium heat. Bring to a boil. Boil for 5 minutes. Remove from heat. Stir in the vanilla and baking soda; mixture will foam. Pour over the pretzel mixture and stir until well coated. Pour into a greased 10×15-inch cake pan. Bake at 250 degrees for 45 minutes, stirring every 15 minutes. Break apart while still warm. Toss with the "M & M's" and candy corn. Spread over waxed paper to cool completely. Store in an airtight container. Yield: 16 cups.

Laurie Tufford, Alpha Zeta
Nevada, Iowa

POPCORN "CAKE"

5 quarts popped popcorn
1 cup (or more) "M & M's" Chocolate Candies
1 cup dry roasted peanuts
1 pound miniature marshmallows
1/2 cup (1 stick) margarine
2 tablespoons vegetable oil

Place the popcorn, "M & M's" and peanuts in a large bowl and mix well. Combine the marshmallows, margarine and oil in a heavy saucepan over medium heat. Cook until marshmallows and margarine are melted and mixture is smooth, stirring constantly. Pour over the popcorn mixture and mix well. Spoon into a 10-inch angel food cake pan, pressing down firmly. Let stand in a cool place to set.
Yield: 20 or more servings.

Sarah Collins, Gamma Eta
New Hampton, Iowa

VOLCANO PARTY PUNCH

Delicious and fun! For Christmas or Valentine's Day, use red gelatin and pink lemonade. For Easter, use burgundy grape gelatin and pink lemonade.

1 (3-ounce) package orange gelatin
1 cup boiling water
1 (6-ounce) can frozen lemonade or limeade
3 cups cold water
Vanilla ice cream
1 (26-ounce) bottle lemon-lime soda

Dissolve the gelatin in the boiling water. Let cool slightly. Pour into a large punch bowl. Add lemonade and cold water and stir well. Drop in spoonfuls of ice cream. Slowly pour in the lemon-lime soda. Watch it erupt! Yield: 16 to 20 servings.

Hazel A. Carr, Xi Master
Abbotsford, British Columbia, Canada

HOT AND SOUR MUSHROOM SOUP

This recipe comes from the Manitoba Division of the Canadian Mushroom Growers Association.

3³/₄ cups beef broth
2 cups water
2 cups sliced fresh mushrooms
1/4 pound boneless pork loin, sliced
1/2 cup bamboo shoots, julienned
2 tablespoons soy sauce
2 tablespoons rice vinegar
1/4 teaspoon crushed red pepper flakes
1/4 teaspoon dark sesame oil
1/4 cup beef broth
2 tablespoons cornstarch
2 tablespoons chopped green onion

Combine 3³/₄ cups beef broth, water, mushrooms, pork, bamboo shoots, soy sauce, rice vinegar, red pepper flakes and sesame oil in a large saucepan over medium-high heat. Bring to a boil; reduce heat. Simmer, uncovered, for 20 minutes or until the pork is cooked through. Combine ¼ cup beef broth and cornstarch in a small bowl and mix until smooth. Add the cornstarch mixture gradually to the simmering soup, cooking until mixture thickens slightly, stirring constantly. Serve hot. Garnish with green onions. Yield: 6 servings.

Frances N. Davie, Preceptor Beta
Winnipeg, Manitoba, Canada

SPICY POTATO SOUP

Serve with jalapeño corn bread.

1 pound lean ground beef	4 cups water
4 cups cubed peeled potatoes	2 teaspoons salt
1 small onion, chopped	1½ teaspoons black pepper
3 (8-ounce) cans tomato sauce	½ to 1 teaspoon hot pepper sauce

Brown the ground beef in a Dutch oven or large skillet, stirring until crumbly; drain. Return the beef to the Dutch oven. Add the potatoes, onion and tomato sauce. Stir in the water, salt, black pepper and hot pepper sauce. Bring to a boil; reduce heat. Simmer, partially covered, for 1 hour or until soup thickens and potatoes are tender. Yield: 6 to 8 servings.

Lori Johnson, Omicron Mu
Fort Stockton, Texas

CHICKEN SOUP

My mom always made a big pot of this soup on Halloween. We children would go out to trick-or-treat and return for a big bowl of steaming soup and French bread. Use your favorite brand of instant split-pea soup mix, and your favorite small pasta. It's very easy and very delicious.

8 cups water	1 cup chopped potatoes
1 package instant split-pea soup mix	½ cup sliced celery
2 to 3 tablespoons chicken bouillon granules	½ cup sliced carrots
	½ cup sliced zucchini
	1 cup chopped cabbage
2 cups chopped boneless skinless chicken or chicken gizzards	Handful of small pasta (optional)

Combine the water, soup mix and bouillon in a 4- to 8-quart stockpot. Bring to a boil. Add the chicken and reduce heat to a simmer. Add the potatoes, celery and carrots. Simmer, uncovered, for 1 hour or until vegetables are tender and chicken is cooked through, adding more water if necessary. Stir in the zucchini, cabbage and pasta. Simmer for 5 to 10 minutes or until pasta is tender. Yield: 8 to 10 servings.

Lesa L. Speyer, Xi Pi
Riverton, Wyoming

MEXICAN CHEF'S SALAD

1½ to 2 pounds ground beef or turkey	¼ cup finely chopped onion
Salt and pepper (optional)	Hot pepper sauce
1 (16-ounce) can kidney beans	2 cups shredded Cheddar cheese
1 large head lettuce, cut or torn into bite-size pieces	1 (8-ounce) bottle Thousand Island salad dressing
4 tomatoes, chopped	1 (10-ounce) bag nacho-flavored chips, regular or taco flavor
1 large cucumber, peeled, chopped	

Brown the ground beef with the salt and pepper in a skillet, stirring until crumbly; drain. Stir in the undrained kidney beans and bring to a simmer. Simmer, uncovered, for 10 minutes. Place the lettuce, tomatoes, cucumber and onion in a large bowl and toss to combine. Stir a couple of dashes of hot pepper sauce into the ground beef mixture. Add to the lettuce mixture. Top with the cheese. Pour the salad dressing over the salad and toss. Crush the tortilla chips slightly and add to the salad. Toss lightly. Serve immediately with additional hot sauce or salsa sauce as desired. Yield: 6 to 8 servings.

Alice Chase, Xi Alpha Tau
Sanford, Maine

Betty Rogers, Xi Lambda Beta, Waco, Texas, prepares Easy Saturday Night Supper by cooking a pound of ground beef with a tablespoon of chili powder until crumbly, mixing in a can of Spanish rice and a can of ranch-style beans, topping with shredded cheese, and baking until the cheese melts. Serve with corn chips, picante sauce, and a salad.

BEEF STEW IN A PUMPKIN SHELL

3 garlic cloves, peeled, quartered
3 tablespoons olive oil or other fat
2 large onions, chopped
2 large tomatoes, chopped
1 large bell pepper, chopped
2 pounds tender beef, cut in 1-inch cubes
1½ teaspoon salt
½ teaspoon pepper
1 teaspoon sugar
8 dried peach halves
3 medium white potatoes, peeled, diced
3 small sweet potatoes, peeled, diced
2 (10-ounce) packages frozen whole kernel corn
2 cups beef broth or consommé
½ cup madeira
1 medium pumpkin
1 tablespoon butter, melted
½ teaspoon salt

Brown the garlic in the olive oil. Add the onion and sauté over medium-low heat until onion is yellow. Add the tomatoes, bell pepper, beef, 1½ teaspoons salt, pepper and sugar and mix well. Simmer, uncovered, for 20 minutes, stirring occasionally. Stir in the peaches, white potatoes, sweet potatoes, corn and broth. Simmer, covered, for 40 minutes longer, adding more broth if necessary. Stir in the madeira. Slice off the top of the pumpkin and reserve. Remove the pumpkin seeds and pulp and rub the inside with 1 tablespoon butter and the ½ teaspoon salt. Pour the beef stew into the pumpkin shell. Replace the top. Place the filled pumpkin in a small nonstick baking pan. Bake at 325 degrees for 1 hour or until the pumpkin is tender. Place carefully on a bed of green leaves to serve. When serving, scoop out a spoonful of pumpkin with every spoonful of stew. Yield: 6 servings.

Phoebe M. Richards, Laureate Mu
Montclair, California

HALLOWEEN BEEF STEW

1 (4-pound) pumpkin
1 pound lean ground beef
1 cup chopped onion
1 tablespoon vegetable oil
⅓ cup chopped red bell pepper
⅓ cup chopped green bell pepper
1 medium garlic clove, minced
1 teaspoon salt
¼ teaspoon thyme
¼ teaspoon pepper
1 (7-ounce) can pitted black olives
1 (8-ounce) can tomato sauce
2 large eggs, beaten

Slice off the top of the pumpkin and reserve. Remove the pumpkin seeds and pulp. Simmer the pumpkin in enough salted water to cover in a large kettle for 20 to 25 minutes or until almost tender; drain. Brown the ground beef with the onion in the oil in a large skillet, stirring until the ground beef is crumbly; drain. Add the bell peppers and garlic. Cook over medium heat for 1 minute longer, stirring occasionally. Remove from heat. Stir in the salt, thyme, pepper, olives, tomato sauce and eggs. Spoon the mixture into the pumpkin shell. Replace the top. Brush the pumpkin with vegetable oil. Bake at 350 degrees for about 1 hour or until pumpkin is tender. Let stand for about 10 minute. Cut into wedges to serve. Yield: 8 servings.

Maxine Houser, Preceptor Eta Omicron
West Sacramento, California

HAMBURGER HALLOWEEN FACES

When my children were young I made these every year for our Halloween party. All the children loved the hamburger faces. Now my children, in their thirties, make this treat for their children.

1½ to 2 pounds 90% fat-free ground beef
4 tablespoons applesauce
1 tablespoon dried onion flakes
1 tablespoon dry mustard
¼ cup seasoned bread crumbs
A.1. steak sauce to taste
2 (8-count) cans refrigerator biscuits

Combine the ground beef, applesauce, onion flakes, mustard, bread crumbs and A.1. sauce in a large bowl and mix well. Shape into eight 3- to 4-inch patties. Remove biscuit dough from cans. Roll each biscuit into a 4- to 5-inch circle. Sandwich each ground beef patty between 2 flattened biscuits. Pinch to seal, enclosing the patty in the dough. Place on a nonstick baking sheet. Use a toothpick, knives and forks to cut a face into each. Bake at 375 degrees for about 30 minutes or until pastry is golden brown and beef is done to taste. Serve warm. Yield: 8 servings.

Judy W. Waggoner, Preceptor Alpha Phi
Midlothian, Virginia

Bobbie Ann Henderson, Alpha Pi, Alpharetta, Georgia, makes Cheddar Quiche in large or miniature sizes by lining a pie plate or muffin cups with pie pastry and filling with a mixture of 2 eggs, 1 cup lowfat mayonnaise, 1 cup lowfat milk, 2 tablespoons cornstarch, 1½ to 2 cups shredded Cheddar cheese, ½ cup sliced green onions, and 1 cup chopped cooked ham, turkey, ground beef, or sausage. Bake at 350 degrees until set.

WITCHES' STEW

To freeze this dish, spoon the mixture into a freezer container and seal securely. When ready to serve, remove from the freezer and thaw in the refrigerator. Then simmer over low heat for 20 minutes or until bubbly—or you may heat it in the microwave.

1/2 pound bacon, crisp-cooked, crumbled	1 (16-ounce) can kidney beans
1 1/2 pounds lean ground beef or turkey	2 cups cooked spaghetti or noodles
Salt and pepper to taste	3 large ripe tomatoes, peeled, coarsely chopped
2 large onions, chopped	
2 large green bell peppers, chopped	
1 (8-ounce) can sliced mushrooms, drained	

Remove the bacon from the skillet to paper towels. Pour off the bacon drippings, leaving 1 tablespoon in the skillet. Add the ground beef, salt and pepper. Sauté over medium heat until the beef loses its color, stirring until crumbly. Stir in the onions and bell peppers. Cook for 10 minutes longer, stirring occasionally. Stir in the bacon, mushrooms, beans, spaghetti, tomatoes and more salt and pepper to taste. Cook until heated through.
Yield: 6 to 8 servings.

Wanda Walters, Omega Lambda
Wellborn, Florida

HOMESTYLE MACARONI AND CHEESE

2 1/4 cups hot water	1/4 cup crushed soda crackers
1 package macaroni and cheese dinner mix	1 tablespoon butter, melted
1/4 teaspoon pepper	1 cup sour cream
1 1/2 cups shredded Cheddar cheese	

Place the water, the packet of cheese mix from the macaroni and cheese dinner mix and the pepper in a 1 1/2-quart casserole and whisk well. Stir in the dry pasta from the dinner mix and 1 cup of the Cheddar cheese. Bake at 375 degrees, covered, for 30 minutes. Combine the remaining 1/2 cup Cheddar cheese, crackers and butter in a small bowl and mix well. Remove the casserole from the oven. Stir in the sour cream. Sprinkle the cracker mixture over the top. Bake, uncovered, for 10 minutes longer.
Yield: 6 servings.

Ellen M. Williams, Alpha Eta Master
Pueblo, Colorado

VEGETABLE SHRIMP LINGUINI

1/4 cup vegetable oil	1 cup dry white wine
1 pound medium shrimp, shelled, deveined	1 teaspoon oregano
2 garlic cloves, minced	1/4 teaspoon crushed red pepper flakes
1 cup water	8 ounces linguini, cooked, drained
1 package Knorr vegetable soup and dip mix	

Heat the oil in a large skillet over medium-high heat. Add the shrimp and garlic. Sauté for 5 minutes or until shrimp turns pink. Remove the shrimp from the skillet. Add the water, soup mix, wine, oregano and red pepper flakes to the skillet. Bring to a boil, stirring constantly. Reduce heat to low. Simmer for 5 minutes. Return the shrimp to the skillet. Simmer for 2 minutes longer. Spoon over the pasta and toss to coat. Yield: 4 servings.

Robin Posey, Alpha Alpha Psi
Destin, Florida

COUNTRY CORN CASSEROLE

1 (16-ounce) package frozen mixed vegetables (corn, broccoli, red pepper)	1 tablespoon butter or margarine
	1 (10-ounce) can Cheddar cheese soup
1/4 cup water	1/4 cup milk
1/2 cup chopped onion	1 1/3 cups crushed saltines

Combine the vegetables and water in a saucepan over medium heat. Bring to a boil; reduce heat. Simmer, covered, for 5 to 6 minutes or until tender; drain. Sauté the onion in the butter in a saucepan over medium heat for 5 minutes or until tender. Add the soup and milk; stir until smooth. Add the saltine crumbs and cooked vegetables and mix well. Spoon into a greased 8×8-inch baking dish. Dot with butter. Bake, uncovered, at 350 degrees for 25 to 30 minutes or until hot and bubbly.
Yield: 6 to 8 servings.

Jackie Kennedy, Preceptor Laureate Beta Rho
Grand Rapids, Michigan

Rhonda Povlot, Alpha Pi, Alpharetta, Georgia, prepares Italian Mushrooms by sautéing a pound of sliced fresh mushrooms in 1 tablespoon butter, adding a mixture of 1/2 cup sour cream, 1 tablespoon flour, 1/2 cup Parmesan cheese, and 1/8 teaspoon pepper. Heat through but do not boil and bake at 425 degrees for 10 minutes or until light brown.

PUMPKIN FRIES

1 (3- to 4-pound) pumpkin	Sugar Cinnamon

Slice off the top of the pumpkin. Scoop out the pulp and seeds. Cut the pumpkin into large chunks. Peel the skin from each chunk and cut the peeled flesh into thick strips. Arrange the strips on a baking sheet sprayed with nonstick cooking spray. Spray the strips with nonstick cooking spray. Bake at 350 degrees for 15 minutes or until golden brown, stirring frequently to prevent burning. Sprinkle with sugar and cinnamon to taste. Cool before serving. Yield: more than 15 servings.

Janelle Nokes, Upsilon
Fayetteville, Arkansas

MYSTERY MARMALADE

2 cups finely chopped cucumbers	Few drops of green food coloring (optional)
4 cups sugar	1/2 bottle liquid fruit pectin
1/3 cup lime juice	
2 tablespoons grated lime zest	

Combine the cucumbers, sugar, lime juice, zest and food coloring in a large saucepan over high heat and mix well. Bring to a full rolling boil. Boil hard for exactly 1 minute, stirring constantly. Remove from heat. Stir in the pectin at once. Skim off the foam. Stir and skim for 5 minutes to cool slightly and prevent floating particles. Ladle quickly into hot sterilized jelly jars, leaving 1/4 inch headspace. Cover at once with hot paraffin. Seal with 2-piece lids. Invert jars of hot marmalade for 5 minutes. Yield: 5 or 6 jars.

Blanche N. Goldsmith, Eta Master
Las Cruces, New Mexico

GLAZED POTATO DOUGHNUTS

3 eggs, beaten	1 teaspoon mace
1 cup sugar	Dash of cinnamon
3 tablespoons butter, softened	1 cup mashed cooked potatoes
2 3/4 cups flour	Oil for deep-frying
4 teaspoons baking powder	1/3 cup boiling water
1 teaspoon salt	1 cup confectioners' sugar
1/4 teaspoon nutmeg	

Cream the eggs, sugar and butter in a mixing bowl until light and fluffy. Sift the flour, baking powder, salt, nutmeg, mace and cinnamon together. Stir the flour mixture into the egg mixture. Stir in the mashed potatoes. Chill, covered, for 2 hours. Roll the dough 1/2 inch thick on a floured surface and cut into doughnuts. Deep fry until brown on both sides, turning once; drain. Place on absorbent paper in a warm place. Dip the warm doughnuts into a warm glaze made by adding the boiling water gradually to confectioners' sugar, stirring well. Yield: 2 1/2 dozen.

Carolyn M. Cline, Laureate Omicron
Jamestown, New York

SOFT PRETZELS

Making pretzels is a great activity for a Halloween party. Serve with mustard for dipping.

1 envelope dry yeast	1 egg, beaten
1 1/2 cups warm water	Coarse salt, sesame seeds, poppy seeds, garlic salt, or cinnamon sugar
3 cups flour	
2 teaspoons sugar	
1 teaspoon salt	

Dissolve the yeast in the warm water in a large bowl. Sift the flour, sugar and salt into the yeast mixture and stir until well mixed. Knead the dough on a lightly floured surface until smooth and elastic, about 5 minutes. Invert the bowl over the dough and let stand for 10 minutes. Preheat the oven to 450 degrees. Divide the dough into 30 pieces. Roll each piece into a thin rope about 18 inches long. Loop into pretzel shapes on a greased baking sheet. Brush with egg. Sprinkle with salt or another topping. Bake for 10 to 15 minutes or until golden brown. Yield: 30 pretzels.

Grace M. Baylor, Laureate Theta
Waynesboro, Pennsylvania

GHOSTLY CAKE WITH FLAMING EYES

Very spooky! Serve with a black kettle filled with root beer with spoonfuls of vanilla ice cream floating on top.

1 (2-layer) yellow cake mix with pudding in mix	1 cup water
	2 sugar cubes
	Licorice string
1 cup water	1 teaspoon lemon extract
3 eggs	
1 (7-ounce) package fluffy white frosting mix	1/3 cup vegetable oil

Use a pastry brush to generously grease a 9×13-inch baking pan with shortening. Flour bottom and sides of the pan. Prepare the cake batter using the package directions. When breaking an egg, crack it in the center and pour out the egg. Select the two best eggshell halves. Wash them and turn them upside down to dry on a paper towel. Pour the batter into the prepared pan. Bake at 350 degrees for 35 to 40 minutes or until a wooden pick inserted in the center comes out clean. Cool in the pan for 10 minutes. Remove to a wire rack to cool completely. Prepare the frosting using the package directions. Measure across one short edge of the cake and mark the center with a wooden pick. Measure 4 inches down each long edge and mark with picks. Cut the cake between the center pick and side picks in a curve to make a rounded top for the ghost's head. Slide the cut corner pieces down the sides to about the center of the cake. Turn the corner pieces cut sides up to make arms that look as if they're "reaching out for you." Attach the arms to the sides of the cake with some of the frosting. Frost the cake with a spatula. Place the 2 eggshell halves round side down on the cake for eyes. Place 1 sugar cube in each shell. Make a mouth of licorice string. Just before serving, pour 1/2 teaspoon lemon extract over each sugar cube. Turn off the lights and light the cubes. Yield: 12 to 15 servings.

Mae Sumner, Alpha Theta Master
Lakeland, Florida

JACK-O'-LANTERN CAKE

The ridges in the bundt cakes make this look like a real pumpkin!

2 (2-layer) yellow or chocolate cake mixes	2 tablespoons (about) milk
3 cups confectioners' sugar	Green food coloring
1/2 cup (1 stick) butter or margarine, softened	Red and yellow food coloring
1 1/2 teaspoons vanilla extract	1 (10-ounce) chocolate candy bar

Prepare the batter for the 2 cakes using the directions on the package. Remove enough batter to make 1 cupcake. Bake the cakes at 350 degrees in bundt pans as directed, baking the cupcake batter in a muffin tin. Combine the confectioners' sugar, butter, vanilla and 1 tablespoon of the milk in a bowl and mix well. Stir in the second tablespoon of milk gradually until frosting is easy to spread but not runny. Remove enough frosting to frost a cupcake. Stir green food coloring into the small amount of frosting. Add red and yellow food coloring to the remaining frosting to make it orange. Place 1 bundt cake upside down on a serving plate and frost. Place the second cake right side up over the first and frost. Place the cupcake in the center of the cake, coating it with green frosting. Cut the candy bar into small triangles and arrange them on the side of the cake to make the eyes, nose

and mouth of the jack-o'-lantern. When ready to serve, slice the top cake first, then the bottom one. Yield: more than 30 servings.

Kathleen M. Grapski, Xi Beta Eta
Gaithersburg, Maryland

PEANUT BUTTER CUPCAKES

1/2 cup peanut butter	1/2 teaspoon salt
1/3 cup shortening	1 cup milk
1 1/2 cups packed brown sugar	1/2 cup packed brown sugar
2 eggs	1/2 cup flour
2 cups flour	1/2 teaspoon cinnamon
2 teaspoons baking powder	2 tablespoons margarine
1/2 teaspoon cinnamon	1/4 cup peanut butter

Beat 1/2 cup peanut butter and shortening in a mixing bowl until creamy. Add 1 1/2 cups brown sugar gradually, beating until light and fluffy. Add the eggs 1 at a time, beating well after each addition. Sift 2 cups flour, baking powder, 1/2 teaspoon cinnamon and salt together. Add to the peanut butter mixture alternately with the milk, mixing well after each addition. Fill paper-lined baking cups 1/2 full. Combine 1/2 cup brown sugar, 1/2 cup flour and 1/2 teaspoon cinnamon in a bowl. Cut in the margarine and 1/4 cup peanut butter until crumbly. Sprinkle over the filled baking cups. Bake at 375 degrees for 18 to 20 minutes. Yield: 1 dozen.

Trudy Ruch, Xi Eta
Omaha, Nebraska

PUMPKIN EATER CUPCAKES

1 (18-ounce) package spice cake mix	2 eggs
1 cup solid-pack pumpkin	1 cup chocolate morsels
2/3 cup water	Whipped topping
	Candy corn

Prepare the cake mix using the package directions, using the 1 cup pumpkin, 2/3 cup water and 2 eggs. Stir in the chocolate morsels. Fill greased and floured muffin cups 2/3 full. Bake at 350 degrees for 15 to 20 minutes or until cake tests done. Cool in the pan for 5 minutes. Remove to a wire rack to cool completely. Cut out cone-shaped sections from the cupcakes and fill with whipped topping. Replace the cut-out sections. Decorate the tops with whipped topping and candy corn. Yield: 2 dozen.

Sharon L. George, Xi Omicron
LaVale, Maryland

PUMPKIN FUDGE

3 cups sugar
2/3 cup evaporated milk
3/4 cup (1½ sticks) margarine
½ cup solid-pack pumpkin
1 teaspoon pumpkin pie spice

2 cups butterscotch chips
1 (7-ounce) jar marshmallow creme
1 teaspoon vanilla extract
½ cup chopped walnuts or pecans

Combine the sugar, evaporated milk, margarine, pumpkin and spice in a heavy saucepan over medium heat. Cook to 234 to 240 degrees on a candy thermometer, soft-ball stage. Remove from heat. Add the butterscotch chips, marshmallow creme, vanilla and nuts and mix well. Pour into a buttered 9×13-inch baking pan. Cool and cut into squares. Yield: 2½ pounds.

Anita Milligan, Beta Beta
Bethany, Missouri

FOUR-FRUIT BARS

To make 16 bars, halve the recipe and use an 8×8-inch baking pan.

2/3 cup golden raisins
2/3 cup dark raisins
2/3 cup dried cranberries
2/3 cup chopped dried apricots
2/3 cup brandy or juice
2 cups flour
2/3 cup packed brown sugar
2/3 cup (1⅓ sticks) margarine or butter, softened

4 eggs
2 cups packed brown sugar
2/3 cup flour
2½ teaspoons vanilla extract
1/3 cup (or more) chopped pecans or walnuts

Combine the golden raisins, dark raisins, cranberries, apricots and brandy in a saucepan over medium heat. Bring to a boil; remove from heat. Let stand for 20 minutes. Combine the 2 cups flour and the 2/3 cup brown sugar in a bowl. Cut in the margarine until crumbly. Press into a greased 9×15-inch baking pan. Bake at 350 degrees for 20 minutes or until golden brown. Beat the eggs at low speed in a medium mixing bowl for 4 minutes. Stir in the 2 cups brown sugar, the 2/3 cup flour and the vanilla. Drain the raisin mixture and stir into the egg mixture. Add the nuts and mix well. Spread evenly over the cooled crust. Bake for 40 minutes. Cool in the pan. Yield: 32 bars.

Mary A. Courten, Laureate Beta Omicron
Cape Coral, Florida

HONEY OATMEAL COOKIES

1 teaspoon baking soda
4 tablespoons milk
2 cups rolled oats
½ cup packed brown sugar
½ cup honey
1 cup shortening

1 teaspoon salt
2 cups flour
2 eggs
3/4 cup chopped walnuts or pecans
1/4 cup raisins

Stir the baking soda into the milk. Combine the milk mixture, oats, brown sugar, honey, shortening, salt, flour and eggs in a large mixing bowl and mix well. Stir in the nuts and raisins. Drop by rounded teaspoonfuls 2 inches apart onto a greased cookie sheet. Bake at 325 degrees for 8 to 10 minutes or until edges begin to brown. Yield: 3 dozen.

June Stone, Laureate Delta Mu
Wichita Falls, Texas

MONSTER COOKIES

1 dozen eggs
2 cups (4 sticks) margarine or butter, softened
2 pounds brown sugar
4 cups sugar
1/4 cup vanilla extract
4 (12-ounce) jars peanut butter

8 teaspoons baking soda
18 cups quick-cooking rolled oats
2⅔ cups chocolate chips
1 pound walnuts or pecans, chopped
1 pound "M & M's" Chocolate Candies

Combine the eggs, margarine, sugars and vanilla in a very large bowl and mix until creamy. Blend in the peanut butter. Add the baking soda and oats and mix well (it may be easier to mix with your hands at this point). Add the chocolate chips, nuts and "M & M's" and mix well. Drop 6 cookies on a greased cookie sheet, using ½ cup dough per cookie. Bake at 350 degrees for 15 to 20 minutes or until edges begin to brown. Let cool a little before removing from the cookie sheet. Yield: 5 dozen.

Charlotte Marcum, Laureate Zeta
Gulf Shores, Alabama

Celeste Frothingham, Xi Epsilon Nu, Colorado Springs, Colorado, makes Coconut Fingers by blending 1 cup softened butter with 3½ tablespoons sugar, mixing in 1 teaspoon vanilla extract, 2 cups flour, and 1 cup coconut. Shape the dough into about 3½ dozen fingers. Bake at 275 degrees for 1 hour on an ungreased cookie sheet and roll the warm cookies in confectioners' sugar.

OLLIE OWL COOKIES

2¹/2 cups flour
2 teaspoons baking
    powder
³/4 cup (1¹/2 sticks)
    butter, softened
1 cup packed brown
    sugar
1 egg

1 teaspoon vanilla
    extract
1¹/2 ounces unsweetened
    baking chocolate,
    melted, cooled
¹/4 teaspoon baking soda
Chocolate chips
Whole cashews

Sift the flour and baking powder together. Cream the butter and brown sugar in a mixing bowl until light and fluffy. Add the unbeaten egg and vanilla and beat well. Blend in the flour mixture. Remove ²/3 of the dough to a floured surface. Blend the melted chocolate into the remaining dough. Chill if desired for easier handling. Roll half the light-colored dough into a 4¹/4×10-inch rectangle. Shape half the dark dough into a 10-inch-long roll. Center the roll over the rectangle. Mold the sides of the light dough around the dark roll, sealing the seam. Wrap in foil. Repeat with the remaining dough. Chill for 2 hours. Cut in ¹/8- to ¹/4-inch-thick slices. Place 2 slices, touching, on a greased cookie sheet for each owl. Pinch up a corner on each slice to make ears. Place a chocolate chip in the center of each slice for eyes. Press a whole cashew, large part toward the bottom, between the slices for the beak. Bake at 350 degrees for 8 to 12 minutes or until desired doneness.
Yield: 3 to 4 dozen.

Karen S. Dobbins, Preceptor Lambda Alpha
Laurie, Missouri

❖ HALLOWEEN THUMBPRINT COOKIES

1 cup (2 sticks) butter or
    margarine, softened
1¹/2 cups sugar
2 egg yolks
2 tablespoons milk
2 teaspoons vanilla
    extract
2 cups flour
²/3 cup baking cocoa
¹/2 teaspoon salt
About 48 Hershey's
    Kisses

Sugar for coating
1 cup confectioners'
    sugar
2 tablespoons butter or
    margarine, softened
4 teaspoons milk
¹/2 teaspoon vanilla
    extract
Yellow and red food
    coloring

Beat the 1 cup butter, 1¹/2 cups sugar, egg yolks, the 2 tablespoons milk and the 2 teaspoons vanilla in a large mixing bowl until well blended. Add a mixture of the flour, baking cocoa and salt to the butter mixture and mix well. Chill the dough, wrapped in plastic wrap, for 1 to 2 hours or until firm enough to handle. Shape the dough into 1-inch balls and roll in sugar. Place 2 inches apart on a lightly greased cookie sheet. Press thumb gently in the center of each ball. Bake at 350 degrees for 10 to 12 minutes or until set. Combine the confectioners' sugar, the 2 tablespoons butter, the 4 teaspoons milk and the ¹/2 teaspoon vanilla in a small mixing bowl and beat at high speed until smooth. Blend in yellow and red food coloring to make an orange filling. Remove the wrappers from the chocolate kisses. Spoon about ¹/4 teaspoon orange filling into the hollow of each warm cookie. Press a chocolate kiss gently in the center. Remove cookies carefully to a wire rack to cool completely. Yield: about 4 dozen.

Roxanne Domek, Xi Alpha Omega
Custer, South Dakota

SOUR CREAM SUGAR COOKIES

1 cup (2 sticks) butter,
    softened
1¹/2 cups sugar
3 eggs
1 teaspoon vanilla
    extract
4 cups flour
1 teaspoon baking soda
¹/2 teaspoon salt

2 teaspoons baking
    powder
1 cup sour cream
2 pounds confectioners'
    sugar
¹/2 cup warm milk
1 cup shortening
2 teaspoons vanilla
    extract

Cream the butter and sugar in a mixing bowl until light and fluffy. Beat in the eggs and 1 teaspoon vanilla. Stir half the flour, the baking soda, salt and baking powder into the butter mixture. Stir in half the sour cream. Stir in the remaining flour and then the remaining sour cream. Chill, wrapped in plastic wrap, for 8 to 12 hours. Roll ¹/8 inch thick on a floured surface. Cut with a cookie cutter. Place on an ungreased cookie sheet. Bake at 350 degrees for 5 to 6 minutes or until firm. Remove to a wire rack to cool. Mix the confectioners' sugar and milk in a mixing bowl. Beat in the shortening and the 2 teaspoons vanilla. Frost the cookies and enjoy. Yield: 4 dozen.

Kathy J. Ferriby, Laureate Beta Tau
Clinton Township, Michigan

Amy Machtolff, Nu Kappa, Guthrie, Oklahoma, prepares Witches' Brew Punch by blending one 14-ounce can sweetened condensed milk and one 46-ounce can chilled pineapple juice together in a large container. Add one chilled 2-liter bottle orange soda and generous scoops of orange sherbet. Serve from a jack-o'-lantern candy bucket used for a punch bowl, in tall glasses over ice or in tall glasses to resemble ice cream sodas.

WITCHES' FINGERS

1 cup (2 sticks) butter, softened	2³/4 cups flour
1 cup confectioners' sugar	1 teaspoon baking powder
1 egg	1 teaspoon salt
1 teaspoon each almond and vanilla extract	³/4 cup whole blanched almonds
	1 tube red decorator gel

Combine the first 5 ingredients in a mixing bowl and beat until smooth. Beat in the flour, baking powder and salt. Chill, covered, for 30 minutes. Work with ¹/4 of the dough at a time, keeping the remaining dough refrigerated. Roll a rounded teaspoon of dough into a finger shape. Press an almond firmly into one end to make a fingernail. Press in the center of the finger to make a knuckle shape. Use a paring knife to make a few slashes to make knuckle wrinkles. Arrange the fingers on lightly greased baking sheets. Bake at 325 degrees for 20 to 25 minutes or until pale golden. Let cool for 3 minutes on the baking sheet. Lift up each almond and squeeze red gel onto the nail bed. Press the almond back in place so the gel oozes from beneath. Remove to a wire rack to cool completely. Yield: about 5 dozen.

Tammy Watson, Theta Xi
Kamloops, British Columbia, Canada

CANDY APPLE PIE

¹/4 cup (¹/2 stick) butter	¹/2 cup red hot cinnamon candies
6 medium Rome apples, peeled, cored, sliced	2 tablespoons water
1 cup sugar	1 (2-crust) pie pastry

Melt the butter in a large skillet over medium-low heat. Add the apples, sugar, candies and water. Cook for 20 minutes or until juice thickens, stirring frequently. Remove from heat. Cool for 15 minutes. Unfold 1 pastry into a 9- or 10-inch pie plate. Remove plastic wrap. Fit pastry into plate and trim edge. Spoon the apple mixture into the pastry-lined pie plate. Top with the remaining pastry, sealing edge and cutting vents. Bake at 425 degrees for 25 to 30 minutes or until golden brown. Serve warm or cool. Yield: 8 servings.

Deborah O'Neill
Cookeville, Tennessee

BANANA TOFFEE PIE

Another way to caramelize condensed milk is to microwave it in a glass bowl at 50% power for about 4 to 5 minutes, stopping to stir midway. Microwave at 30% power for 8 to 12 minutes longer until thick and caramel-colored, stirring frequently.

1 (14-ounce) can sweetened condensed milk	1 cup whipping cream, whipped
1 baked (10-inch) deep-dish pie shell	Crushed toffee bits (optional)
2 to 3 bananas, diagonally sliced	

Cook the condensed milk in the top of a double boiler over simmering water for about 30 minutes or until thick and caramel-colored, stirring frequently. Let cool. Pour the caramelized milk into the pie shell. Layer the bananas, whipped cream and toffee bits over the caramel layer. Chill for at least 1 hour before serving. Yield: 6 to 8 servings.

Anne M. Rector, Preceptor Alpha Kappa
Trenton, Ontario, Canada

❖ CRANAPPLE COOKIE GOBBLER

4 tart apples, peeled, sliced	3 tablespoons flour
1 (16-ounce) can whole-berry cranberry sauce	1 teaspoon cinnamon
¹/3 cup packed brown sugar	1 roll refrigerator sugar cookie dough

Layer the apples in a 9×13-inch baking dish. Mix the cranberry sauce, brown sugar, flour and cinnamon together in a bowl. Layer the cranberry mixture over the apples. Cut the cookie dough into ¹/2-inch slices and arrange over the cranberry mixture. Bake at 350 degrees for 30 minutes or until cookies are golden. Serve hot in individual bowls. Yield: 4 to 6 servings.

Kathleen J. Shafer, Beta Zeta
Mifflinburg, Pennsylvania

CHOCOLATE PUDDING GRAVEYARD

2 (4-ounce) packages instant chocolate pudding mix	Miniature chocolate chips
3¹/2 cups cold milk	Candy corn
4 to 5 cups whipped topping	Candy pumpkins
1 (16-ounce) package chocolate sandwich cookies, crushed	Rectangular light-colored cookies

Prepare the pudding mixes in a large bowl using the package directions, reducing the total amount of milk by 1/2 cup. Let stand for 5 minutes. Stir in 3 cups whipped topping and half the cookie crumbs. Spoon into a 9×13-inch dish. Sprinkle with the remaining cookie crumbs. This is the "graveyard." Chill, covered, for 1 hour. Stand light-colored cookies on end on the cake for the "tombstones." Write on them with decorator icing (RIP and BOO, for example). Spoon whipped topping onto the cake in fat droplets to make small fat ghosts. Try making the ghosts in 3 layers with a flip on the top droplet. Use miniature chocolate chips for eyes and nose. Scatter candy corn and pumpkins over the surface. Yield: 15 servings.

Carol J. Harper, Alpha Delta Phi
Lowry City, Missouri

FUDGE TRUFFLE CHEESECAKE

1 1/2 cups vanilla wafer
  crumbs (about 45
  wafers)
1/2 cup confectioners'
  sugar
1/3 cup baking cocoa
1/3 cup (2/3 stick) butter
  or margarine, melted
24 ounces cream cheese,
  softened
1 (14-ounce) can
  sweetened condensed
  milk

2 cups semisweet
  chocolate chips,
  melted
4 eggs
2 teaspoons vanilla
  extract
1 cup semisweet
  chocolate chips
  (optional)

Combine the first 4 ingredients in a small bowl and mix well. Press into the bottom and 1 inch up the side of a 9-inch springform pan. Beat the cream cheese in a large mixing bowl until fluffy. Add the condensed milk gradually, beating until smooth. Add the melted chocolate, eggs, vanilla and chocolate chips and mix well. Spoon into the prepared pan. Bake at 300 degrees for 1 hour and 5 minutes or until center is set. Chill. Garnish as desired. Refrigerate any leftovers. Yield: 16 servings.

Judy Flannery, Laureate Alpha Epsilon
Yukon, Oklahoma

CARAMEL DIPPING SAUCE

2 cups sugar
1 cup light corn syrup
3/4 cup (1 1/2 sticks) butter
2 cups evaporated milk

Dash of salt
1 teaspoon vanilla
  extract

Combine the sugar, corn syrup, butter, evaporated milk and salt in a heavy saucepan over medium-high

heat. Bring to a full rolling boil, stirring constantly. Reduce heat a little. Simmer for 30 minutes, stirring frequently. Remove from heat. Stir in the vanilla. Serve cold with apple slices or banana chunks for dipping, or serve warm over ice cream or with marshmallows. Refrigerate leftovers. Yield: 3 1/2 cups.

Martha Krempel, Alpha Tau
Columbus, Indiana

BLACKBERRY COBBLER

5 cups blackberries or
  huckleberries
1 1/2 tablespoons lemon
  juice
2 cups flour
3 cups sugar
1 cup milk
1 teaspoon salt

1/3 cup (2/3 stick)
  margarine, melted
2 teaspoons baking
  powder
2 tablespoons
  cornstarch
1 1/2 cups boiling water

Wash the berries and spread in an ungreased 9×11-inch baking pan. Sprinkle with the lemon juice. Combine the flour, 1 1/2 cups of the sugar, milk, 1/2 teaspoon of the salt, margarine and baking powder in a bowl and mix well. Spoon the flour mixture evenly over the berries, covering them to the edge of the pan. Combine the cornstarch, remaining 1 1/2 cups sugar and remaining 1/2 teaspoon salt in a bowl and mix well. Sprinkle the cornstarch mixture over the flour mixture. Pour the boiling water slowly over the top, covering the whole surface. Bake at 350 degrees for 1 hour and 10 minutes or until crust is golden brown. Serve warm with ice cream.
Yield: 12 servings.

Annie Tester, Preceptor Gamma Kappa
Pilot Rock, Oregon

POPCORN POPS

1 cup light corn syrup
1/2 cup sugar
1 (3-ounce) package
  flavored gelatin

9 cups popped popcorn
9 or 10 Tootsie Roll
  Pops

Combine the corn syrup and sugar in a heavy saucepan over medium-high heat. Bring to a boil and cook until sugar dissolves, stirring constantly. Remove from heat. Add the gelatin, stirring just until blended. Place the popcorn in a large bowl. Pour the gelatin mixture over the popcorn and mix well. Quickly form popcorn balls around the Tootsie Roll Pops with buttered hands. Wrap the popcorn pops in plastic wrap to keep fresh. Yield: 9 or 10 servings.

Karen Wade, Lambda Sigma
Hallsville, Missouri

PUMPKIN CHEESECAKE

1½ cups ginger snaps
   cookie crumbs
⅓ cup (⅔ stick) butter,
   melted
16 ounces cream cheese,
   softened
¾ cup packed brown
   sugar
4 eggs, separated

1 tablespoon cinnamon
½ teaspoon ground
   ginger
½ teaspoon allspice
¼ teaspoon nutmeg
½ teaspoon salt
1 (14-ounce) can solid-
   pack pumpkin

Combine the cookie crumbs with the butter and mix well. Press into a lightly greased 10-inch springform pan. Bake at 325 degrees for 8 minutes or until lightly browned. Let stand to cool. Beat the cream cheese in a large mixing bowl. Add the brown sugar and egg yolks gradually, beating until smooth. Blend in the cinnamon, ginger, allspice, nutmeg and salt. Beat in the pumpkin until well blended. Beat the egg whites in a separate bowl until stiff peaks form. Fold the stiffly beaten egg whites gently into the pumpkin mixture. Pour over the cooled crust. Bake at 325 degrees for about 1 hour or until set. Remove from oven and cool. Chill, covered, for 2 to 3 hours before serving. Remove the side of the pan. Garnish with sweetened whipped cream. Yield: 16 servings.

Linda McMullan, Alpha Rho
Hope, British Columbia, Canada

PUMPKIN CREAM CHEESE SWIRLS

6 tablespoons butter,
   melted
1¾ cups sugar
3 large eggs
1 cup canned pumpkin
1¾ cups flour
1½ teaspoons cinnamon

1 teaspoon baking soda
½ teaspoon baking
   powder
½ teaspoon nutmeg
8 ounces cream cheese,
   softened

Blend the butter and 1½ cups of the sugar in a mixing bowl. Beat in 2 of the eggs, pumpkin and ⅓ cup water. Mix the flour, cinnamon, baking soda, baking powder and nutmeg in a separate bowl. Add the flour mixture to the pumpkin mixture and beat until blended. Spread evenly in a buttered and floured 10×15-inch cake pan. Combine the cream cheese, remaining egg and remaining ¼ cup sugar in a mixing bowl and beat until smooth. Drop the cream cheese mixture in 24 evenly spaced 1-tablespoon portions over the batter. Swirl lightly to marbleize. Bake at 350 degrees for 30 minutes or until set. Cool in pan on a wire rack. Yield: 24 servings.

Donna Ramsey, Psi Masters
Fort Collins, Colorado

❖ PUMPKIN TRIFLE

May substitute a 30-ounce can of pumpkin pie mix for the canned pumpkin, but omit the spices.

1 (2-layer) store-bought
   or homemade spice
   cake
4 (4-ounce) packages
   instant butterscotch
   pudding mix
2½ cups milk
1 teaspoon cinnamon

¼ teaspoon nutmeg
¼ teaspoon ground
   ginger
¼ teaspoon allspice
1 (29-ounce) can solid-
   pack pumpkin
2 cups whipping cream,
   whipped

Crumble half the spice cake into a trifle bowl. Prepare the pudding using the package directions, using 2½ cups milk. Blend the cinnamon, nutmeg, ginger and allspice into the pumpkin. Mix the pudding and pumpkin mixture together. Layer half the pudding mixture and half the whipped cream over the spice cake crumbs. Crumble ¾ of the remaining spice cake over the whipped cream. Repeat the pudding mixture and whipped cream layers. Crumble the remaining spice cake over the top.
Yield: more than 25 servings.

Betty Scharfenberg, Xi Alpha Lambda
Cold Lake, Alberta, Canada

KAHLUA TIRAMISU

Be sure to use pasteurized eggs for this dessert.

6 egg yolks
1¼ cups sugar
1 pound mascarpone
   cheese, softened
4 tablespoons Kahlúa
1½ cups whipping
   cream, whipped

2 cups espresso
2½ (3-ounce) packages
   ladyfingers
Toasted almonds
Baking cocoa to taste

Beat the egg yolks and sugar in a mixing bowl at high speed for 1 minute. Place the yolk mixture in the top of a double boiler over boiling water. Reduce heat to low. Cook for 10 to 15 minutes or until slightly thickened, stirring constantly. Remove from heat and let cool. Add the cheese to the yolk mixture and beat well. Blend in 2 tablespoons of the Kahlúa. Fold the whipped cream into the yolk mixture. Stir the remaining 2 tablespoons Kahlúa into the espresso. Dip the ladyfingers in the espresso mixture. Line a 9×13-inch pan with the dipped ladyfingers. Layer half the egg yolk mixture, half the almonds and baking cocoa over the ladyfingers. Repeat the layers. Chill, covered, until serving time. Yield: 15 servings.

Joanne Wiemers, Xi Beta Iota
Mankato, Minnesota

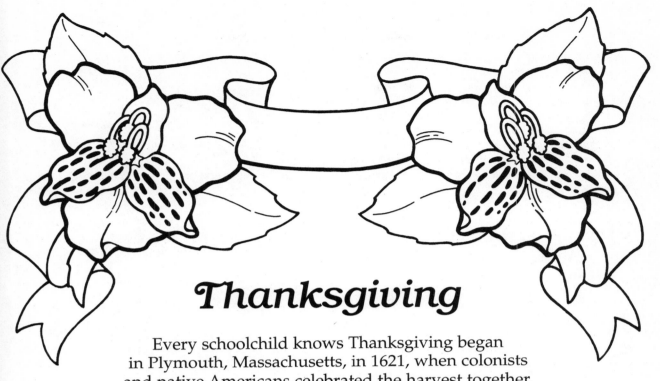

Thanksgiving

Every schoolchild knows Thanksgiving began
in Plymouth, Massachusetts, in 1621, when colonists
and native Americans celebrated the harvest together.
And most of us remember that Thanksgiving
became a nationwide holiday during the Civil War
when President Lincoln declared a day of truce and
prayer in November 1863.
In fact, Thanksgiving Day continues to occur
only through presidential proclamation. Every year
since 1863, our presiding chief has authorized the
holiday by issuing a proclamation designating the
fourth Thursday of November as Thanksgiving Day
in the U.S. Who knows—maybe some day
some president will change her mind and make it a
Wednesday. She may even decide to cook a goose
instead of a turkey! Whatever your choice,
you'll be thankful for the ideas in this chapter.

PUMPKIN SNOWMAN

If you have a leftover uncut pumpkin from Halloween, use it as a yard decoration or a centerpiece for Thanksgiving. Spray the pumpkin with white paint and glue a white styrofoam ball on top. Tie a length of cloth around the neck for a scarf and add a selection of buttons from your button box to form the eyes, mouth, and buttons down the front. Insert a small carrot for the nose and branches for arms. All pumpkins are different in size and shape so you will have a unique pumpman.

Lynn Hough, Delta Mu Alpha
Live Oak, California

FIRE-BRIGHT PINE CONES

Thanksgiving and Christmas are always more fun with a fire in the fireplace, and children can help make the fire more colorful for all to enjoy. Collect fallen pine cones. Make up a solution of 8 ounces baking soda dissolved in 2 quarts water in a large container. Add pine cones, soak overnight, drain, and place in mesh bags to dry. The dry pine cones can be added a few at a time to the fire in the fireplace for interesting color accents. A solution of borax or salt with the same proportions of water will each produce a different color.

Judith A. Faught, Xi Beta
Phenix City, Alabama

CLAY POT CANDLE HOLDERS

Make these inexpensive but elegant holders using colors appropriate to the season or holiday. For Thanksgiving or Christmas I like gold and white. Paint a 5-inch clay pot with gold paint and let dry. Cover the hole in the bottom with tape on the inside. Stencil or sponge white stars on the outside of the pot. Select a clear glass chimney that looks good with the pot and sponge gold stars on the chimney. Fill the clay pot with sand, insert a 10-inch white taper in the sand, and place the chimney over the taper.

Gretchen Hild, Alpha Nu
Norfolk, Nebraska

WHEN THE FLOWERS DIE

If you have large outdoor clay pots on your patio or at your front door, you know how bare they look once the flowers die. Make them beautiful again for winter by discarding the dead flower stems and covering the soil with evergreen branches. Add natural or artificial seasonal color and pine cones. This creates a welcoming atmosphere during the dreary cold months.

Joyce Lambert, Preceptor Gamma Tau
Longmont, Colorado

PUMPKIN DIP

Our family enjoys this dip for dessert.

4 cups confectioners' sugar, sifted	2 teaspoons cinnamon
16 ounces cream cheese, softened	1 teaspoon ground ginger
1 (30-ounce) can pumpkin pie filling	1 small pumpkin, hollowed out, chilled

Cream the sugar and cream cheese in a large mixing bowl until light and fluffy. Beat in the pie filling, cinnamon and ginger. Store in an airtight container in the refrigerator. Fill the pumpkin with the dip at serving time. Serve with gingersnaps, graham crackers or apple pieces for dipping. Yield: 7 cups.

Beverly Rippey, Preceptor Beta Phi
Bryan, Texas

SAUERKRAUT BALLS

Great as an hors d'oeuvre or vegetable side dish. The key to success with this recipe is to make sure the ingredients really are finely chopped. A food mill is useful for this task.

1 medium onion, finely chopped	2 cups well-drained sauerkraut, finely chopped
3 tablespoons butter or margarine	1/8 teaspoon seasoned salt
1 cup finely chopped ham	1/3 teaspoon Worcestershire sauce
1 cup finely chopped corned beef	2 cups milk
1/2 garlic clove, crushed	2 1/2 cups sifted flour
1/3 cup flour	2 cups fine bread crumbs
1 egg, beaten	Vegetable oil for deep-frying
1/2 cup prepared beef bouillon	

Sauté the onion in the butter in a skillet for 2 to 3 minutes. Stir in the ham, corned beef and garlic. Cook over medium-low heat for 10 minutes, stirring occasionally. Stir in 1/3 cup flour, egg, bouillon, sauerkraut, salt and Worcestershire sauce. Cook until thickened, stirring constantly. Chill, covered, for 2 to 4 hours. Shape into walnut-size balls. Mix the milk and 2 1/2 cups flour together to make a smooth batter. Dip the balls in the batter. Roll in bread crumbs. Deep-fry at 375 degrees until lightly browned. Drain on paper towels. Serve warm. Yield: 4 1/2 dozen.

Carolyn Dixon, Preceptor Alpha Lambda
Springfield, Missouri

PERCOLATOR PUNCH

Not only does this punch taste great, it creates a wonderful aroma. Serve at special gatherings.

2 (32-ounce) bottles
  cranberry juice
  cocktail
1 (32-ounce) can
  unsweetened
  pineapple juice
1 cup packed brown
  sugar

4 teaspoons whole
  cloves
12-inch cinnamon
  sticks, broken
Peel of 1/2 orange, cut
  into strips
3 1/2 cups light rum
  (optional)

Combine the cranberry cocktail, pineapple juice and brown sugar in a 30- to 40-cup percolator. Combine the cloves, cinnamon sticks and orange peel in the percolator basket. Perk using the manufacturer's instructions. Add the rum just before serving. Yield: 30 to 40 cups.

Ilene Scott, Xi Zeta Chi
Port Elgin, Ontario, Canada

GINGER CARROT SOUP

Serve as a first course for a roast pork, turkey, or chicken dinner. You may purée the soup in a blender or with a hand-held blender; please don't use an egg beater.

1/2 tablespoon olive oil
1/4 teaspoon dark
  sesame oil
2 garlic cloves, crushed
1/2 teaspoon minced
  fresh gingerroot
5 large carrots, sliced
  (about 4 cups)
1/4 teaspoon salt
1 teaspoon ground
  ginger

1 teaspoon curry powder
1/2 teaspoon thyme
9 cups light (not too
  salty) chicken stock
2 tablespoons lemon
  juice
2 tablespoons soy sauce
1 tablespoon peanut
  butter

Heat the olive and sesame oils in a large wok over medium heat. Add the garlic and gingerroot. Cook for about 3 minutes or until golden brown. Add the carrots. Stir-fry for about 5 minutes. Stir in the salt, ground ginger, curry powder and thyme. Add 1 cup of the chicken stock, lemon juice, soy sauce and peanut butter. Cook until peanut butter is melted, stirring constantly. Add 2 more cups of stock. Bring to a boil; reduce heat so mixture boils gently. Cook until mixture is reduced by 1/3, stirring frequently. Add 1 more cup of stock. Cook until mixture is reduced by 1/3 again, stirring frequently. Continue adding stock, 1 cup at a time, and reducing mixture until 7 cups of stock have been used and carrots are very tender (takes about 40 minutes). Purée in 3 or 4 batches. Place the purée in a saucepan over medium heat; purée will be thick. Add the remaining 2 cups stock and cook until heated through, stirring constantly. Garnish with a swirl of cream or sour cream and a sprinkle of paprika. Yield: 6 to 8 cups.

Valerie Bottyan, Alpha
Winnipeg, Manitoba, Canada

AUTUMN APPLE SALAD

Very refreshing after eating a big Southern Thanksgiving dinner.

1 (20-ounce) can crushed
  pineapple
2/3 cup sugar
1 (3-ounce) package
  lemon gelatin
8 ounces cream cheese,
  softened

1 cup diced unpeeled
  apples
1/2 cup chopped walnuts
  or pecans
1 cup chopped celery
1 cup whipped topping
Lettuce leaves

Combine the undrained pineapple and sugar in a saucepan over medium-high heat and bring to a boil. Boil gently for 3 minutes, stirring frequently. Add the lemon gelatin, stirring until dissolved. Add the cream cheese, stirring until mixture is thoroughly combined. Let cool. Fold in the apples, nuts, celery and whipped topping. Pour into a 9-inch-square baking dish. Chill until firm. Cut into squares and serve on lettuce leaves. Yield: 9 to 12 servings.

Dot Kennedy, Xi Zeta Iota
Winter Haven, Florida

CRANBERRY SALAD

Try chopping the cranberries, orange, and apples in a blender or food processor.

10 ounces fresh
  cranberries, chopped
1 orange, peeled,
  chopped
2 apples, peeled, cored,
  chopped
2 cups sugar

1 (3-ounce) package
  lemon gelatin
1 (3-ounce) package
  raspberry gelatin
1 1/2 cups pecans or
  walnuts, chopped

Combine the cranberries, orange and apples in a large bowl. Cover with the sugar. Let stand until sugar is dissolved. Dissolve the gelatin in 2 cups hot water. Stir in 1 cup cold water. Stir the gelatin mixture into the cranberry mixture. Add the pecans and mix well. Chill until set. Yield: 20 servings.

Cynthia Thigpen, Alpha Rho Lambda
Farwell, Texas

❖ CRANAPPLE GREEN SALAD

To sugar pecans, cover the bottom of a skillet with sugar over low heat. When the sugar begins to crystallize, place the pecans in the skillet and stir with a wooden spoon. Cool on waxed paper.

Romaine, torn into bite-size pieces
1 cup dried cranberries
2 green apples, chopped
4 ounces bleu cheese, crumbled
1 cup sugared pecans
Salt and pepper to taste
1/4 cup apple cider vinegar
3 tablespoons minced shallots
2 teaspoons honey
1/2 cup light olive oil
Minced garlic to taste
2 teaspoons Dijon mustard

Combine the romaine, cranberries, apples, cheese, pecans, salt and pepper in a salad bowl. Shake the vinegar, shallots, honey, oil, garlic and mustard in a covered jar until well blended. Pour over the romaine mixture. Toss and serve. Yield: 8 servings.

Jo An Pidd, Alpha Mu Master
Gold River, California

ORIENTAL CRANBERRY RICE SALAD

This dish was a big hit at our family Thanksgiving dinner. The sesame oil was a new flavor for us. Be sure to use the dark flavorful sesame oil, not the pale sesame oil sold in health food stores.

2 cups instant rice
2 cups chicken broth
8 green onions, sliced
4 ribs celery, sliced
2 cups thawed frozen peas
1 cup slivered almonds
2 cups dried cranberries
4 tablespoons red wine vinegar
2 tablespoons soy sauce
2 teaspoons sugar
1/2 cup olive oil
4 teaspoons dark sesame oil

Cook the rice using the package directions, substituting the chicken broth for water. Let cool. Combine the rice, onions, celery, peas, almonds and cranberries in a large bowl. Combine the vinegar, soy sauce, sugar, olive oil and sesame oil in a smaller bowl and whisk to blend. Pour over the rice mixture and mix lightly. Chill, covered, until serving time. Yield: 8 to 10 servings.

Nina Rohlfs, Preceptor Tau
Unadilla, Nebraska

HEAVENLY ORANGE RICE

The light fruity flavor offers a great contrast to all the other heavenly Thanksgiving food.

1 (16-ounce) can crushed pineapple
2 (3-ounce) packages orange gelatin
3 cups boiling water
2 cups cooked rice (1 cup uncooked)
16 to 20 large marshmallows, cut up
1/2 cup chopped apple
2 tablespoons lemon juice
1 cup whipping cream, whipped

Drain the pineapple and reserve the juice. Dissolve the gelatin in the boiling water in a 4-quart bowl. Add the cooked rice and marshmallows. Stir until marshmallows are almost dissolved. Stir in the reserved pineapple juice. Chill until partially thickened. Stir in the pineapple, apple and lemon juice. Fold in the whipped cream. Chill until thick. Yield: 6 to 8 servings.

Kathy Provance, Alpha
West Fargo, North Dakota

RICE SALAD

3/4 cup water
3/4 cup Italian dressing
1 1/2 cups uncooked instant rice
3 cups thawed frozen green peas
6 tablespoons chopped green onions
3/4 cup chopped fresh mushrooms
3/4 cup chopped cucumber
6 tablespoons chopped black olives
1 1/2 cups mayonnaise

Combine the water and Italian dressing in a medium saucepan. Bring to a boil. Stir in the rice. Remove from heat. Let stand, covered, for 5 to 10 minutes or until liquid is absorbed and rice is tender. Stir in the peas, green onions, mushrooms, cucumber, olives and mayonnaise. Chill, covered, until ready to serve. Serve cold. Yield: 6 to 8 servings.

R. Gene Farley, Laureate Gamma Iota
Tallahassee, Florida

ORANGE TAPIOCA SALAD

3 cups water
1 (3-ounce) package orange gelatin
1 (4-ounce) package instant vanilla pudding
1 (3-ounce) package tapioca pudding
1 (15-ounce) can mandarin oranges, drained
1 (8-ounce) can crushed pineapple, drained
8 ounces whipped topping

Bring the water to a boil in a large saucepan over medium-high heat. Whisk in the gelatin and pudding mixes. Return to a boil, stirring occasionally. Boil for 1 minute. Remove from heat. Let cool completely. Gently fold in the oranges, pineapple and whipped topping. Remove to a serving bowl. Chill, covered, for at least 2 hours before serving. Yield: 12 to 14 servings.

Maureen Carpenter, Preceptor Mu
Brookings, Oregon

AUTUMN COLESLAW

4 cups shredded cabbage	1/4 cup sugar
1 cup sliced celery	2 tablespoons cider
1 unpeeled Red	vinegar
Delicious apple,	2 teaspoons prepared
diced	horseradish
1/2 cup raisins	1/2 teaspoon salt
1 cup mayonnaise	1/2 cup chopped walnuts

Combine the cabbage, celery, apple and raisins in a large bowl. Combine the mayonnaise, sugar, vinegar, horseradish and salt in a small bowl and whisk until blended. Pour over the cabbage mixture. Stir until evenly coated. Chill, covered, for 1 to 6 hours. Stir in the walnuts just before serving. Garnish with apple slices if desired. Yield: 10 servings.

Grace Sheldon, Preceptor Beta Alpha
Gastonia, North Carolina

BROCCOLI SALAD

A glass salad bowl will show off the beautiful colors of this salad. A red onion is preferred to white. To blanch the sliced carrots, drop them in boiling water for 1 minute, drain, and rinse in cold water. As a luncheon meal, the salad will serve 4 to 6 people.

1 large red or white	Mustard Salad Dressing
onion	1/4 cup golden raisins
2 cups chopped fresh	1/2 pound side bacon,
broccoli	chopped small,
1 cup chopped fresh	crisp-cooked, drained
cauliflower	1 (8-ounce) can
1 cup very thinly sliced	mandarin oranges,
carrots, blanched	drained

Slice the onion very thin, then halve and separate the slices. Combine the onion, broccoli, cauliflower and carrots in a large bowl. Add the Mustard Salad Dressing and toss to combine. Chill, covered, until ready to serve. Add the raisins, bacon and oranges at serving time and toss. Serve in a medium-size glass bowl. Yield: 6 to 8 servings.

MUSTARD SALAD DRESSING

2 eggs	1/4 cup water
1/2 cup sugar	1/2 cup low-calorie
1 teaspoon cornstarch	mayonnaise-type
1 teaspoon dry	salad dressing
mustard	
1/4 cup white wine	
vinegar	

Combine the eggs, sugar, cornstarch and mustard in a heavy nonstick saucepan over low heat. Add the vinegar and water gradually. Cook until smooth and thickened, stirring constantly. Remove from heat. Add the salad dressing and stir until smooth. Let cool.

Virginia Reed, Xi Delta Upsilon
Golden, British Columbia, Canada

GROUND BEEF PUMPKIN CASSEROLE

1 medium pumpkin	3 ribs celery
1/4 cup honey	1/4 cup soy sauce
1/4 cup packed brown	1 cup orange juice
sugar	1 teaspoon ground
1 (16-ounce) package	ginger
long grain and wild	2 tablespoons parsley
rice	flakes
1 pound lean ground	1 (8-ounce) can button
beef	mushrooms, drained
1 teaspoon salt	2 tablespoons
1 1/2 teaspoons pepper	margarine, softened
1/2 cup chopped onion	4 ounces sliced almonds
1/2 cup chopped green	
bell pepper	

Wash the pumpkin. Cut off the top and set aside. Scoop out all pulp and seeds. Coat the inside of the pumpkin with a mixture of the honey and brown sugar. Cook the rice using the package directions; do not overcook. Brown the ground beef in a medium-size skillet, stirring until crumbly; drain. Combine the salt, pepper, onion, bell pepper, celery, soy sauce, orange juice, ginger and parsley in a small skillet over medium heat. Bring to a boil. Stir in the mushrooms. Remove from heat. Place the rice, ground beef and bell pepper mixture in a large bowl. Toss lightly to combine. Coat the outside of the pumpkin with the margarine. Place the pumpkin in a sturdy baking pan. Fill the pumpkin with the rice mixture. Sprinkle with the almonds. Replace the pumpkin top. Bake at 300 degrees for 2 hours. Let stand for 10 to 15 minutes at room temperature before serving. Serve directly from the pumpkin. Yield: 6 to 8 servings.

Jan Allred, Laureate Zeta Delta
Beaumont, Texas

HOT BROWNS

My husband prefers the day after Thanksgiving to Thanksgiving Day—he loves the Hot Browns I make with the leftover turkey.

6 tablespoons butter	1/4 cup sliced mushrooms
4 tablespoons flour	4 slices bread, toasted
1 cup chicken stock	Sliced turkey
1 cup milk	1 tomato, sliced
1/2 cup shredded Cheddar cheese	8 slices bacon, crisp-cooked, drained

Melt 4 tablespoons of the butter in a skillet over medium-low heat. Add the flour and cook until golden, stirring constantly. Add the chicken stock and milk gradually. Cook until thickened, stirring constantly. Add the cheese. Heat until melted, stirring occasionally. Remove from heat. Sauté the mushrooms in the remaining 2 tablespoons butter in a small skillet for about 5 minutes. Line a 12-inch-square baking dish with the bread. Layer several slices of turkey, a tomato slice, 2 bacon slices and a tablespoon of mushrooms over each bread slice. Pour the cheese mixture over all. Broil 6 inches from the heat source for 5 to 10 minutes or until brown and bubbly. Yield: 4 servings.

Molly Moore, Preceptor
Loganville, Georgia

CHICKEN BISCUIT SQUARES

Add peas, corn, or water chestnuts to the filling if you like. This is a dish the kids will eat day after day!

1 pound boneless skinless chicken breast, cubed	1/4 teaspoon salt or garlic salt
	Pepper to taste
8 ounces cream cheese, softened	2 (8-count) cans crescent rolls
1/4 cup (1/2 stick) butter, softened	Seasoned bread crumbs

Brown the chicken in a skillet over medium heat until cooked through Combine the cream cheese, butter, salt and pepper in a bowl and mix well. Stir the chicken into the cream cheese mixture. Unroll the crescent roll dough. Separate into 8 squares, pressing the perforations to seal. Mound 1/4 to 1/3 cup chicken mixture over each square. Pinch dough edges together to enclose the filling. Arrange on a baking sheet. Sprinkle with bread crumbs. Bake at 350 degrees for 20 minutes or until biscuits are brown. Yield: 6 to 8 servings.

Sandy Jazdzewski, Xi Alpha Xi
Appleton, Wisconsin

FOUR-CHEESE QUICHE

My family members eat this on Thanksgiving morning while preparing a feast for 20 to 30 friends and relatives—and have done so for 30 years! The quiche may be made ahead of time and frozen.

1 unbaked (10-inch) deep-dish pie shell	3 eggs
	1/2 cup half-and-half
8 slices bacon, crisp-cooked, crumbled	1/2 cup cottage cheese
	1 tablespoon flour
3 green onions, chopped, sautéed in bacon drippings	1/2 teaspoon dillweed
	1/4 teaspoon salt
	2 tablespoons grated Parmesan cheese
1/2 cup shredded Cheddar cheese	
1/2 cup shredded Monterey Jack cheese	

Prick the pastry shell all over with a fork. Bake at 425 degrees for 10 minutes. Reduce oven temperature to 350 degrees. Layer the bacon, green onions, Cheddar cheese and Monterey Jack cheese in the pie crust. Process the eggs, half-and-half, cottage cheese, flour, dillweed, salt and Parmesan cheese in a blender until smooth. Pour over the cheese layer. Bake for 35 to 45 minutes or until a knife inserted near the center comes out clean. Yield: 6 to 8 servings.

Karen A. Bouvier, Xi Phi Iota
Hesperia, California

BROCCOLI CASSEROLE

This is a family holiday favorite that traveled from California to Georgia.

2 (16-ounce) packages frozen chopped broccoli, thawed	1 cup chopped yellow onion
	2 cups shredded Cheddar cheese
1 (10-ounce) can cream of mushroom soup	1/4 teaspoon salt
1 (10-ounce) can cream of chicken soup	3/4 cup uncooked instant rice
1/4 cup (1/2 stick) butter, melted	1 (7-ounce) can sliced mushrooms, drained
1 (8-ounce) can water chestnuts, drained	

Combine the broccoli, soups, butter, water chestnuts, onion, 1 1/2 cups of the cheese, salt, rice and mushrooms in a bowl and mix well. Pour into a greased 2-quart baking dish. Sprinkle with the remaining cheese. Bake, uncovered, at 350 degrees for 45 to 60 minutes. Yield: 10 to 12 servings.

Jean Anderson, Xi Mu Chi
Gerber, California

BAKED BROCCOLI WITH ONION

This is a fix-ahead vegetable that everyone enjoys at our Thanksgiving dinners.

1 pound fresh broccoli, or 1 (10-ounce) package frozen broccoli	2 tablespoons flour
	1/2 teaspoon salt
	Dash of pepper
	1 cup milk
1 medium onion, coarsely chopped	3 ounces cream cheese, softened
4 tablespoons butter or margarine	2 ounces sharp Cheddar cheese, shredded
1 cup soft bread crumbs	

Cut the broccoli in half lengthwise, then cut into 1-inch pieces. Cook in boiling water for 5 to 10 minutes or until tender. Cook the onion in boiling water for 5 to 10 minutes or until tender. Place the broccoli and onion in a 1 1/2-quart casserole. Melt 2 tablespoons of the butter in a skillet over medium heat. Brown the bread crumbs in the butter. Remove from heat. Melt the remaining 2 tablespoons butter in a skillet over medium-low heat. Whisk in the flour, salt and pepper. Add the milk gradually. Cook until thick and bubbly, stirring constantly. Reduce the heat. Blend in the cream cheese. Pour the cream cheese mixture over the broccoli and onion and mix lightly. Top with the Cheddar cheese. Chill, covered, until serving time. One hour before serving time, bake at 350 degrees for 30 minutes. Sprinkle the bread crumbs over the top. Bake for 30 minutes longer. Yield: 12 servings.

Phyllis M. Krause, Xi Beta Upsilon
Falls City, Nebraska

BROCCOLI AND BLEU CHEESE

1 pound broccoli, trimmed, stems peeled	4 ounces bleu cheese
	1/2 cup walnut pieces
	1/4 cup milk
6 ounces cream cheese, softened	1/4 teaspoon pepper

Cook the broccoli for 3 minutes in boiling water; drain. Combine the broccoli, cream cheese and bleu cheese in a saucepan over low heat. Heat until cheeses are melted, stirring frequently. Stir in the milk and pepper. Cook, covered, for about 5 minutes or until broccoli is hot and sauce is bubbling. Yield: 4 servings.

Claire Rettenmund, Laureate Nu
Flint, Michigan

THREE-CORN CASSEROLE

1 (15-ounce) can whole kernel corn	1 (4-ounce) jar chopped pimentos
1 (15-ounce) can cream-style corn	1 (7-ounce) package corn muffin mix
1/2 cup (1 stick) cold margarine, diced	2 eggs, beaten
	1 cup sour cream
1 small green bell pepper, chopped	1 1/2 to 2 cups shredded Cheddar cheese
1 small onion (or 6 green onions), chopped	

Combine the first 3 ingredients in a bowl and mix well. Sauté the bell pepper and onion in a little margarine for about 5 minutes. Add to the corn mixture. Stir in the pimentos, corn muffin mix and eggs. Mix well. Pour into a greased 9×13-inch baking dish. Top with sour cream and Cheddar cheese. Bake at 350 degrees for about 45 minutes, stirring halfway through baking time. Yield: 8 to 10 servings.

Phyllis A. Paine, Beta Lambda
Mt. Pleasant, Iowa

CORN-STUFFED ONIONS

8 large sweet onions, peeled	1 cup soft bread crumbs
	1 (7-ounce) can whole kernel corn, drained
1/2 pound bulk pork sausage	2 tablespoons butter or margarine
2 tablespoons chopped parsley	1/2 teaspoon paprika

Cut a slice from the top of each onion. Use a small knife to scoop out enough of the onion to leave a cavity about 1 to 1 1/2 inches deep. Chop enough of the removed onion to make 1/2 cup and set aside. Place the hollowed onions in a large kettle. Add just enough water to cover. Bring to a boil; reduce heat. Simmer, covered, for 20 minutes or just until tender (do not overcook); drain. Preheat the oven to 400 degrees. Brown the sausage in a skillet until cooked through, stirring until crumbly; drain. Add the reserved chopped onion. Sauté for 6 to 8 minutes or until onion is tender. Remove from heat. Stir in the parsley, bread crumbs and corn. Melt the butter in a 9×13-inch baking dish in the oven. Stir in the paprika. Brush the butter mixture over the hollow onions to coat well. Fill the onions with the sausage mixture. Arrange the stuffed onions in the same baking dish. Bake, covered loosely with foil, for 15 minutes. Bake, uncovered, for 5 minutes longer or until heated through and filling is lightly browned. Yield: 8 servings.

Dolores Patton, Laureate Eta Beta
Hilltop Lakes, Texas

HOLIDAY CREAMED CORN

2 (10-ounce) packages frozen corn, thawed, drained	Pinch of white pepper
	1 teaspoon salt
2 cups whipping cream or coffee cream	2 tablespoons sugar
	2 tablespoons butter, melted
8 ounces milk	2 tablespoons flour

Combine the corn, cream, milk, pepper, salt and sugar in a saucepan over medium heat. Bring to a boil; reduce heat. Simmer for 5 minutes, stirring occasionally. Blend the butter and flour together. Add to the corn mixture and mix well. Cook until thickened and heated through, stirring constantly. Yield: 6 to 8 servings.

Carol McLennan, Preceptor Alpha Tau
Lawton, Oklahoma

CHEESY EGGPLANT CASSEROLE

1 medium eggplant, peeled, diced	1/4 cup evaporated milk
	1 cup crushed soda crackers
1 (2-ounce) jar chopped pimentos	Salt and pepper to taste
2 cups shredded Cheddar cheese	Bread crumbs
	Shredded cheese
3 eggs, beaten	
1/4 cup (1/2 stick) margarine, melted	

Cook the eggplant in salted water until tender; drain. Combine the eggplant, pimentos, cheese, eggs, margarine, milk, soda crackers, salt and pepper in a bowl and mix well. Spoon into a greased 1 1/2-quart baking dish. Bake at 350 degrees for about 25 minutes. Remove from oven. Sprinkle with bread crumbs and more shredded cheese. Bake for 10 minutes longer or until cheese melts. Garnish with pimento strips and parsley for a festive look. Yield: 6 to 8 servings.

Clemmie Purcell, Laureate Tau
Gainesville, Georgia

SAVORY EGGPLANT CASSEROLE

2 medium to large eggplants, peeled, diced	1/2 teaspoon salt
	1/4 teaspoon pepper
1/2 cup chopped onion	1/2 cup seasoned bread crumbs
2 teaspoons olive oil or butter	1 egg
1 or 2 garlic cloves, crushed	1 1/4 cups shredded Cheddar cheese

Boil the eggplants in enough water to cover until tender. Drain very well. Sauté the onion in the olive oil in a skillet over medium-low heat for 5 to 10 minutes or until tender. Stir in the garlic. Mash the eggplant in an oven-safe casserole. Stir in the salt, pepper, onion mixture and breadcrumbs. Taste and add more salt if necessary. Add the egg and 1/2 cup of the cheese and mix well. Top with the remaining cheese. Bake at 350 degrees for 30 minutes. Yield: 4 servings.

Blanca Nelson, Preceptor Kappa Lambda
Ingleside on the Bay, Texas

RICH CREAMED POTATOES

5 or 6 medium potatoes	1 cup sour cream
1 (10-ounce) can cream of chicken soup	1 cup shredded Cheddar cheese
1/4 cup (1/2 stick) butter, softened	

Scrub the potatoes. Boil in enough water to cover for 20 minutes or until tender. Let cool. Peel the potatoes when cool enough to handle. Grate into a bowl. Heat the soup and butter in a saucepan over medium heat until butter is melted. Stir in the sour cream and cheese. Fold the sour cream mixture into the potatoes. Pour into a buttered 1 1/2-quart baking dish. Bake at 350 degrees for 45 minutes or until golden brown. Yield: 10 to 12 servings.

Roxanne Jones, Laureate Alpha Pi
Mountain View, California

CHICKEN AND PUMPKIN CASSEROLE

1 large pumpkin	2 tablespoons butter or margarine
3 cups chicken broth	
2 cups uncooked brown rice	3 to 4 tablespoons curry powder
1 cup uncooked wild rice	1 bunch scallions, green part only, chopped
4 or 5 boneless skinless chicken breasts	4 tart apples, cored, chopped
1 large yellow onion, chopped	1 pound cashews
2 garlic cloves, minced	

Slice off the top of the pumpkin and set aside. Remove the seeds and pulp. Bring the broth to a boil in a saucepan over medium heat. Stir in the rices; reduce heat. Simmer, uncovered, for 30 minutes; liquid may not be completely absorbed. Remove from heat. Cut the chicken into bite-size pieces. Sauté the onion and garlic in the butter in a skillet over medium-low heat until onion is light brown. Remove the onion from the skillet. Add the chicken. Sauté for about 2 minutes; do not cook through. Stir in the curry powder. Combine the rice mixture, onion mixture, chicken mixture, scallions and apples in a large bowl and mix well. Stir in the cashews. Place the pumpkin on a baking sheet. Fill with the chicken mixture. Replace the pumpkin top. Bake at 325 degrees for 1 to 1½ hours or until fork easily penetrates pumpkin shell. Yield: 6 to 8 servings.

Marie Umbriac, Preceptor Alpha Upsilon
Tamaqua, Pennsylvania

CHEESY SPINACH CASSEROLE

2 (10-ounce) packages frozen chopped spinach	½ cup (1 stick) margarine, softened
8 eggs, beaten	½ cup milk
1 pound brick cheese, shredded	½ cup flour
8 ounces cream cheese, softened	Salt and pepper to taste

Thaw the spinach and squeeze out excess moisture. Combine the spinach, eggs, brick cheese, cream cheese, margarine, milk, flour, salt and pepper in a large bowl and mix well. Bake at 375 degrees in a greased 9×13-inch baking pan for 45 minutes. Yield: 10 servings.

Monica Samson, Chi Omicron
Naperville, Illinois

SPINACH RICE CASSEROLE

This dish can be made ahead of time and refrigerated overnight. Be sure to add additional baking time.

1 cup uncooked brown rice	¼ cup chopped walnuts
1 (10-ounce) package frozen chopped spinach	1 tablespoon sesame seeds
2 eggs, beaten	1 teaspoon soy sauce
½ cup plain yogurt	½ teaspoon oregano
1 or 2 garlic cloves, pressed	Dash of nutmeg
¼ cup grated Parmesan cheese	Dash of cayenne pepper
	¼ cup wheat germ (optional)

Cook the rice in 2 cups water using the package directions. Thaw the spinach and squeeze out excess moisture. Combine the rice, spinach, eggs, yogurt, garlic, cheese, walnuts, sesame seeds, soy sauce, oregano, nutmeg and cayenne pepper in a large bowl and mix well. Spoon into a lightly oiled 2-quart casserole. Sprinkle with the wheat germ. Bake, uncovered, at 350 degrees for 35 minutes. Yield: 6 to 8 servings.

Mary McLoud, Laureate Theta Delta
Oak Park, California

TURBAN SQUASH CASSEROLE

This delicious Thanksgiving casserole also makes an attractive centerpiece.

1 large turban squash	1 cup grated Parmesan cheese
1 pound sausage	
½ cup chopped onion	1 teaspoon nutmeg
1 cup sliced mushrooms	Salt and pepper to taste
1 cup diced celery	½ cup bread crumbs
1 cup sour cream	½ cup shredded Cheddar cheese
1 egg, beaten	

Cut the "turban" off the squash and reserve it; level as needed. Scoop out the seeds. Sprinkle lightly with salt. Place cut side down on a nonstick baking sheet. Bake at 375 degrees for 1 hour or until tender. Scoop out the pulp, leaving a ½-inch shell. Brown the sausage with the onion, mushrooms and celery in a skillet, stirring until sausage is crumbly; drain. Combine the sausage mixture, sour cream, egg, half the Parmesan cheese, nutmeg, salt and pepper in a large bowl and mix well. Fill the squash shell with the sausage mixture. Top with the bread crumbs, remaining Parmesan cheese and Cheddar cheese. Bake at 350 degrees for 20 to 25 minutes. Place the squash on the turban stand to serve. Yield: 6 to 12 servings.

Patricia Butler, Xi Alpha Omicron
Layton, Utah

STUFFED ACORN SQUASH

We originally got the idea for this recipe by cooking with the scooped-out pumpkin pulp when my daughters made jack-o'-lanterns for Halloween.

3 large acorn squash	1 roll ground sausage
1 (6-ounce) package herb-seasoned stuffing mix	2 apples, chopped
	Sugar and cinnamon to taste

Cut the squash in half and remove seeds. Spray cut sides with nonstick cooking spray. Place cut sides down on an 11×14-inch baking pan. Bake at 300 degrees for 1 to 1½ hours or until tender. Scoop out the pulp, leaving ½-inch shells. Place the shells skin side down on the baking pan. Prepare the stuffing using the package directions. Brown the sausage with the apples in a skillet, stirring until sausage is crumbly and cooking until apples are tender; drain. Add the stuffing, squash pulp, sugar and cinnamon and mix well. Fill the squash cavities with the sausage mixture. Bake, covered, for 20 to 30 minutes or until hot and lightly browned. Yield: 6 servings.

Reba A. Plaisance, Preceptor Epsilon
Baton Rouge, Louisiana

ACORN SQUASH DESSERT

Acorn squash, 1/2 per
   guest
1/2 cup orange juice

1/4 cup honey
Vanilla ice cream

Bake the squash halves at 350 degrees until tender, about 1 hour. Let cool slightly. Blend the orange juice and honey. Fill the squash cavities with vanilla ice cream. Drizzle with the orange juice mixture. Yield: 1/2 squash per guest.

Carol Cape
Myrtle Beach, South Carolina

BAKED SQUASH CASSEROLE

1 1/2 pounds zucchini,
   chopped, cooked
1 medium onion, diced
1 cup diced carrots
1 (4-ounce) can water
   chestnuts, drained
1/2 cup diced celery
1 (2-ounce) jar chopped
   pimentos, drained

1 cup sour cream
1 (10-ounce) can cream
   of chicken soup
1/2 cup (1 stick) butter or
   margarine, melted
1 (6-ounce) package
   herb-seasoned
   stuffing mix

Drain the zucchini, leaving it a little soupy. Combine the zucchini, onion, carrots, water chestnuts, celery and pimentos in a large bowl and mix gently. Stir in a mixture of the sour cream and soup. Place the butter and stuffing mix in a bowl and toss to combine. Fold 1/2 to 2/3 of the stuffing mixture into the squash mixture. Add salt and pepper to taste. Spread in a greased 9×13-inch baking dish. Top with the remaining stuffing mix. Bake, covered, at 350 degrees for about 45 minutes. Yield: 9 to 12 servings.

Joan E. Anderson, Laureate Alpha Chi
Cocoa, Florida

PINEAPPLE SWEET POTATO BAKE

2 (40-ounce) cans sweet
   potatoes, heated,
   drained
1/2 cup (1 stick) butter,
   softened
3/4 cup packed brown
   sugar
1/2 teaspoon salt, or
   to taste

1 teaspoon cinnamon, or
   to taste
1 (20-ounce) can
   pineapple tidbits,
   drained
1 cup packed brown
   sugar
1/2 teaspoon cinnamon
1/2 cup chopped pecans

Place the sweet potatoes in a large mixing bowl and beat at high speed. Add half the butter and 3/4 cup brown sugar gradually, mixing at high speed. Beat in the salt and 1 teaspoon cinnamon. Stir in the pineapple. Pour into a 9×13-inch baking dish. Combine the remaining 1/2 stick butter, 1 cup brown sugar and 1/2

teaspoon cinnamon in a saucepan over medium-low heat. Cook until butter is melted, stirring frequently. Stir in the pecans. Pour the pecan mixture evenly over the sweet potatoes. Bake at 350 degrees for 35 to 45 minutes. Top with halved marshmallows for the last 10 minutes of baking time if desired. Yield: more than 20 servings.

Ruth Ann Adams, Member-at-Large
Kansas City, Missouri

SWEET POTATO CASSEROLE

3 cups mashed cooked
   sweet potatoes
3/4 cup sugar
1/4 cup milk
2 eggs, slightly beaten
1 teaspoon vanilla
   extract
1 cup flaked coconut

1/2 cup (1 stick)
   margarine or butter,
   softened
1 cup packed brown
   sugar
1/2 cup flour
1 cup broken walnuts or
   pecans

Combine the sweet potatoes, sugar, milk, eggs, vanilla and coconut in a large bowl and mix well by hand. Spread in a greased 9-inch deep-dish pie plate or 9×13-inch baking dish. Combine the butter, brown sugar, flour and nuts in a bowl and mix well. Spread over the top of the sweet potato mixture. Bake at 350 degrees for 20 minutes. Yield: 6 to 8 servings.

Brenda Audet, Preceptor Eta
Hampden, Maine

SUGARLESS SWEET POTATOES

The discovery that I am a diabetic put me on a journey of cooking experimentation. Now I am learning how to cook so that I can eat meals that my family will enjoy, too.

3 large sweet potatoes
   (about 2 1/2 pounds)
1 1/2 tablespoons apple
   pie spice
1/2 teaspoon ground
   cloves

1/4 cup orange or
   tangerine juice
1/2 cup brown sugar
   substitute
Cinnamon

Boil the unpeeled sweet potatoes in enough water to cover for 20 minutes or until tender. Peel when cool enough to handle. Mash the sweet potatoes in a large bowl with a hand masher or an electric mixer. Add the apple pie spice, cloves, juice and brown sugar substitute and mix well. Spoon into a buttered 2-quart casserole. Sprinkle with cinnamon. Dot with butter if desired. Bake at 350 degrees for 20 minutes or until heated through. Yield: 5 (1/2-cup) servings.

Linda L. Stroh, Preceptor Alpha Rho
Slidell, Louisiana

BAKED SWEET POTATOES

6 medium sweet
   potatoes
2 tablespoons orange
   juice
1/2 teaspoon grated
   orange zest
2 tablespoons brown
   sugar

2 tablespoons butter or
   margarine, softened
1/2 teaspoon salt
1/4 teaspoon cinnamon
1 egg
1/2 cup milk

Scrub the sweet potatoes and cut off the woody portions. Boil in enough water to cover for about 20 minutes or until tender; drain. Peel the sweet potatoes and cut up. Mash in a bowl with a potato masher or an electric mixer at low speed. Stir in the orange juice and zest, brown sugar, butter, salt and cinnamon. Add the egg and milk; beat until fluffy, adding additional milk if necessary. Spoon into a greased 1-quart casserole. Bake, covered, at 350 degrees for 45 to 50 minutes or until light brown.
Yield: 6 to 8 servings.

Pat Snyder, Laureate Beta Phi
Mississauga, Ontario, Canada

HOLIDAY SWEET POTATOES

If pressed for time, put the potatoes in the refrigerator to get them cool enough to peel.

Fresh sweet potatoes,
   1 per person
1 cup (2 sticks) butter
1/2 cup brown sugar or
   brown sugar
   substitute

1 1/2 cups chopped
   walnuts
Marshmallows, halved
   (optional)

Boil the unpeeled potatoes in enough water to cover for about 20 minutes or until soft but not mushy. Melt the butter in a saucepan over low heat. Stir in the brown sugar and walnuts. Remove from heat. Peel the potatoes when they are cool enough to handle. Cut into vertical 1/2-inch slices. Layer half the potatoes cut side down in a greased 9×13-inch baking dish. Spoon desired amount of the walnut mixture over the potatoes. Make a second layer with the remaining potatoes and cover with desired amount of the walnut mixture. Top with marshmallows. Bake, covered, at 350 degrees for 20 to 25 minutes or until light brown. Yield: 6 to 8 servings.

Eileen Michaud, Alpha Alpha Psi
Destin, Florida

PECAN SWEET POTATO BAKE

1 (40-ounce) can sweet
   potatoes, drained,
   mashed
1 cup sugar
2 eggs, beaten
1/2 cup milk
1/2 teaspoon salt
1/3 stick butter, melted

1 teaspoon vanilla
   extract
1 cup packed brown
   sugar
1/2 cup flour
1/3 cup (2/3 stick) butter,
   melted
1 cup chopped pecans

Combine the sweet potatoes, sugar, eggs, milk, salt, 1/3 stick butter and vanilla in a large bowl and mix well. Pour into a buttered 9×13-inch baking pan. Combine the brown sugar, flour, 2/3 stick butter and pecans in a bowl and mix well. Crumble the brown sugar mixture evenly over the sweet potato mixture. Bake, uncovered, at 350 degrees for 35 to 45 minutes or until heated through and lightly browned.
Yield: 12 servings.

Michele Lacy, Laureate Gamma Upsilon
Westerville, Ohio

VEGETABLES AU GRATIN

We like to use this versatile dish for Thanksgiving because of the variety of vegetables it contains. You may add half a can of green beans and use only half the can of carrots if desired.

3/4 cup (1-inch squares)
   green bell pepper
1/4 cup (1/2 stick)
   margarine, melted
1 garlic clove, crushed
1/4 cup flour
2/3 cup milk
3/4 teaspoon salt
1/8 teaspoon pepper
1/8 teaspoon basil
1/8 teaspoon oregano
1/4 teaspoon sugar

1 cup shredded sharp
   Cheddar cheese
1 (14-ounce) can
   pear-shaped or small
   tomatoes
1 (8-ounce) can small
   onions, drained
1 (16-ounce) can sliced
   carrots, drained
1 (10-ounce) package
   frozen corn, thawed

Sauté the bell pepper in the margarine in a skillet over medium-low heat for 3 to 4 minutes. Stir in the garlic, flour, milk, salt, pepper, basil, oregano, sugar and half the cheese. Heat until cheese is melted, stirring frequently. Combine the tomatoes, onions, carrots and corn in a large casserole. Pour the cheese mixture over the vegetables. Sprinkle the remaining 1/2 cup cheese over the top. Bake, covered, at 350 degrees for 50 minutes. Yield: 8 to 10 servings.

Linda Rager, Xi Psi
Sioux Falls, South Dakota

SLOW-COOKER DRESSING

1 whole chicken, boiled
   until tender, deboned
8 slices white bread
1 (8-inch) pan corn
   bread, cooked
   day before
1 medium onion,
   chopped
1/4 cup chopped celery
2 teaspoons sage
Salt and pepper to taste
4 eggs, beaten
2 (10-ounce) cans cream
   of chicken soup

Reserve the broth from the boiled chicken. Cut the chicken into bite-size pieces. Crumble the white bread and corn bread into a large bowl. Add the onion, celery, sage, salt and pepper and mix well. Add a mixture of the eggs and soup and mix well. Pour in 2 soup cans of the warm reserved chicken broth. Stir in the chicken. Place the mixture in a slow cooker. Dot with 2 tablespoons of butter. Cook on Medium for 4 hours. Yield: 12 to 16 servings.

Syble Ann Shoults, Xi Alpha Xi
Bessemer, Alabama

CORN BREAD DRESSING

This is a wonderful recipe for those who cannot tolerate gluten. Use the dressing to stuff a 10- to 12-pound turkey, or bake in a baking dish as described in the recipe.

2 cups chopped celery
1 cup chopped onion
1/2 cup (1 stick) butter or
   margarine
6 cups corn bread, cubed
1 tablespoon sage
1 tablespoon poultry
   seasoning
Chopped cooked poultry
   giblets (optional)
2 eggs, lightly beaten
1 cup chicken broth

Sauté the celery and onion in the butter until tender. Combine the onion mixture, corn bread, sage, poultry seasoning and giblets in a large bowl and mix well. Add a mixture of the eggs and chicken broth to the corn bread mixture and stir gently. Place in a greased 2-quart casserole. Bake, covered, at 400 degrees for 20 minutes. Bake, uncovered, for 10 minutes longer. Yield: 8 to 10 servings.

Phyllis Kraich, Laureate Beta Epsilon
Akron, Colorado

Pat Crockett, Laureate Alpha, Myrtle Creek, Oregon, makes Garlic Cheese Grits by cooking 1 cup grits according to package directions, stirring in 12 ounces garlic cheese and 1/4 cup margarine until melted, pouring into a greased casserole, topping with 1/2 cup cracker crumbs, and baking at 350 degrees for 1 hour.

RHUBARB STUFFING

Rhubarb is plentiful in the spring in Pennsylvania. I freeze it in 5-cup containers so I will have it for Thanksgiving. Guests can never guess the special ingredient, but they love this stuffing. You can use frozen rhubarb if you do not have access to fresh.

5 cups chopped rhubarb
1/2 cup sugar
1 medium onion,
   chopped
1/2 cup (1 stick) butter or
   margarine
3 cups corn bread
   stuffing mix
1/2 cup walnuts

Place the rhubarb and sugar in a large bowl and toss to combine. Sauté the onion in 2 tablespoons of the butter in a skillet over medium heat for 5 to 10 minutes or until tender. Stir into the rhubarb mixture. Add the stuffing mix and walnuts and mix gently. Melt the remaining 6 tablespoons butter. Drizzle over the stuffing mixture and toss lightly. Spoon into a greased 2-quart baking dish. Bake, uncovered, at 325 degrees for 40 to 45 minutes or until the stuffing is heated through and top is browned.
Yield: 6 to 8 servings.

Connie R. Nygren, Lambda Chi
Danville, Pennsylvania

HOLIDAY SAGE DRESSING

1 (16-ounce) package
   butter crackers
1 1/2 pounds gizzards
Turkey neck
1 1/2 large onions
1 1/2 cups cut-up celery
4 hard-cooked eggs
3 teaspoons poultry
   seasoning
1 tablespoon sage
1 (4-ounce) can oysters,
   coarsely chopped
   (optional)

Crush the butter crackers in a large bowl. Boil the gizzards and neck in water until tender. Remove the gizzards and neck, reserving the broth. Remove the meat from the neck. Process the gizzards and neck meat in a food processor until finely chopped. Add to the butter crackers. Process the onions, celery and eggs until finely chopped. Stir into the cracker mixture. Stir in the poultry seasoning, sage and oysters. Add enough water to the reserved broth to make 4 cups. Add to the stuffing mixture and mix well. Bake at 350 degrees in a nonstick 9×13-inch baking dish for 20 to 30 minutes or until heated through and lightly browned. Yield: 12 to 15 servings.

Mary Bryan, Theta Chi
Steinhatchee, Florida

SCALLOPED OYSTERS

This recipe can be halved and baked in an 8-inch-square baking dish.

4 (8-ounce) cans oysters
4 cups coarse cracker
   crumbs
1 cup (2 sticks) butter or
   margarine, melted
Pepper to taste

1½ cups nondairy
   canned milk
½ teaspoon
   Worcestershire sauce
1 teaspoon salt

Drain the oysters, reserving ½ cup of the liquid. Combine the crumbs and butter in a bowl and mix well. Layer ⅓ of the crumb mixture and ½ of the oysters in a greased 9×13-inch baking dish. Sprinkle with pepper. Repeat the layers and sprinkle with pepper. Layer the remaining ⅓ of the crumbs over the top. Drizzle with a mixture of the reserved oyster liquid, canned milk, Worcestershire sauce and salt. Bake at 350 degrees for 40 to 60 minutes or until golden brown. Yield: 8 to 12 servings.

Peggy Mead, Xi Zeta Psi
Moberly, Missouri

SCALLOPED APPLES

10 cups sliced peeled
   tart apples (about 8
   medium)
⅓ cup sugar
2 tablespoons
   cornstarch

½ to 1 teaspoon
   cinnamon
¼ teaspoon nutmeg
2 tablespoons butter or
   margarine

Place the apples in a 2½-quart microwave-safe bowl. Combine the sugar, cornstarch, cinnamon and nutmeg in a small bowl and mix well. Sprinkle over the apples and toss to coat. Dot with butter. Microwave, covered, on high for 15 minutes or until apples are tender, stirring every 5 minutes. Yield: 8 servings.

Melissa La Hay, Alpha Delta Psi
Park Hills, Missouri

CRANBERRY JAM

Jars of this Cranberry Jam make great holiday gifts.

1 (10-ounce) package
   frozen strawberries,
   thawed
1 medium orange, seeded

2 cups cranberries
¼ cup water
3 cups sugar
½ bottle of pectin

Crush the strawberries. Process the orange and cranberries in a food processor until finely chopped. Combine the finely chopped orange and cranberries with the strawberries, water and sugar in a large saucepan over low heat. Cook for 2 minutes, stirring constantly. Bring to a boil. Boil hard for 1 minute, stirring constantly. Remove from heat. Stir in the pectin. Skim and stir for 4 to 5 minutes to prevent fruit from floating. Pour into hot sterilized jelly jars; seal with 2-piece lids. Process in a boiling water bath for 10 minutes. Yield: 3 pints.

Mildred M. Steeves, Preceptor Alpha Lambda
Emporia, Kansas

CRANBERRY PEAR RELISH

This Thanksgiving relish looks beautiful when served in a crystal pedestal dish.

1½ cups sugar
½ cup water
3 cups cranberries
2 medium pears, cored,
   cubed (about 2 cups)
½ teaspoon nutmeg

½ teaspoon allspice
4 inches stick cinnamon
Bay leaves (optional)
Strips of lemon peel
   (optional)

Combine the sugar and water in a large saucepan. Bring to a boil, stirring constantly until sugar is dissolved. Boil, uncovered, for 5 minutes. Stir in the cranberries, pears, nutmeg, allspice and cinnamon sticks. Return to a boil. Boil for 3 to 4 minutes or until cranberry skins pop, stirring frequently. Remove from heat. Pour into a bowl. Chill, covered, until serving time. Remove cinnamon sticks before serving. Garnish with bay leaves and lemon peel. Yield: 3¼ cups.

Marie Beck, Alpha Epsilon
Plymouth, Minnesota

ALL-BRAN BREAD

4 cups All-Bran cereal
2 cups raisins
2 cups molasses
½ cup (1 stick)
   margarine
3 cups boiling water

4 eggs
4 cups flour
4 teaspoons baking soda
2 teaspoons salt
3 teaspoons cinnamon

Combine the cereal, raisins, molasses, margarine and boiling water in a very large bowl and mix well. Let stand until cool. Add the eggs and mix well. Sift the flour, baking soda, salt and cinnamon together. Stir into the egg mixture. Pour into four 5×9-inch loaf pans. Bake at 350 degrees for 40 to 45 minutes or until bread tests done. Yield: 4 loaves.

Vera M. Bangert Rohan, Laureate Zeta
Mesa, Arizona

PUMPKIN COFFEE CAKE

1/4 cup packed brown sugar	1 cup sour cream
1/4 cup sugar	1 cup canned or cooked pumpkin
1/2 teaspoon cinnamon	1 teaspoon vanilla
2 tablespoons cold butter or margarine	2 cups flour
1/2 cup chopped pecans	1/2 teaspoon pumpkin pie spice
1/2 cup (1 stick) butter or margarine, softened	1 teaspoon baking soda
1 cup sugar	1 teaspoon baking powder
2 eggs	1/4 teaspoon salt

Combine the brown sugar, 1/4 cup sugar and cinnamon in a small bowl. Cut in 2 tablespoons butter until the mixture resembles coarse crumbs. Stir in the pecans. Cream 1/2 cup butter and 1 cup sugar in a mixing bowl until light and fluffy. Add the eggs 1 at a time, beating well after each addition. Combine the sour cream, pumpkin and vanilla in a separate bowl and mix well. Combine the flour, pumpkin pie spice, baking soda, baking powder and salt and mix well. Add the dry ingredients to the egg mixture alternately with the sour cream mixture, blending well after each addition. Pour into a greased and floured 9×13-inch baking pan. Sprinkle with the pecan mixture. Bake at 325 degrees for 40 to 50 minutes or until a wooden pick inserted near the center comes out clean. Yield: 16 to 20 servings.

Maureen Armstrong, Xi Gamma
Auburn, Maine

GERMAN STREUSEL KUCHEN

1 cup (2 sticks) butter, softened	2 teaspoons vanilla extract
1 cup plus 2 tablespoons sugar	1 (20-ounce) jar apricot preserves
4 eggs	2 1/2 cups flour
4 cups flour	3/4 cup sugar
1 tablespoon baking powder	1/4 teaspoon cinnamon
3/4 cup milk	1 cup (2 sticks) butter, softened

Cream 1 cup butter and 1 cup plus 2 tablespoons sugar in a mixing bowl until light and fluffy. Add the eggs 1 at a time, beating well after each addition. Mix the flour and baking powder together. Beginning and ending with the flour mixture, add the flour mixture and milk alternately, mixing well after each addition. Stir in the vanilla. Spread in a greased 11 1/2×17 1/2-inch baking dish. Spread the apricot preserves over the batter. Combine 2 1/2 cups flour, 3/4 cup sugar and cinnamon in a bowl and mix well. Cut 1 cup butter into the cinnamon mixture until the mixture resembles coarse crumbs. Sprinkle evenly over the apricot jam layer. Bake at 375 degrees for 40 to 45 minutes or until the cake tests done. Yield: 12 to 14 servings.

Shirley J. Duffey, Laureate Epsilon Kappa
Lady Lake, Florida

OATMEAL BREAD

Excellent for leftover turkey sandwiches.

1 cup (heaping) quick-cooking oats	1 cake yeast
1 tablespoon butter	3/4 cup warm water
1 tablespoon salt	1/2 cup molasses
2 3/4 cups boiling water	8 cups flour

Combine the oats, butter and salt in a large bowl. Add the boiling water and mix well. Let stand until lukewarm. Dissolve the yeast in 3/4 cup warm water. Add the yeast mixture and molasses to the oat mixture and mix well. Add the flour and mix well. Let rise in the bowl, covered, until doubled in bulk. Knead 5 to 10 strokes on a floured surface. Shape into loaves and place in 3 buttered loaf pans. Let rise, covered, until doubled in bulk. Bake at 350 degrees for 1 hour or until bread tests done. Yield: 3 loaves.

Jean Van Stelten, Epsilon Master
Manchester, New Hampshire

PUMPKIN BREAD

I use this delicious bread as the center of my "gift plates" for the holidays.

1/2 cup (1 stick) margarine, softened	1 teaspoon cinnamon
8 ounces cream cheese, softened	1/2 teaspoon baking powder
2 1/2 cups sugar	1/4 teaspoon ground cloves
4 eggs	1 cup chopped walnuts or pecans
1 (16-ounce) can pumpkin	2 cups confectioners' sugar
3 1/2 cups flour	3 tablespoons milk
2 teaspoons baking soda	
1 teaspoon salt	

Cream the margarine, cream cheese and sugar in a mixing bowl until light and fluffy. Add the eggs 1 at a time, mixing well after each addition. Add the pumpkin and mix well. Combine the flour, baking soda, salt, cinnamon, baking powder and cloves in a bowl and mix well. Add the dry ingredients gradually to the pumpkin mixture, stirring until moistened. Stir in the nuts. Pour into 2 greased and floured 9-inch loaf pans. Bake at 350 degrees for 1 hour or until a wooden pick inserted in the center comes out clean. Remove the loaves to a wire rack. Let cool for 5 to 10 minutes. Drizzle a mixture of the confectioners' sugar and milk over the loaves. Yield: 2 loaves.

Denise Monette, Xi Theta
Socorro, New Mexico

SWEET POTATO BREAD

1¹/₂ cups self-rising flour
1 cup sugar
¹/₂ teaspoon cinnamon
1 teaspoon nutmeg
¹/₂ cup vegetable oil
2 tablespoons milk
2 eggs

1 cup mashed cooked
*   sweet potatoes*
1 cup chopped pecans
¹/₂ cup golden raisins,
*   dates or dried*
*   cranberries*

Combine the flour, sugar, cinnamon and nutmeg in a large bowl and mix well. Combine the oil, milk and eggs in a small bowl and blend well. Add the egg mixture to the dry ingredients and stir until moistened. Add the sweet potatoes, pecans and raisins and mix well. Pour into a 9-inch loaf pan sprayed with nonstick cooking spray. Bake at 350 degrees for 1 hour and 15 minutes. Remove from the pan. Cool on a wire rack. Yield: 12 servings.

Linda M. Tucker, Xi Gamma Pi
Lafayette, Tennessee

BRAN MUFFINS

These low-fat, low-sugar muffins are healthful as well as delicious.

1¹/₂ cups 100% bran
*   cereal*
1 cup skim milk
¹/₂ cup flour
¹/₂ cup whole wheat
*   flour*
¹/₃ cup sugar

2¹/₂ teaspoons baking
*   powder*
¹/₂ teaspoon baking soda
¹/₂ teaspoon salt
1 egg or egg substitute
¹/₄ cup vegetable oil

Preheat the oven to 400 degrees. Combine the cereal and milk in a medium bowl. Let stand for 5 minutes. Combine the flours, sugar, baking powder, baking soda and salt in a small bowl and stir well. Stir the egg and oil into the cereal mixture. Add the flour mixture, stirring just until moistened; do not overmix. Fill 12 buttered muffin cups ²/₃ full. Bake for 18 to 20 minutes or until muffins test done. Yield: 12 servings.

Jean Hoehn, Laureate Epsilon Alpha
Lynn Haven, Florida

PRALINE MUFFINS

1 cup coarsely chopped
*   pecans*
1 cup packed light
*   brown sugar*
¹/₂ cup flour
¹/₄ teaspoon baking
*   powder*

¹/₄ teaspoon salt
2 eggs
¹/₂ teaspoon vanilla
*   extract*
2 tablespoons butter,
*   melted*

Combine the pecans, brown sugar, flour, baking powder and salt in a bowl and mix well. Add a mixture of the eggs, vanilla and butter and mix well. Fill greased muffin cups ¹/₂ full. Bake at 300 degrees for 20 to 30 minutes or until muffins test done. Yield: 6 servings.

K. K. Davis, Alpha Delta
Searcy, Arkansas

BEST APPLE CAKE

1 (2-layer) yellow
*   cake mix*
10 medium Granny
*   Smith apples*

¹/₂ cup sugar
2 tablespoons cinnamon

Prepare the cake mix using the package directions; pour the batter into a greased 10×15-inch cake pan. Pat out any bubbles in the batter. Peel, core and slice the apples. Arrange the apple wedges rounded side up over the batter. Sprinkle a mixture of sugar and cinnamon evenly over the top. Bake at 375 degrees for 55 to 60 minutes or until the cake tests done. Serve warm with whipped cream or ice cream. Yield: 24 servings.

Karen H. Berg
Chino Valley, Arizona

APPLE CAKE

3 cups flour
1 teaspoon baking soda
1 teaspoon salt
1 to 2 teaspoons
*   vegetable oil*
2 cups sugar, or 1 cup
*   brown sugar*

1 large egg
3 cups chopped peeled
*   apples*
2 teaspoons vanilla
*   extract*
1 cup chopped walnuts
¹/₂ teaspoon allspice

Combine the flour, baking soda, salt, oil, sugar, egg, apples, vanilla, walnuts and allspice in a bowl and mix well. Pour into a greased and floured tube pan. Bake at 325 degrees for 1 hour and 10 to 15 minutes or until the cake tests done. Cool in the pan for 10 minutes. Invert onto a serving plate. Yield: 4 to 6 servings.

Cynde Fischer, Xi Beta Phi
Bend, Oregon

❖ CARROT CAKE

2 cups sugar	3 large carrots, grated
1½ cups vegetable oil	1 cup chopped black
2 cups self-rising flour	walnuts
1 teaspoon vanilla	1 cup sugar
extract	½ cup buttermilk
½ teaspoon cinnamon	½ teaspoon baking soda
4 eggs	1 tablespoon corn syrup

Combine 2 cups sugar, oil, flour, vanilla and cinnamon in a large bowl and mix well by hand. Add the eggs and beat well. Stir in the carrots and nuts. Pour into a lightly greased tube pan. Bake at 350 degrees for 1 hour and 15 minutes. Remove the cake from the oven. Combine 1 cup sugar, buttermilk, baking soda and corn syrup in a saucepan over medium heat. Bring to a boil. Pour over the warm cake still in the pan. Let cool completely in the pan on a wire rack. Remove from the pan. Yield: 15 servings.

Teresa L. Toler, Xi Gamma Epsilon
Bidwell, Ohio

HARVEST CAKE

This pumpkin cake with its warm feeling is great for October and November family get-togethers. Remember, the cake must be cooled completely before frosting.

2 cups sugar	½ cup (1 stick) butter,
2 cups canned pumpkin	softened
1¼ cups vegetable oil	8 ounces cream cheese,
4 eggs	softened
2 cups flour	1 pound confectioners'
1 teaspoon salt	sugar
2 teaspoons cinnamon	1 teaspoon vanilla
2 teaspoons baking soda	extract
2 teaspoons baking	½ cup chopped pecans
powder	

Combine the sugar, pumpkin and oil in a large mixing bowl and mix well. Add the eggs 1 at a time, beating for 1 minute after each addition. Stir in a mixture of the flour, salt, cinnamon, baking soda and baking powder and mix well. Pour into a greased and floured 9×13-inch baking pan. Bake at 350 degrees for 35 to 45 minutes or until cake tests done. Cool completely in the pan on a wire rack. Blend the butter and cream cheese together in a bowl. Add the confectioners' sugar and vanilla and beat until creamy. Stir in the pecans. Frost the cooled cake. Yield: 12 to 15 servings.

Kathryn D. Brown, Preceptor Epsilon Theta
St. Petersburg, Florida

PUMPKIN PECAN CAKE

2 cups crushed vanilla	4 eggs
wafers (about 50)	⅔ cup (1⅓ sticks) butter
1 cup chopped pecans	or margarine,
¾ cup (1½ sticks) butter	softened
or margarine,	3 ounces cream cheese,
softened	softened
1 (18-ounce) package	3 cups confectioners'
spice cake mix	sugar
1 (16-ounce) can solid-	2 teaspoons vanilla
pack pumpkin	extract
¼ cup butter or	½ cup caramel ice cream
margarine, softened	topping

Beat the vanilla wafers, pecans and ¾ cup butter in a mixing bowl at medium speed for 1 minute or until crumbly. Press into 3 greased and floured 9-inch round cake pans. Combine the cake mix, pumpkin, ¼ cup butter and eggs in a large mixing bowl and beat at medium speed for 3 minutes. Spread over the vanilla wafer layer in each pan. Bake at 350 degrees for 30 minutes or until a wooden pick inserted near the center comes out clean. Cool in the pans for 10 minutes. Remove to a wire rack to cool completely. Combine ⅔ cup butter, cream cheese, confectioners' sugar and vanilla in a small mixing bowl. Beat for 3 minutes or until light and fluffy. Spread the frosting thinly between the three layers and over the top and side of the cooled cake. Spread the caramel topping over the top of the cake, allowing some to drip down around the side. Keep refrigerated. Yield: 16 to 20 servings.

Eileen Ayers, Alpha Theta Master
Lakeland, Florida

CREAM SHERRY CAKE

1 (2-layer) package	½ cup vegetable oil
yellow cake mix	1 teaspoon nutmeg
1 (4-ounce) package	¾ cup Bristol cream
instant vanilla	sherry
pudding mix	Confectioners' sugar
4 eggs, beaten	to taste

Combine the cake mix and pudding mix in a large bowl. Beat in the eggs. Add the oil, nutmeg and sherry and mix well. Pour into a greased and floured bundt pan. Bake at 350 degrees for 45 minutes to 1 hour or until cake springs back from a gentle touch. Cool in the pan for 30 minutes. Remove to a serving plate and sprinkle with confectioners' sugar. Yield: 16 to 24 servings.

Willie Mae Coffman, Iota Master
New Braunfels, Texas

CHOCOLATE CHIP OATMEAL COOKIES

You can make a Chocolate Chip Oatmeal Cookie Jar to give as a gift. Layer the flour, chocolate chips, pecans, raisins, oats, baking soda, and sugars in a quart jar. Add the lid and a circle of cloth tied with a ribbon. Include the recipe!

1¼ cups whole wheat pastry flour
1 cup semisweet chocolate chips
½ cup chopped pecans
½ cup raisins
1½ cups rolled oats
½ teaspoon baking soda
¼ cup sugar
½ cup packed brown sugar
1 tablespoon vanilla extract
1 tablespoon milk
1 egg
½ cup (1 stick) butter, softened, or shortening

Combine the flour, chocolate chips, pecans, raisins, oats, baking soda, sugar and brown sugar in a large bowl and mix well. Add the vanilla, milk, egg and butter and mix well. Drop by teaspoonfuls on a non-stick cookie sheet. Bake at 350 degrees for 10 minutes. Yield: about 4 dozen.

Patricia Hart, Alpha Omega
Paris, Tennessee

CRANBERRY OAT SQUARES

1½ cups pre-sifted flour
¼ teaspoon baking soda
1 cup packed brown sugar
1¾ cups rolled oats
¾ cup (1½ sticks) butter, softened
1 (15-ounce) can whole cranberry sauce

Combine the flour and baking soda in a large bowl and mix well. Add the brown sugar and oats and mix well. Work in the butter with your fingertips. Pat half the flour mixture in a lightly greased 9×9-inch baking pan. Spread the cranberry sauce evenly over the flour layer. Pat the remaining flour mixture evenly over the cranberry sauce. Bake at 375 degrees for 45 minutes. Cut into squares when cool. Yield: 20 squares.

Talifer-Jo Whitby, Laureate Gamma Nu
Richmond Hill, Ontario, Canada

Maxine Knecht, Xi Eta Pi, West Bend, Iowa, makes Apple Nut Pie by mixing ¾ cup flour, 1 cup packed brown sugar, 1½ teaspoons baking powder, ½ teaspoon salt, a dash of cinnamon, 2 eggs, and 1½ teaspoons vanilla extract. Add 1½ cups chopped peeled apples and ¾ cup nuts, pour into a greased pie plate, and bake at 350 degrees for 25 to 30 minutes. Serve with whipped cream or ice cream.

DATE RAISIN BARS

1⅓ cups flour
¼ teaspoon salt
1 teaspoon baking powder
2 cups chopped pitted dates
1 cup chopped walnuts
½ cup golden raisins
3 eggs, well beaten
1 cup light corn syrup
1 teaspoon vanilla extract
Confectioners' sugar

Sift the flour, salt and baking powder into a bowl. Stir in the dates, walnuts and raisins. Blend the eggs, corn syrup and vanilla together in another bowl. Add to the flour mixture and mix well. Spread in a greased 9×13-inch baking pan. Bake at 350 degrees for 45 minutes or until light brown. Cut into bars when cool. Roll in confectioners' sugar. Store in an airtight container. Yield: 3 dozen.

Mary D. McDermitt, Xi Epsilon Rho
St. Marys, Ohio

PECAN PIE BARS

1 (2-layer) package yellow cake mix
½ cup (1 stick) margarine, melted
3 eggs
½ cup packed brown sugar
1½ cups dark corn syrup
1 teaspoon vanilla extract
1 cup chopped pecans

Butter the bottom and sides of a 9×13-inch baking pan. Set aside ⅔ cup of the dry cake mix. Combine the remaining dry cake mix, margarine and 1 of the eggs in a large mixing bowl and mix until crumbly. Press into the prepared pan. Bake at 350 degrees for 10 to 15 minutes. Combine the brown sugar, corn syrup, vanilla and remaining 2 eggs in a mixing bowl. Beat at medium speed for 1 to 2 minutes. Spread over the partially baked crust. Sprinkle with the pecans. Return to the oven and bake for 30 to 35 minutes longer or until golden brown. Serve with whipped topping. Yield: 12 to 18 servings.

Donna L. Cotter, Preceptor Phi
Madison, Wisconsin

Shay Gebauer, Mu, Sioux City, Iowa, makes Old-Fashioned Butterscotch Filling for pouring into a graham cracker crust and topping with meringue, or for serving as pudding. Brown ⅓ cup butter in a saucepan. Blend in 1 cup sugar, ¼ cup flour and ½ teaspoon salt. Add 2 cups milk and 2 egg yolks and cook until thickened, stirring constantly. Add 1 teaspoon vanilla extract.

SPICE ROCK COOKIES

2¹/₂ cups flour	3 eggs, well beaten
¹/₄ teaspoon salt	1 teaspoon baking soda
1 teaspoon cinnamon	1 tablespoon hot water
1¹/₂ cups packed brown sugar	1 cup dates or raisins
¹/₂ cup shortening or low-fat margarine	1 cup chopped pecans or walnuts

Sift the flour, salt and cinnamon together. Cream the brown sugar and shortening in a mixing bowl until light and fluffy. Beat in the eggs. Add the sifted dry ingredients; mix well. Mix the baking soda and hot water and stir into the flour mixture. Stir in the dates and nuts. Drop by teaspoonfuls onto a greased cookie sheet. Bake at 350 degrees for about 12 minutes or until done. Yield: 3 dozen.

June D. Andrews, Preceptor Chi
Covington, Virginia

PEACH TART

Cheesecake lovers love this recipe . . . and it can be made very low-fat! Just use fat-free condensed milk, light sour cream, and a sugar-free graham cracker crust.

1 (7-ounce) can sliced peaches	1 teaspoon lemon juice
1 cup sour cream	1 (9-inch) graham cracker pie shell
1 (8-ounce) can sweetened condensed milk	¹/₄ cup chopped almonds

Drain the peaches, reserving 5 tablespoons of the syrup. Combine the sour cream and condensed milk in a bowl and blend well. Add the reserved peach syrup and lemon juice and blend well. Pour into the pie shell. Top with the almonds and the peaches. Bake at 350 degrees for 20 to 25 minutes or until set. Let cool slightly before serving. Yield: 6 to 8 servings.

Cindy Mathis, Laureate Zeta
Houston, Texas

CHOCOLATE PECAN PIE

1 cup (2 sticks) margarine	1 cup chopped pecans
2 cups sugar	4 eggs, beaten
1 cup semisweet chocolate chips	2 unbaked (9-inch) pie shells

Melt the margarine in a large saucepan over low heat. Add the sugar and stir until dissolved. Add the chocolate chips and heat until melted, stirring constantly. Stir in the pecans. Remove from heat and cool slightly. Add the eggs and mix well. Pour into the pie shells. Bake at 350 degrees for 45 minutes. Yield: 12 servings.

Shirley Smith, Laureate Delta Omicron
Pace, Florida

SUGARLESS APPLE PIE

1 (2-crust) pie pastry	1¹/₂ teaspoons cinnamon
1 (14-ounce) can water-pack sliced apples	¹/₃ teaspoon nutmeg
13 packets artificial sweetener	³/₄ teaspoon ground cloves
2 tablespoons cornstarch	Dash of ginger (optional)
	1 tablespoon butter

Unfold the pastry into a pie plate. Fit pastry into plate and trim edge. Drain the apples and pour into the pie shell. Combine 12 packets of the artificial sweetener, cornstarch, cinnamon, nutmeg, cloves and ginger in a bowl and mix well. Sprinkle over the apples. Dot with butter. Top with the remaining pastry, sealing edge and cutting vents. Sprinkle additional cinnamon and the remaining packet of artificial sweetener over the top pastry. Bake at 425 degrees for 30 to 45 minutes or until golden brown. Yield: 6 to 8 servings.

Gayle Osburn, Delta Xi
Blanchard, Oklahoma

PUMPKIN ICE CREAM PIE

1¹/₂ cups crumbled gingersnaps	³/₄ teaspoon cinnamon
¹/₃ cup melted butter	¹/₂ teaspoon nutmeg
1 quart vanilla ice cream	¹/₄ teaspoon ground cloves
1 cup canned pumpkin	¹/₂ teaspoon salt
¹/₂ cup packed brown sugar	Whipped cream (optional)

Mix the cookie crumbs and butter together in a bowl. Press over the bottom and up the side of a 9-inch pie plate sprayed with nonstick cooking spray. Chill, covered, until ready to use. Stir the ice cream in a large bowl until slightly softened. Add the next 6 ingredients and mix well. Spread the ice cream mixture in the prepared pie plate. Freeze for 4 hours or until firm. Spread whipped cream over the surface of the ice cream filling before or after freezing. Garnish with a few crumbs of gingersnaps if desired. Let stand at room temperature for 5 to 10 minutes before serving. Yield: 8 servings.

Margaret Gebhardt, Alpha Epsilon
Minneapolis, Minnesota

PIE CRUST

My husband's grandmother gave me this recipe 32 years ago, and it has never failed. Use for any pie, cobbler, or tart recipe.

2¹/₂ cups flour
1 teaspoon salt
2 tablespoons sugar
1 cup shortening
²/₃ cup milk
1 egg yolk

Mix the flour, salt and sugar together in a large bowl. Cut in the shortening with a pastry blender until mixture resembles coarse crumbs. Beat the milk and egg yolk together with a fork. Add the yolk mixture to the flour mixture and stir until well mixed. Shape into a ball. Use immediately or chill, wrapped in plastic wrap, until ready to use.
Yield: 2 (2-layer) pie pastries.

Peggy Jourden, Preceptor Alpha
Albuquerque, New Mexico

ORANGE-GLAZED PUMPKIN PIE

2 cups canned pumpkin
1 cup packed light
    brown sugar
³/₄ teaspoon salt
2 eggs
2 tablespoons grated
    orange zest
¹/₂ teaspoon ground
    cloves
1¹/₂ teaspoons cinnamon
¹/₂ teaspoon mace
¹/₄ cup boiling water
1¹/₂ cups evaporated
    milk
1 unbaked (9-inch) pie
    shell
¹/₄ cup orange juice
4 teaspoons cornstarch
¹/₄ cup sugar
2 tablespoons water
¹/₃ cup evaporated milk

Combine the pumpkin, brown sugar, salt, eggs and 1 tablespoon of the orange zest in a large bowl and mix well. Combine the cloves, cinnamon, mace and boiling water in a small bowl and mix well. Stir into the pumpkin mixture. Add the 1¹/₂ cups evaporated milk gradually, stirring until well blended. Pour into the pie shell. Bake at 375 degrees for 50 to 55 minutes or until set. Heat the orange juice in a saucepan over low heat. Combine the cornstarch and sugar in a small bowl and stir in enough of the 2 tablespoons water to make a smooth paste. Stir gradually into the orange juice. Stir in the remaining 1 tablespoon orange zest and a pinch of salt. Cook over low heat until thick and clear, stirring constantly. Cool slightly. Stir in the ¹/₃ cup evaporated milk. Spread over the cooled pumpkin pie, leaving a 1-inch border free of the orange glaze. Garnish with fresh orange sections.
Yield: 6 to 8 servings.

Jeanette A. Foor, Alpha Alpha
Altoona, Pennsylvania

PUMPKIN CREAM PIE

³/₄ cup cold milk
1 (4-ounce) package
    instant vanilla
    pudding mix
¹/₂ cup solid-pack
    pumpkin
³/₄ teaspoon pumpkin pie
    spice
²/₃ cup semisweet
    chocolate chips
3¹/₂ cups whipped
    topping
1 (9-inch) graham
    cracker pie shell

Pour the milk into a mixing bowl. Add the pudding mix and whisk for 1 minute or until blended. Let stand for 5 minutes. Blend in the pumpkin, spice, chocolate chips and 2 cups of the whipped topping. Spoon into the pie crust. Chill, covered, for 4 hours. Garnish with the remaining whipped topping and additional chocolate chips. Yield: 8 servings.

Betty Jo Benuche, Laureate Beta
Bradenton, Florida

SUGAR-FREE PUMPKIN PIE

1 cup cold 2% milk
1 (16-ounce) can
    pumpkin
1 teaspoon cinnamon
¹/₄ teaspoon ground
    cloves
¹/₂ teaspoon ginger
1 small package vanilla
    instant sugar-free
    pudding mix
1 (9-inch) graham
    cracker pie shell

Pour the milk into a large bowl. Add the pumpkin, cinnamon, cloves, ginger and pudding mix and whisk until well blended. Pour into the pie shell. Chill, covered, for 4 hours. Yield: 6 to 8 servings.

Naomi E. Golden, Alpha Nu Master
Van Buren, Ohio

❖ PUMPKIN BREAD PUDDING

6 cups bread cubes,
    toasted
2 cups half-and-half
1¹/₂ cups sugar
3 large eggs, lightly
    beaten
1 (15-ounce) can
    pumpkin
¹/₂ cup raisins
¹/₂ cup chopped pecans
3 tablespoons butter,
    melted
2 teaspoons pumpkin
    pie spice
1 teaspoon grated
    orange zest

Layer the bread cubes in a lightly greased 7×11-inch baking dish. Pour the half-and-half over the bread. Combine the remaining ingredients in a bowl and mix well. Fold gently into the bread mixture. Bake at 350 degrees for 50 to 60 minutes or until set and lightly browned. Serve with whipped cream.
Yield: 8 servings.

Natasha Kellerman, Beta Gamma
Batesville, Indiana

PUMPKIN CHEESECAKE

12 (2¹/₂-inch-square)
honey graham
crackers, crushed
1¹/₃ cups instant non-fat
dry milk
³/₄ cup part-skim ricotta
cheese
³/₄ cup egg substitute
²/₃ cup 1% cottage cheese
¹/₂ cup canned pumpkin
¹/₄ cup packed light
brown sugar
1 tablespoon lemon
juice
¹/₂ teaspoon cinnamon
¹/₂ teaspoon vanilla
extract

Sprinkle the cracker crumbs evenly over the bottom of an 8-inch springform pan sprayed with nonstick cooking spray. Combine the dry milk, ricotta cheese, egg substitute, cottage cheese, pumpkin, brown sugar, lemon juice, cinnamon and vanilla in a blender or food processor container. Process until smooth. Pour into the prepared pan, reserving ¹/₄ cup of the pumpkin batter. Drizzle the reserved batter in circles over the main batter. Bake at 350 degrees for 50 to 60 minutes or until a knife inserted near the center comes out clean. Let cool. Chill, covered, until serving time. Yield: 8 servings.

Ann-Joy Hardy, Xi Zeta Iota
Winter Haven, Florida

PUMPKIN FLAN

1¹/₃ cups sugar
6 eggs
2 cups canned or cooked
pumpkin
³/₄ teaspoon salt
¹/₂ teaspoon ginger
¹/₂ teaspoon cinnamon
¹/₄ teaspoon allspice
2 cups heavy cream

Combine ²/₃ cup of the sugar and ¹/₄ cup water in a small skillet. Bring to a boil. Boil until sugar dissolves, stirring and washing down any sugar crystals clinging to the side of the pan with a brush dipped in cold water. Cook the syrup over medium heat until a deep caramel color, swirling the skillet. Pour into a 2-quart glass loaf pan, tilting the pan to coat the bottom evenly. Let the caramel stand to harden. Combine the eggs with the remaining ²/₃ cup sugar in a bowl and mix well. Beat in the pumpkin, salt, ginger, cinnamon, allspice and cream. Pour over the caramel layer in the pan. Set the pan into a larger pan of hot water; water should reach halfway up the side of the loaf pan. Bake in the water bath at 350 degrees for 1¹/₄ hours. Remove from oven and let cool. Chill, covered, for 8 to 12 hours before serving. Run a thin knife around the edge of the pan and invert onto a serving plate. Serve sliced, accompanied by cinnamon whipped cream. Yield: 10 servings.

Ethel Armitage, Laureate Beta Delta
Delta, British Columbia, Canada

PUMPKIN PARFAIT

1 cup crushed ginger
snaps
¹/₄ cup sugar
1¹/₄ cups margarine,
melted
1 cup packed brown
sugar
2 teaspoons cinnamon
¹/₄ teaspoon ground
cloves
3 cups canned pumpkin
¹/₂ teaspoon salt
¹/₂ teaspoon ginger
2 quarts vanilla ice
cream or frozen
yogurt, softened

Combine the cookie crumbs, sugar and margarine in a small bowl and mix well. Press into a 9×13-inch baking dish sprayed with nonstick cooking spray. Combine the brown sugar, cinnamon, cloves, pumpkin, salt, ginger and ice cream in a large bowl and mix well. Pour over the crumb layer. Sprinkle with additional cookie crumbs. Freeze until firm, about 4 hours. Serve topped with whipped cream.
Yield: 12 to 16 servings.

Pamela Toews
Albany, Oregon

PUMPKIN PIE CAKE

2 (15-ounce) cans solid-
pack pumpkin
1 (13-ounce) can
evaporated milk
3 eggs
¹/₂ teaspoon salt
2 teaspoons pumpkin
pie spice
1 cup sugar
1 (2-layer) yellow
cake mix
1³/₄ sticks margarine,
melted
1 cup chopped pecans

Combine the pumpkin, evaporated milk, eggs, salt, pumpkin pie spice and sugar in a bowl and mix well. Pour into a buttered 9×13-inch glass baking dish. Sprinkle the dry cake mix evenly over the pumpkin layer. Drizzle the margarine evenly over the cake mix layer. Bake at 350 degrees for 25 minutes. Sprinkle the pecans over the cake. Return to the oven and bake for 25 minutes longer. Serve hot or cold with whipped topping. Yield: 18 servings.

Verna Edgemon Green, Preceptor Mu Omega
Weslaco, Texas

Marsha Bertsch, Preceptor Alpha Gamma, Yankton, South Dakota, makes Berry-Filled Amaretto Cream Cups. Combine 8 ounces softened cream cheese, ¹/₂ cup sugar, and ¹/₄ cup amaretto in a bowl and blend until smooth and creamy. Fold in 1 cup unsweetened whipped cream. Spoon into 8 mounds on a waxed paper-lined tray and shape into shallow cups. Freeze until firm. Fill the frozen cups with a mixture of berries and serve immediately.

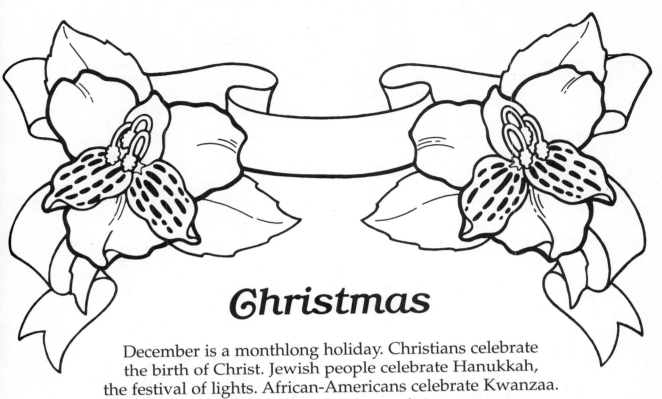

Christmas

December is a monthlong holiday. Christians celebrate
the birth of Christ. Jewish people celebrate Hanukkah,
the festival of lights. African-Americans celebrate Kwanzaa.
And some of our favorite holiday traditions come to us
from even earlier Germanic and Celtic peoples who
celebrated the winter solstice on December 21.
Their pagan customs included decorating with holly,
mistletoe, Yule logs, and wassail bowls. The Christmas tree
originated as the "paradise tree," a symbol for Eden.
The feast of St. Nicholas, the patron saint of children,
originally fell on December 6, and it was the Dutch who
introduced the idea of distributing gifts to tiny tots.
Every December brings opportunities for creating
new holiday traditions: warm family gatherings, parties
for friends, lovely decorations, cheerful music, and
tantalizing food. These ideas and recipes will
make every December event joyous.

CHRISTMAS MICE

*M*ake these adorable mice to perch on a plate of cookies or just to eat. Combine 2 cups of smooth peanut butter, ½ cup softened margarine, and 3 cups of confectioners' sugar in a bowl and mix until smooth. Divide into portions and shape each portion into a ball that can then be molded into a teardrop shape for the mouse body. Place the body on waxed paper and press lightly to flatten the back. Insert roasted peanut halves about a third of the way from the pointed end for ears, cinnamon red hots or small green candies for eyes, and another piece of candy for the nose. Attach a four-inch piece of licorice lace to the wide end for a tail. This will make about two dozen mice.

Deb Blaz, Xi Eta Epsilon
Angola, Indiana

CHRISTMAS MOBILES

*C*lose the hook of a wire coat hanger into a loop and pull the bottom wire down until the hanger elongates into a diamond shape. Dip yarn of any desired color into a solution of starch and wrap around the hanger, criss-crossing between opposite sides of the hanger. Secure the yarn and hang the hanger up to dry. Decorate the frame by adding small angels, miniature ornaments, or other seasonal items. The mobiles can be made for any season or holiday with a change in yarn color and decorations, such as flowers and butterflies for spring/Easter, or spiders and bats for Halloween.

To use the mobile as a centerpiece or table decoration, turn the framework upside-down, insert the loop in a flowerpot filled with florist foam, and attach the decorations.

Vivian Dehay, Preceptor
Santa Rosa, California

CINNAMON ORNAMENTS

*W*onderful-smelling, delightful ornaments to add to your traditional decorations are easy to make. Mix 3/4 cup of applesauce and a 4-ounce package of ground cinnamon in a bowl until the dough is very stiff. Roll out on a work surface to a ¼-inch thickness. Use cookie cutters of various shapes to cut out the ornaments. Make a hole in the top of each ornament with a straw or skewer. Place the ornaments carefully on a wire rack to dry. Let dry for a day or two, turning occasionally. Be sure that the ornaments are completely dry before threading ribbon or yarn through the holes for hanging. The ornaments can be painted with paste, food coloring, or frosting. This recipe will make twelve to fifteen ornaments.

Marcella Younker, Xi Alpha Tau
Knoxville, Iowa

HOLIDAY LANTERNS

*M*ake beautiful and useful lanterns from large, empty aluminum cans. Be sure that the tops have been removed carefully with a can opener to avoid sharp edges and snags. Small designs such as stars and crescent moons can be cut out with metal cutters, but children can make their own designs if the cans are filled with water and frozen. The ice will permit using a large nail or punch to hammer designs such as snowmen into the can without the can denting inward. A pair of holes at the top of the can on opposite sides will allow a wire handle to be added. Secure a candle to the inside bottom of the lantern.

During the Christmas holidays, we have a house full of children and each makes a lantern. On a nice evening we all go for a walk down the road and through the woods singing carols, the children toting their lanterns.

Donna Adams, Lambda Epsilon
Kenora, Ontario, Canada

WINE BOTTLE TREE

*M*ake a beautiful presentation for any bottled gift, such as bubble bath or lotion. Place a wine bottle in a small round basket. Measure the distance from the top of the basket to the top of the bottle. Double the measure. Cut a circle from lightweight cardboard, with a diameter equal to the doubled measurement. Make a cut from the outer edge to the center and overlap the cut edges to make a cone that fits over the bottle; secure the cone with tape or staples. Cover the cardboard cone with gift wrap, extending the wrap slightly inside the cone for a finished look. Cut two stars from the remaining gift wrap, glue wrong sides together with a toothpick or pipe cleaner between. Let the star dry, insert the toothpick in the top of the cone, and slip the cone over the bottle.

Roxanne E. Cooper, Xi Beta Mu
Elkins, West Virginia

LIGHTS AND SMELLS OF CHRISTMAS

*T*his is a great craft project for kids—quick, easy, and not very messy. Use a clean quart jar, making sure it is completely dry. Coil a 35-count string of tiny clear lights inside the jar, leaving the plug and attached length of cord outside the jar. Fill the jar with your favorite holiday potpourri. Secure a doily or piece of lace or net over the jar top with a rubber band. Tie a piece of ribbon over the rubber band. Plug in the lights and enjoy the glow and the fragrance.

Judy Moore, Preceptor Gamma Theta
Pendleton, Oregon

UNUSUAL CHRISTMAS WREATH

During the fall, pick dried cockleburrs—be sure to wear gloves as they are very prickly. Trim the stems to ¼ inch, dip the stem end in glue, and affix the burrs to a styrofoam wreath until it is completely covered. Glue on dried flowers of your choice to make a pleasing arrangement. When the glue is completely dry, spray the entire wreath with polyurethane, let it dry, and hang it up. When I give the wreaths as gifts, everyone loves them. This may sound strange, but the cockleburrs look like tiny pine cones and the wreaths are so sturdy that I have mounted them on stakes to use as grave decorations.

Marian Eastman, Laureate Lambda
Tendoy, Idaho

HOLIDAY PLACE MARKERS

Make simple, practical, and beautiful keepsake mementos of holiday fellowship. Use a plain colored Christmas ball for each person. Write each person's name on a ball with silver or gold marking pens. Add the date if you wish and arrange the balls to match your seating plan.

Kari Collett, Alpha Epsilon Nu
Warrensburg, Missouri

CANDLES IN THE FIREPLACE

Instead of a fire in your fireplace, make an arrangement of candles of varying heights, and of diameters greater than 2 inches. The more candles, the more dazzling the effect. You may arrange greenery such as evergreen, holly, or magnolia leaves or branches among the candles, but do not leave the fireplace unattended.

Sherri Griffis, Alpha Delta
Forest, Virginia

COUNTRY RUFFLE WREATHS

We made these as favors for our chapter's Breakfast with Santa. A couple of sisters who could sew did the basics, then everyone worked to assemble them.

These measurements will make two wreaths. Start with ⅛ yard of any seasonal calico print. Cut the fabric into two 2½-by-18-inch pieces using pinking shears. Fold one of the strips in half lengthwise with the right sides out and stitch a ⅜-inch seam to form a casing. Cut an 18-inch piece of ⅝-inch ribbon into two 9-inch pieces. Fold a pipe cleaner in half over a safety pin and thread the safety pin through the fabric casing to gather the fabric onto about 4 inches of the pipe cleaner; twist the ends of the pipe cleaner together to form a circular wreath. Shape the remaining length of the pipe cleaner into a hook or loop for hanging. Tie a ribbon piece into a bow and attach to the wreath with glue or a couple of stitches. Repeat with the remaining fabric, ribbon, and another pipe cleaner to make the second wreath.

Christine Berry, Delta Pi
Adrian, Missouri

CHRISTMAS TREE GARLAND

This garland is easy to make and can help customize a Christmas tree, window, or stairway to match your Christmas theme.

Select 1 yard each of three different fabrics. Cut the fabric into 1½-by-3-inch rectangles with pinking shears. Using a length of twine or ribbon, tie the rectangles alternately along the twine, then tie wood, plastic, or glass decorations at intervals of six to 12 inches along the garland. Scrunch the fabric rectangles close together for a fuller look or spread apart to let the twine or ribbon show through.

I have made these garlands using denim, eyelet, or handkerchief fabric for a country look. We have also made them by using gingham prints and adding tiny wood birdhouses.

Denise Monette, Xi Theta
Socorro, New Mexico

PUNCHBOWL CENTERPIECE

Make a pretty setting for your punchbowl by cutting a small slice from the bottoms of two oranges and three apples so they will sit levelly. Cut an indentation in the top of each to allow a tealight to fit inside. Place the punchbowl in the center of a large tray; arrange pine branches around the bowl and space the candleholder fruit around the bowl. Sprinkle a few fresh cranberries on the greens for additional color. Light the candles when the guests arrive. This is especially attractive with a cranberry punch.

Jan Schweer
Atlantic, Iowa

CHRISTMAS GIFT WRAP

Create your own customized wrapping paper by starting with brown wrapping paper, paper bags, or freezer paper. Use rubber stamps of any seasonal design such as gingerbread men, gum drops, evergreen trees, stars, etc. Ink pads come in many colors so the possibilities are endless. Children love to help prepare the wrapping paper.

Nadeane Allard, Xi Beta Omega
Valentine, Nebraska

QUICK TABLE COLOR TRICK

Instead of just placing a tablecloth on the table, use two different cloths twisted together and placed down the center of the table as a runner. Add whatever else you choose to carry out your theme. Vary colors to suit the occasion.

Aleksandra Stolley, Delta Gamma
Corpus Christi, Texas

SOUTHERN FRIENDSHIP ANGEL

Collect magnolia grandiflora seed pods and spray them with gold paint. Attach a 1¼-inch styrofoam ball at the top for a head with hot glue. Cover the ball with glue and press Spanish moss over the ball for hair. Make a large bow from ribbon to attach to the back to resemble wings and use metallic ribbon to shape a halo and a bow around the neck.

Linda Ling, Preceptor Gamma
Memphis, Tennessee

COUNTDOWN TO CHRISTMAS

I remember my grandmother helping me understand how many days it was until Christmas.

Use a favorite cookie recipe that the children can help make. Before baking, make a hole in each cookie that can be used to hang the cookies. Make 25 cookies and wrap each in plastic wrap. Decorate a 2-foot tree to place on the kitchen table or counter, thread ribbon through the holes of the cookies, and add them to the tree. Each day until December 24th, allow the children to eat one cookie. Save the last cookie for Santa.

Barbara Mullen, Tau Omicron
Forsyth, Missouri

SCENTED TRIVET

Select fabric that matches the holiday, decor, or theme of your choice. The size of your trivets is your choice, also—8-, 10-, or 12-inch sizes are all useful. Cut the fabric into rectangles of your selected size. Place right sides of two fabric pieces together and sew around the edges on three sides, leaving one of the sides open to permit filling. Turn right side out. Fold the trivet in half with the open side at the top and mark the fold top and bottom (draw a line to connect the marks if necessary). Stitch from top to bottom, securing each end of the stitching with back stitches. Fold each side to the center stitching line, mark and stitch as before. The trivet will have four channels to fill with a scented mixture. Make as much mixture as you need to fill the channels using the following proportions: 2 cups rice, ½ cup whole cloves, ¼ cup whole allspice, and a few drops of oil of cinnamon or oil of cloves. Fill the channels to ¾-inch of the top, turn the raw edges to the inside and stitch securely. Place a hot dish or teapot on the trivet and the heat will release the fragrance of the spices. To revive the fragrance, simply place the trivet on the counter and rap it several times with a wooden spoon.

June Harmann, Laureate Beta Delta
Paseo, Washington

CANDY WREATH

Use metal needlework rings of whatever size you desire; I usually use the 4-inch rings and 2 pounds of candy. Select hard candy that is individually wrapped in colorful wrappers. Select three rolls of curling ribbon: one each of red, green, and white, or whatever goes well with your candy wrappers is fine. Cut the ribbon into 6-inch lengths. Tie one end of each ribbon piece onto one end of a candy piece and then tie the ribbon onto the ring; use scissors to curl the remaining end of the ribbon. Continue until the ring is completely covered with candy and ribbon. Attach a large bow to the top of the wreath. Tie a colorful pair of child's plastic scissors to the wreath on a length of ribbon to invite sampling.

Barbara Kajfasz, Xi Eta
Kirkland, Quebec, Canada

VEGETABLE TREE CENTERPIECE

Start with a 12-inch green styrofoam cone placed on a large tray. Decorate the tree with toothpick-skewered broccoli florets, cucumber slices, olives, sugar snap peas, sliced red, green, and yellow bell peppers, cherry tomatoes and other bite-size vegetables. Cut a star from a yellow bell pepper for the top. Don't worry about covering the tree completely at first because you can go back and simply tuck small broccoli bits without toothpicks into the bare spots. Add additional bite-size vegetables as well as dishes of your favorite vegetable dip to the tray.

Kelli Cole
Shady Point, Oklahoma

IF YOUR CHRISTMAS CACTUS WON'T BLOOM

When your cactus won't cooperate during the holidays, hang tiny ornaments on it as you would a tree and place it in a prominent place. One of the best memories my sister and I have is the time my cactus didn't bloom but I made the best of it.

Laura Kerr, Gamma Laureate
Ganandque, Ontario, Canada

CHEDDAR ALE CHEESE BALLS

6 cups (1½ pounds) shredded sharp Cheddar cheese
3 ounces cream cheese, softened
4 tablespoons butter or margarine, softened
¾ cup ale or beer
1 teaspoon dry mustard
½ teaspoon crushed red pepper
¾ cup chopped English walnuts
½ cup (or more) chopped parsley

Combine the Cheddar cheese, cream cheese and butter in a large mixing bowl and beat at high speed until smooth. Beat in the ale gradually. Beat in the mustard and red pepper. If mixture is very soft, chill, covered, until firm enough to hold a shape. Divide in half and shape into 2 balls. Combine the walnuts and parsley on a sheet of waxed paper. Roll the cheese balls in the nut mixture, coating well. Place on a serving platter. Serve with assorted crackers. Keep leftovers refrigerated. Yield: 25 servings.

Ruth Ellen Shaffer, Upsilon Master
Lancaster, Ohio

ARTICHOKE CHILE DIP

1 (14-ounce) jar artichoke hearts (not marinated), drained, chopped
1 cup mayonnaise
1 cup grated Parmesan cheese
1 (8-ounce) can chopped green chiles
1 cup shredded Cheddar cheese

Mix the artichokes, mayonnaise, Parmesan cheese, chiles and Cheddar cheese together in a large bowl by hand. Spread in an 8-inch-square baking dish sprayed with nonstick cooking spray. Bake, uncovered, at 350 degrees for 20 to 25 minutes or until heated through. Serve with tortilla chips.
Yield: 8 to 10 servings.

Jennifer Moore, Beta Iota Pi
Pasadena, Texas

Cecelia Welsh, Preceptor Zeta Sigma, Blue Springs, Missouri, makes an elegant Super-Easy Avocado Appetizer by whipping ½ cup whipping cream and then folding in ½ cup chili sauce, ½ cup mayonnaise, 1 tablespoon Worcestershire sauce, and 3 tablespoons lemon juice. She peels and seeds 4 avocados, slices the avocados thinly, and fans the slices on small plates. She then adds a decorative drizzle of whipped cream sauce and serves the remaining sauce at the table.

ARTICHOKE CASSEROLE

Serve this holiday party dip with bagel chips or sliced, toasted baguettes.

1 (14-ounce) can artichoke hearts (not marinated), drained, chopped
1 cup shredded mozzarella cheese
1 cup freshly grated Parmesan cheese
1 cup mayonnaise
1 tablespoon chopped garlic
4 ounces cream cheese, softened
⅓ cup chopped parsley

Mix the ingredients together in a bowl. Place in a 2-quart casserole sprayed with nonstick cooking spray. Bake, uncovered, at 350 degrees for about 25 minutes or until heated through. Yield: 10 servings.

Joyce O. Morgan, Laureate Alpha Rho
Christiansburg, Virginia

CORN DIP

3 (11-ounce) cans Mexicorn
1 cup sour cream
1 cup mayonnaise
1 to 3 jalapeño peppers, chopped
2 cups shredded Cheddar cheese
4 green onions, chopped
1 (4-ounce) can chopped green chiles

Combine the Mexicorn, sour cream, mayonnaise, jalapeños, cheese, green onions and chiles in a bowl and mix well. Chill, covered, for 8 to 12 hours. Serve with chips or crackers. Yield: 8 to 10 servings.

Tammy Brasher, Xi Chi Theta
Yoakum, Texas

CHICKEN ENCHILADA DIP

16 ounces cream cheese, softened
1½ cups shredded Cheddar cheese
2 or 3 cooked chicken breasts, chopped
1 teaspoon minced garlic
1 (10-ounce) can extra-hot tomatoes with green chiles, drained
Leaves of 1 bunch cilantro, chopped
4 green onions, chopped

Stir the cream cheese and Cheddar cheese together in a bowl until well blended. Add the chicken, garlic, tomatoes with green chiles, cilantro and green onions and mix well. Chill, covered, until serving time, or serve at room temperature. Serve with tortilla chips. Yield: 10 to 12 servings.

Liz Missildine, Preceptor Nu Sigma
Palestine, Texas

CRANBERRY DIP

Great for a holiday buffet or open house. If you want to prepare the dip in the microwave, mix the ingredients in a 1-quart microwave-safe bowl. Microwave, uncovered, on High for 3 to 5 minutes, stirring once or twice.

1 (16-ounce) can jellied cranberry sauce	1 tablespoon lemon juice
3 tablespoons prepared horseradish	1 garlic clove, minced
2 tablespoons honey	1/2 teaspoon ground red pepper
1 tablespoon Worcestershire sauce	Orange pieces
	Pineapple tidbits
	Vienna sausages, sliced

Combine the cranberry sauce, horseradish, honey, Worcestershire sauce, lemon juice, garlic and red pepper in a saucepan over medium-high heat. Bring to a boil; reduce heat. Simmer, covered, for about 5 minutes. Serve warm with orange pieces, pineapple tidbits and Vienna sausages. Yield: 1 1/2 cups.

Gladys Weems, Laureate Eta Iota
Highland, California

HOT MUSHROOM SPREAD

Do not use mayonnaise-type salad dressing for this spread—be sure to use real mayonnaise.

2 cups mayonnaise	1 (16-ounce) can sliced mushrooms, drained
2 cups shredded Cheddar cheese	1 envelope Italian dressing mix
1/2 cup grated Parmesan cheese	

Combine the mayonnaise, Cheddar cheese, Parmesan cheese, mushrooms and dry dressing mix in a bowl and mix well. Spread in an 8-inch-square baking dish sprayed with nonstick cooking spray. Bake, uncovered, at 350 degrees for 10 minutes or until bubbly. Serve with crackers. Yield: 3 1/2 cups.

Tresa Ward, Laureate Delta
Louisville, Kentucky

SUN-DRIED TOMATO DIP

To make Pita Toasts, cut pita bread into 3-inch wedges. Brush with a mixture of 1/2 cup melted margarine, 1 tablespoon garlic salt, and 2 tablespoons parsley flakes. Broil for 3 to 4 minutes on each side.

1 (7-ounce) jar oil-packed sun-dried tomatoes, chopped	1/2 cup mayonnaise
7 ounces ricotta cheese	1 tablespoon hot pepper sauce
4 ounces cream cheese, softened	1/2 green onion, chopped
	1 teaspoon garlic salt

Combine the sun-dried tomatoes, ricotta cheese, cream cheese, mayonnaise, hot pepper sauce, green onion and garlic salt in a bowl and mix well. Chill, covered, for 4 to 6 hours. Serve with warm pita toasts. Yield: 6 to 8 servings.

Jeanne Curtis, Xi Delta Tau
Princeton, Missouri

APPLE WREATH WITH CARAMEL DIP

8 ounces cream cheese, softened	3/4 cup half-and-half
3/4 cup packed brown sugar	1/4 cup Kahlúa
1 cup sour cream	1 (4-ounce) package instant vanilla pudding mix
2 teaspoons vanilla extract	Red apples
2 teaspoons lemon juice	Green apples (Granny Smith)

Beat the cream cheese and brown sugar in a mixing bowl until smooth. Add the sour cream, vanilla, lemon juice, half-and-half, Kahlúa and dry pudding mix 1 at a time, beating well after each addition. Chill, covered, for 1 to 12 hours. Core the apples and cut in wedges. Toss with additional lemon juice, coating well. Arrange red and green wedges alternately on a serving plate to form a wreath. Place a bowl in the center for the dip. May also serve with crackers and/or assorted fresh fruit. Yield: 3 1/2 cups.

Elizabeth A. Brookley, Preceptor Alpha Epsilon
Melbourne, Florida

HOLIDAY CREAM CHEESE WREATH

16 ounces cream cheese, softened	1/4 cup chopped green onion
1/2 cup mayonnaise-type salad dressing	10 slices bacon, crisp-cooked, crumbled
1/3 cup grated Parmesan cheese	

Combine the cream cheese and salad dressing in a bowl and mix well. Add the Parmesan cheese, green onion and bacon 1 ingredient at a time, mixing well after each addition. Place a glass in the center of a serving plate and spoon the mixture around the plate, forming a "wreath." Chill, covered, until serving time. Remove the glass. Make a wreath with parsley and pimentos at the top. Yield: 3 cups.

Norma D. Chaney, Laureate Alpha Lambda
Parkersburg, West Virginia

SMALL BITS ANTIPASTO

All my father's grandparents came from the same city in northern Italy, San Giorgio Canavese. This authentic recipe is theirs! Make enough for yourself and to give to family and friends as holiday treats.

2 cups sliced carrots	2 (6-ounce) cans water-
2 cups sliced cauliflower	pack white tuna
1 cup drained cocktail	1¼ cups ketchup
onions	½ cup olive oil
1 cup chopped dill	1¼ cups chili sauce
pickles	1 or 2 garlic cloves,
1 cup sliced stuffed green	crushed
olives	¼ cup lemon juice
2 cups chopped	
mushrooms	

Cook the carrots and cauliflower in boiling water until tender-crisp; drain. Combine the carrots, cauliflower, onions, pickles, olives, mushrooms and tuna in a large bowl. Stir in a mixture of the ketchup, olive oil, chili sauce, garlic and lemon juice and mix well. Chill, covered, for at least 24 hours before serving. Serve with crackers or celery. Yield: 2 quarts.

Catherine Cuthbertson, Xi Gamma Zeta
Tucson, Arizona

BRUSCHETTE

6 ripe tomatoes, finely	½ teaspoon salt
chopped	2 tablespoons red wine
¼ cup finely chopped	vinegar
fresh basil	2 to 4 tablespoons olive
3 garlic cloves, crushed	oil
2 to 4 tablespoons	1 teaspoon chopped
chopped pickled	parsley
jalapeño peppers	1 loaf Italian bread

Shake the tomatoes in a colander gently for a few seconds to remove excess liquid and seeds. Combine the tomatoes and the next 7 ingredients in a glass bowl and mix well. Chill, covered, for 2 to 4 hours. Cut the bread diagonally in ½-inch slices and toast. Serve the vegetable mixture near room temperature. Stir before serving. Spoon over toasted bread slices and serve at once. Yield: 6 to 12 servings.

Cheryl Ingeberg, Preceptor Alpha
Regina, Saskatchewan, Canada

Vergie Stockton, Beta Omicron, Ft. Worth, Texas, makes Tuna Pecan Finger Sandwiches the day ahead using a large can of tuna rinsed with boiling water and drained well, 1 cup mayonnaise, and 1 cup chopped pecans, spread on thin-sliced bread.

OKRA PINWHEELS

Try to find the Talk o'Texas brand of crisp okra pickles for this recipe.

1 (16-ounce) jar crisp	8 ounces low-fat cream
okra pickles	cheese, softened
½ pound square ham	
slices	

Cut off the crowns of the okra pods; drain the pods on paper towels. Lay the ham slices on a flat surface. Spread a generous amount of cream cheese evenly over each slice. Place an okra pod along one edge of each slice and roll evenly. Secure each roll with 3 or 4 wooden picks along the seam. Chill, covered, for 8 to 12 hours. At serving time, remove the toothpicks and slice the rolls ¼ to ⅜ inch thick with a sharp knife. Arrange on a serving tray. Garnish with cherry tomatoes and parsley sprigs. Yield: 48 pinwheels.

Karen Bradshaw, Xi Epsilon
Addison, Texas

MEXICAN PINWHEELS

Select mild to hot picante sauce according to your taste.

8 ounces cream cheese,	⅛ teaspoon garlic
softened	powder
1 cup sour cream	12 (10-inch) flour
1 (4-ounce) can chopped	tortillas
green chiles, drained	1 (16-ounce) jar picante
1 (4-ounce) can chopped	sauce
black olives, drained	

Combine the cream cheese, sour cream, green chiles, olives and garlic powder in a bowl and mix well. Spread some of the cream cheese mixture evenly over one side of each tortilla. Roll each tortilla into a tight roll to enclose the cream cheese filling. Chill, wrapped in plastic wrap, for 2 to 12 hours. Cut into ½-inch pieces at serving time. Serve with picante sauce. Yield: 15 to 20 servings.

Nan Warren, Xi Epsilon Alpha
Muskogee, Oklahoma

Sonya Lee, Xi, Brandon, Mississippi, prepares Cran-Raspberry Liqueur for gifts by processing 3 cups sugar, 3 cups vodka, 2 cups finely chopped cranberries, and a 12-ounce package of frozen unsweetened raspberries in a food processor, sealing in a quart jar and storing in a cool place for a month, mixing well at least once a week. Strain through cheesecloth and pour into pretty bottles.

YULE LOG SANDWICH LOAF

Be sure to use canned ham chunks, not deviled ham. Use fat-free cream cheese and sour cream if you like. Select a long, thin, flat serving dish for the log; place 3 or 4 stacks of bread next to each other on the dish to make sure it is long enough.

2 (5-ounce) cans cooked
   ham chunks
Mayonnaise or salad
   dressing
2 (5-ounce) cans cooked
   chicken chunks,
   white meat
1/2 cup (1 stick)
   margarine, softened
Loaf of white bread,
   thinly sliced, crusts
   trimmed

1 (14-ounce) tub
   pimento cheese
1 cup sour cream
16 ounces cream cheese,
   softened
Stuffed green olives,
   halved

Drain the ham. Mash it well in a bowl and mix with enough mayonnaise to make it of spreading consistency. Drain, mash and mix the chicken the same way in a separate bowl. Spread a very thin layer of margarine over one side of each slice of bread. Lay 3 or 4 bread slices end to end on the serving dish. Spread a layer of ham mixture over the bread. Layer 3 or 4 bread slices over the ham; spread a layer of pimento cheese over the bread. Cover with another layer of bread, a layer of chicken mixture and another layer of bread. Repeat this process until all bread has been used. The last layer should be bread; stacks should be even and there should be no space between them. There will nearly always be a little of something left over. Mix the sour cream gradually into the cream cheese in a mixing bowl, beating at low speed until of spreading consistency. Frost the top and sides of the loaf with the sour cream mixture. Garnish the top with the olive halves, red side up. Lay parsley sprigs around the loaf on the serving dish. Lay a pretty knife alongside the loaf and allow party guests to help themselves. Yield: 15 to 25 servings.

Barbara Johnson-Clark, Xi Delta Sigma
Hendersonville, Tennessee

ROASTED WATER CHESTNUTS

1 pound sliced bacon
1 (6- to 8-ounce) can
   water chestnuts,
   drained

1 cup packed brown
   sugar
1 cup ketchup

Cut the bacon slices crosswise in half or thirds. Wrap each bacon piece around a water chestnut; secure with a wooden pick. Arrange on a nonstick baking sheet. Bake at 350 degrees for about 30 minutes or until bacon is cooked through. Combine the brown sugar and ketchup in a slow cooker and mix well. Stir in the wrapped water chestnuts. Cook on Low for 3 hours. Yield: 5 to 8 servings.

Amanda Swavely, Preceptor Epsilon
Palmer, Alaska

SUGAR-COATED PEANUTS

1 cup sugar
1/2 cup water

2 cups raw peanuts,
   skins on

Dissolve the sugar in the water in a saucepan over medium heat, stirring constantly. Add the peanuts and cook over medium heat until nuts are completely sugared and no syrup is left, stirring constantly. Spread over an ungreased baking sheet. Bake at 300 degrees for 30 minutes, stirring at 5-minute intervals. Let cool. Store in an airtight container. Yield: 2 cups.

Victoria Gonzales, Xi Psi Xi
Friendswood, Texas

FIRECRACKERS

Makes a wonderful homemade gift. Keebler Zesta is a good brand of fat-free saltines for this recipe.

40 fat-free saltines
2 teaspoons of your
   favorite grilling spice
Crushed red pepper
   flakes

1 (10-ounce) brick
   Cracker Barrel extra-
   sharp Cheddar
   cheese, shredded

Preheat the oven to 475 degrees. Arrange the crackers in a single layer, sides touching, in a 10×15-inch cake pan. Sprinkle with the grilling spice, then with as many pepper flakes as you dare. Layer the cheese evenly over the crackers. Place the pan on the center shelf of the oven. Close the oven door and turn off the oven. Leave in oven for 4 hours. The hot oven will melt and brown the cheese, producing an even coating of crisp brown. Remove from oven and let cool. Break apart and store in an airtight container. Will keep for several weeks. Yield: 40 crackers.

Mary Anne Wilkerson, Zeta Sigma
Burlington, North Carolina

Margaret Wilburn, Preceptor Delta Pi, Houston, Texas, makes Hot Holiday Jelly by blending a cup of pineapple preserves, a cup of apple jelly, a small jar of horseradish, and 2 to 3 tablespoons dry mustard. Pour into half-pint jars for gifts. Serve over a block of cream cheese with crackers.

CARAMEL POPCORN

Perfect for packing in tins and sharing with neighbors and co-workers.

2 cups packed brown sugar	1 teaspoon burnt sugar flavoring
1 cup (2 sticks) margarine	1 teaspoon vanilla extract
1/2 cup white corn syrup	8 quarts popped popcorn
1/2 teaspoon baking soda	

Combine the brown sugar, margarine and corn syrup in a heavy saucepan over medium heat. Cook for 5 minutes, stirring constantly. Stir in the baking soda, burnt sugar flavoring and vanilla. Pour over the popcorn, stirring until coated. Spread over baking sheets. Bake at 250 degrees for 1 hour, stirring every 10 to 15 minutes to prevent burning. Yield: 8 quarts.

Susan Bratt, Alpha Gamma Iota
Kansas City, Missouri

CEREAL SNACK MIX

3 cups chocolate puff cereal	1/2 cup (1 stick) margarine
3 cups rice chex	1/4 cup light corn syrup
1 1/2 cups small twisted pretzels	1/4 teaspoon cream of tartar
1 cup peanuts	1/4 teaspoon baking soda
1 cup packed brown sugar	1/2 teaspoon vanilla extract

Combine the cereals, pretzels and peanuts in a 9×13-inch baking dish. Combine the brown sugar, margarine and corn syrup in a heavy saucepan over medium heat. Bring to a boil, stirring constantly; then boil for 4 minutes without stirring. Remove from heat. Stir in the cream of tartar and baking soda. Stir in the vanilla. Pour over the cereal mixture, stirring to coat well. Bake at 300 degrees for 30 minutes, stirring halfway through the baking time. Spread over foil and let cool. Yield: 2 quarts.

Mary Jo Lavenhagen, Xi Phi
Philo, Illinois

TEXAS ALMOND MIX

1 (12-ounce) package each rice chex, corn chex and honeycomb cereal	2 cups dry roasted peanuts
	2 cups pecan halves
1 (15-ounce) package small pretzels	3 (6-ounce) packages white almond bark

Combine the cereals, pretzels and nuts in 2 large bowls or pans, half of each in each bowl, and mix well. Melt the almond bark and pour over the cereal mixtures. Toss until well coated. Spread over waxed paper and let cool for 1 hour. Break apart. Yield: more than 40 servings.

Joan Sittel, Nu Master
Amarillo, Texas

SPICY SUGARED WALNUTS

1/2 cup sugar	1/4 teaspoon ground cloves
1/2 teaspoon salt	
1 teaspoon cinnamon	1/2 cup water
1/4 teaspoon nutmeg	1 cup walnut halves

Combine the sugar, salt, cinnamon, nutmeg, cloves and water in a 1-quart microwave-safe bowl and mix well. Microwave, covered, on High for 4 minutes or until bubbly. Stir in the walnuts. Pour the mixture over a waxed paper-lined baking sheet; separate the nuts quickly with a fork. Let cool. Yield: about 1 cup.

Debby Eagleburger, Preceptor Alpha Eta
Kansas City, Kansas

❖ CHERRY MOCHA WARMER

2 cups very hot strongly brewed coffee	2 cups milk, scalded
	3/4 cup crème de cacao
4 ounces semisweet baking chocolate, chopped	3/4 cup cherry brandy
	1 cup whipping cream
3/4 cup sugar	4 tablespoons sifted confectioners' sugar
1/8 teaspoon salt	
4 cups half-and-half, scalded	Maraschino cherries with stems

Chill a small bowl and the beaters of an electric mixer in the freezer. Combine the coffee, chocolate, sugar and salt in the top of a double boiler over hot water. Heat until chocolate is melted and smooth, whisking constantly. Whisk the half-and-half and milk into the chocolate mixture. Stir in the crème de cacao and brandy. Keep warm. Whip the cream in the chilled bowl until soft peaks form. Add the confectioners' sugar gradually, beating until stiff peaks form. Top the beverage with a dollop of whipped cream and a maraschino cherry. Yield: 14 (6-ounce) servings.

Margie Kelarek, Laureate Eta Beta
Hilltop Lakes, Texas

Sarah Duinink, Lambda Beta, Otley, Iowa, blends 1 1/2 cups strongly brewed coffee, 1/2 cup sweetened condensed milk, 1/2 cup half-and-half, and 1/2 teaspoon vanilla extract and serves the mixture over crushed ice for Cappuccino on Ice.

FROTHY EGGNOG PUNCH

To make a stronger punch, add 1 cup of sherry or rum.

12 eggs, separated	1 pint vanilla ice cream
1 cup sugar	6 (16-ounce) bottles
1 quart whole milk	lemon-lime soda,
1 tablespoon sherry or	chilled
rum	Nutmeg

Beat the egg whites until soft peaks form. Beat the egg yolks in a large mixing bowl; beat in the sugar gradually. Beat in the milk gradually until well blended. Stir in the sherry. Fold in the egg whites. Pour into a large punch bowl. Float scoops of ice cream over the surface of the punch. Pour in the lemon-lime soda slowly. Sprinkle with nutmeg. Yield: 25 servings.

Lucy K. Brushaber, Preceptor Epsilon Theta
Pinellas Park, Florida

STRAWBERRY SOUP

1 pound strawberries	1 tablespoon grenadine
2 cups sour cream	syrup
6 tablespoons sifted	4 tablespoons half-and-
confectioners' sugar	half
2 tablespoons vanilla	
extract	

Combine the strawberries and sour cream in a large mixing bowl and beat at low speed until well mixed. Beat in the confectioners' sugar, vanilla and grenadine until smooth. Add the half-and-half, beating just until well blended. Chill and serve, stirring well before serving. Yield: 6 servings.

Shirley Boston-Otis, Preceptor Iota
Independence, Missouri

CHRISTMAS BROTH

3 cups vegetable juice	2 tablespoons sherry
cocktail	2 tablespoons butter,
2 cups chicken broth	softened
2 tablespoons brown	2 tablespoons finely
sugar	chopped parsley

Combine the vegetable juice, chicken broth, brown sugar and sherry in the top of a double boiler over simmering water. Heat almost to the boiling point. Stir in the butter. Serve in warmed individual soup plates or cups. Sprinkle each serving with parsley, making a wreath shape. Yield: 6 servings.

Fran Robbins, Preceptor Alpha Phi
Orleans, Ontario, Canada

ONION WINE SOUP

5 large onions, chopped	1 tablespoon vinegar
1/4 cup butter, melted	2 teaspoons sugar
5 cups beef broth	1 cup light cream
1/2 cup celery leaves	1 tablespoon minced
1 large potato, sliced	parsley
1 cup dry white wine	Salt and pepper to taste

Sauté the onions briefly in the butter in a large saucepan over medium heat. Stir in the broth, celery leaves and potato. Bring to a boil; reduce heat. Simmer, covered, for 30 minutes. Purée the mixture in a blender or food processor. Return the purée to the saucepan. Blend in the wine, vinegar and sugar. Simmer for 5 minutes. Stir in the cream, parsley, salt and pepper. Cook until heated through, stirring constantly; do not boil. Yield: 6 to 8 servings.

Jean McGuire, Laureate Tau
Sioux Falls, South Dakota

POTATO HAM SOUP

1/2 cup chopped onion	3 cups cubed cooked
1/2 cup chopped celery	ham
1/2 cup (1 stick) butter	3 cups cubed cooked
1/4 cup flour	potatoes
3 cups hot water	1 cup sour cream
3 to 4 cups chopped	Salt and pepper to taste
cabbage	

Sauté the onion and celery in the butter until tender. Add the flour and stir well. Stir in the hot water, cabbage and ham. Cook over low heat for 20 minutes, stirring occasionally. Stir in the potatoes, sour cream, salt and pepper. Heat until sour cream is well blended into the mixture. Simmer until ready to serve. Yield: 6 servings.

Judy Wilkerson, Xi Gamma Lambda
Shattuck, Oklahoma

❖ INSALATA A SORPRESA

If you can't find thin green beans, use regular green beans and slice lengthwise.

4 ounces thin green	1/8 teaspoon black
beans, ends trimmed	pepper
3/4 cup toasted walnut	1 red bell pepper,
pieces	julienned
4 tablespoons honey	2 unpeeled apples,
1/4 cup apple cider	julienned
vinegar	2 heads Belgian endive,
1/3 cup vegetable oil	julienned

Preheat the oven to 400 degrees. Parboil the green beans for 3 minutes. Combine the walnuts, half the honey and a pinch of salt in a small bowl and mix well. Spread the walnut mixture over a greased baking sheet and bake for 5 minutes. Let cool. Combine the vinegar, oil, the remaining 2 tablespoons honey, 1/4 teaspoon salt and the black pepper in a blender or food processor container. Process until well blended and creamy. Place the green beans, bell pepper, apples, endive and vinegar dressing in a large bowl and toss to combine. Sprinkle each serving with the honey-roasted walnuts. Yield: 8 to 10 servings.

Shirley Simpson, Preceptor Beta Mu
Carterville, Illinois

FRUITY GELATIN BEET SALAD

1 (16-ounce) can julienned beets	2 tablespoons water 1 (3-ounce) package
1 (8-ounce) can crushed pineapple	raspberry gelatin 3 teaspoons lemon juice
2 tablespoons apple cider vinegar	1 teaspoon sugar 1/4 cup chopped walnuts

Drain the beets and pineapple, reserving the liquid from both. Mix reserved liquids with the vinegar and water, making a total of 2 cups. Heat the liquid in a saucepan over medium heat; bring to a boil. Add the gelatin, stirring to dissolve. Remove from heat. Stir in the beets, pineapple, lemon juice, sugar and walnuts. Pour into an 8×8-inch baking dish. Chill, covered, until ready to serve. Yield: 9 servings.

Lucile Curtner, Laureate Theta Zeta
West Covina, California

RED HOT SALAD

3/4 cup red hot cinnamon
    candies
	2 envelopes unflavored
	    gelatin

1 cup water	4 tablespoons cold
1 (29-ounce) can pears	water

Combine the red hots and 1 cup water in a 1-quart microwave-safe dish. Microwave on High until boiling; microwave on Low until candies are melted, stirring occasionally. Drain the pears, reserving the liquid. Place the pears rounded side up in a 5-cup mold. Heat the pear liquid in a saucepan over medium heat until hot. Stir the gelatin into the cold water. Combine the red hots liquid, hot pear liquid and gelatin mixture in a bowl and stir until completely dissolved. Pour over the pears in the mold. Chill, covered, for 8 to 12 hours. Yield: 8 servings.

Maxine Yoder, Laureate Alpha Theta
Elkhart, Indiana

CHRISTMAS LUNCHEON SALAD

Serve with hot crescent rolls, butter, and a nice dessert champagne. For a colorful Christmasy look, use red placemats, white dinner plates, and decorative napkins. Make a centerpiece of a large crystal bowl filled with whole pomegranates and red and green Christmas balls, accented with holly.

1 large head romaine	Olive oil and red wine
1 cup pomegranate seeds	vinegar to taste
1 cup chopped walnuts	Salt and pepper
1 cup crumbled bleu cheese	to taste Cherry tomatoes
1 medium purple onion, thinly sliced	

Combine the first 9 ingredients in a large salad bowl and toss to combine. Chill, covered, until serving time. Toss again. Add 3 or 4 tomatoes to each serving. Yield: 8 to 12 servings.

Marje Chase, Laureate Epsilon Omega
Alhambra, California

WILD RICE CRANBERRY SALAD

1 cup wild rice, cooked	3 green onions, chopped
1 cup wheatberries, cooked	1/2 cup roasted pecans 1/4 cup olive oil
1/2 cup dried cranberries	Juice of 1 lemon
1 tablespoon chopped fresh cilantro	Salt to taste

Combine the ingredients and mix well. Chill, covered, for at least 1 hour before serving. May also serve hot as a side dish. Yield: 10 servings.

Wendy Bennett, Xi Pi Rho
Napa, California

LEMON CHICKEN

6 boneless skinless chicken breasts	1/2 teaspoon tarragon 1/2 teaspoon salt
1/4 cup (1/2 stick) butter or margarine	1 chicken bouillon cube 1 lemon, thinly sliced
1 tablespoon flour	

Cut each chicken breast into 10 or 12 strips. Melt the butter in a skillet over medium heat. Add the chicken. Sprinkle with the flour, tarragon and salt. Cook for 5 minutes or until chicken has no pink color, stirring constantly. Add the bouillon cube to 3/4 cup hot water, stirring until dissolved. Pour over the chicken. Add the lemon slices. Reduce heat; simmer, covered, for 3 minutes. Yield: 4 or 5 servings.

Jacqueline Miller, Laureate Delta
Newport News, Virginia

APPLE SAUSAGE OMELET

5 teaspoons margarine	6 eggs
3 Italian sausages, cut into 1/4-inch slices	1/4 cup water
	1 tablespoon chopped parsley
1 potato, peeled, thinly sliced	1 1/2 teaspoons salt
1 medium onion, peeled, cut into thin rings	1 teaspoon pepper
1 small Granny Smith apple, peeled, cored, thinly sliced	

Melt 1 teaspoon of the margarine in a skillet over medium heat. Add the sausages. Sauté until brown and cooked through; drain on paper towels. Melt the remaining 4 teaspoons margarine in a nonstick 10-inch skillet. Add the potato and onion. Cook over low heat for 5 minutes until softened. Add the apple. Cook for 5 minutes longer, stirring occasionally. Beat the eggs, water, parsley and salt together in a bowl. Add the egg mixture to the potato mixture, swirling the skillet so eggs spread evenly. Cover the skillet and cook over medium heat for 15 minutes or just until eggs are set. Invert carefully onto a serving platter. Sprinkle with the pepper and additional chopped parsley. Serve immediately. Yield: 6 servings.

Marian Kubic, Laureate Delta Alpha
Oceanside, California

BREAKFAST BENEDICT

8 hard-cooked eggs, halved lengthwise	1 (1-pound) roll pork sausage
1/4 cup melted margarine	1/4 cup flour
1/2 teaspoon Worcestershire sauce	2 1/2 cups milk
	1/4 teaspoon salt
1 tablespoon chopped green onion	1/8 teaspoon pepper
1/2 teaspoon Dijon mustard	1/2 cup shredded Cheddar cheese
8 English muffin halves, toasted	Paprika to taste

Remove the yolks from the eggs to a bowl and mash with a fork. Add the margarine, Worcestershire sauce, green onion and mustard to the yolks and mix well. Fill the egg whites with the yolk mixture. Arrange the filled eggs over English muffin halves in a lightly greased 9×13-inch baking dish. Brown the sausage in a skillet, stirring until crumbly; do not drain. Add the flour to the sausage and cook for a few minutes, stirring constantly. Add the milk gradually. Cook for about 5 minutes or until thickened, stirring constantly. Season with salt and pepper. Pour the sauce over the eggs and muffins. Sprinkle with the cheese and paprika. Bake at 325 degrees for 25 to 30 minutes or until hot and bubbly. Yield: 8 servings.

Jackie Chartvant, Nu Beta
Troy, Michigan

BREAKFAST CASSEROLE

2 pounds ground pork sausage	2 teaspoons dry mustard
	Salt and pepper to taste
12 eggs, beaten	3 cups shredded sharp Cheddar cheese
4 cups milk	
12 slices bread, cubed	

Remove sausage from casing if necessary. Brown the sausage in a skillet, stirring until crumbly; drain and cool. Beat the eggs and milk together in a large bowl. Add the bread, mustard, salt and pepper. Stir until bread is soft. Stir in the cheese and sausage. Pour into a greased 9×13-inch baking dish. Chill, covered, for 8 to 12 hours. Bake at 350 degrees for 40 to 45 minutes or until lightly browned. Let stand for 5 minutes. Cut into squares. Yield: 9 to 12 servings.

Elaine R. Hackenberg, Preceptor Alpha Upsilon
Nesquehoning, Pennsylvania

BREAKFAST PIZZA

This recipe comes together quickly on a hectic Christmas morning. You may use cooked ham instead of smoked salmon if you like.

1 (10-inch) focaccia, or baked pizza crust	2 tablespoons each chopped fresh dill, chives and parsley
8 eggs	
1/4 cup yogurt or sour cream	2 tablespoons butter
	6 ounces thinly sliced smoked salmon
1/4 teaspoon salt	
1/4 teaspoon pepper	

Preheat the oven to 350 degrees. If the focaccia is thicker than 1 inch, cut in half horizontally and save one half for future use. Warm the focaccia in the oven for about 10 minutes. Whisk the eggs with the yogurt, salt, pepper, dill, chives and parsley in a large bowl. Melt the butter in a large nonstick skillet over medium heat. Add the egg mixture, stirring as the eggs cook and form soft curds; do not overcook. Spoon the egg mixture over the warm focaccia. Layer the salmon over the egg mixture. Garnish with ground black pepper, fresh chives or green onions and dill. Cut in wedges to serve. Yield: 6 servings.

Donna Luus, Laureate Alpha Omega
Sault Ste. Marie, Ontario, Canada

CHRISTMAS MORNING BAKE

With this recipe you'll be able to sit and relax and enjoy Christmas morning with your family.

16 slices white bread, crusts trimmed
Thin slices of bacon or ham
Slices of sharp Cheddar cheese
6 eggs
1/2 teaspoon salt
1/2 teaspoon pepper
1/2 to 1 teaspoon dry mustard
1/4 cup minced onion
1/4 cup finely chopped green bell pepper
1 to 2 teaspoons Worcestershire sauce
3 cups whole milk
Dash of Tabasco sauce
1/2 cup (1 stick) butter, melted
Crushed cornflakes

Layer 8 slices of the bread in a buttered 9×13-inch baking dish; cover the bottom of the pan completely, adding more bread if necessary. Layer bacon and cheese over the bread. Add another layer of bread. Beat the eggs, salt and pepper in a bowl. Beat in the mustard, onion, bell pepper, Worcestershire sauce, milk and Tabasco sauce. Pour evenly over the bread. Let stand in the refrigerator, covered, for 8 to 12 hours. Drizzle with the butter when ready to bake. Add a layer of cornflakes. Bake, uncovered, at 350 degrees for 1 hour. Let stand for 10 minutes before serving. Yield: 8 servings.

Sheri-Lyn George, Delta Zeta
Langley, British Columbia, Canada

SPINACH SEAFOOD PASTA

1 rounded teaspoon minced garlic
2 tablespoons olive oil
1 cup chicken broth
1 (14-ounce) can Italian-style diced tomatoes
8 ounces bow tie pasta
10 ounces fresh spinach
3/4 pound imitation crab meat, cut or shredded
Grated Parmesan cheese

Sauté the garlic in the olive oil until brown. Add the chicken broth and undrained tomatoes. Bring to a boil; reduce heat. Simmer, uncovered, for 10 minutes. Cook the pasta using the package directions. Wash and dry the spinach and tear into bite-size pieces. Place the spinach in the bottom of a large bowl. Place the drained pasta over the spinach. Pour the tomato mixture over the pasta. Top with the crab meat. Toss to combine. The heat from the pasta will wilt the spinach. Sprinkle with Parmesan cheese. Serve with garlic bread. Yield: 6 to 8 servings.

Pat Bleick, Xi Alpha Gamma Lambda
Palestine, Texas

SPICED TOMATOES

1 (20-ounce) can Roma tomatoes
1 1/2 cups packed light brown sugar
1/4 cup margarine
Salt to taste
1 teaspoon cloves or allspice, or 1/2 teaspoon each

Drain the tomatoes, reserving the juice. Combine the tomato juice, brown sugar, margarine, salt and cloves in a cast-iron skillet over medium-high heat. Add the tomatoes. Bring to a boil; reduce heat. Simmer, uncovered, for 1 hour. Yield: 1 1/2 cups.

Beverly Gooch, Preceptor Gamma
Memphis, Tennessee

TURNIP PUFF

5 cups diced cooked turnips
1 (10-ounce) jar applesauce
2 tablespoons butter, softened
2 eggs, beaten
2 tablespoons flour
1 tablespoon brown sugar
1 tablespoon baking powder
Salt and pepper to taste

Mash the turnips in a large bowl. Add the remaining ingredients and mix well. Bake at 350 degrees in a 1 1/2-quart baking dish for 45 minutes. Yield: 12 servings.

Donna O'Neil, Laureate Alpha Zeta
Trenton, Ontario, Canada

BLUEBERRY RHUBARB JAM

5 cups cut-up rhubarb
1 cup water
4 cups sugar
1 (16-ounce) can blueberry pie filling
2 (3-ounce) packages raspberry gelatin

Simmer the rhubarb in the water in a saucepan for 5 to 10 minutes or until tender. Add the sugar and bring to a boil. Boil gently for 5 minutes, stirring constantly. Stir in the pie filling. Cook for 6 minutes longer, stirring constantly. Remove from heat. Add the gelatin, stirring until dissolved. Pour into hot sterilized jelly jars, leaving 1/4 inch headspace; seal with 2-piece lids. Invert jars for 5 minutes. Yield: 8 cups.

Alma D. Laser, Alpha Delta Master
Johnstown, Colorado

Susan Bousquet, Xi Chi, Omaha, Nebraska, makes Creamed Corn with 20 ounces frozen corn kernels, 2 tablespoons sugar, 1/4 cup butter, 8 ounces cream cheese, and 6 tablespoons water, cooked in a slow cooker on Low for 4 to 5 hours.

SPICED PEACHES

1 (29-ounce) can peach halves	1/2 cup vinegar
3/4 cup packed brown sugar	2 (3-inch) sticks cinnamon
	Whole cloves

Drain the peaches, reserving the syrup. Combine the peach syrup, brown sugar, vinegar and cinnamon sticks in a heavy saucepan over medium heat. Bring to a boil. Boil gently for 5 minutes, stirring constantly. Remove from heat. Place the peaches in a bowl. Insert a whole clove into each peach half. Pour the hot peach syrup mixture over the peaches. Let stand, covered, in the refrigerator for 8 to 12 hours. Serve peaches drizzled with syrup. Yield: 6 to 10 servings.

Mary Ellen Bradley, Preceptor Kappa
Landisville, Pennsylvania

SPICY ORANGE PEACHES

1 (17-ounce) can peaches	1/8 teaspoon cinnamon
1/4 cup vinegar	1 (3-ounce) package orange gelatin
1/2 cup sugar	3/4 cup cold water
12 whole cloves	

Drain the peaches, reserving 3/4 cup of the syrup. Coarsely chop the peaches. Combine the reserved syrup, vinegar, sugar, cloves and cinnamon in a heavy saucepan over medium heat. Bring to a slow boil. Stir in the peaches; reduce heat. Simmer for 10 minutes, stirring occasionally. Strain through muslin. Discard the cloves. Measure the liquid carefully, adding boiling water if necessary to make 1 cup. Dissolve the gelatin in the hot liquid. Stir in the peaches and cold water. Chill until slightly thickened. Pour into a 3-cup mold or serving bowl. Chill, covered, until ready to serve. Yield: about 2 1/2 cups.

Helen Jean Pretz, Laureate Beta Epsilon
Ponte Vedra Beach, Florida

Myrna L. Kruse, Theta Master, Tulsa, Oklahoma, makes Brandied Cranberries by microwaving a package of cranberries and 1 cup sugar on High for 8 minutes, then stirring in 1/4 cup sugar and 1/4 cup brandy. Serve warm or give as gifts.

Robyn Brewer, Laureate Mu, Beaverton, Oregon, keeps Hot Buttered Rum Mix in the freezer. Mix a pound of melted butter, 1 quart softened vanilla ice cream, 2 pounds brown sugar, 2 tablespoons cinnamon, and 1 teaspoon nutmeg. Combine 2 tablespoons of the mix, 6 to 8 ounces boiling water, and rum to taste.

OVERNIGHT COFFEE CAKE

The beauty of this delicious breakfast coffee cake is that it can be prepared the night before serving.

10 tablespoons butter, softened	1 teaspoon baking soda
1 cup sugar	1/2 teaspoon salt
1 cup packed light brown sugar	1 cup buttermilk
2 large eggs	3/4 cup coarsely chopped pecans
2 cups flour	1/2 teaspoon cinnamon
1 tablespoon cinnamon	2 tablespoons melted butter
1 teaspoon baking powder	

Cream 10 tablespoons butter, sugar and 1/2 cup of the brown sugar in a mixing bowl for 2 to 3 minutes or until light and fluffy. Add the eggs 1 at a time, beating well after each addition. Combine the flour, 1 tablespoon cinnamon, baking powder, baking soda and salt. Add the dry ingredients and buttermilk alternately to the egg mixture, mixing well after each addition. Pour into a lightly greased and floured 9×13-inch baking pan. Combine the remaining 1/2 cup brown sugar, pecans and 1/2 teaspoon cinnamon. Sprinkle over the batter in the pan. Drizzle with the melted butter. Chill, covered with plastic wrap, for 8 to 12 hours. Bake, uncovered, at 350 degrees for 30 minutes. Yield: 15 servings.

Dee E. Borger, Laureate Psi
Centerville, Ohio

BRAZIL NUT BREAD

1 pound pitted dates	1/2 teaspoon baking powder
1 cup well-drained maraschino cherries	1/2 teaspoon salt
1 pound (3 cups) shelled Brazil nuts	3 eggs
3/4 cup flour	1 teaspoon vanilla extract
3/4 cup sugar	

Place the dates, cherries and nuts in a large bowl. Sift the flour, sugar, baking powder and salt over the fruits and nuts. Stir until well coated. Beat the eggs in a bowl until foamy. Add the vanilla and mix well. Pour over the nut mixture and blend thoroughly. Pour into a paper-lined 5×9-inch loaf pan. Bake at 300 degrees for 1 3/4 hours. Cool in the pan until lukewarm. Remove to a wire rack to cool completely. Wrap the cooled cake in foil or plastic wrap. Yield: 12 servings.

Paula Disterhaupt, Xi Gamma Nu
Garland, Texas

CHERRY CHEESE BREAD

I like giving this tasty, easy-to-make bread to friends, or donating it to a holiday sale, where it always sells very quickly.

8 ounces cream cheese, softened
1 cup (2 sticks) butter, softened
1¹/2 cups sugar
4 eggs
2¹/4 cups flour
¹/2 cup chopped drained maraschino cherries
¹/2 cup chopped English walnuts or pecans
1¹/2 teaspoons baking powder
1¹/2 teaspoons vanilla extract

Cream the cream cheese, butter and sugar in a mixing bowl until light and fluffy. Add the eggs 1 at a time, beating well after each addition. Mix ¹/4 cup of the flour with the cherries and nuts in a small bowl. Mix the remaining 2 cups flour with the baking powder in a separate bowl. Stir the vanilla into the egg mixture. Fold in the flour mixture. Fold in the cherry mixture. Pour into a greased and floured bundt pan. Bake at 325 degrees for about 1 hour or until cake tests done. Cool in the pan for 10 minutes. Remove to a wire rack to cool completely. Dust with sifted confectioners' sugar. Yield: 16 servings.

Norma J. Newmeister, Preceptor Lambda
Cedar Rapids, Iowa

GOLDEN PANCAKES

This recipe is also excellent for making waffles. Bake extra waffles and freeze them—when reheated in a toaster they are as delicious as if they were freshly made.

1 cup cream-style cottage cheese
6 eggs
¹/2 cup sifted flour
¹/4 teaspoon salt
¹/4 cup vegetable oil
¹/4 cup milk
¹/2 teaspoon vanilla extract

Combine the cottage cheese, eggs, flour, salt, oil, milk and vanilla in a blender container and process at high speed for 1 minute, stopping to stir once. Pour ¹/4 cup at a time onto a hot, lightly greased griddle. Cook until brown on both sides, turning once. Serve with syrup, margarine or fruit. Yield: 20 (4-inch) pancakes.

Plina Thomas, Xi Xi
Blytheville, Arkansas

FLUFFY SCONES

2 cups flour
4 teaspoons baking powder
1 teaspoon salt
Optional ingredients:
¹/2 cup shredded cheese, ¹/4 cup raisins, ¹/4 cup mixed dried fruit or 1 tablespoon mixed dried herbs such as oregano and basil
¹/2 cup (1 stick) butter, softened
1 cup milk, cream or buttermilk

Combine the flour, baking powder, salt and optional ingredient in a bowl and mix well. Cut the butter into the dry ingredients until mixture is comprised of pea-sized bits. Add the milk and mix with a fork until a soft dough forms. Turn onto a floured surface. Pat and knead 8 to 10 times. Roll to desired thickness (biscuits will double in size when baking). Cut into shapes and arrange on a nonstick 10×14-inch baking sheet. Let stand in the refrigerator, covered, for 30 minutes before baking. Bake at 425 degrees for 12 to 15 minutes or until beginning to lightly brown. Yield: 6 to 8 servings.

Greer Rosequist, Preceptor Alpha Omega
Sidney, British Columbia, Canada

APPLE PANCAKES

3 large Granny Smith apples
3 tablespoons butter
3 tablespoons sugar
¹/2 teaspoon cinnamon
1 tablespoon lemon juice
4 eggs
²/3 cup flour
²/3 cup milk
Grated zest of 1 lemon
2 tablespoons melted butter

Peel, core and slice the apples. Melt the 3 tablespoons butter in a large skillet over medium heat. Add the apples and sauté for 3 minutes. Sprinkle the sugar, cinnamon and lemon juice over the apples. Sauté over high heat for 2 to 3 minutes longer or until apples are tender and pale golden. Remove from heat. Combine the eggs, flour, milk, lemon zest and the 2 tablespoons melted butter in a mixing bowl and beat until batter is very smooth. Layer the apples in a 9×13-inch baking dish sprayed with nonstick cooking spray. Pour the batter evenly over the apples. Bake at 425 degrees for 20 to 25 minutes or until golden; do not open the oven door while baking. Yield: 4 servings.

Jeanette Barrett, Lambda Epsilon
Kenora, Ontario, Canada

FLUFFY INDIANA WAFFLES

2 cups flour
4 teaspoons baking
   powder
1 teaspoon salt
1 tablespoon sugar
4 tablespoons
   margarine, melted
3 eggs, separated
2 cups milk

Mix the first 4 ingredients in a bowl. Beat in a mixture of the margarine, egg yolks and milk. Beat the egg whites until stiff peaks form. Fold into the flour mixture. Pour 1/2 cup batter onto a hot waffle iron. Bake using manufacturer's directions. Yield: 12 servings.

Madeline Kruckeberg, Preceptor Delta Epsilon
Ft. Wayne, Indiana

CINNAMON BUNS

1 envelope dry yeast
3/4 cup lukewarm water
1/4 cup shortening
1 teaspoon salt
1/4 cup sugar
1 egg
2 1/4 cups flour
1/2 cup (1 stick) butter or
   margarine, melted
1 cup packed brown
   sugar
1 to 2 teaspoons
   cinnamon
1 cup confectioners'
   sugar
1 teaspoon vanilla
   extract
Chopped nuts (optional)

Dissolve the yeast in the water in a mixing bowl. Add the shortening, salt, sugar, egg and 1 cup of the flour. Beat for 2 minutes or until smooth. Stir in the remaining 1 1/4 cups flour and blend well. Let rise, covered, in a warm place until doubled in bulk. Stir down the dough. Roll into an 8×10-inch rectangle on a lightly floured surface. Spread with the melted butter. Sprinkle heavily with the brown sugar and cinnamon. Roll up from a wide edge to enclose the filling. Cut into 1-inch slices. Arrange cut side down in an oiled 9-inch pie plate. Let rise until doubled in bulk. Bake at 375 degrees for 12 to 15 minutes or until golden brown. Glaze buns while warm with a mixture of confectioners' sugar, vanilla and enough water to make of desired thickness. Sprinkle with chopped nuts. Yield: 6 to 8 servings.

Pat Haines, Laureate Delta Psi
San Angelo, Texas

Joyce E. Hasson, Laureate Rho, Jackson, Michigan, makes Pineapple Stickies by mixing a 9-ounce can of drained crushed pineapple with 1/4 cup melted butter and the icing from a package of refrigerator cinnamon rolls, spooning into muffin cups, adding the rolls, and baking for 20 minutes. Let stand for 5 minutes, invert and garnish each with a maraschino cherry.

POPPY SEED BUNS

1/2 cup (1 stick) butter or
   margarine
1 1/2 cups sugar
1/2 teaspoon salt
1 teaspoon vanilla
   extract
1 cup milk, scalded
1 envelope dry yeast
4 eggs, well beaten
5 cups flour
1 cup water
1 cup poppy seeds
1/2 teaspoon cinnamon
1 egg yolk

Add the butter, 1/2 cup of the sugar, salt and vanilla to 3/4 cup of the hot milk and stir until butter is melted; let cool. Cool the remaining 1/4 cup milk to lukewarm. Sprinkle with the yeast. Stir the yeast mixture and eggs into the butter mixture. Beat in the flour, 1/2 at a time. Let rise, covered, in a warm place until doubled in bulk. Divide dough into 3 parts. Roll each part into a 12-inch circle. Combine the remaining 1 cup sugar, water, poppy seeds and cinnamon in a heavy saucepan over medium heat. Cook until slightly thickened, stirring constantly. Remove from heat. Let stand for 1 minute. Strain through a sieve. Spread evenly over the circles of dough. Cut into wedges; roll up from the wide ends. Shape into crescents on a greased baking sheet. Brush with a mixture of the egg yolk and 1 teaspoon water; sprinkle with additional sugar. Sprinkle with grated orange zest or finely chopped nuts if desired. Bake at 350 degrees for 15 to 20 minutes or until golden. Yield: 2 dozen.

Darlene Bright
Minnedosa, Manitoba, Canada

NUT ROLLS

2 envelopes dry yeast
1/2 cup sugar
1 cup warm water
6 cups flour
1 teaspoon salt
1 cup shortening
3 egg whites
1/2 cup warm water
1/2 cup evaporated milk
4 cups ground walnuts
   or pecans
1 cup sugar
2 cups packed brown
   sugar

Combine the yeast, 1/2 cup sugar and 1 cup warm water in a bowl. Let stand until yeast dissolves. Stir the flour and salt together in a bowl. Cut in the shortening until mixture resembles coarse crumbs. Add the egg whites, 1/2 cup warm water, evaporated milk and yeast mixture. Let rise, covered, in a warm place until doubled in bulk. Punch the dough down. Divide dough into 8 pieces and roll each into a circle on a floured surface, adding more flour if too sticky. Mix the nuts, 1 cup sugar and brown sugar to make the filling. Moisten the dough by brushing with additional evaporated milk, then sprinkle with the nut mixture. Roll up as for a jelly roll. Place 2 rolls on a baking sheet. Brush the rolls with beaten egg. Bake at 350 degrees for 30 minutes. Brush the hot rolls with a mixture of 1 tablespoon sugar and a little hot water. Yield: 8 rolls.

Helen Elswick, Laureate Omega
Gary, West Virginia

GERMAN CHRISTMAS STOLLEN

3/4 cup milk, scalded	*2 3/4 cups unsifted flour*
1/4 cup sugar	*1/4 cup raisins*
1/2 teaspoon salt	*1 (4-ounce) package*
1/4 cup margarine	*candied fruit*
1/4 cup warm (110 to 115	*1/2 cup chopped pecans*
degrees) water	*1 tablespoon margarine,*
1 envelope dry yeast	*melted*

Combine the first 4 ingredients in a small bowl, stirring until margarine is melted. Cool to lukewarm. Measure the warm water into a large bowl. Add the yeast, stirring until dissolved. Add the milk mixture and 2 cups of the flour and beat until smooth. Stir in the remaining flour, raisins, candied fruit and pecans. Turn out onto a lightly floured surface and knead for 5 minutes. Place in a greased bowl, turning to coat the surface. Let rise, covered, in a warm place for about 1 hour or until doubled in bulk. Punch the dough down. Roll into a rectangle about 1/2 inch thick. Brush with the 1 tablespoon melted margarine. Fold in half lengthwise. Place on a greased baking sheet. Let rise again until doubled. Bake at 350 degrees for 40 minutes or until golden. Let cool. Yield: 1 loaf.

Irene Linvill, Phi Master
Neodesha, Kansas

SWEDISH RYE BREAD

1 envelope plus 1/2	*1 cup packed brown*
teaspoon dry yeast	*sugar*
1 1/2 cups warm water	*1/4 cup molasses*
1 teaspoon sugar	*1 tablespoon salt*
1 1/2 cups milk, scalded	*3 cups rye flour*
1/3 cup shortening	*5 cups flour*

Dissolve the yeast in the warm water in a large bowl. Stir in the sugar. Combine the milk, shortening, brown sugar, molasses and salt in a bowl and mix well. Let cool to lukewarm and add to the yeast mixture. Stir in the flours 1/2 cup at a time. Knead for 10 minutes on a floured surface, adding up to 1 cup white flour if necessary; dough should be sticky, so add as little flour as possible. Place in a greased bowl, turning to coat the surface. Let rise, covered, in a warm place for about 1 1/2 hours or until doubled in bulk. Punch the dough down. Knead a few more times on a floured surface. Divide into 3 parts. Shape

into loaves and place in greased 5×8-inch bread pans. Let rise until double. Bake at 350 degrees for 45 minutes or until bread tests done. Yield: 3 loaves.

Carol Carson, Laureate Alpha Zeta
Kane, Pennsylvania

BOURBON ORANGE POUND CAKE

1 cup (2 sticks) unsalted	*2 tablespoons fresh*
butter, softened	*orange juice*
1 cup sugar	*2 tablespoons bourbon*
5 large eggs, separated	*2 to 3 tablespoons fresh*
2 1/2 cups self-rising flour	*orange juice*
Grated zest of 2 oranges	*1 to 2 tablespoons*
1/4 cup bourbon	*bourbon*
1 1/2 cups apricot jam	

Cream the butter and sugar in a mixing bowl until light and fluffy. Beat the egg yolks in another bowl until thick and pale in color. Add the eggs to the butter mixture and mix well. Sift the flour over the butter mixture; stir it in with the orange zest and the 1/4 cup bourbon. Beat the egg whites until peaks that are stiff but not dry form. Fold into the batter. Butter a 5×9-inch loaf pan and line with parchment paper. Pour the batter into the prepared pan. Bake at 350 degrees for 50 to 55 minutes or until a cake tester inserted in the center comes out clean; do not overbake. Heat the apricot jam in a saucepan over medium heat. Bring to a simmer; simmer for 1 minute. Strain through muslin. Reserve 1 cup of the strained jam for the sauce. Stir the 2 tablespoons orange juice and the 2 tablespoons bourbon into the remaining strained jam to make the glaze. As soon as the cake is removed from the oven, poke holes in the top with fork tines. Pour half the glaze over the cake. Let stand for 5 minutes. Pour the remaining glaze over the cake. Cool in the pan for 10 minutes. Remove to a wire rack to cool completely. Combine the 1 cup reserved strained jam, the 2 to 3 tablespoons orange juice and the 1 to 2 tablespoons bourbon in a bowl and mix to make the sauce. Slice the cooled cake. Serve on a pool of sauce or drizzle sauce over the cake. Yield: 12 to 14 servings.

Cynthia Tubbs, Alpha Omega
Paris, Tennessee

Michelle S. Warren, Omicron Mu, Ft. Stockton, Texas, mixes 4 cups pecans, 1 pound chopped dates, 9 ounces candied pineapple, 1 pound candied cherries, 2 cans coconut, and 2 cans sweetened condensed milk, presses into a loaf pan, and bakes at 300 degrees for 1 hour for Fruitcake Loaf.

BUCHE DE NOEL

4 eggs, separated	1/4 teaspoon salt
1 cup sugar	Confectioners' sugar
1/2 teaspoon vanilla extract	2 tablespoons rum
1 cup sifted cake flour	Chocolate Filling
1/2 teaspoon baking powder	

Beat the egg yolks at high speed in a mixing bowl until thick and lemon-colored. Add half the sugar gradually, beating constantly. Stir in the vanilla. Beat the egg whites in a separate bowl until soft peaks form. Add the remaining 1/2 cup sugar gradually, beating until stiff peaks form. Fold the yolk mixture into the egg white mixture. Pour into a greased and floured 10½×15½-inch baking pan sprayed with nonstick cooking spray. Bake at 375 degrees for 10 to 12 minutes. Remove the cake from the oven and loosen from the side of the pan. Invert onto a towel sprinkled with confectioners' sugar. Drizzle the rum over the cake. Roll the cake and towel together from a long side; let cool. Unroll the cake. Spread with half the Chocolate Filling. Reroll, without including the towel this time. Cut a 4-inch piece diagonally from the cake. Place the cut edge of the shorter piece against the longer roll on a serving plate so that the cake resembles a log shape. Frost with the remaining Chocolate Filling. Mark with fork tines to make frosting resemble bark. Decorate as desired.
Yield: 12 servings.

CHOCOLATE FILLING

1½ ounces unsweetened chocolate	1/2 cup (1 stick) butter, softened
2/3 cup sugar	1 tablespoons rum
1/3 cup water	1 teaspoon instant coffee crystals
2 egg yolks	

Melt the unsweetened chocolate; let cool. Heat the sugar and water in a small saucepan over medium heat. Cook to 240 degrees on a candy thermometer, soft-ball stage. Beat the egg yolks at high speed in a mixing bowl until thick and lemon-colored. Add the hot sugar mixture to the egg yolks very gradually, beating constantly; continue beating until mixture is completely cool. Beat in the butter, 1 tablespoon at a time. Add the chocolate, rum and coffee crystals and beat until thick.

LaRue Robinson, Laureate Alpha Upsilon
Garden City, Kansas

I CAN'T BELIEVE I LIKE FRUITCAKE!

Hardly anyone admits to liking fruitcake—but everyone like this one. It's been a favorite of our family and friends since 1968.

2 cups flour	1½ pound pitted dates, coarsely cut
2 teaspoons baking powder	4 eggs
1/2 teaspoon salt	1 cup sugar
1 pound candied pineapple chunks	2 pounds (8 cups) pecan halves
1 pound whole candied cherries	Light corn syrup

Sift the flour, baking powder and salt into a large bowl. Add the pineapple, cherries and dates and mix well with your hands to coat each piece. Beat the eggs in a mixing bowl until frothy; beat in the sugar gradually. Pour the egg mixture over the floured fruit and mix well with your hands. Mix in the pecans. Butter three 5×9-inch loaf pans and line with brown paper. Press the fruit mixture firmly into the prepared pans. Bake at 275 degrees for 1½ hours. Cool in the pans for about 5 minutes. Remove from pans and peel off paper. Brush the tops with corn syrup. Remove to a wire rack to cool completely. Wrap well and store in a cool place. Yield: about 36 slices.

Dianne Henry, Epsilon Zeta
Broomfield, Colorado

GINGERBREAD COOKIES

My five-year-old son loves to help me decorate these cookies for family and friends.

1/3 cup (2/3 stick) butter or margarine, softened	1 teaspoon baking soda
	1 teaspoon salt
1/3 cup packed brown sugar	2 teaspoons cinnamon
	1 teaspoon ground ginger
1 egg	1 teaspoon ground cloves
2/3 cup molasses	
2¾ cups flour	

Cream the butter and brown sugar in a mixing bowl until light and fluffy. Beat in the egg and molasses until well mixed. Combine the flour, baking soda, salt, cinnamon, ginger and cloves in a separate bowl and mix well. Add the dry ingredients to the molasses mixture and mix well. Roll the dough 1/4 inch thick on a floured surface. Cut with cookie cutters. Place on a greased cookie sheet. Bake at 350 degrees for 10 to 15 minutes or until golden on the bottom. Decorate with colored icing. Yield: 2 to 4 dozen.

Tami Luciow, Gamma Phi
Maple Ridge, British Columbia, Canada

JAM CAKE

Every Christmas my grandmother made this instead of fruitcake.

1 cup (2 sticks) butter or
   shortening, softened
2 cups sugar
5 eggs, beaten
3 cups sifted flour
1/2 teaspoon cinnamon
1 1/2 teaspoons ground
   cloves
1 1/2 teaspoons allspice

1/4 teaspoon salt
1 teaspoon baking soda
1 cup buttermilk
1 cup raisins or chopped
   dates
1 cup chopped walnuts
   or pecans
1 cup blackberry jam

Cream the butter and sugar in a mixing bowl until light and fluffy. Beat in the eggs. Combine the flour, cinnamon, cloves, allspice and salt and mix well. Dissolve the baking soda in the buttermilk. Add to the egg mixture alternately with the dry ingredients, mixing well after each addition. Dredge the raisins and nuts lightly in additional flour and stir into the batter. Add the jam, stirring to mix well. Butter two 9-inch cake pans and line with paper. Pour the batter 2 inches deep into the prepared pans. Bake at 325 degrees for 40 minutes. Ice with caramel icing, or any flavor you like. Yield: 16 servings.

Sharon Lorenz, Laureate Zeta
Louisville, Kentucky

ORANGE SLICE CAKE

1 cup (2 sticks) butter
4 eggs, beaten
2 cups sugar
1/2 cup buttermilk
3 1/2 cups flour
1 teaspoon baking soda
1/4 teaspoon salt
1 1/2 pounds orange slice
   candy, chopped

1 1/3 cups shredded
   coconut
8 ounces dates, chopped
1 cup pecans, chopped
2 cups confectioners'
   sugar
1 cup orange juice
1 teaspoon vanilla
   extract

Melt the butter in a saucepan over medium heat, being careful not to burn it. Remove from heat. Combine the eggs, sugar, buttermilk and butter and mix well. Add a mixture of the flour, baking soda and salt to the egg mixture and mix well. Stir in the candy, coconut, dates and pecans. Pour the batter into a greased and floured bundt pan. Bake at 325 degrees for 1 hour. Combine the remaining ingredients in a saucepan over medium heat and bring to a boil. Pierce holes in the warm cake with a fork. Pour the glaze over the warm cake in the pan. Let stand for 8 to 12 hours. Remove from pan. Yield: 32 servings.

Gloria Mann, Nu Rho
Killeen, Texas

SYRUP CAKE

6 eggs, separated, at
   room temperature
1 cup farina or cream of
   wheat
1 teaspoon vanilla
   extract
1/4 teaspoon almond
   extract (optional)

4 cups water
1 1/2 cups sugar
1 teaspoon lemon juice
1/2 teaspoon grated
   lemon zest

Beat the egg whites in a mixing bowl until stiff but not dry peaks form. Fold in the farina. Beat the egg yolks until pale yellow. Beat in the vanilla and almond extract. Fold the yolk mixture into the egg white mixture. Pour into an 8-inch-square baking pan sprayed with nonstick cooking spray. Bake at 375 degrees for 25 minutes or until cake tests done. Remove from oven. Cut into diamond-shaped pieces while cake is still in the pan. Combine the water, sugar, lemon juice and zest in a heavy saucepan over medium heat. Bring to a boil; reduce heat. Simmer for 15 minutes or until thick and syrupy. Pour the syrup over the warm cake very slowly so that all is absorbed by the cake. Cover with foil. Let cool completely. Yield: 16 servings.

Jane C. Wargo, Delta Master
Rochester, New York

MRS. CLAUS' SECRET FUDGE

2 cups (4 sticks) butter
1 pound Velveeta cheese
1 cup baking cocoa
4 pounds confectioners'
   sugar

1 tablespoon vanilla
   extract
1 1/2 cups chopped pecans
   or walnuts (optional)

Place the butter and cheese in a large microwave-safe bowl. Microwave on Medium until butter and cheese are melted, stirring occasionally. Combine the butter mixture, baking cocoa, confectioners' sugar, vanilla and nuts in a large bowl and mix well; the mixture will get thick, but keep on mixing, using hands if necessary. Spread over waxed paper and pat into a rectangle. Cut into squares. Yield: 50 or more pieces.

Mary Ellen Grossman, Laureate Beta Nu
Lawrenceburg, Indiana

Patricia A. Gillmore, Xi Omega, Murphysboro, Illinois, makes Cookies and Cream Fudge by melting 18 ounces white chocolate with a can of sweetened condensed milk and 1/8 teaspoon salt, then stirring in 2 cups coarsely crushed cream-filled sandwich cookies. Spread in a foil-lined pan and chill until firm.

HOLIDAY FUDGE

2 cups semisweet chocolate chips	1/2 cup coarsely chopped pecans or walnuts
1 (14-ounce) can sweetened condensed milk	1/4 cup coarsely chopped mixed candied fruit

Line a 5×9-inch loaf pan with lightly buttered waxed paper, allowing the paper to hang over the sides of the pan. Melt the chocolate in the top of a double boiler over hot, not boiling, water. Remove to a medium bowl. Add the condensed milk, nuts and candied fruit and mix well. Pat into the prepared pan. Chill, covered, for 2 to 4 hours or until firm. Use the waxed paper to pull the block of fudge from the pan. Cut into 1-inch squares. Yield: 32 servings.

Sarah Stephens, Tau Master
Austin, Texas

VICTORIA FUDGE

3 cups sugar	1/4 cup chopped figs or dates
1/4 cup butter	1 teaspoon (or less) almond extract or rose flavoring
3/4 cup heavy cream	
1 cup flaked coconut	
1/4 cup chopped candied pineapple	
1/4 cup chopped candied cherries	

Combine the sugar, butter and cream in a heavy saucepan. Cook, uncovered, over medium heat to 234 to 238 degrees on a candy thermometer, soft-ball stage. Remove from heat. Cool to lukewarm; beat until creamy. Add the pineapple, cherries, figs and almond extract and mix well. Pour into a well-buttered shallow baking pan. Let stand until firm. Cut into squares. Yield: 32 servings.

Vicki L. Hadler, Laureate Rho
Greensburg, Indiana

WALNUT SOUR CREAM FUDGE

2 cups sugar	1/4 cup candied cherries, quartered
1/2 cup sour cream	1 cup coarsely chopped walnuts
1/3 cup white corn syrup	
2 tablespoons margarine	
1/4 teaspoon salt	
2 teaspoons vanilla extract	

Combine the sugar, sour cream, corn syrup, margarine and salt in a heavy saucepan over medium heat. Bring to a boil slowly, stirring until sugar dissolves. Cook, uncovered, over medium heat to 236 degrees on a candy thermometer, soft-ball stage; do not stir. Remove from heat and let stand for 15 minutes; do not stir. Add the vanilla. Beat for about 8 minutes or until mixture begins to lose its gloss. Stir in the cherries and walnuts and pour quickly into a buttered shallow pan. Let cool until firm. Cut into squares. Yield: 24 servings.

Peggy Fox, Xi Gamma Alpha
Norfolk, Nebraska

ALMOND BUTTER CRUNCH WHEELS

1 cup blanched slivered almonds	1/2 cup sugar
1/2 cup (1 stick) butter	1 tablespoon light corn syrup

Line the bottom and side of a 9-inch cake pan with heavily buttered foil. Combine the almonds, butter, sugar and corn syrup in a 10-inch skillet over medium heat. Bring to a boil, stirring constantly. Boil until mixture turns golden brown, stirring constantly. Spread quickly in the prepared pan. Let cool for about 15 minutes or until firm. Remove from the pan by lifting the edges of the foil; remove the foil. If you are careful, the foil may be used for several batches. Let cool completely. May be served as a disk or broken into bite-size pieces. Yield: 12 servings.

Corinne Martins, Preceptor Theta
Buhl, Idaho

ALMOND BUTTER TOFFEE

1/2 cup (1 stick) butter	2 tablespoons sliced almonds
1 cup sugar	1 (4-ounce) milk chocolate bar
1/2 teaspoon salt	
1/4 cup water	

Place the butter in a 2-quart microwave-safe bowl. Pour the sugar over the butter. Add the salt and water. Microwave on High for 7 minutes, stirring once or twice. Continue to microwave, 30 seconds at a time, until mixture is the color of light brown sugar. Butter a baking sheet; sprinkle with the almonds. Pour the sugar mixture over the almonds; do not scrape the bowl. Let cool. Microwave the chocolate bar on High in a microwave-safe bowl for 1 to 1 1/2 minutes or until melted; remember that the chocolate will keep its shape when microwaved even after it has melted. Spread evenly over the candy. Let cool completely. Hit the pan on the countertop and break candy into pieces. Yield: 16 servings.

Nancy Cummings, Xi Kappa Pi
Belleville, Illinois

ALMOND COCONUT CANDY

1 pound flaked coconut
2 pounds confectioners'
    sugar
1 cup (2 sticks) butter,
    melted
1 (14-ounce) can
    sweetened condensed
    milk

1/2 teaspoon vanilla
    extract
1/4 teaspoon salt
6 cups chocolate chips
3 tablespoons paraffin
Almonds

Combine the coconut, confectioners' sugar, butter, condensed milk and vanilla in a bowl and mix well. Let stand, covered, in the refrigerator until cool. Roll into 1-inch balls. Arrange on a baking sheet and chill for 1 or 2 hours. Melt the chocolate chips and paraffin in the top of a double boiler over simmering water; mix well. Dip each ball in the chocolate mixture. Press an almond into each dipped ball. Return to the refrigerator and chill. May also be frozen. Yield: 5 dozen.

Judy Thornton, Laureate Zeta Epsilon
Potter Valley, California

CINNAMON CRACKING CANDY

2 3/4 cups sugar
3/4 cup light corn syrup
3/4 cup water
1/2 teaspoon oil of
    cinnamon

1 teaspoon red food
    coloring

Combine the sugar, corn syrup and water in a heavy saucepan over medium heat. Cook for 5 to 10 minutes, stirring constantly. Turn heat to high and cook, uncovered, to 300 degrees on a candy thermometer, hard-crack stage. Remove from heat. Stir in the oil of cinnamon and food coloring. Pour over a buttered baking sheet. Let stand until hard. Crack into pieces. Yield: 20 to 30 servings.

Lynda Hadley, Delta Beta
Pleasant Grove, Alabama

CHRISTMAS CHEER CANDY

3 cups sugar
1 cup light corn syrup
1 1/2 cups light cream
1 teaspoon vanilla
    extract
1 cup walnuts, chopped

1 cup pecans, chopped
8 ounces candied
    pineapple
8 ounces candied
    cherries

Combine the sugar, corn syrup and cream in a heavy saucepan over medium heat. Cook, uncovered, to 234 to 240 degrees on a candy thermometer, soft-ball stage, stirring constantly. Remove from heat. Stir in the vanilla. Beat at high speed until mixture begins to thicken and turn light in color. Stir in the nuts, pineapple and cherries. Pour into a buttered 10×15-inch cake pan. Let cool. Cut into squares. Let stand in an airtight container for 2 or 3 weeks to mellow. May be frozen. Yield: 40 servings.

Nell Lister, Laureate Delta Mu
Wichita Falls, Texas

CRANBERRY CANDY

1 (16-ounce) can jellied
    cranberry sauce
1 (3-ounce) package
    lemon gelatin
2 (3-ounce) packages
    orange, raspberry or
    cranberry gelatin

1 cup sugar
1 cup chopped pecans or
    walnuts (optional)
Confectioners' sugar

Melt the cranberry sauce in a saucepan over low heat. Bring to a boil. Stir in the gelatin and sugar. Boil for 1 minute or until dissolved, stirring constantly. Remove from the heat. Stir in the pecans. Pour into a well-buttered 8×11-inch baking pan. Let cool at room temperature for 8 to 12 hours. Invert onto a 9x13-inch baking sheet covered with confectioners' sugar. Cut into squares. Dust with confectioners' sugar. Let stand in a cool place for 5 days; do not refrigerate. Yield: 40 servings.

Beverly Christian Dull, Master Epsilon
Roseburg, Oregon

FOREVER AMBER BALLS

This candy will keep in the freezer for 1 to 3 months, and tastes especially good when served frozen.

1 pound orange slice
    candy, finely chopped
2 (14-ounce) cans
    sweetened condensed
    milk
7 ounces flaked coconut

1 cup finely chopped
    pecans
1 teaspoon vanilla
    extract
1 pound confectioners'
    sugar

Combine the orange candy, condensed milk, coconut, pecans and vanilla in a bowl and mix well. Spread in a 9×13-inch baking pan. Bake at 325 degrees for 30 to 35 minutes. Cool slightly. Roll into balls using hands and a teaspoon. Dredge in confectioners' sugar. Yield: more than 30 servings.

Mary Bogan, Beta Iota Mu
Houston, Texas

PEANUT BRITTLE

1 cup sugar
1/2 cup light corn syrup
1³/4 to 2 cups dry roasted
    peanuts
1 teaspoon butter or
    margarine

1 teaspoon vanilla
    extract
1 teaspoon baking soda

Combine the sugar and corn syrup in a 2-quart microwave-safe dish. Microwave on High for 4 minutes. Stir in the peanuts with a wooden spoon. Microwave on High for 3 minutes longer. Stir in the butter and vanilla. Microwave on High for 2 to 2¹/2 minutes or until the mixture separates into hard threads that crack when pressed between the fingers. Add the baking soda, stirring until mixture is light and foamy. Pour over a generously greased baking sheet, spreading quickly to the edges with the back of a wooden spoon. Stretch the candy into a thin sheet with palms of hands as it cools. Let cool completely. Break into pieces. Store in an airtight container in a cool place. Yield: 20 servings.

Ruth Townsend, Laureate Lambda
Lower Sackville, Nova Scotia, Canada

PECAN PRALINES

2 cups packed brown
    sugar
1 cup sugar
1 (14-ounce) can
    sweetened condensed
    milk

1/2 cup water
2 teaspoons maple
    extract
2 cups chopped pecans

Combine the sugars, condensed milk, water and maple extract in a medium saucepan. Cook over medium heat to exactly 236 degrees on a candy thermometer, soft-ball stage. Remove from heat. Add the pecans and mix well. Drop by tablespoonfuls onto buttered waxed paper. Let cool. Store in an airtight container. Yield: about 42 servings.

Helen J. Smith, Laureate Zeta Eta
College Station, Texas

CREAMY PRALINES

1 teaspoon baking soda
1 cup buttermilk
3 cups sugar
2 tablespoons light corn
    syrup

1 cup (2 sticks) butter
1 teaspoon vanilla
    extract
3 cups pecan halves

Stir the baking soda into the buttermilk. Combine the buttermilk mixture, sugar, corn syrup and butter in a heavy saucepan. Cook over medium heat to 234 to 240 degrees on a candy thermometer, soft-ball stage.

Stir in the vanilla and pecans. Cool the candy quickly by placing the saucepan in a large pan of cold water. Let stand for 3 to 5 minutes or until candy thickens. Drop by teaspoonfuls onto waxed paper. Let cool completely before serving. Yield: 3 dozen.

Linda P. Tutwiler
Alva, Oklahoma

AMBROSIA COOKIES

1 cup (2 sticks) butter or
    margarine, softened
1 cup firmly packed
    dark brown sugar
1 cup sugar
2 eggs
2 cups flour
1¹/2 cups uncooked
    rolled oats
2 teaspoons baking
    powder
1/2 teaspoon baking soda
1/2 teaspoon salt
1 cup chopped dates
1 cup golden raisins

1 cup flaked coconut
1 cup chopped pecans
1 teaspoon grated
    orange zest
1 teaspoon grated
    lemon zest
1 teaspoon vanilla
    extract
1/2 teaspoon almond
    extract
1/2 teaspoon orange
    extract
About 4 dozen candied
    cherries, halved

Cream the butter, brown sugar and sugar in a mixing bowl at medium speed until light and fluffy, adding the brown sugar and sugar gradually. Add the eggs 1 at a time, beating well after each addition. Combine the flour, oats, baking powder, baking soda and salt; mix well. Add the flour mixture, dates, raisins, coconut, pecans, orange zest, lemon zest, vanilla, almond extract and orange extract to the creamed mixture; mix well. Drop by rounded teaspoonfuls 2 inches apart onto lightly greased cookie sheets; press a cherry half lightly into each cookie. Bake at 350 degrees for 14 to 16 minutes or until edges begin to brown. Cool on cookie sheets for 10 minutes. Remove to wire racks to cool completely; cookies will firm as they cool. Yield: about 8 dozen.

Cynthia Perry, Alpha Omega
Paris, Tennessee

Denise Devillier, Omega Gamma, Winnie, Texas, makes Almond Brandy Spread to serve with gingersnaps or shortbread. Plump a cup of golden raisins in peach brandy overnight and drain. Soften an envelope of unflavored gelatin in 1/4 cup cold water and heat until dissolved. Blend in a mixture of 12 ounces cream cheese, 1/2 cup butter, 1/2 cup sour cream, and 1/2 cup sugar. Mix in 1 cup sliced almonds and zest of 2 lemons. Pour into crocks and chill.

CANDY CANE COOKIES

My children loved it when Christmastime came around and they would get to help make and decorate these candy canes, laughing and giggling. If you use self-rising flour in this recipe, omit the salt.

1/2 cup (1 stick) butter or margarine, softened	2 1/2 cups flour
1/2 cup shortening	1 teaspoon salt
1/2 cup confectioners' sugar	1/2 teaspoon red food coloring
1 egg	1/2 cup crushed peppermint candy
1 1/2 teaspoons almond extract	1/2 cup sugar
1 teaspoon vanilla extract	

Preheat the oven to 375 degrees. Combine the butter, shortening, confectioners' sugar, egg, almond extract and vanilla in a mixing bowl and mix until smooth. Blend in the flour and salt. Divide dough in half; blend the food coloring into 1/2 of the dough. Combine the peppermint candy and sugar in a separate bowl and mix well. Shape teaspoonfuls of dough into 4-inch ropes, rolling them back and forth on a lightly floured surface to make smooth, even cylinders. Place a red rope and a white rope side by side for each cookie; press together lightly and twist. Repeat. Arrange the cookies on an ungreased cookie sheet, curving down the tops to form the candy canes. Bake for about 9 minutes or until set and very lightly brown. Sprinkle the hot cookies with the peppermint mixture. Remove from the cookie sheet to a wire rack to cool completely. Yield: 4 dozen.

Cynthia Miller
Beaumont, Texas

CHOCOLATE CARAMEL BARS

I give these cookies to special friends during the Christmas holidays—some of them start asking me in October if they are still on the list to receive them!

38 caramels	1 cup rolled oats
6 tablespoons heavy cream	1/2 teaspoon baking soda
1 cup flour	3/4 cup (1 1/2 sticks) butter, softened
3/4 cup packed brown sugar	1 cup semisweet chocolate chips

Heat the caramels and cream in a heavy saucepan over medium heat until caramels are melted, stirring frequently. Combine the flour, brown sugar, rolled oats and baking soda in a bowl and mix well. Cut in the butter until the mixture resembles coarse crumbs. Pat half the flour mixture into an 8-inch-square baking dish sprayed with nonstick cooking spray. Bake at 325 degrees for 20 minutes. Pour the caramel mixture over the baked crust. Sprinkle evenly with the chocolate chips. Crumble the remaining half the flour mixture evenly over the chips. Bake for 20 minutes longer. Let cool and cut into squares. They freeze very well. Yield: 30 bars.

Shirley Balasko, Preceptor Beta Phi
Englewood, Colorado

PEANUT BUTTER BROWNIES

These brownies were my mom's specialty at Christmastime. She scattered Christmas sprinkles over the white frosting.

1 cup peanut butter	1 cup flour
1/2 cup shortening	2 teaspoons vanilla extract
2 cups sugar	Vanilla Frosting
4 eggs	

Cream the peanut butter, shortening and sugar in a mixing bowl until light and fluffy. Add the eggs 1 at a time, beating well after each addition. Beat in the flour and vanilla. Spread in a greased 9×13-inch baking pan. Bake at 350 degrees for 20 minutes. Check the center with a wooden pick; if doughy, bake for 5 to 10 minutes longer. Let cool. Frost with Vanilla Frosting. Yield: 2 dozen.

VANILLA FROSTING

1/2 cup shortening	3 cups confectioners' sugar
1/4 teaspoon salt	1/2 cup milk
1 teaspoon vanilla extract	

Combine the shortening, salt, vanilla and 1 cup of the confectioners' sugar in a bowl. Add small amounts of the milk alternately with the remaining confectioners' sugar, beating until smooth and creamy.

Diana K. Adams, Theta
Vincennes, Indiana

Cara Nelson, Beta Gamma, Smithers, British Columbia, Canada, makes moist Whipped Shortbread Cookies by combining 2 cups softened butter, 1/2 cup cornstarch, 1/2 cup confectioners' sugar, 3 cups flour, and 1 teaspoon vanilla extract and beating until fluffy. Spoon or press with a cookie press onto ungreased cookie sheets and bake at 350 degrees for 8 to 10 minutes.

WHITE CHOCOLATE BROWNIES

1¼ cups flour
½ teaspoon baking
    powder
Pinch of salt
1 cup white chocolate
    chips
¾ cup sugar
½ cup (1 stick)
    margarine

2 eggs, lightly beaten
1 teaspoon vanilla
    extract
1 cup semisweet
    chocolate chips
2 cups milk chocolate
    chips
1 cup chopped pecans or
    macadamia nuts

Combine the flour, baking powder and salt and mix well. Combine the white chocolate chips, sugar and margarine in a medium saucepan over medium-low heat. Heat until all is melted and smooth, stirring frequently. Remove from heat and cool slightly. Stir in the eggs and vanilla. Add the flour mixture and stir until well mixed. Add the semisweet chocolate chips and mix well. Spread in a buttered 9-inch springform pan. Bake at 350 degrees for 20 to 25 minutes or until a wooden pick inserted in the center comes out clean. Remove from oven. Sprinkle with the milk chocolate chips. Return to oven to bake for 1 minute longer. Remove from oven. Spread the melted chocolate over the surface. Sprinkle with pecans. Let cool in the pan for 30 minutes. Chill, covered, in the refrigerator for 1 hour. Slice into wedges. Yield: 16 servings.

Sandy Franklin, Xi Iota Lambda
Olney, Illinois

WHITE CHRISTMAS COOKIES

2¼ cups flour, sifted
1 teaspoon baking soda
1 teaspoon salt
1 cup unsalted butter,
    softened
¾ cup firmly packed
    light brown sugar
¾ cup sugar
3 eggs

1 teaspoon vanilla
    extract
2 cups white chocolate
    chips
¾ cup salted
    macadamia nuts,
    chopped
1¼ cups golden raisins
    (optional)

Combine the flour, baking soda and salt and mix well. Cream the butter and sugars in a mixing bowl until light and fluffy. Add the eggs 1 at a time, beating well after each addition. Beat in the vanilla. Beat in the flour mixture gradually. Stir in the chocolate chips, nuts and raisins. Drop by teaspoonfuls 2 inches apart onto lightly greased cookie sheets. Bake at 350 degrees for 8 to 10 minutes or until pale golden. Cool on a wire rack. Yield: 6 dozen.

Tish Hamilton, Kappa
Highlands, Texas

ORANGE CHOCOLATE CHIP COOKIES

1⅓ cups butter, softened
1⅓ cups sugar
8 ounces cream cheese,
    softened
3 eggs
2⅔ teaspoons vanilla
    extract

2⅔ cups flour
1½ teaspoons salt
1 tablespoon grated
    orange zest
2 cups semisweet
    chocolate chips

Cream the butter and sugar in a mixing bowl until light and fluffy. Beat in the cream cheese, eggs and vanilla. Add a mixture of the flour and salt gradually to the creamed mixture. Stir in the orange zest and chocolate chips. Drop by rounded teaspoonfuls onto ungreased cookie sheets. Bake at 350 degrees for 15 minutes or until edges are browned.
Yield: 8 dozen small cookies.

Linda Newman, Xi Beta Theta
Tucumcari, New Mexico

ENGLISH TOFFEE COOKIES

2 cups (4 sticks) butter,
    softened
2 cups sugar
2 eggs, separated
2 teaspoons cinnamon

2 teaspoon salt
4 cups cake flour
2 teaspoons vanilla
    extract
2 cups chopped pecans

Cream the butter and sugar in a mixing bowl until light and fluffy. Beat in the egg yolks 1 at a time. Add the cinnamon, salt, flour, vanilla and half the pecans and mix well. Press the mixture into a buttered 10×15-inch cake pan. Beat the egg whites with a mixer until stiff peaks form. Spread the egg whites over the mixture in the pan. Sprinkle with the remaining 1 cup pecans. Bake at 375 degrees for 30 minutes. Cool and cut into 1-inch squares.
Yield: 6 dozen.

Carol A. Granat, Preceptor Alpha Alpha
Las Vegas, Nevada

OATMEAL RAISIN COOKIES

1 cup (2 sticks) butter or
    margarine, softened
2 cups sugar
2 eggs, beaten
1½ cups flour
1 teaspoon baking soda
⅛ teaspoon salt

1 cup ground raisins
2 cups ground
    rolled oats
1 teaspoon vanilla
    extract
1 cup ground pecans
    (optional)

Cream the butter and sugar in a mixing bowl until light and fluffy. Beat in the eggs. Stir in the raisins. Sift the flour, baking soda and salt over the egg mixture and mix well. Stir in the rolled oats and vanilla. Stir in the pecans last. Chill, covered, for 2 to 3 hours.

Shape dough into small balls. Place 2 inches apart on a greased cookie sheet. Bake at 325 degrees for 12 to 15 minutes or until golden brown. Remove to a wire rack before they cool. Yield: 5 to 6 dozen.

Mary Belle Morgan, Zeta Xi
Dongola, Illinois

HAWAIIAN NUT COOKIES

1 cup (2 sticks) butter, softened	2¼ cups flour
1 cup firmly packed brown sugar	1 teaspoon baking soda
	1 cup shredded coconut
½ cup sugar	¾ cup chopped macadamia nuts
1 large egg	

Combine the butter, sugars and egg in a mixing bowl and beat until creamy. Add a mixture of the flour and baking soda ½ cup at a time, blending after each addition. Stir in the coconut and nuts. Drop by rounded teaspoonfuls 2 inches apart on an ungreased cookie sheet. Bake at 375 degrees for 8 minutes or until golden brown. Yield: 3 dozen.

Norma Bullerman, Beta Delta
Calmar, Iowa

HOLIDAY FRUIT AND NUT HUNKS

1 teaspoon baking soda	1 teaspoon cinnamon
2 tablespoons hot water	1 pound pecans, chopped
1 cup (2 sticks) butter, softened	1 pound raisins
	1 pound dates, chopped
1½ cups sugar	½ cup chopped maraschino cherries
3 eggs	
3 cups flour	

Dissolve the baking soda in the hot water. Cream the butter and sugar in a mixing bowl until light and fluffy. Beat in the eggs and the baking soda mixture. Beat in the flour and cinnamon. Stir in the remaining ingredients. Drop by teaspoonfuls on a greased cookie sheet. Bake at 350 degrees for 7 to 10 minutes if you like chewy hunks, 10 to 12 minutes for crispy hunks. Yield: 4 to 5 dozen.

Sharon Erikson, Eta Pi
Gretna, Louisiana

Mary Lou Jones, Laureate Delta Delta, Oak Grove, Missouri, makes Snicker Bar Pies by creaming 8 ounces cream cheese, 1½ cups confectioners' sugar, and ½ cup peanut butter, folding in 16 ounces whipped topping and 5 chopped Snicker bars and spreading in 2 graham cracker or chocolate crumb pie shells. Chill overnight.

KIFFLINGS

2 cups (4 sticks) butter, softened	3 teaspoons vanilla extract
⅔ cup sugar	1 pound pecans or walnuts, ground
4 cups flour	

Cream the butter and sugar in a mixing bowl until light and fluffy. Add the flour and vanilla and mix well. Add the nuts and knead until well mixed. Shape into small balls and place on a nonstick cookie sheet. Shape the dough balls into small crescents. Bake at 275 degrees for 1 hour. Let cool. Roll in confectioners' sugar. Yield: 4 dozen.

Marie Christine Betts, Preceptor Alpha Alpha
Burnaby, British Columbia, Canada

FUDGE MELTAWAYS

1¼ cups butter, softened	1 egg, slightly beaten
2 ounces unsweetened chocolate	1 cup flaked coconut
	½ cup finely chopped pecans or walnuts
¼ cup sugar	
2 teaspoons vanilla extract	1 tablespoon milk
	2 cups sifted confectioners' sugar
2 cups graham cracker crumbs	

Melt ½ cup of the butter and half the chocolate in a small saucepan over low heat, stirring occasionally; remove from heat. Combine ¼ cup sugar, 1 teaspoon of the vanilla, graham cracker crumbs, egg, coconut and nuts in a large mixing bowl and mix well. Blend in the melted chocolate. Press into an ungreased 9-inch-square pan. Let stand, covered, in the refrigerator. Combine ¼ cup of the butter, milk, confectioners' sugar and remaining 1 teaspoon vanilla in a medium mixing bowl and mix well. Spread evenly over the chocolate layer. Chill. Melt remaining ½ cup butter and remaining chocolate in a small saucepan over low heat, stirring occasionally. Spread evenly over the confectioners' sugar layer. Let stand in the refrigerator. Cut into squares before fudge is too firm. Yield: 5 to 6 dozen.

Cynthia Marie Keene, Xi Chi Kappa
McKinleyville, California

Judy Pruett, Alpha Delta, Lynchburg, Virginia, melts ¼ cup butter in a baking pan and adds layers of 1 cup graham cracker crumbs, 7 ounces coconut, 1 cup chocolate chips, 1 cup butterscotch chips, ½ cup peanut butter chips, 1 can sweetened condensed milk, and 1 cup chopped pecans for Easy Christmas Eight-Layer Cookies. Bake at 325 degrees for 30 minutes. Cool and cut.

HOLLY COOKIES

My artistic sister Kathy made these delicious cookies every Christmas, and they were masterpieces— almost too beautiful to eat! Serve with a cup of hot English tea.

2 cups flour	2/3 cup raspberry jam
1 cup sugar	2 cups confectioners'
1 teaspoon cinnamon	sugar
3/4 teaspoon baking	1/2 teaspoon vanilla
powder	extract
1/4 teaspoon salt	Green food coloring
1/2 cup (1 stick) butter or	2 to 3 tablespoons milk
margarine, softened	Red hot cinnamon
1 egg, slightly beaten	candies
1/4 cup milk	

Preheat the oven to 375 degrees. Combine the flour, sugar, cinnamon, baking powder and salt in a medium mixing bowl. Cut in the butter until mixture resembles small peas. Make a well in the center. Combine the egg and milk and add all at once to the butter mixture. Stir until moistened. Roll the dough to 1/8-inch thickness on a lightly floured surface. Cut into 2-inch circles or flowers with a cookie cutter. Place on ungreased baking sheets. Bake for 8 to 10 minutes or until light brown on the bottom. Remove to a wire rack to cool completely. Spread about 1/2 teaspoon raspberry jam between each pair of cookies, rounded sides facing out. Blend the confectioners' sugar, vanilla, food coloring and enough milk to make of desired consistency. Decorate with the green icing and red hot cinnamon candies.
Yield: about 4 1/2 dozen.

Jane E. Ross, Zeta Zeta
Pine, Arizona

NORWEGIAN SPICE COOKIES

1 cup (2 sticks) butter,	1 teaspoon baking soda
softened	3/4 teaspoon ground
1 cup sugar	cloves
1 egg	1 tablespoon dark corn
3 teaspoons cinnamon	syrup

Cream the butter and sugar in a mixing bowl until light and fluffy. Beat in the egg. Sift the cinnamon, baking soda and cloves over the creamed mixture and mix well. Beat in the corn syrup. Chill for 1 hour. Shape into small balls and place on a nonstick cookie sheet. Flatten each ball with the bottom of a buttered and sugared glass. Bake in a preheated 350-degree oven for 10 minutes. Yield: 100 small cookies.

Joyce L. Voss, Preceptor Beta Zeta
Twin Oaks, Oklahoma

WHITE CHOCOLATE PECAN COOKIES

1/2 cup sugar	2 eggs
1 cup packed brown	2 1/2 cups flour
sugar	1 teaspoon baking soda
1 cup butter-flavored	1/2 teaspoon salt
shortening	1 cup white chocolate
1 1/2 teaspoons vanilla	chips
extract	1 1/2 cups chopped pecans

Cream the sugars and shortening in a large bowl until light and fluffy. Beat in the vanilla and eggs. Add a mixture of the flour, baking soda and salt and mix well. Stir in the chocolate chips and pecans. Drop by teaspoonfuls 2 inches apart onto a well-greased cookie sheet. Bake in a preheated 375-degree oven for 10 to 12 minutes or until golden brown. Remove the cookies to a wire rack to cool. Yield: 6 dozen.

Sue Helms, Preceptor Kappa
Jonesboro, Arkansas

CRISP SUGAR COOKIES

Children enjoy "squashing" these cookies, decorating them, and, of course, devouring them.

1/2 cup (1 stick)	2 1/2 teaspoons vanilla
margarine, softened	extract
1 1/2 cups shortening	5 cups flour
3 cups sugar	2 teaspoons baking soda
3 eggs	1 teaspoon salt

Cream the margarine, shortening and sugar in a mixing bowl until light and fluffy. Add the eggs 1 at a time, beating well after each addition. Beat in the vanilla. Sift together the flour, baking soda and salt. Add the dry ingredients to the creamed mixture and mix well. Chill, covered, for at least 1 hour. Preheat the oven to 325 degrees. Shape the dough into small balls and place on a nonstick cookie sheet. Flatten the balls with the bottom of a drinking glass or a cookie press. Decorate with colored sugars. Bake for 10 minutes or until light golden around the edges.
Yield: about 5 dozen.

Rhonda Phillips, Beta Epsilon Tau
Houston, Texas

TOFFEE SQUARES

1 cup (2 sticks) butter,	2 cups flour
softened	1/4 teaspoon salt
1 cup packed brown	8 ounces sweet baking
sugar	chocolate, melted
1 egg yolk	1/2 cup chopped walnuts
1 teaspoon vanilla	or pecans
extract	

Cream the butter and brown sugar in a mixing bowl until light and fluffy. Beat in the egg yolk and vanilla. Add a mixture of the flour and salt and mix until moistened. Pat into a 10×13-inch rectangle on a greased baking sheet. Bake at 350 degrees for 20 minutes. Spread with melted chocolate while still warm and sprinkle with nuts. Let cool and cut into squares. Yield: 1 to 3 dozen.

Marie Hass, Beta Epsilon
Madison, Wisconsin

WELSH COOKIES

Chill the dough before rolling and cutting these cookies to make it easier to handle. Or you may form the dough into 2½-inch rolls, wrap in waxed paper, chill, slice, and bake. If you like, you may substitute ½ teaspoon mace for ½ teaspoon of the nutmeg. Another tip: It's best to use fresh baking powder.

1 cup currants	1 teaspoon salt
4 cups flour	1 tablespoon nutmeg
4 teaspoons baking powder	1¼ cups shortening
1½ cups sugar	2 eggs
	½ cup milk

Soak the currants in enough hot water to cover for at least 30 minutes. Sift the flour, baking powder, sugar, salt and nutmeg together into a large bowl. Cut in the shortening until the mixture resembles coarse crumbs. Combine the eggs and milk in a small bowl and beat well. Add the egg mixture to the flour mixture and mix well. Squeeze the liquid from the currants. Mix the currants into the dough. Roll the dough into 3/8-inch thickness on a floured surface, trying not to use too much extra flour when rolling. Cut into 2½-inch rounds. Bake on an electric skillet set at 350 degrees for about 3 minutes on each side or until golden. Yield: 5 dozen.

Janis Bradbury, Preceptor Beta
Chandler, Arizona

CHERRY ALMOND MOUSSE PIE

1 (14-ounce) can sweetened condensed milk	8 ounces cream cheese, softened
1 ounce unsweetened chocolate	1 cup cold water
½ teaspoon almond extract	1 (3-ounce) package instant vanilla pudding mix
1 baked (9-inch) pie shell	1 cup whipping cream, whipped
1 (10-ounce) jar maraschino cherries, drained	½ cup chopped toasted almonds
	Chocolate curls (optional)

Combine 1 cup of the condensed milk and the chocolate in a heavy saucepan over low heat. Cook for 4 to 5 minutes or until chocolate is melted and mixture is thickened, stirring constantly. Stir in ¼ teaspoon of the almond extract. Pour into the pie shell. Chop the cherries, reserving 8 whole cherries for garnish. Beat the cream cheese in a mixing bowl until light. Beat in the remaining condensed milk and the water gradually. Add the dry pudding mix and the remaining ¼ teaspoon almond extract and mix well. Fold in the whipped cream. Stir in the chopped cherries and toasted almonds. Pour the cherry mixture over the pie. Chill, covered, for 4 hours before serving. Garnish with whole cherries and chocolate curls. Yield: 8 to 10 servings.

Janice Wilson, Laureate Delta Delta
Oak Grove, Missouri

CHRISTMAS CHERRY PIE

1 (15-ounce) can dark sweet juice-pack cherries, drained	1 tablespoon vanilla extract
1 (15-ounce) can crushed pineapple, drained	1 (3-ounce) package orange gelatin
2 cups sugar	1 cup chopped pecans
½ cup flour	6 ripe bananas, mashed well
1 tablespoon red food coloring	2 baked (9- or 10-inch) pie shells

Combine the cherries and pineapple in a medium saucepan over medium-low heat. Stir in the sugar, flour and food coloring. Cook until thick, stirring constantly. Remove from heat. Stir in the vanilla and gelatin. Let cool. Stir in the pecans and bananas. Pour into the pie shells. Chill, covered, until ready to serve. Serve with whipped cream or whipped topping. Yield: 12 servings.

Michelle R. Smith, Preceptor Chi
Mt. Vernon, Illinois

Suzanne Golay, Xi Epsilon Rho, Perry, Oklahoma, makes use of high-quality fruit to make a light, tangy Grapefruit Pie. She cuts the sections from 3 grapefruit, then drains and sets them aside. Then she mixes a 3-ounce package of strawberry gelatin with 2 tablespoons cornstarch, 1 cup sugar, and 2 cups cold water in a saucepan and cooks over medium heat until clear and thickened, stirring constantly. After blending in 2 drops of red food coloring, a pinch of salt, and a tablespoon of margarine, she lets the mixture cool, folds in the grapefruit, and pours the mixture into a baked pie shell. Chill until firm and serve with whipped topping.

RUM CHIFFON PIE

This is an old recipe that I have used for 50 years, always receiving compliments when I make it. The pie is festive, light, and fluffy. You can cut up a chocolate candy bar to make the slivered chocolate.

1 tablespoon unflavored gelatin	1/8 teaspoon salt
1/4 cup cold water	3 tablespoons rum
3 eggs, separated	1 baked (9- or 10-inch)
3/4 cup sugar	pie shell
1 1/2 cups milk	1 cup whipped cream
	Slivered sweet chocolate

Soften the gelatin in the cold water. Beat the egg yolks. Beat the egg whites in a separate bowl until stiff peaks form. Combine the yolks, sugar, milk and salt in a saucepan over medium heat. Cook for about 8 minutes or until mixture coats the spoon, stirring constantly. Stir in the gelatin mixture. Cook until thickened, stirring constantly; do not boil. Remove from heat. Fold in the egg whites and rum. Pour into the pie shell. Top with whipped cream and chocolate. Chill until set. Refrigerate leftovers. Yield: 6 or 7 servings.

Louise Rogers, Preceptor
Sturgis, South Dakota

RUM CUSTARD PIE

My mother found this recipe about 65 years ago in the Denver Post. *Our family has enjoyed it all these years.*

1 1/2 cups finely ground Brazil nuts	1/2 cup sugar
3 tablespoons sugar	1/8 teaspoon salt
1 envelope unflavored gelatin	1 1/2 cups milk, scalded
1/4 cup cold water	1 1/2 cups sliced maraschino cherries
3 eggs, separated	2 tablespoons light rum
	1/2 cup whipped cream

Combine the nuts and the 3 tablespoons sugar in a bowl and mix well. Press the nut mixture over the bottom and up the side of a 9-inch pie plate. Bake at 400 degrees for 8 minutes or until lightly browned. Soften the gelatin in the cold water. Place the egg yolks in the top of a double boiler over hot, not boiling, water. Beat the yolks with a fork. Beat in 1/4 cup of the sugar and the salt. Add the milk gradually, cooking until the mixture coats a metal spoon, stirring constantly. Remove from heat. Stir in the gelatin mixture. Chill until the mixture mounds slightly when dropped from a spoon. Beat the egg whites at medium speed until soft peaks form. Add the remaining 1/4 cup sugar gradually, beating constantly at high speed until stiff peaks form. Fold into the egg

yolk mixture. Pour into the Brazil nut crust. Chill, covered, for 8 to 12 hours. Spoon whipped cream in dollops around the edge of the pie. Top with 1/4 cup shaved Brazil nuts. Yield: 8 servings.

Norma T. Klapmeyer, Laureate Pi
Roswell, New Mexico

WINTER APPLE PIE

I found this recipe in a newspaper about 20 years ago and it has become our traditional Christmas dinner dessert.

1 cup seedless raisins	1/4 teaspoon salt
1/2 cup ground carrot	1/2 cup hot water
1/2 cup sugar	1 cup coarsely chopped
1 tablespoon cornstarch	apples
1/2 teaspoon cinnamon	1 (2-crust) pie pastry
1/4 teaspoon nutmeg	
1/4 teaspoon ground cloves	

Combine the raisins, carrot and a mixture of the sugar, cornstarch, cinnamon, nutmeg, cloves and salt in a medium saucepan over medium heat. Stir in the water. Bring to a boil; reduce heat. Simmer for about 5 minutes. Stir in the apples. Remove from heat. Pour into a pastry-lined pie plate. Top with the remaining pastry, sealing edge and cutting vents. Bake at 375 degrees for about 20 minutes or until golden brown. Yield: 6 to 8 servings.

Joanne Mayer, Xi Alpha Theta
Lively, Ontario, Canada

MINCEMEAT MALLOW CHEESECAKE

1 cup vanilla wafer crumbs	16 ounces light cream cheese, softened
1/4 cup margarine, melted	2 teaspoons grated orange zest
4 cups miniature marshmallows	8 ounces whipped topping
1/3 cup orange juice	1 3/4 cups mincemeat

Combine the crumbs and margarine in a bowl and mix well. Press the crumb mixture into a 9-inch springform pan. Bake at 325 degrees for 10 minutes. Let cool. Place the marshmallows and orange juice in the top of a double boiler over simmering water. Cook until marshmallows are melted, stirring until smooth. Chill until thickened. Combine the cream cheese and orange zest in a mixer bowl and beat until well blended and fluffy. Beat in the marshmallow mixture; fold in the whipped topping. Spread the mincemeat over the cooled crust. Pour the cream cheese mixture over the mincemeat. Chill until firm.

Garnish with additional mincemeat and chopped candied fruit to form a wreath shape if desired. Yield: 10 to 12 servings.

Joy Easingwood, Xi Master
Langley, British Columbia, Canada

FESTIVE RASPBERRY CHEESECAKE

1³/₄ cups graham cracker crumbs	¹/₄ teaspoon vanilla extract
2 tablespoons sugar	3 eggs
¹/₄ cup butter or margarine, melted	1 (12-ounce) package frozen unsweetened raspberries
24 ounces cream cheese, softened	³/₄ cup sugar
1 cup sugar	¹/₃ cup water
2 teaspoons grated lemon zest	3 tablespoons cornstarch

Stir the crumbs and the 2 tablespoons sugar together in a bowl. Mix in the melted butter. Press the mixture evenly over the bottom of a lightly greased 9-inch springform pan. Bake at 350 degrees for 10 minutes. Let cool. Reduce oven temperature to 300 degrees. Beat the cream cheese in a large mixer bowl. Add 1 cup sugar gradually, beating until fluffy. Add the lemon zest and vanilla. Add the eggs 1 at a time, beating well after each addition. Pour the mixture over the cooled crust. Bake for about 1 hour or until center is firm. Chill for 3 hours. Combine the raspberries and ³/₄ cup sugar in a saucepan. Blend the water and cornstarch until smooth and pour over the raspberries. Cook over medium heat until thickened, stirring constantly. Let cool. Pour over the cream cheese mixture. Chill, covered, until serving time. Yield: 10 servings.

Barbara Grinde, Preceptor Pi
Polson, Montana

RUM AND EGGNOG CHEESECAKE

1 cup graham cracker crumbs	16 ounces light cream cheese, softened
¹/₂ cup sugar	1 (14-ounce) can sweetened condensed milk
¹/₄ cup butter or margarine, melted	
1 envelope unflavored gelatin	2 teaspoons vanilla extract
¹/₄ cup light rum	1¹/₂ cups whipping cream
¹/₄ cup boiling water	
3 eggs, separated	Nutmeg

Combine the graham cracker crumbs, 2 tablespoons of the sugar and the melted butter in a medium bowl and mix well. Press firmly into a lightly greased 9-inch springform pan. Bake at 350 degrees for 10 minutes. Let cool. Sprinkle the gelatin over the rum in a small bowl; let stand for 5 minutes. Add the boiling water and stir until gelatin is dissolved. Whisk the egg yolks and 2 tablespoons of the sugar together in a small saucepan over medium heat. Whisk in the gelatin mixture. Bring to a boil, stirring constantly. Remove from heat. Beat the cream cheese, condensed milk, egg yolk mixture and vanilla at high speed in a large mixing bowl until smooth. Chill for 20 to 30 minutes or until partially set. Beat the egg whites at medium speed until soft peaks form. Add the remaining ¹/₄ cup sugar gradually, beating constantly at high speed until stiff peaks form. Beat ¹/₂ cup of the whipping cream at high speed in a small bowl until firm peaks form. Fold the egg whites into the cream cheese mixture, then fold in the whipped cream. Pour over the prepared crust. Chill, covered, for 3 to 12 hours or until set. Beat the remaining whipping cream at serving time and spread over the top of the cheesecake; sprinkle with nutmeg. Yield: 10 servings.

Gleniss Osecki
Porcupine Plain, Saskatchewan, Canada

MOCHA COOKIES AND CREAM

1 teaspoon instant coffee granules	8 ounces nonfat whipped topping
1 tablespoon hot water	8 chocolate wafers, crushed
²/₃ cup chocolate sweetened condensed milk	6 rolled sugar wafers
¹/₄ teaspoon vanilla extract	

Dissolve the coffee granules in the hot water in a small cup. Pour the condensed milk into a small bowl. Stir in the coffee and vanilla. Pour the coffee mixture into a medium bowl. Fold in the whipped topping. Add the chocolate wafers, stirring gently. Divide the mixture among 6 dessert glasses. Serve with sugar cookies. Yield: 6 servings.

Anita Schwab, Mu Eta
Brechin, Ontario, Canada

Sheila Pomeroy, Alpha Chi, Vancouver, British Columbia, Canada, makes Five Minutes to Heaven by preparing a small package of vanilla instant pudding, folding in 2 cups of whipped cream, and alternating layers of pudding mixture and unsalted soda crackers in a pan, ending with crackers. Top with cherry pie filling and chill.

BREAD PUDDING WITH LEMON SAUCE

I make this with homemade sourdough bread when I can.

1 loaf of French bread	**½ cup raisins (optional)**
4 cups milk	**½ cup (1 stick) plus 3**
3 eggs	**tablespoons butter**
3 cups sugar	**Juice of 1 to 2 lemons**
1 cup shredded coconut	
3 teaspoons vanilla	
extract	

Tear the bread into bite-size pieces and place in a large bowl. Combine the milk, eggs, 2 cups of the sugar, coconut, 2 teaspoons of the vanilla and raisins in a bowl and mix well. Pour over the bread. Let soak for 30 minutes or until almost all liquid is absorbed. Place 3 tablespoons of the butter in a 9×13-inch baking dish and melt in the oven; tilt the dish to coat the bottom. Pour in the bread mixture. Bake at 350 degrees for 40 to 45 minutes or until brown. Combine the remaining ½ cup butter, 1 cup sugar, 1 teaspoon vanilla and lemon juice in a saucepan over low heat. Heat for about 5 minutes or until butter is melted and mixture is hot, stirring frequently. Serve over the warm pudding. Yield: 12 to 16 servings.

Maxine Keith, Laureate Delta Omicron
Pace, Florida

❖ THE EASIEST AND BEST BREAD PUDDING YOU WILL EVER PUT IN YOUR MOUTH

It is best when served warm but also reheats well in the microwave.

5 eggs	**4 cups half-and-half**
2 cups sugar	**1 cup shredded coconut**
4 tablespoons packed	**(optional)**
light brown sugar	**1 loaf of French bread**
2 teaspoons vanilla	**Lemon Sauce**
extract	
½ cup (1 stick) butter,	
melted	

Combine the eggs, sugars, vanilla, butter, half-and-half and coconut in a bowl, whisking after each addition. Tear the bread into bite-size pieces and soak it in the egg mixture for 5 minutes. Pour into a 9×13-inch baking dish sprayed with nonstick cooking spray. Bake at 375 degrees for 50 to 55 minutes or until brown. Serve with Lemon Sauce.
Yield: 10 to 25 servings.

LEMON SAUCE

4 eggs	**1 pound confectioners'**
¼ cup lemon juice	**sugar**
1 cup (2 sticks) butter,	
melted	

Combine the eggs, lemon juice and hot melted butter in a blender container. Add the confectioners' sugar gradually, processing until smooth. Sauce will keep 1 week in the refrigerator.

Katrina Dawson, Alpha Alpha Phi
Milton, Florida

FRUITCAKE PUDDING

2 cups cubed aged or	**Milk**
leftover fruitcake	**1 tablespoon vanilla**
¼ to ½ cup sugar	**extract**
3 eggs or egg substitute	**¼ cup shredded coconut**

Place the fruitcake in a 1½-quart casserole sprayed with nonstick cooking spray. Sprinkle with the sugar. Beat the eggs well in a 2-cup measuring cup with a fork or wire whisk. Add enough milk to make 2 cups of liquid; stir in the vanilla. Pour over the fruitcake. Sprinkle with coconut. Let the fruitcake mixture stand for about 15 minutes. Bake, uncovered, at 350 degrees for 45 minutes or until a knife inserted in the center comes out clean. Serve with whipped cream or whipped topping if desired. Yield: 6 to 8 servings.

Eugenia Wallace, Laureate Kappa
Lexington, Kentucky

OLD-FASHIONED DATE PUDDING

A three-generation Christmas Eve tradition.

½ cup sugar	**¾ cup milk**
1 teaspoon baking	**1 cup chopped dates**
powder	**2 cups packed brown**
1½ cups flour	**sugar**
½ teaspoon baking soda	**1¼ cups boiling water**
½ teaspoon salt	**3 tablespoons butter**

Sift the sugar, baking powder, flour, baking soda and salt together into a large bowl. Add the milk and dates and mix well. Pour into a 2-quart buttered casserole. Combine the brown sugar, boiling water and butter in a bowl and mix well. Pour over the date mixture. Bake at 350 degrees for 35 minutes. Serve warm with half-and-half or whipped cream.
Yield: 6 to 8 servings.

Dee Zimmerman, Alpha Kappa Preceptor
Eau Claire, Wisconsin

Special Occasions

Special occasions enliven every month of the year.
Between St. Patrick's Day shamrocks and Founders'
Day feasts, we honor our mothers and fathers,
commemorate anniversaries, surprise friends
with showers, dance at weddings, and light
birthday candles. The truth is, we don't have to
wait for special occasions. We'll use any excuse to
throw a party and share good times.

With a deft turn of the hand and a little extra
creativity, we can create occasions that memories
are made of. This chapter reveals small details,
big ideas, and yummy recipes that transform the
ordinary into the extraordinary. Read this section
when you want to add a little magic to
your celebrations of life.

MOTHER'S DAY MEMORY JAR

Make a lovely jar for your memories. Cover the lid of a large canning jar with polyfill and a piece of fabric secured with glue and ribbon. Decorate with lace, buttons, and other feminine trimmings.

Prepare a stack of small slips of paper. Write notes to your mother that are special—thank-yous for remembered favors, moments of shared pleasure, recognition of mom's sacrifices, whatever flits through your mind. It may take only a day or two to fill the jar, or it may take several weeks. Start another jar when the first one is filled.

Give mom the jar with instructions to read one a week. My mother and I live hours apart, but the notes help us keep in touch with our memories and good times together.

Dawn-Marie Miller, Xi Eta Theta
Wamego, Kansas

AFTER-MEETING BABY SHOWER

Decorate the room with balloons, streamers, baby t-shirts, rattles, and pacifiers. Use diapers carefully folded and tied with ribbon as favors. (If you wish, winner of the door prize can be the holder of the diaper bearing a dab of mustard in it.) The diapers are not to be taken home, but to be given as extras to the mother-to-be.

Here are a couple of thematic games: Have each guest bring a picture of herself as an infant or toddler. Don't show them to anyone before the party. Place the pictures on a table, set a time limit, and see if the guests can identify who is who.

If the guest of honor is willing, have each guest cut from a large ball a length of string that she thinks will fit around the mother-to-be. Supply prizes for the winners.

Linda Curtis, Preceptor Gamma Theta
Pendleton, Oregon

TREASURED MEMORY REMINDERS

Keep a glass container in the living room or family room. Whenever you have a celebration that warrants a bottle of wine or champagne, uncork the bottle and note with a fine-tip permanent marker the date of the celebration and the reason; place the cork in the glass container. Whenever you need a happy thought, pull out a cork and relive those moments and friends. Don't forget to replace the cork for more memories later.

Lynda J. Solder, Alpha Omega
Shippensburg, Pennsylvania

HUSBAND'S GARTER

Our men have their own extension of our chapter. Every year on St. Patrick's Day we have a progressive dinner. At the last house we have dessert and honor our men. The first year they received a garter to wear on an arm, and our president gave a funny speech to thank them for "putting up with us." Each year since they get a speech and a pin representing the president's theme for the year. The men add each pin to their garters.

The first year we inducted an honorary male member over the phone. He not only accepted the honor but responded with a thank-you card that read: "I will try to perform my duty, to the utmost of my ability."

Terri Pellegrino, Zeta Eta
Roosevelt, Arizona

MARDI GRAS PARTY

We had so much fun at our first Mardi Gras party that it has replaced our usual St. Patrick's Day party.

Plan ahead by purchasing an assortment of plain masks when they are available in October for Halloween. Before the party, give each member a mask to decorate, wear to the party, and use to compete for prizes.

Decorate with gold, purple, and green balloons, themed plates and napkins, and lots of beads for decorating and greeting guests. Play Cajun music and serve a menu of Mardi Gras-style food and drinks. Present a program on the history of Mardi Gras.

Cyndi Johnson, Preceptor Nu
Trenton, Missouri

HOMECOMING PARTY

Although all of our members graduated from different schools, we decided to have a homecoming celebration. We had each member and spouse fill out a questionnaire that answered questions such as high school or college names, school colors, and mascots. Using that information, we made pennants out of poster board to use for decorations. Everyone came dressed in their school's colors—one member even came in her old cheerleading outfit from the '70s.

Pots of chili were labeled "Quarterback Crunch" for the hot, and "Armchair Quarterback" for the mild. Members supplied the appetizers and drinks. The music was a selection of favorites from the '50s thru the '80s. We shared memories, school songs, and a bonfire. It has been our most successful couples social to date.

Melody Sublette-Peyton, Omicron Chi
Spirit Lake, Iowa

MOTHER'S GARDEN FAVORS

*T*his dessert was a feature of a Mother's Night Out celebration. Line new 2-inch clay pots with foil. Fill the pots with prepared chocolate pudding, sprinkle crushed chocolate cookies over the top, and add a cluster of small silk flowers. The pots and flowers were to take home as a memento after eating the pudding.

Ann Harms, Laureate Gamma Sigma
Anson, Texas

MOON AND STARS RUSH PARTY

*T*hese ideas are a composite from many members so you can pick and choose to meet your needs.

Prepare halos for the guests by making head-size wire circles. Add ribbon streamers to be decorated with glitter, a moon, and stars, attached with glue. As the guests arrive, place a halo on each head, add a star sticker or two to forehead or cheek, and sprinkle with glitter. (The stickers and glitter can also be added to the invitations to set the theme.)

A fun game using the star theme can be prepared in advance by making a list of famous star couples from the worlds of movies, TV, cartoons, history, politics, etc. Cut out a number of 4-inch stars and cut the stars apart using different edged scissors or squiggled as for jigsaw pieces. Then using your list, write half of a star couple on each half star. Give each guest half a star and allow the guests to search out the person holding the other half of the star. Now let the two guests holding the matching stars perform a charade identifying the couple for the other guests to guess.

After refreshments, give each guest a fresh yellow rose to take home.

Terry Patlovany, Delta Sigma
Broomfield, Colorado

INSPIRATION ISN'T HARD TO FIND

*Y*ou probably already have what you need to decorate for a party or wrap a gift. Let your imagination roam. Table coverings can be made from old maps, bath towels, fabric remnants, aluminum foil, or colored plastic wrap. Any of the named table coverings will also wrap a package of almost any size, and a disposable table cloth can always double as a package wrap.

Nancy Tosetti, Omicron Delta
Witt, Illinois

Wilena Walton, Laureate Iota, Maysville, Kentucky, serves a mixture of 1 cup each shredded Swiss cheese, chopped onion, and mayonnaise as Swiss Miss Dip for veggies or crackers.

POT-O'-GOLD FAVORS

*P*aint 1½- to 2-inch clay pots with gold paint and fill with gold foil-wrapped candy kisses. Add a leprechaun on a popsicle stick.

Louise Stith, Preceptor Gamma Psi
Vacaville, California

YELLOW ROSES FOR ALL OCCASIONS

*F*loat yellow rose candles in a small amount of water in a decorative glass bowl. Add some frozen or fresh cranberries and some fresh greens for a striking centerpiece.

Irene L. Sheridan, Chi Master
Lee's Summit, Missouri

SUNFLOWER CHEESE BALL

For a special sisterly gathering, use invitations and napkins decorated with sunflowers and display sunflowers on the tables. This great sunflower cheese ball will add to the festivities.

1½ cups lightly salted roasted sunflower seeds	2 tablespoons sour cream
8 ounces cream cheese, softened	1 teaspoon chicken bouillon granules
3 ounces bleu cheese, crumbled	⅛ teaspoon ground red pepper
¼ cup finely chopped celery	1 (15-ounce) package nacho cheese tortilla chips
¼ cup finely chopped green onions	

Combine 1 cup of the sunflower seeds, the cream cheese, bleu cheese, celery, green onions, sour cream and bouillon in a medium bowl and mix well. Shape into a ball. Coat with the remaining ½ cup sunflower seeds. Let stand in the refrigerator, wrapped in plastic wrap, for 8 to 12 hours to marry the flavors. Let stand at room temperature for 20 to 30 minutes before serving. Press tortilla chips around the side of the cheese ball, allowing them to extend, so as to resemble flower petals. Serve with additional chips. Yield: 2 cups.

Alice White, Preceptor Gamma Kappa
Chesapeake, Virginia

Minnie Miller, Preceptor Delta Tau, Ridgecrest, California, makes Artichoke Crowns by topping drained canned artichoke bottoms with a dollop of cream cheese, a smoked oyster, and a sliver of green onion or pimento.

BLEU CHEESE AND GARLIC DIP

16 ounces cream cheese, softened
2 tablespoons crumbled, crisp-fried bacon, drained
¼ cup half-and-half
5 garlic cloves, roasted, chopped
1 cup crumbled bleu cheese
¼ cup chopped green onions
¼ cup sliced almonds, toasted

Process the cream cheese in a food processor until smooth. Add the bacon, half-and-half and garlic and process until well blended. Remove the bacon mixture to a large bowl. Fold in the bleu cheese and green onions. Place in a 1-quart casserole. Bake, uncovered, at 350 degrees for 20 minutes or until bubbly and brown. Garnish with the almonds. Serve with crackers. Yield: 15 servings.

Joann Duffy, Alpha Beta Eta
Sun City Center, Florida

MOCK GUACAMOLE

2 (10-ounce) cans cut-up asparagus, drained
¾ to 1 cup finely chopped tomato
¼ cup chopped onion
2 tablespoons lemon juice
1 tablespoon reduced-fat mayonnaise
½ teaspoon garlic salt
½ teaspoon chili powder
¼ teaspoon Tabasco sauce

Process the asparagus in a food processor or blender until smooth. Remove to a bowl. Stir in the tomato, onion, lemon juice, mayonnaise, garlic salt, chili powder and Tabasco sauce. Place in a paper towel-lined wire mesh strainer or colander; drain for 1 hour. Chill, covered, for at least 3 hours. Yield: 2 cups.

Lillian H. Harrell, Preceptor Eta
Mobile, Alabama

SHRIMP MOLD

1 envelope unflavored gelatin
1 (10-ounce) can cream of mushroom soup
8 ounces cream cheese, softened
1 cup mayonnaise
¼ cup finely chopped celery
¼ cup finely chopped green onions
1 (4-ounce) can tiny shrimp

Combine the gelatin and soup in a saucepan over medium heat. Bring to a boil; remove from heat. Add the cream cheese, whisking until smooth. Add the mayonnaise, celery, green onions and shrimp and mix well. Pour the mixture into a bowl or mold

sprayed with nonstick cooking spray. Chill, covered, for 8 to 12 hours. Serve out of the bowl, or unmold if desired; serve with assorted crackers. Yield: 3 cups.

Nancy Kuntzmann, Preceptor Alpha Lambda
Portland, Oregon

❖ MEXICAN CAJUN DELIGHT

2 envelopes unflavored gelatin
5 large avocados
½ cup finely chopped onions
3 tablespoons lemon juice
¼ cup mayonnaise
1 teaspoon salt
1 teaspoon black pepper
½ teaspoon cayenne pepper
¼ cup finely chopped green onions
½ cup finely chopped celery
½ cup finely chopped green bell pepper
1 pound fresh mushrooms, sliced
2 tablespoons margarine
1 pound flaked cooked crab meat
1 pound cooked shrimp, finely chopped
8 ounces cream cheese, softened
½ teaspoon powdered steak seasoning
½ teaspoon garlic powder
1 cup sour cream
2 tablespoons finely chopped onion

Dissolve 1 envelope of the gelatin in ¼ cup hot water; cool. Chop 2 of the avocados; purée 2 of them. Combine the chopped and puréed avocados, the ½ cup onions, lemon juice, mayonnaise, ½ teaspoon of the salt, ½ teaspoon of the black pepper and ¼ teaspoon of the cayenne pepper in a bowl and mix well. Stir in the dissolved gelatin. Spoon the mixture into a springform pan. Chill, covered, in the refrigerator for about 30 minutes. Dissolve the remaining envelope of gelatin in ¼ cup hot water. Sauté the green onions, celery, bell pepper and mushrooms in the margarine for 5 to 10 minutes or until tender. Stir in the crab meat, shrimp, cream cheese, steak seasoning, garlic powder, ½ teaspoon salt, ½ teaspoon black pepper, ¼ teaspoon cayenne pepper and the dissolved gelatin. Let cool completely. Adjust the seasonings to taste. Spread over the avocado layer in the springform pan. Chill for about 15 minutes. Combine the sour cream and the 2 tablespoons chopped onion in a bowl and mix well. Spread evenly over the seafood layer. Chill, covered, for at least 8 hours or until set. Slice the remaining avocado. Remove the side of the springform pan. Garnish with the sliced avocado and parsley if desired. Serve with tortilla chips. Yield: 20 servings.

Merline McCoy, Alpha Psi Master
Village Mills, Texas

TOMATO PESTO TORTE

1 (8- to 12-ounce) package sun-dried tomatoes	1/4 to 1/2 cup grated Parmesan cheese
16 ounces light cream cheese, softened	1/2 to 2 garlic cloves, crushed
1 cup sour cream	1/2 teaspoon salt
1/3 cup butter, softened	1 (8-ounce) carton pesto

Place the tomatoes in a bowl. Pour boiling water over the tomatoes. Soak until soft. Drain well. Process in a food processor until finely chopped. Divide among 2 or 3 flat lidded containers, spreading tomatoes over the bottom. Process the cream cheese, sour cream, butter, Parmesan cheese, garlic and salt in a clean food processor container until very smooth. Divide the cheese mixture into 2 or 3 portions and spread gently over the tomatoes. Divide the pesto into 2 or 3 portions and spread gently over the cheese mixture. Attach the container lids securely and chill for 8 to 12 hours or freeze; make sure containers are not over-filled or they may explode. To serve each torte, run a warm knife around the edges. Invert onto a serving plate and let container slowly release. It may be necessary to touch up the top of the torte. Serve with assorted crackers and raw vegetables. Yield: 24 servings.

Joni L. Burd, Xi Xi
Phoenix, Arizona

GOLDEN COCKTAIL BALLS

2 cups shredded Cheddar cheese	1 cup sifted flour
1/2 cup (1 stick) butter, softened	1/2 teaspoon salt
	1 teaspoon paprika
	48 small stuffed olives

Combine the cheese, butter, flour, salt and paprika in a bowl and blend well. Drain the olives and pat dry. Shape the cheese dough around the olives, enclosing them in dough. Arrange 1 1/2 inches apart on an ungreased baking sheet. Bake at 370 degrees for 12 minutes. Serve warm. Yield: 48 servings.

Dorothy Hoefer, Laureate Phi
Higginsville, Missouri

GLAZED HAM BALLS

3/4 pound ground ham	1 cup packed brown sugar
3/4 pound ground pork	
1 1/2 cups dry bread crumbs	1/4 cup pineapple juice
3/4 cup milk	1/4 cup vinegar
2 eggs, well beaten	1 teaspoon prepared mustard

Combine the ham, pork, bread crumbs, milk and eggs in a bowl and mix well. Shape into balls. Place in an 8-inch-square baking pan. Bake at 350 degrees for about 40 minutes or until cooked through. Combine the brown sugar, pineapple juice, vinegar and mustard in a small saucepan over medium heat and bring to a boil. Boil gently for 6 minutes. Remove the ham balls from the oven; drain. Pour the mustard sauce evenly over the ham balls. Return to the oven and bake for 25 minutes longer. Yield: 4 servings.

Janelle Brophy, Gamma Xi
Wellman, Iowa

SPINACH BALLS

2 (10-ounce) packages frozen chopped spinach, thawed, drained	6 eggs, slightly beaten
	2 large onions, chopped
	1 tablespoon garlic salt
	1 tablespoon pepper
2 cups herb stuffing mix	3/4 cup (1 1/2 sticks) butter or margarine, melted
2 cups grated Parmesan cheese	1 teaspoon thyme

Combine the spinach, stuffing mix, cheese, eggs, onions, garlic salt, pepper, butter and thyme in a bowl and mix well. Shape into small balls and arrange on a greased baking sheet. Bake at 350 degrees for 20 minutes. Yield: 3 dozen.

Cathy Baber, Theta Chi
Chesapeake, Virginia

ARTICHOKE APPETIZER

1 cup chopped onion	1 teaspoon salt
1 cup water	1/4 teaspoon pepper
4 (6-ounce) jars marinated artichokes, drained	1/4 teaspoon oregano
	6 drops of hot pepper sauce
8 eggs, well beaten	4 cups shredded Cheddar cheese
1/2 cup bread crumbs	

Cook the onion in the water in a small saucepan over medium heat for 5 minutes or until tender; drain. Chop the artichokes and pat with paper towels until most of the oil is removed. Combine the eggs, bread crumbs, salt, pepper, oregano and hot sauce in a large bowl and mix well. Stir in the onion, artichokes and cheese. Spread in a greased 7×11-inch baking dish. Bake at 350 degrees for 18 to 20 minutes or until bubbly and slightly browned. Let stand until completely cooled. Cut into 1-inch squares. Garnish with a pimento strip over each square. Yield: 32 pieces.

Emelie A. Graham, Omicron Lambda
Blythe, California

BRIE AND CRANBERRY PIZZA

Serve with fresh vegetables and a light wine.

1 (8-count) can crescent
    rolls
8 ounces Brie cheese,
    rind removed

3/4 cup canned whole
    cranberry sauce
1/2 cup chopped pecans

Unroll crescent roll dough. Separate into triangles. Arrange in an oiled 12-inch pizza pan with the points toward the center; press to seal. Bake in a preheated 425-degree oven for 5 to 6 minutes or until light brown. Cut the Brie into 1/2-inch cubes. Scatter over the partially baked crust. Stir the cranberry sauce in a bowl; spread evenly over the cheese. Sprinkle with the pecans. Bake for 6 to 7 minutes longer or until cheese is melted and crust is golden brown. Let cool for 5 minutes. Cut into wedges or squares. Yield: 16 appetizers.

Sharon Horn, Xi Zeta
Brandon, Manitoba, Canada

GREEN DEVILS

These green deviled eggs are especially nice for Saint Patrick's Day. The best way to hard-cook eggs is to cover them with cold water in a saucepan, bring to a boil, then remove from heat and let stand, covered, for 20 minutes.

1/3 cup thawed frozen
    chopped spinach
1 dozen hard-cooked
    eggs, peeled
1/4 cup mayonnaise
1/4 cup bacon bits

1 tablespoon cider
    vinegar
1 tablespoon sugar
1 1/2 teaspoons pepper
1/4 teaspoon salt

Drain the spinach and squeeze dry. Halve the eggs lengthwise. Scoop out the yolks; mash in a bowl with a fork. Add the spinach, mayonnaise, bacon bits, vinegar, sugar, pepper and salt; mix well. Spoon the yolk mixture into the egg whites. Chill, covered, until ready to serve. Yield: 24 halves.

Anita J. Mawer, Xi Sigma Mu
Simi Valley, California

SHRIMP-FILLED SALMON ROLLS

3/4 pound cooked tiny
    shrimp
3/4 cup whipping cream,
    whipped
2 teaspoons minced
    fresh dill
1 tablespoon prepared
    horseradish

Salt and freshly ground
    pepper to taste
6 thin slices cold
    smoked salmon
2 tablespoons salmon
    roe
6 sprigs fresh dill
2 limes, cut into wedges

Combine the shrimp, whipped cream, 2 teaspoons minced dill and horseradish in a medium bowl and mix well. Season with the salt and pepper. Spread the shrimp mixture over the salmon slices. Roll each slice into a cone shape, enclosing the filling. Garnish with the roe, sprigs of dill and lime wedges. Serve chilled. Yield: 6 rolls.

Juanita Lunn, Preceptor Theta Rho
Eustis, Florida

PEPPERONI PIE SQUARES

1 1/2 cups flour
2 cups milk
2 large eggs
1/2 teaspoon oregano
1/4 teaspoon pepper
1/4 teaspoon chopped
    fresh parsley

1 pound muenster
    cheese, diced
1 (8-ounce) package
    sliced pepperoni,
    chopped
1 (15-ounce) can pizza
    sauce

Mix the flour, milk, eggs, oregano, pepper, parsley, cheese and pepperoni in a large bowl. Pour into a lightly greased 9×13-inch baking dish. Bake at 350 degrees for 30 minutes. Let cool slightly. Cut into squares. Warm the pizza sauce and serve with the squares for dipping. Yield: 8 to 10 servings.

Diane C. Walsh, Preceptor Alpha
Sarasota, Florida

CINNAMON CREAM CHEESE ROLLS

2 loaves very thinly
    sliced diet white
    bread, crusts trimmed
16 ounces cream cheese,
    softened
2 egg yolks

1/2 cup sugar
3/4 cup (1 1/2 sticks)
    butter, softened
1 cup sugar
2 tablespoons cinnamon

Roll the bread slices as flat as possible with a rolling pin. Arrange the slices in a single layer over damp paper towels, 6 slices per paper towel. Let stand for 1 hour. Combine the cream cheese, egg yolks, 1/2 cup sugar and butter in a bowl and mix until smooth. Spread the cream cheese filling evenly over the bread slices. Roll each slice as for a jelly roll. Cut each roll in half. Dip the rolled halves in additional butter (melted) and roll in a mixture of the 1 cup sugar and the cinnamon. Arrange on a baking sheet and freeze. Place the frozen rolls in storage bags to be kept in the freezer until needed. Arrange the frozen rolls on a baking sheet when ready to serve. Bake in a preheated 325-degree oven for 10 to 15 minutes or until golden, turning once. Yield: 4 dozen.

Linda Howard, Laureate Eta
Gadsden, Alabama

COFFEE MOCHA PUNCH

Perfect for a brunch or early tea. You may use skim milk, 1%, 2%, or whole milk.

1/4 cup sugar	1 quart milk
4 tablespoons instant coffee granules	1/2 gallon vanilla ice cream or frozen yogurt, slightly softened
6 tablespoons chocolate syrup	
3 cups boiling water	

Combine the sugar, coffee granules, chocolate syrup and boiling water in a bowl and mix well. Chill, covered, in the refrigerator until 30 minutes before serving time. Pour the coffee mixture into a punch bowl. Cut the ice cream into 2-inch pieces. Add the milk and ice cream to the coffee mixture. Stir and serve. Yield: 3 quarts.

Denia Petruzella, Rho
Birmingham, Alabama

FROZEN DAIQUIRI PUNCH

Mix this punch and freeze it right in the punch bowl. It can be made ahead—a day, a week, even a month. The alcohol content will keep it slushy.

1 (26-ounce) bottle white rum	2 limeade cans water
2 (2-liter) bottles lemon-lime soda	Few drops of green food coloring
2 (6-ounce) cans frozen limeade	

Combine the rum, soda, limeade, water and food coloring in a punch bowl. Freeze until ready to serve. Remove from the freezer at least 1 hour before serving. May be refrozen. Yield: 4 quarts.

Flo Sampson, Preceptor Alpha Nu
Port Moody, British Columbia, Canada

LEPRECHAUN LIME DRINK

Serve on Saint Patrick's Day.

1 quart lime sherbet, softened	2 tablespoons sugar
1/2 cup frozen limeade, thawed	2 (12-ounce) cans lemon-lime soda, chilled
	1 to 2 cups crushed ice

Blend the sherbet, limeade and sugar in a mixing bowl. Stir in the soda and ice and mix well. Pour into glasses and garnish with lime slices. Yield: 2 quarts.

Marian Blankenship
Glenwood, Iowa

LOW-FAT GRASSHOPPER

1 quart low-fat vanilla frozen yogurt	2 1/2 to 3 teaspoons crème de cacao
2 1/2 to 3 teaspoons crème de menthe	

Combine the yogurt, crème de menthe and crème de cacao in a deep container and mix until blended, softened and pourable; a few small lumps are fine. Serve in wineglasses. You may substitute low-fat vanilla ice cream for the frozen yogurt. Yield: 5 to 6 servings.

Carole A. Gaulden, Laureate Nu
Jupiter, Florida

MANGO MARGARITAS

1 cup mashed chopped peeled mango	2 tablespoons triple sec or orange liqueur
6 tablespoons gold tequila	2 tablespoons fresh lime juice
6 tablespoons confectioners' sugar	2 1/2 cups ice cubes

Purée the mango in a blender. Add the tequila, confectioners' sugar, triple sec and lime juice and blend until smooth. Add the ice cubes and process until slushy. Yield: 4 servings.

Linda Lewis, Alpha Alpha Chi
Ft. Myers, Florida

HUNGARIAN MUSHROOM SOUP

2 cups sliced mushrooms	2 cups sour cream
1/2 medium onion, chopped	1 teaspoon dillweed
1/2 cup (1 stick) butter	1 teaspoon paprika
1/2 cup flour	1/2 cup dry white wine
4 cups half-and-half	Salt and pepper to taste

Sauté the mushrooms and onion in the butter in a 5-quart kettle over medium heat until tender. Whisk in the flour and cook for 3 or 4 minutes or until light brown, stirring constantly. Stir in the half-and-half. Cook over medium heat until thick, stirring constantly. Stir in the sour cream, dillweed, paprika, wine, salt and pepper. Serve hot. Yield: 8 servings.

Sandy Holt, Xi Delta Tau
Hillsboro, Oregon

Karen Smith, Smithers, British Columbia, Canada, combines a can of cream of chicken soup, 2 cups milk, a can of chicken, 2 cups chopped cooked broccoli, 1/2 cup frozen corn, and 1/2 cup shredded Cheddar cheese and simmers for Quick Chicken Broccoli Chowder.

PIZZA SOUP

1¼ cups sliced fresh
  mushrooms
½ cup finely chopped
  onion
1 teaspoon vegetable oil
2 cups water
1 (15-ounce) can pizza
  sauce
1 cup chopped fresh
  tomatoes

1 cup chopped pepperoni
½ cup crumbled cooked
  Italian sausage
¼ teaspoon Italian
  seasoning
¼ cup grated Parmesan
  cheese
Shredded mozzarella
  cheese

Sauté the mushrooms and onion in the oil in a large saucepan over medium-low heat for 5 minutes or until tender. Add the water, pizza sauce, tomatoes, pepperoni, sausage and Italian seasoning. Bring to a boil; reduce heat. Simmer, covered, for 20 minutes, stirring occasionally. Stir in the Parmesan cheese just before serving. Garnish with mozzarella cheese. Serve with cheese bread or garlic toast.
Yield: 4 servings.

Mickey A. Sweeten, Preceptor Gamma
Boise, Idaho

TACO SOUP

Great for fall and winter potlucks, and very simple to make.

2 pounds lean ground
  beef
1 small white onion,
  diced
2 cups water
2 (15-ounce) cans diced
  tomatoes
2 (15-ounce) cans golden
  hominy
2 (15-ounce) cans ranch-
  style beans
2 (15-ounce) cans pinto
  beans

1 (15-ounce) can black
  beans
1 (15-ounce) can chick-
  peas
1 (4-ounce) can chopped
  green chiles
1 envelope ranch
  dressing mix
1 envelope taco
  seasoning mix
¼ teaspoon ground
  ginger
Salt and pepper to taste

Brown the ground beef with the onion in a skillet, stirring until the ground beef is crumbly; drain. Place the ground beef mixture in a stock pot. Add the water, tomatoes, hominy, ranch-style beans, pinto beans, black beans, chick-peas and chiles; do not drain any of the canned ingredients. Stir in the dressing mix, taco seasoning mix, ginger, salt and pepper. Simmer, uncovered, for 1½ hours, stirring occasionally. Serve sprinkled with crumbled tortilla chips and shredded cheese if desired. Yield: 30 servings.

Carol Stevens, Preceptor Delta Phi
Groveland, California

TOMATO ONION SOUP

4 cups sliced onions
¼ cup (½ stick) butter
2 tablespoons flour
1½ teaspoons salt
¼ teaspoon pepper
2 (20-ounce) cans beef
  broth

2 cups water
1 (28-ounce) can
  tomatoes
½ teaspoon sugar

Sauté the onions in the butter in a large skillet until tender. Stir in the flour, salt, pepper, broth and water. Bring to a boil, stirring constantly. Purée the undrained tomatoes in a blender. Add the tomatoes and sugar to the onion mixture. Bring to a boil; reduce heat. Simmer, covered, for 15 minutes. Garnish individual servings with croutons and shredded cheese. Yield: 8 servings.

Marion Ritchie, Preceptor Alpha Beta
Blaine, Washington

SEAFOOD CAJUN GUMBO

Use of a slow cooker makes this gumbo an easy meal to come home to. If you want to make it more quickly, simply combine the ingredients in a kettle and simmer until vegetables are tender and flavors are blended.

2 cups vegetable juice
  cocktail
1 (16-ounce) can
  vegetable or chicken
  broth
⅓ cup brown or
  wild rice
1 rib celery, chopped
½ green bell pepper,
  chopped
1 tomato, chopped

¼ cup diced onion
1 (16-ounce) can okra
4 mushrooms, chopped
Salt and pepper to taste
1 to 2 tablespoons
  (or to taste) Cajun
  seasoning
½ to 1 pound fresh
  seafood (scallops,
  shrimp, crawfish,
  etc.)

Combine the vegetable juice cocktail, vegetable broth, rice, celery, bell pepper, tomato, onion, okra, mushrooms, salt, pepper, Cajun seasoning and seafood in a slow cooker. Cook on Low for 6 to 12 hours. Yield: 4 to 8 servings.

Louise McCrea, Laureate Alpha
Boise, Idaho

Hazel Lisotta, Laureate Eta Sigma, Nederland, Texas, browns a pound of ground beef, adds a can each of beef broth, stewed tomatoes, tomatoes with green chiles and 2 cans each of cream-style corn and tamales, cut-up, to make Easy Tamale Soup.

GRAPE SALAD

2 pounds white seedless
  grapes
2 pounds red seedless
  grapes
8 ounces cream cheese,
  softened
1 cup sour cream

1 cup sugar
1 teaspoon vanilla
  extract
1 cup packed brown
  sugar
1 cup chopped pecans

Wash the grapes the day before using and pat dry. Combine the cream cheese, sour cream, sugar and vanilla in a bowl and blend well. Place the grapes in a large bowl. Fold in the cream cheese mixture. Spread evenly in a 9×13-inch dish. Sprinkle evenly with the brown sugar and pecans. Chill until ready to serve. Yield: more than 20 servings.

Betty A. Moore, Sigma Master
Lansing, Michigan

CHICKEN AND PRAWN SALAD

1 pound chicken thighs,
  cooked, boned, thinly
  sliced
1/4 cup light soy sauce
1 tablespoon oyster
  sauce
1/2 teaspoon five-spice
  powder
2 tablespoons lemon
  juice
2 teaspoons minced
  garlic
1 teaspoon grated fresh
  gingerroot
Cornmeal
Vegetable oil for
  deep-frying
4 ounces snow peas
2 cups bean sprouts

2/3 cup slivered almonds,
  toasted
16 ounces egg noodles,
  cooked
1 pound prawns with
  tails, cooked, peeled
1 (8-ounce) can bamboo
  shoots, rinsed,
  drained
1 red bell pepper, sliced
2 tablespoons light soy
  sauce
1/2 teaspoon dark
  sesame oil
1/3 cup vegetable oil
1 teaspoon fish sauce
1 teaspoon honey
1 teaspoon minced
  garlic

Combine the chicken, the 1/4 cup soy sauce, oyster sauce, five-spice powder, half the lemon juice, the 2 teaspoons garlic and gingerroot in a large bowl and mix well. Chill, covered, for 3 to 12 hours. Drain the chicken and discard the marinade. Toss the chicken in cornmeal until well coated. Deep-fry in hot oil until well browned; drain. Boil or steam the snow peas for 1 to 2 minutes or until of desired tenderness. Combine the snow peas, bean sprouts, almonds, noodles, prawns, bamboo shoots and bell pepper in a large bowl and mix well. Whisk together the 2 tablespoons soy sauce, sesame oil, the 1/3 cup vegetable oil, fish sauce, honey, the 1 teaspoon garlic and the

remaining 1 tablespoon lemon juice and pour over the chicken mixture. Toss and serve. Yield: 8 servings.

Jean Richardt, Lambda Epsilon
Kenora, Ontario, Canada

CHICKEN SALAD

3 or 4 chicken breasts,
  cooked, chopped
1/2 bunch green grapes,
  halved
4 ribs celery, chopped
1 cup shredded Cheddar
  cheese
1 (15-ounce) can
  pineapple chunks

2 Pippin apples, cut into
  small chunks
2 teaspoons lemon juice
1/4 to 1/2 cup mayonnaise
Chopped walnuts or
  pecans (optional)
Chopped avocado
  (optional)

Combine the chicken, grapes, celery, cheese, pineapple, apples, lemon juice and mayonnaise in a large bowl and mix well. Stir in chopped nuts or avocado. Chill, covered, until ready to serve over lettuce leaves. Yield: 6 to 10 servings.

Sharon Rahe, Beta Sigma Phi
Madera, California

SMOKED TURKEY SALAD

2 pounds fresh smoked
  turkey breast, cubed
2 ribs celery, diced
1 1/2 bunches green
  onions, thinly sliced
1 red bell pepper,
  julienned
1 yellow bell pepper,
  julienned
4 slices bacon, crisp-
  cooked, crumbled

Salt to taste
1 teaspoon freshly
  ground pepper
3/4 cup mayonnaise
1/3 cup honey mustard
1 ounce Jack Daniel's
  whiskey
2 tablespoons chopped
  fresh basil

Combine the turkey, celery, green onions, bell peppers, bacon, salt and pepper in a large bowl. Whisk together the mayonnaise, honey mustard, whiskey and basil in a small bowl and pour over the turkey mixture. Toss well. Chill, covered, until ready to serve. Serve in cantaloupe halves if desired. Yield: 8 servings.

Susan Gafnea, Xi Alpha Xi
Hueytown, Alabama

Hazel Ivey, Beta Epsilon Omicron, Brackettville, Texas, mixes 1 cup each of 6 different kinds of fresh or canned fruit, 1/4 cup jicama strips, and 1/4 cup orange juice, and tops with a mixture of 1/2 cup sour cream, 2 tablespoons brown sugar, and 2 teaspoons rum to make Jicama Rum Cream Salad.

❖ SPRINGTIME SHRIMP SALAD

This recipe makes 2 large or 4 small servings. To prepare the shrimp so that it remains tender, cook no longer than 2 to 3 minutes in simmering water, then rinse in cold water to stop the cooking process. Use Haas avocados if you can find them.

1/3 cup fresh lime juice	4 green onions
1 tablespoon Dijon mustard	Leaf lettuce
Salt and pepper to taste	1 red bell pepper, stemmed, seeded, cut into 1/2-inch strips
1/2 to 3/4 cup olive oil	
1 tablespoon chopped green onion	1 cup chopped plum tomatoes
Finely grated zest of 1 lime	1 pound large shrimp, peeled, deveined, cooked
1 or 2 ripe avocados, pitted, peeled, sliced	3 tablespoons chopped mint leaves
2 tablespoons fresh lime juice	

Whisk together the 1/3 cup lime juice, mustard, salt and pepper in a small bowl. Add the olive oil in a fine stream, whisking constantly until thickened. Stir in the 1 tablespoon green onion and lime zest. Place the avocado in a separate bowl. Add the 2 tablespoons lime juice and toss to coat. Cut the 4 green onions into thin diagonal slices, including 3 inches of the green. Line 2 plates with whole lettuce leaves. Layer the bell pepper, tomatoes, sliced green onions, avocado and shrimp over the lettuce. Pour half the lime dressing gently over each salad. Sprinkle mint leaves over the salads just before serving. Yield: 2 servings.

Karen Casson, Xi Beta Delta
Encampment, Wyoming

BROCCOLI PASTA SALAD

Very good whether eaten fresh or even after a couple of days in the refrigerator.

2 or 3 heads broccoli	1/2 (8-ounce) can whole kernel corn, drained
2 cups cooked vegetable rotini	3/4 cup ranch dressing
1/4 cup chopped pimentos	

Remove the broccoli stems and reserve for another purpose. Cut the broccoli florets into bite-size pieces. Combine the broccoli, rotini, pimentos and corn in a large bowl. Add the dressing and mix well. Chill, covered, for at least 1 hour before serving. Yield: 8 servings.

Pat Owens, Beta Beta Master
Odessa, Texas

GREEK PASTA SALAD

To prevent clumping, toss hot pasta with olive oil.

1/3 cup olive oil	1 bunch green onions, chopped
2 tablespoons lemon juice	1 (4-ounce) can chopped black olives, drained
3 tablespoons mayonnaise	1 (4-ounce) can sliced black olives, drained
3 rounded tablespoons Greek seasoning	12 ounces angel hair pasta, cooked, cooled
1 (4-ounce) jar chopped pimentos, drained	

Combine the olive oil, lemon juice, mayonnaise and Greek seasoning in a large bowl and blend well. Stir in the pimentos, green onions and chopped and sliced olives. Pour over the pasta in a sealable container and mix well. Chill, covered, for at least 3 hours before serving stirring and mixing several times. Will keep well in the refrigerator for several days. Yield: 10 servings.

Susie Permenter, Xi Tau Zeta
Orange, Texas

RICE SALAD

May be served cold or heated in the microwave.

4 cups cooked white rice	4 tablespoons soy sauce
1 (12-ounce) can whole kernel corn	1/2 cup vegetable oil
1 cup unsalted peanuts	2 tablespoons lemon juice
1 red bell pepper, diced	Garlic powder and pepper to taste
1 medium carrot, grated	
2 green onions, chopped	
1 cup sunflower seeds	
3 tablespoons chopped fresh parsley, or 2 tablespoons dried parsley	

Combine the rice, corn, peanuts, bell pepper, carrot, green onions, sunflower seeds, parsley, soy sauce, oil and lemon juice in a large bowl and toss to combine. Add the garlic powder and pepper. Spread in a 9×13-inch dish. Chill, covered, until ready to serve. Yield: 12 servings.

Norma Main, Xi Master
Langley, British Columbia, Canada

Jane McDaniel, Laureate Beta Gamma, Tyler, Texas, mixes chicken, broccoli florets, celery, and sliced pimento-stuffed olives with a dressing of mayonnaise flavored with curry powder for a Broccoli Chicken Salad.

CAN'T BE BEETS!

2 (15-ounce) cans sliced
   beets
White or cider vinegar
1 cup (or less) sugar
2 (3-ounce) packages
   lemon gelatin
4 or 5 ribs celery,
   chopped

2 to 5 green onions,
   sliced
1 or 2 cucumbers,
   seeded, chopped
1/2 cup sour cream
Garlic salt or powder
   to taste

Drain the juice from the beets into a large measuring cup. Add enough vinegar to the beet juice to make 2 cups liquid. Combine the liquid and sugar in a large saucepan over medium heat. Heat until sugar is dissolved, stirring constantly. Stir in the lemon gelatin. Remove from heat. Let stand for 5 minutes. Chop the beets into small pieces. Stir the beets, celery and green onions into the gelatin mixture. Pour into a mold or glass dish. Chill, covered, until set. Serve a mixture of the cucumbers, sour cream and garlic salt in a separate bowl for spooning over the salad if desired. Yield: 8 to 10 servings.

Linda Stires, Xi Gamma Mu
Indianapolis, Indiana

NORWEGIAN BEET SALAD

1 (6-ounce) beet, peeled,
   shredded
1 (6-ounce) carrot,
   peeled, shredded
1 (6-ounce) apple,
   peeled, shredded
1 cup chopped pecans or
   walnuts

1/2 cup shredded coconut
2 tablespoons lemon
   juice
1 tablespoon minced
   gingerroot
1 tablespoon sesame or
   olive oil
Salt and pepper to taste

Combine the beet, carrot and apple in a bowl and mix well. Add the pecans, coconut, lemon juice, gingerroot and sesame oil and mix well. Add salt and pepper. Sprinkle with chopped parsley.
Yield: 6 to 8 servings.

Dorothy H. Ebert, Laureate Zeta
Hope, Idaho

Jackie Hoskins, Preceptor Gamma Eta, Merritt Island, Florida, prepares Three-Way Bleu Cheese Cream by blending 2 cups cottage cheese until smooth and adding 1 cup crumbled bleu cheese, 2 tablespoons sliced green onions, 2 tablespoons lemon juice, 1 teaspoon Worcestershire sauce and 1 cup sour cream and processing until smooth and creamy. Use as a dip with crackers, chips, or vegetables, as a salad dressing with greens, or as a topping on baked potatoes.

BROCCOLI SLAW

A quick blanching improves the texture and color of broccoli—simply dip it in boiling water for a minute or so and rinse with cold water before chopping.

2 cups thinly sliced
   cabbage
1 head broccoli, stems
   peeled, chopped
1 (8-ounce) can water
   chestnuts, drained
1 small onion, diced
1 cup diced celery
1/2 pound bacon, crisp-
   cooked, crumbled

1/2 cup raisins
1 cup slaw dressing or
   mayonnaise
2 tablespoons vinegar
1 tablespoon sugar
1/2 cup shelled sunflower
   seeds

Combine the cabbage, broccoli, water chestnuts, onion, celery, bacon and raisins in a bowl and mix well. Blend the slaw dressing, vinegar and sugar in a small bowl. Pour the vinegar mixture over the broccoli mixture and stir well. Chill, covered, until ready to serve. Add the sunflower seeds. Toss and serve. Yield: 8 servings.

Jan Coe, Preceptor Mu
Florence, South Carolina

COUNTRY CLUB SALAD

1 (10-ounce) package
   frozen brussels
   sprouts
1 (10-ounce) package
   frozen broccoli florets
1 (10-ounce) package
   frozen cauliflower
   florets
1 (6-ounce) package
   frozen baby carrots
1 (8-ounce) can water
   chestnuts, sliced
1/2 pound mushrooms,
   quartered

1 (14-ounce) can
   artichoke hearts,
   drained, halved
1 fresh zucchini, peeled,
   sliced
2 cups mayonnaise
1 cup sour cream
1 cup prepared
   horseradish
2 tablespoons lemon
   juice
1 teaspoon MSG
1 teaspoon salt

Place the brussels sprouts, broccoli, cauliflower and carrots in a large bowl. Pour hot water over the vegetables to thaw; drain. Rinse with cold water and drain again. Add the water chestnuts, mushrooms, artichokes and zucchini and mix well. Combine the mayonnaise, sour cream, horseradish, lemon juice, MSG and salt in a small bowl and blend well. Add to the vegetable mixture and mix well. Serve chilled. Yield: 12 servings.

Janis Chase, Xi Alpha Theta
Bartlesville, Oklahoma

OLIVE SALAD

1 (10- to 13-ounce) jar green olives	1 medium onion, chopped
1/4 cup white vinegar	1 cup sliced carrots
3 tablespoons olive oil	1 cup cauliflower florets
1 (4-ounce) can chopped black olives	1/2 teaspoon garlic powder
	1/4 teaspoon oregano

Drain the green olives, reserving the juice in a small bowl. Add the vinegar and olive oil to the juice and mix well. Combine the next 6 ingredients with the green olives in a bowl and mix well. Stir in the vinegar mixture. Marinate, covered, in a sealed glass jar for 8 to 12 hours, turning the jar several times. Yield: 8 to 10 servings.

Sara H. Conley, Laureate Beta Alpha
Tampa, Florida

ROASTED POTATO SALAD

2 1/2 pounds small red potatoes	1 tablespoon grainy mustard
1 garlic clove, chopped	2 teaspoons minced chives
5 tablespoons olive oil	
Salt and pepper to taste	1 teaspoon fresh rosemary
1 1/2 tablespoons red wine vinegar	

Scrub the potatoes and cut into quarters. Place in a single layer in a large baking dish. Add the garlic, 3 tablespoons of the olive oil, salt and pepper and toss to combine. Bake, uncovered, at 425 degrees for 30 to 40 minutes or until potatoes are tender, tossing every 10 minutes. Whisk together the vinegar and mustard in a large bowl. Whisk in the remaining 2 tablespoons olive oil until smooth. Add the roasted potatoes and mix gently. Add more salt and pepper to taste. Let cool to room temperature. Sprinkle with the chives and rosemary just before serving. Yield: 6 servings.

Joanne Bowen, Xi Beta Rho
Shelbyville, Indiana

SPICY SALAD

If you prepare the salad in a ring mold, fill the center with the horseradish sauce.

3 (3-ounce) packages raspberry gelatin	2 cups sour cream
1 1/4 cups hot water	1 tablespoon creamed horseradish
3 (16-ounce) cans stewed tomatoes, cut up	1/4 teaspoon salt
	1/2 teaspoon sugar
6 drops of Tabasco sauce	

Dissolve the gelatin in the hot water in a large bowl. Stir in the undrained tomatoes and Tabasco sauce.

Pour into a mold. Chill until set. Unmold onto a lettuce-lined serving plate. Serve with a mixture of the sour cream, horseradish, salt and sugar in a small bowl. Yield: 12 servings.

Georgia R. Clark
Springfield, Massachusetts

PIGS IN BLANKETS

You may bake these steak rolls as directed or cook in a slow cooker on Medium for 4 to 5 hours. When cooked in the slow cooker, a delicious gravy is made.

3 thin slices round steak	9 to 12 slices dill pickle
Prepared mustard	Paprika
Chopped onion	Flour
4 to 6 slices bacon, halved	Salt and pepper

Cut each slice of round steak into 3 or 4 pieces. Pound to make even thinner slices. Spread mustard over each slice. Layer chopped onion, a half slice of bacon and a pickle slice over the mustard on each steak slice. Sprinkle with paprika. Roll into tight cylinders, securing with wooden picks or string. Roll in a mixture of flour, salt and pepper. Brown the rolls in hot oil in a skillet. Remove to a 9×13-inch baking dish. Bake, covered, at 350 degrees for 1 1/2 hours. Yield: 9 to 12 servings.

Constance Busto, Preceptor Zeta Phi
Elgin, Illinois

ONION SWISS STEAK

3 pounds boneless blade or chuck steak	2 carrots, finely chopped
1/2 cup flour	1 1/2 cups beef broth
1/2 teaspoon salt	1 (15-ounce) can diced tomatoes
1/4 teaspoon pepper	1 1/2 teaspoons Worcestershire sauce
1/4 cup vegetable oil	
6 onions, cut into 1/2-inch wedges	1/4 teaspoon thyme

Cut the steak into strips. Dredge in a mixture of the flour, salt and pepper, coating generously; pound the flour mixture into the steak. Heat 2 tablespoons of the oil in a skillet over medium-high heat. Brown the steak in the hot oil in batches, adding more oil as needed. Remove to an ovenproof 9×13-inch baking pan. Stir in the onions, carrots, broth, tomatoes, Worcestershire sauce and thyme. Bake, covered, at 325 degrees for 1 1/2 hours or until meat is fork-tender. Adjust seasoning if necessary. Yield: 8 servings.

Gloria Eberhardt, Preceptor Epsilon Nu
Kitchener, Ontario, Canada

SWISS PEPPER STEAK

For ease of handling and to make thinner slices, freeze the steak before slicing.

3 pounds round steak, thinly sliced
1 large green bell pepper
1 large red bell pepper
1 large yellow bell pepper
1 large onion, chopped
1 (6-ounce) can sliced mushrooms, drained
1 (16-ounce) can crushed tomatoes
Onion salt and pepper to taste
1 teaspoon garlic salt

Dredge the steak slices in flour. Brown the steak in hot oil in a skillet. Place the steak in a 12×15-inch baking pan. Slice the bell peppers and sauté with the onion in the same skillet until tender. Layer the bell pepper mixture, mushrooms and tomatoes over the steak. Season with onion salt and pepper. Sprinkle with the garlic salt. Bake, covered, at 350 degrees for 1½ hours. Yield: 10 servings.

Shirley Smith Hull, Upsilon Master
Albuquerque, New Mexico

SAUSAGE STEW

1 pound beef stew meat
¼ cup chopped onion
2 cups water
1 (12-ounce) can beer
2 teaspoons beef bouillon granules
1 teaspoon salt
½ teaspoon thyme
¼ teaspoon pepper
1 bay leaf
3 carrots, cut into ½-inch slices
1 pound cooked Polish sausage, sliced
2 cups uncooked noodles
½ medium head cabbage, shredded

Brown the stew meat in hot oil in a large skillet. Remove the meat. Sauté the onion in the same skillet until tender; drain. Stir in the water, beer, bouillon, salt, thyme, pepper and bay leaf. Bring to a boil; reduce heat. Simmer, covered, for 30 minutes. Stir in the carrots, sausage, noodles and cabbage. Bring to a boil; reduce heat. Simmer, covered, for 10 to 15 minutes or until noodles are tender. Discard the bay leaf. Yield: 8 to 12 servings.

Debbie Stuart, Preceptor Pi
Polson, Montana

CORNED BEEF AND CABBAGE

Serve with Irish brown bread.

1 onion
4 whole cloves
4 pounds corned beef
2 sprigs of parsley
8 whole peppercorns
2 pounds cabbage, wedged, cored
1 cup sour cream
1 tablespoon prepared horseradish

Peel the onion and stud it with the whole cloves. Combine the corned beef, onion, parsley and peppercorns in a large kettle and cover with water. Simmer, covered, for 2½ to 3 hours or until corned beef is tender. Add the cabbage and simmer, covered, for 30 minutes longer or until cabbage is tender. Ladle some of the broth over the corned beef and cabbage and serve a mixture of the sour cream and horseradish on the side. Yield: 8 servings.

Ellen Hanlon, Nu Beta
Rochester Hills, Michigan

CORNED BEEF CASSEROLE

1 (12-ounce) can corned beef, chopped
4 pounds potatoes, cooked, diced
2 cups drained sauerkraut
1½ cups finely chopped celery
1 cup shredded Swiss cheese
2 cups mayonnaise
2 to 3 teaspoons prepared mustard
1 teaspoon salt
¼ teaspoon garlic powder
⅛ teaspoon black or white pepper

Combine the corned beef, potatoes, sauerkraut, celery, cheese, mayonnaise, mustard, salt, garlic powder and pepper in a large bowl and mix well. Spoon into a greased 9×13-inch baking pan. Bake at 350 degrees for 30 minutes. Yield: 12 to 15 servings.

Doris Calkins, Laureate Eta Lambda
Spring Valley, California

CORNED BEEF AND CABBAGE CASSEROLE

Serve with Irish soda bread.

1 medium head cabbage, shredded (about 8 cups)
1 small onion, chopped
1 cup water
1 (15-ounce) can white hominy, rinsed, drained
¾ pound thinly sliced corned beef, chopped
¼ teaspoon salt
¼ teaspoon black pepper
¼ teaspoon hot pepper sauce

Combine the cabbage, onion and water in a large saucepan. Bring to a boil; reduce heat. Simmer, covered, for 15 minutes or until cabbage is tender. Stir in the hominy, corned beef, salt, pepper and hot pepper sauce. Simmer for 5 minutes longer or until heated through. Yield: 6 servings.

Angea Carroll, Xi Xi Sigma
Copperas Cove, Texas

CORNED BEEF STEW

My family called this delicious stew "Shirley Temple Stew." Once when my older sister was babysitting her six younger siblings, who rarely seemed to appreciate her cooking, she cleverly told us this stew was Shirley Temple's favorite dish . . . and we loved it!

3 cups water
1 onion, sliced
3 sliced cooked white
   potatoes
1 (12-ounce) can corned
   beef, chopped
3 tablespoons flour
Salt and pepper to taste

Bring the water to a boil in a large saucepan. Add the onion and simmer until tender. Add the potatoes and corned beef. Thicken with the flour. Season to taste. Serve over hot biscuits or toast. Yield: 6 servings.

Ellen Phillips, Xi Kappa Lambda
Costa Mesa, California

MEAT LOAF

2/3 cup chopped onion
2 pounds carrots, peeled,
   shredded
Salt and pepper to taste
2 eggs
1 cup bread crumbs
1/4 cup milk
1/2 teaspoon thyme
1 tablespoon salt
1/4 teaspoon pepper
1 1/2 teaspoons parsley
   flakes
2 pounds lean ground
   beef
1/2 cup ketchup
2 tablespoons brown
   sugar
1/4 teaspoon dry mustard

Sauté the onion in hot oil in a skillet over medium-low heat until tender. Stir in the carrots, and salt and pepper to taste. Remove from heat. Mix the eggs, bread crumbs, milk, thyme, the 1 tablespoon salt, the 1/4 teaspoon pepper, parsley flakes and ground beef in a large bowl. Pat the beef mixture into a rectangle about 3/4 to 1 inch thick over waxed paper. Spread the carrot mixture evenly over the rectangle. Roll as for a jelly roll, sealing the edge. Place seam side down on a baking sheet. Blend together the ketchup, brown sugar and mustard in a small bowl. Pour evenly over the meat loaf. Bake at 350 degrees for 1 hour or until cooked through. Yield: 6 to 8 servings.

Doris M. Swinehart, Xi Alpha Omicron
Necedah, Wisconsin

Lisa Morford, Mu, Dakota Dunes, South Dakota, combines 2 pounds sliced eye of round, 1 envelope onion soup mix, 3/4 cup white wine, 1/2 cup sour cream, 1 can mushroom soup, and canned mushrooms and bakes, covered, at 300 degrees for 3 hours to make No-Peek Beef. Serve with potatoes, rice, or noodles.

ROYAL THREE MEAT LOAF

Ask the butcher to prepare the three packages of ground meat for you.

2 pounds ground sirloin
1 pound ground veal
1 pound ground pork
1 cup cottage cheese
1 cup bread crumbs
1 1/2 cups finely chopped
   onion
3 eggs, beaten
1 cup finely chopped
   green bell pepper
1 cup chili sauce
Salt and pepper to taste
Dash of cinnamon
1/2 cup good red wine
1/2 cup tomato sauce

Combine the sirloin, veal and pork in a large bowl and mix well. Add the cottage cheese, bread crumbs, onion, eggs, bell pepper and half the chili sauce and mix well. Season with salt, pepper and cinnamon. Shape into 3 loaves in greased disposable loaf pans. Pour 1/3 of the red wine over each loaf. Spread a mixture of the tomato sauce and the remaining 1/2 cup chili sauce over the loaves. Bake at 400 degrees for 30 minutes, basting frequently with the drippings. Reduce oven temperature to 350 degrees. Bake for 50 to 60 minutes longer or until cooked through. Yield: 10 servings.

Julie Spangenberg, Xi Alpha Delta
Austin, Texas

BAKED BARBECUED MEATBALLS

Be sure not to omit the liquid smoke. It is an essential ingredient.

2 eggs, beaten
1 (8-ounce) can
   evaporated milk
2 cups rolled oats
1/2 teaspoon garlic
   powder
2 teaspoons salt
2 teaspoons chili
   powder
3 pounds lean ground
   beef
2 cups ketchup
1/2 cup chopped onion
2 teaspoons liquid
   smoke
1 to 1 1/2 cups packed
   brown sugar

Combine the eggs, evaporated milk, oats, garlic powder, salt and chili powder in a large bowl and mix well. Add the ground beef to the egg mixture and mix well. Shape the beef mixture into 1-inch balls. Combine the ketchup, onion, liquid smoke and brown sugar in a small saucepan over low heat. Arrange the meatballs in a 9×13-inch baking pan. Bake at 350 degrees for 20 minutes; drain. Pour the warm ketchup mixture evenly over the meatballs. Bake for 1 hour longer. Yield: 12 to 15 servings.

Kari Weohn, Zeta Nu
Queen City, Missouri

BEEF CABBAGE CASSEROLE

1/2 to 1 pound lean
   ground beef
1 small or 1/2 large head
   cabbage
1/4 cup uncooked rice

1/4 cup chopped onion
1 (15-ounce) can tomato
   sauce or spaghetti
   sauce

Brown the ground beef in a skillet, stirring until crumbly; drain well. Cut the cabbage into 1/2-inch-thick slices. Layer the cabbage slices, rice, onion and beef in a 2-quart baking dish. Drizzle with the tomato sauce. Bake, covered, at 350 degrees for 1 hour and 20 minutes. Yield: 4 servings.

Norma Halstead, Preceptor Beta Mu
Carterville, Illinois

REAL TEXAS CHILI

The chili may be poured into loaf pans, cut into six 1-pound blocks after it sets in the freezer, then wrapped and frozen for future use.

6 pounds lean ground
   beef
1 1/2 tablespoons sugar
1 1/2 teaspoons oregano
1/2 cup plus 1 tablespoon
   chili powder
2 1/4 teaspoons cumin
1 1/2 teaspoons cayenne
   pepper

4 1/2 teaspoons paprika
4 1/2 teaspoons salt
9 garlic cloves, finely
   chopped
8 cups water
1/2 cup plus 1 tablespoon
   cornmeal
1 1/2 tablespoons flour

Brown the ground beef slightly in a large kettle, stirring until crumbly. Combine the sugar, oregano, chili powder, cumin, cayenne pepper, paprika and salt in a bowl and mix well. Add the spice mixture and garlic to the beef and mix well. Stir in the water. Cook over low heat for 2 hours, stirring occasionally. Add a mixture of the cornmeal and flour to the chili. Cook for 10 minutes or until thickened, stirring frequently. Yield: 12 to 24 servings.

Alva Nell Lister, Laureate Delta Mu
Wichita Falls, Texas

Cynthia Nordin, Beta Epsilon Tau, Humble, Texas, makes Armadillo Eggs. Stuff 15 jalapeño peppers with Monterey Jack cheese. Mix a 5-ounce package of biscuit mix with 2 cups shredded Monterey Jack cheese and 1 1/2 pounds hot or mild sausage. Wrap around the jalapeños to cover completely and shape like eggs. Dip in beaten egg, roll in Shake 'n Bake for pork, and bake at 350 degrees for 30 minutes. Eat hot or cold.

SLOW-COOKER LASAGNA

1 pound lean ground
   beef
1 large onion, chopped
2 garlic cloves, minced
1 (29-ounce) can tomato
   sauce
1 cup water
1 (6-ounce) can tomato
   paste

1 teaspoon salt
1 teaspoon oregano
1 (8-ounce) package
   lasagna noodles
4 cups shredded
   mozzarella cheese
1/2 cup grated Parmesan
   cheese
1 1/2 cups cottage cheese

Brown the ground beef with the onion and garlic in a skillet, stirring until the ground beef is crumbly; drain. Stir in the tomato sauce, water, tomato paste, salt and oregano. Spread 1/4 of the beef mixture in an ungreased 5-quart slow cooker. Layer 1/3 of the noodles over the beef layer, breaking noodles as necessary. Combine the mozzarella, Parmesan and cottage cheese in a bowl and mix well. Layer 1/2 of the cheese mixture over the noodle layer. Repeat the layers twice. Top with the remaining beef mixture. Cook on Low for 4 to 5 hours or until noodles are tender. Yield: 6 to 8 servings.

Millissa A. Duffey, Theta
Vincennes, Indiana

BOURBON-BASTED HAM

1 (10- to 12-pound) ham
   butt
1 cup bourbon
1 cup packed brown
   sugar

1 teaspoon grated
   orange zest
1/4 teaspoon ground
   cloves
Whole cloves

Roast the ham in a roasting pan at 325 degrees for 2 hours. Combine the bourbon, brown sugar, orange zest and ground cloves in a bowl and mix well. Let bourbon mixture stand for 30 minutes, stirring often until sugar is dissolved. Remove the skin from the ham. Score the fat into 1-inch diamonds. Insert a whole clove in each diamond point. Brush with half the bourbon mixture. Bake for 1 hour longer, basting frequently with the remaining bourbon mixture. Yield: 24 servings.

Nancy Long, Eta Omicron
Washington, Georgia

Tammy Gilmer, Alpha Chi, Orofino, Idaho, lines a 9×13-inch pan with hash brown squares, covers with a mixture of mushroom and celery soups, 1/2 soup can milk, 1 cup sour cream, chopped onion, pepper, and 3 cups ham or sausage links, tops with 2 cups shredded Cheddar cheese, and bakes at 350 degrees for about 1 1/2 hours to make Anytime Casserole.

BROCCOLI HAM RING

1/4 pound cooked ham, coarsely chopped	*1 1/2 cups shredded Swiss cheese*
1/4 pound fresh broccoli, coarsely chopped	*2 tablespoons Dijon mustard*
1 small onion, coarsely chopped	*1 teaspoon lemon juice*
1/2 cup coarsely chopped fresh parsley	*2 (8-count) cans crescent rolls*

Combine the ham, broccoli, onion, parsley, cheese, mustard and lemon juice in a bowl and mix well. Unroll the crescent dough. Separate into triangles. Arrange the triangles in a circle on a 13-inch pizza pan with narrow ends to the outside. The points of the wide ends of adjacent triangles should overlap slightly and an uncovered 3-inch-diameter circle should be left in the center. Spoon the ham mixture evenly over the wide halves of the triangles. Fold the narrow ends back over the filling, tucking them under the wide ends. Filling will not be completely covered. Bake at 350 degrees for 20 to 25 minutes or until golden brown. Yield: 6 to 8 servings.

Melissa Heskett, Xi Gamma Chi
Hayes Center, Nebraska

ROAST LOIN OF PORK

1 (3- to 3 1/2-pound) pork loin roast	*1 onion, chopped*
2 garlic cloves, slivered	*1 cup dry white wine*
2 tablespoons vegetable oil	*1 cup hot chicken broth*
Salt and pepper to taste	*1 tablespoon cornstarch*
2 carrots, cut into 1-inch pieces	*2 tablespoons water*
2 ribs celery, cut into 1-inch pieces	*2 tablespoons sour cream*
	1 tablespoon Dijon mustard

Stud the roast with the garlic slivers and brush with the vegetable oil. Season with salt and pepper. Place in a roasting pan. Roast in a 350-degree oven for 30 minutes per pound, adding the carrots and celery after 45 minutes of cooking. Remove to a heated serving platter. Let stand for 15 minutes before carving. Place the onion in the drippings in the roasting pan over high heat; reduce heat to medium. Cook for 5 minutes, stirring constantly. Stir in the wine. Cook over medium heat until reduced by half, stirring constantly. Stir in the chicken broth and a mixture of the cornstarch and water. Bring to a boil, stirring constantly. Mixture will thicken. Remove from heat. Stir

in the sour cream and mustard. Serve the sour cream mixture in a gravy bowl with mashed potatoes and the roast. Yield: 4 to 6 servings.

Marilyn Finucan, Lambda Lambda
Brechin, Ontario, Canada

BARBECUED SPARERIBS

4 pounds pork spareribs	*1/4 cup chili sauce*
1 medium onion, quartered	*1/4 cup Worcestershire sauce*
2 teaspoons salt	*2 tablespoons chopped onion*
1/4 teaspoon pepper	*1 tablespoon lemon juice*
1/2 cup cider vinegar	*1/2 teaspoon dry mustard*
1/2 cup packed brown sugar	*1 garlic clove*
1/2 cup ketchup	

Place the ribs, quartered onion, salt and pepper in a large kettle. Add enough water to cover ingredients. Bring to a boil; reduce heat. Simmer, uncovered, for 1 1/2 hours. Combine the vinegar, brown sugar, ketchup, chili sauce, Worcestershire sauce, 2 tablespoons chopped onion, lemon juice, mustard and garlic in a saucepan to make the barbecue sauce. Bring to a boil; reduce heat. Simmer, uncovered, for 1 hour or until thick, stirring occasionally. Arrange the ribs on a rack in a broiler pan. Brush with the barbecue sauce. Broil 5 inches from the heat source for 5 minutes. Turn. Brush with additional barbecue sauce. Broil for 5 minutes longer. Yield: 4 servings.

Gloria Korth, Iota Kappa
Caledonia, New York

LAMB SHANKS

4 lamb shanks	*1 (8-ounce) can tomato sauce*
1 teaspoon dill	
1/2 teaspoon oregano	*1/4 cup brown sugar*
1 teaspoon rosemary	*1 cup California white table wine*
1 large garlic clove	
1 large onion, thinly sliced	*1 1/2 teaspoons salt*
	1/8 teaspoon pepper

Place the lamb in a roasting pan. Combine the dill, oregano, rosemary, garlic, onion, tomato sauce, brown sugar, wine, salt and pepper in a bowl and mix well. Pour over the lamb. Bake, covered, at 325 degrees for 3 hours. Bake, uncovered, for 30 minutes longer. Remove the lamb to a serving platter and keep warm. Pour the liquid into a saucepan over high heat. Cook until slightly reduced. Thicken with cornstarch if desired. Pour over the lamb.
Yield: 4 to 6 servings.

Irene Coward
Cloverdale, California

BAKED CHICKEN

10 skinless boneless
  chicken breasts
10 (4-inch) slices Swiss
  cheese
2 (10-ounce) cans cream
  of chicken soup
1/4 cup dry white wine
  (optional)

1 1/4 cups crushed herb-
  seasoned stuffing mix
1/2 cup (1 stick) butter or
  margarine, melted
16 ounces angel hair
  pasta, cooked

Arrange the chicken breasts in a lightly greased 9×13-inch baking pan. Top with cheese slices. Combine the soup and wine in a bowl and mix well. Spoon evenly over the chicken. Sprinkle with the stuffing mix. Drizzle the butter over the stuffing layer. Bake, uncovered, at 350 degrees for 45 minutes to 1 hour or until chicken is cooked through. Add the pasta to the pan about 10 minutes before removing it from the oven, stirring to mix the pasta with the liquid. Yield: 10 servings.

Laraine Mizell, Gamma Xi
Claxton, Georgia

CHICKEN BROCCOLI CASSEROLE

4 chicken breasts,
  cooked
1 bunch fresh broccoli
2 (10-ounce) cans cream
  of mushroom soup
1 cup mayonnaise

2 (4-ounce) cans sliced
  mushrooms
1 cup slivered almonds
1 (10-ounce) can French-
  fried onion rings

Cut the chicken into bite-size pieces. Cook the broccoli until almost tender and cut into bite-size pieces. Combine the soup and mayonnaise in a bowl and stir until very smooth. Layer the broccoli, chicken, mushrooms and almonds in a 9×13-inch baking pan. Pour the soup mixture evenly over the almond layer. Push the soup mixture into the layers with a spoon. Bake at 350 degrees for 45 minutes. Top with the onion rings. Bake for 15 minutes longer. Yield: 6 to 8 servings.

Jean Poynor, Epsilon Master
Eureka Springs, Arkansas

SAUTEED CHICKEN

4 boneless skinless
  chicken breasts
2 eggs, beaten
1 cup Italian bread
  crumbs

Olive oil
8 ounces mushrooms,
  sliced
1 pound muenster
  cheese, sliced

Cut the chicken in 1/2-inch strips. Dip the strips in the eggs and shake lightly. Roll in the bread crumbs. Sauté in olive oil until golden brown. Sauté the mushrooms in a little olive oil until tender. Layer half the chicken, half the mushrooms and half the cheese in a buttered 4-quart casserole. Repeat the layers. Bake, covered, for 40 minutes or until cheese is melted. Yield: 6 servings.

Helga M. Broer, Preceptor Eta
Rockville, Maryland

SWEET GARLIC CHICKEN

2 to 3 boneless skinless
  chicken breasts
1 tablespoon vegetable
  oil
1 tablespoon finely
  chopped onion
  (optional)
1 (14-ounce) can diced
  tomatoes

1 or 2 garlic cloves,
  finely chopped
1/4 cup packed brown
  sugar
3 to 4 teaspoons
  Worcestershire sauce
Pinch of basil
Pinch of oregano
Salt and pepper to taste

Cook the chicken in the oil in a skillet over medium heat until cooked through, stirring frequently. Remove the chicken from the skillet and cut into bite-size pieces. Return the chicken to the skillet and add the onion. Cook for 1 or 2 minutes or until onion is tender. Add the undrained tomatoes, garlic, brown sugar, Worcestershire sauce, basil, oregano, salt and pepper. Bring to a boil, stirring frequently; remove from heat. Serve over rice. Yield: 4 servings.

Michelle West, Theta Theta
Coffeyville, Kansas

CHICKEN PAPRIKASH

1/4 cup garlic butter
4 to 6 boneless skinless
  chicken breasts
2 small to medium
  onions, chopped
2 tablespoons paprika

2 (10-ounce) cans
  chicken broth
2 rounded tablespoons
  flour
4 to 6 ounces sour cream
Salt to taste

Melt the garlic butter in a skillet over medium-low heat. Brown the chicken in the butter. Sprinkle the onions and half the paprika over the chicken. Pour 1 can of the chicken broth over the chicken. Bring to a boil; reduce heat. Simmer for 20 minutes. Remove the chicken to a serving platter and keep warm. Pour the onion broth into a blender container. Add the flour, remaining chicken broth and remaining 1 tablespoon paprika and process until smooth. Return to the skillet over medium-high heat. Bring to a boil; remove from heat. Whisk in the sour cream. Pour over the chicken breasts. Yield: 4 to 6 servings.

Gaye Jean Saks, Preceptor Delta Nu
Richmond Heights, Ohio

CHORIZO CHICKEN

Serve with a salad and refried beans.

8 ounces Monterey Jack
  cheese
4 whole boneless
  skinless chicken
  breasts
1 (4-ounce) can chopped
  green chiles
1/4 pound chorizo
  sausage, cooked,
  chopped

1/2 cup bread crumbs
1/4 tablespoon chili
  powder
1/2 teaspoon cumin
Salt and pepper to taste
1/4 cup (1/2 stick) butter,
  melted

Cut the cheese into 8 slices. Pound the chicken 1/4 inch thick between sheets of waxed paper. Spread each piece of chicken with equal parts green chiles and chorizo. Top each with 1 slice of cheese. Roll to enclose filling and secure with a pick. Combine the bread crumbs, chili powder, cumin, salt and pepper in a shallow bowl and mix well. Dip each chicken roll in the butter, then roll in the bread crumb mixture. Place the chicken rolls seam side down in a 9×9-inch baking dish. Cover each with a slice of cheese. Chill, covered, for 1 hour. Bake, covered, at 400 degrees for 30 minutes or until cooked through. Yield: 4 servings.

Julie Griffin, Xi Epsilon Mu
Englewood, Colorado

SAVORY MARINATED CHICKEN

Serve as an appetizer, or as an entrée over rice.

1/2 cup soy sauce
1/2 cup packed brown
  sugar
1/2 teaspoon ground
  ginger
2 tablespoons dried
  minced onion

1/2 cup whiskey
1 pound boneless
  skinless chicken, cut
  into bite-size pieces
2 tablespoons white
  wine

Combine the soy sauce, brown sugar, ginger, onion and whiskey in a bowl and mix well. Add the chicken and stir. Marinate, covered, in the refrigerator for 3 to 4 hours, stirring every 30 minutes. Place the chicken in a single layer in a large baking pan. Bake at 350 degrees for 1 hour, basting every 10 minutes with the marinade. Remove the chicken from the pan. Scrape the pan drippings into a skillet. Add the wine and cook over medium-low heat for 1 minute, stirring constantly. Add the chicken and cook for 1 minute, stirring constantly. Yield: 4 to 6 servings.

Kimberly Couvillion, Theta Delta
El Campo, Texas

SOUR CREAM CHICKEN

4 to 6 boneless skinless
  chicken breasts
1 envelope ranch
  dressing mix
1 (10-ounce) can cream
  of mushroom soup

1 cup sour cream
1 cup shredded Cheddar
  cheese
1 (3-ounce) can French-
  fried onions

Place the chicken breasts in a single layer in a shallow baking dish. Sprinkle with the dry ranch dressing mix. Combine the soup and sour cream in a bowl and mix well. Spread over the chicken. Layer the cheese and onions over the soup layer. Bake at 350 degrees for 45 minutes to 1 hour or until chicken is cooked through. Yield: 4 to 6 servings.

Sharon C. Johnson, Preceptor Alpha Zeta
Granbury, Texas

CHICKEN WITH SUN-DRIED TOMATOES

4 boneless skinless
  chicken breasts
3 tablespoons butter or
  margarine
1 large shallot, minced
3/4 cup heavy cream
1/2 cup dry white wine
  (optional)

3 tablespoons chopped
  sun-dried tomatoes
1 cup sliced fresh
  mushrooms
1/2 cup chopped green
  bell pepper
1/2 teaspoon dillweed
Salt and pepper to taste

Slice each chicken breast diagonally into 6 pieces. Melt the butter in a large skillet over medium heat. Sauté the chicken in the butter for about 3 minutes or until cooked through. Remove the chicken to a serving platter. Add the shallot to the butter in the skillet and sauté for 5 minutes. Stir in the cream, wine, sun-dried tomatoes, mushrooms, bell pepper and dillweed. Bring to a boil, stirring constantly. Cook over high heat for about 8 minutes or until reduced to a medium-thick sauce, stirring constantly. Reduce heat. Stir in the chicken and simmer for 2 or 3 minutes. Season with salt and pepper. Yield: 4 servings.

Betty Keenan
Edmonton, Alberta, Canada

Linda Anderson, Preceptor Alpha Phi, Greely, Ontario, Canada, makes Roasted Chicken with a Twist. She mixes 1/4 cup melted butter with 1/2 cup honey, 1 teaspoon prepared mustard, and 1 teaspoon curry powder, pours the mixture over 3 or 4 chicken breasts or thighs, and bakes at 350 degrees for 40 minutes.

SWEET-AND-SOUR CHICKEN

2 carrots, peeled, halved
  lengthwise, cut into
  1-inch lengths
1 (20-ounce) can
  pineapple chunks
1/4 cup packed brown
  sugar
3 1/2 tablespoons
  cornstarch
1/2 cup ketchup
1/3 cup apple cider
  vinegar
1 tablespoon soy sauce
1 tablespoon flour
1/2 teaspoon salt
1/4 teaspoon pepper

1 egg
4 boneless skinless
  chicken breasts, cut
  into 1-inch cubes
Vegetable oil for frying
1 cup coarsely chopped
  onion
1 green bell pepper, cut
  into 1-inch squares
1 garlic clove, sliced
2 cups coarsely chopped
  peeled cucumber
  (optional)
6 button mushrooms,
  sliced (optional)
3 cups hot cooked rice

Blanch the carrots for 1 minute in boiling water. Drain, reserving 3/4 cup of the water. Drain the pineapple, reserving 3/4 cup of the juice. Stir together the brown sugar and 2 1/2 tablespoons of the cornstarch in a 3-quart saucepan. Add the reserved water and pineapple juice, ketchup, vinegar and soy sauce. Cook over medium-low heat until thickened and bubbly, stirring constantly. Cook for 1 minute longer, stirring constantly. Remove from heat. Stir together the flour, the remaining 1 tablespoon cornstarch, salt and pepper in a small bowl. Add the egg, stirring until smooth. Add the chicken pieces, stirring to coat. Pour the oil 1/2 inch deep in a heavy skillet over medium heat. Add the chicken a few pieces at a time to the hot oil. Cook until browned on all sides, turning as necessary. Remove the chicken with a slotted spoon; drain on a paper towel. Keep warm. Add the onion, bell pepper and garlic to the oil in the skillet. Cook for 2 minutes. Remove the vegetables and drain on paper towels. Add the carrots, cucumber and mushrooms to the skillet. Cook for 2 minutes. Remove the vegetables and drain on paper towels. Stir all vegetables and the pineapple into the vinegar mixture in the saucepan over medium-low heat. Stir in the chicken. Serve over rice. Yield: 6 to 8 servings.

Beverly Eppright, Nu Lambda
Oronogo, Missouri

Carolyn Gilbert, Preceptor Gamma, Christopher, Illinois, sprinkles a whole chicken inside and out with seasoned salt, places it so it sits on a beer can filled with 1/2 can beer and 1/4 cup barbecue sauce , the can on a foil pie plate. Grill, covered, for 1 1/4 hours, turning the plate 1/4 turn every 15 minutes to make Chicken on a Beer Can.

CAJUN CHICKEN SPAGHETTI

1 tablespoon cayenne
  pepper
1 teaspoon ground
  cloves
1 tablespoon garlic
  powder
1 tablespoon salt
1 tablespoon black
  pepper
1/4 cup (1/2 stick)
  unsalted butter
2 pounds boneless
  skinless chicken
  breast, cut into bite-
  size pieces

1 large yellow onion,
  chopped
10 large fresh
  mushrooms, sliced
2 (14-ounce) cans
  chicken broth
1 bunch green onions,
  chopped
1/2 cup whipped
  margarine
8 to 10 ounces angel hair
  pasta, cooked,
  drained

Mix the first 5 ingredients in a small bowl. Heat a 10-inch or larger black iron skillet over high heat. Melt the butter in the skillet. Add the chicken and sauté until brown. Add the yellow onion and sauté for 3 minutes. Add the mushrooms and sauté for 3 minutes longer. Add the seasoning mixture and sauté for 4 minutes longer. Add the chicken broth and simmer for 15 minutes. Add the green onions and simmer for 4 minutes longer. Add the margarine, beating it into the chicken mixture. Remove from heat. Add the angel hair pasta and mix well. Let stand for a few minutes before serving. Yield: 4 to 6 servings.

Denise Trouard, Xi Rho
Sulphur, Louisiana

ROTINI TRIESTA

1/2 cup flour
2 whole boneless
  skinless chicken
  breasts, cubed
1/2 cup olive oil
2 garlic cloves, minced
Salt and pepper
  to taste
Chopped fresh parsley
  to taste

1 (14-ounce) can
  artichoke hearts,
  drained, halved
1 cup chopped sun-dried
  tomatoes
1 cup sliced portobello
  mushrooms
1 pound fresh asparagus
1 pound rotini, cooked,
  drained

Lightly flour the chicken pieces. Heat the olive oil in a large skillet. Sauté the chicken in the oil until almost cooked through. Stir in the garlic, salt, pepper and parsley. Add the next 4 ingredients. Simmer, covered, for 10 to 15 minutes or until asparagus is tender. Serve the chicken mixture over the rotini. Sprinkle with Parmesan cheese. Yield: 6 to 8 servings.

Janice DiBeneditto, Laureate Iota
Waterbury, Connecticut

SANTA FE PASTA

1 medium green bell pepper	1/2 teaspoon salt
1/2 pound boneless skinless chicken breasts	1/2 teaspoon black pepper
1/2 cup sliced green onion	1/4 teaspoon cayenne pepper
1 garlic clove, minced	1 (12-ounce) can low-fat evaporated milk
1 tablespoon vegetable oil	1 tablespoon cornstarch
1 1/2 ounces sun-dried tomatoes, chopped	1/4 cup fresh cilantro leaves
1/2 teaspoon chili powder	1/2 pound pasta, cooked, drained

Cut the bell pepper and chicken into 2-inch strips. Cook the green onion and garlic in the oil in a large skillet over medium-high heat for 1 to 2 minutes. Add the bell pepper, chicken, sun-dried tomatoes, chili powder, salt, black pepper and cayenne pepper. Cook for 4 to 5 minutes or until chicken is cooked through. Combine a small amount of the evaporated milk with the cornstarch in a bowl and mix well. Add the cornstarch mixture, cilantro and the rest of the evaporated milk to the chicken in the skillet. Cook over medium-high heat until slightly thickened, stirring occasionally. Serve over pasta. Yield: 4 servings.

Beverly Wilczek, Iota Omicron
Loveland, Colorado

BAKED CHICKEN SANDWICHES

10 cups chopped cooked chicken	1 cup chopped water chestnuts
1 cup cream of mushroom soup	1 cup chicken broth
2 tablespoons chopped pimentos	20 bread slices, crusts trimmed
2 tablespoons chopped green onion	4 eggs, beaten
	2 tablespoons milk
	Crushed potato chips

Combine the chicken, soup, pimentos, green onion and water chestnuts in a large bowl and mix well. Stir in the chicken broth. Spread the chicken mixture between bread slices, making 10 sandwiches. Wrap in foil and freeze for 24 hours. Dip the frozen sandwiches in a mixture of the eggs and milk. Roll in potato chips. Arrange in baking dishes. Bake at 300 degrees for 1 hour. Yield: 10 sandwiches.

George Anne Bedford, Laureate Zeta Gamma
Deer Park, Texas

CREPE PARTY PURSES

These creations look beautiful at the place settings at a Mother's Day dinner or sorority get-together.

1 1/4 cups milk	1/4 teaspoon white pepper
1 cup flour	1/2 cup reduced-sodium chicken broth
1 egg	
1 teaspoon vegetable oil	1/3 cup dry white wine
1/4 teaspoon baking powder	5 ounces boursin cheese
1/4 teaspoon salt	1/8 teaspoon crushed tarragon
6 green onions	1 red bell pepper, chopped (optional)
1 tablespoon olive oil	
1 1/2 cups chopped cooked chicken breast	

Combine the milk, flour, egg, oil, baking powder and salt in a blender container and process until smooth. Heat a very lightly greased nonstick 7-inch skillet over medium-high heat. Remove from heat. Spoon 2 tablespoons of the flour mixture into the center of the skillet. Lift and tilt the skillet to evenly spread the batter. Return to heat. Cook for 1 minute or until light brown. Turn with a spatula. Cook the second side for 30 seconds. Slide the crepe carefully onto a plate lined with paper towels. Repeat with the remaining batter, keeping cooked crepes covered. Thinly slice the white bulbs of the green onions. Reserve 12 whole green top pieces. Bring 1/2 cup water to a boil in a saucepan. Add the green onion tops and cook for 30 seconds. Rinse immediately with cold water in a colander; drain. Heat the olive oil in a large skillet over medium-high heat. Add the sliced onion blulbs, chicken and white pepper. Cook just until chicken is heated through. Add the broth and wine. Bring to a boil; reduce heat. Simmer, uncovered, for 5 to 7 minutes or until liquid is reduced by half. Add the cheese and tarragon. Cook until cheese is melted, stirring constantly. Strain the sauce and keep warm. Spoon about 2 tablespoons chicken mixture over each crepe. Pull up the sides to make a "purse." Tie the purse closed with a cooked onion top. Spoon 1 tablespoon sauce onto each plate; set the purse in the center. Garnish with red bell pepper if desired.
Yield: 12 servings.

Roxanna E. Cooper, Xi Beta Mu
Elkins, West Virginia

Shelly Allison, Nu Kappa, Guthrie, Oklahoma, mixes 8 ounces cream cheese with 1/4 cup orange marmalade and 1/2 cup pecans to spread on toasted croissants. Add sliced turkey, canned cranberry sauce, and lettuce for Turkey Croissants.

CHICKEN AND BROCCOLI BRAID

2 cups chopped cooked
   chicken
1 cup chopped broccoli
1/2 cup chopped green
   bell pepper
1 cup shredded Cheddar
   cheese
1 garlic clove
1/2 cup mayonnaise

1 teaspoon dillweed
1/4 teaspoon salt
2 (8-count) cans crescent
   rolls
1 egg white, lightly
   beaten
2 tablespoons slivered
   almonds

Combine the chicken, broccoli, bell pepper and cheese in a bowl and mix well. Press the garlic through a garlic press over the chicken mixture. Add the mayonnaise, dillweed and salt; mix well. Open 1 can of crescent rolls and unroll the dough. Separate into rectangles and place in a single layer on a baking sheet. Roll the dough to the edges of the baking sheet, sealing the perforations. Spread half the filling down the center. Cut each side into 1½-inch diagonal strips 3 inches deep. Lift the strips across the filling to meet in the center, twisting each strip 1 turn, alternating strips to form a braid. Tuck up the ends to form a rim at the end of the braid. Brush the egg white over the dough. Sprinkle with almonds. Bake at 375 degrees for 25 to 28 minutes or until deep golden brown. Repeat procedure with other can of dough. Yield: 2 loaves.

Greta Kidd Hinson, Epsilon Kappa
Elkin, North Carolina

CHICKEN LASAGNA

6 lasagna noodles
1 (10-ounce) package
   frozen chopped
   spinach, thawed
2 cups chopped cooked
   chicken
2 cups shredded Cheddar
   cheese
1/3 cup finely chopped
   onion
1/4 teaspoon freshly
   ground nutmeg
1 tablespoon cornstarch
1 tablespoon soy sauce
1/2 teaspoon salt

1/4 teaspoon pepper
1 (10-ounce) can cream
   of mushroom soup
1 cup sour cream
1 (4-ounce) can sliced
   mushrooms, drained
1/3 cup mayonnaise or
   salad dressing
Tabasco sauce to taste
1 cup grated Parmesan
   cheese
2 tablespoons butter or
   margarine
2 tablespoons chopped
   pecans

Cook the noodles using the package directions; drain. Drain the spinach well; press between paper towels. Combine the spinach, the next 13 ingredients and half the Parmesan cheese in a large bowl and mix well. Melt the butter in a small skillet and sauté the

pecans for 3 minutes to make a butter pecan topping. Arrange 2 noodles in a lightly greased 7×11-inch baking dish. Spread half the chicken mixture over the noodles. Repeat the noodle and chicken layers twice. Sprinkle with the remaining 1/2 cup Parmesan cheese and the butter pecan topping. Bake, covered, at 350 degrees for 55 to 60 minutes or until lightly browned. Let stand for 15 minutes before serving.
Yield: 8 servings.

Gina Otten, Tau Lambda
Coral Springs, Florida

HONEY GINGER CHICKEN

1 (2½- to 3-pound)
   chicken, cooked
1/4 cup soy sauce
2 tablespoons honey
1 garlic clove, pressed
1/4 cup peanut oil
1 tablespoon minced
   fresh gingerroot

2 scallions, sliced
1 teaspoon finely
   chopped red bell
   pepper
1/2 teaspoon red pepper
Fresh coriander to taste
1 head iceberg lettuce,
   shredded

Shred the chicken meat. Chill, covered, until serving time. Combine the soy sauce, honey and garlic in a small bowl and mix well. Let stand for 10 minutes. Combine the next 6 ingredients in a saucepan over medium heat and bring to a boil; reduce heat. Simmer for 3 minutes. Add the red pepper mixture to the soy sauce mixture and blend well to make the sauce. Pour the sauce over the chicken and toss to combine. Serve over lettuce on a platter.
Yield: 4 servings.

Karen L. Baker, Nu Gamma
Southfield, Michigan

GRILLED SALMON

1 large onion, thinly
   sliced
1 orange, thinly sliced
1 pound salmon fillets
   or steaks

1 cup (2 sticks) butter
3/4 cup packed brown
   sugar

Line a disposable rectangular baking pan with the onion and orange slices, reserving a few slices for garnish. Place the salmon skin side down over the onion and orange slices. Melt the butter in a saucepan over medium-low heat. Add the brown sugar, stirring until dissolved. Pour the brown sugar mixture over the salmon. Grill over hot coals until the salmon flakes easily with a fork, basting frequently with the juices. Garnish with the reserved onion and orange slices. Yield: 3 to 4 servings.

Sally Reis, Delta Theta
Longwood, Florida

SEAFOOD SAKA

Serve this exquisite topping over swordfish, tuna, mahimahi, or just about any fish.

4 vine-ripened tomatoes, chopped
2 yellow tomatoes, chopped
1/2 red bell pepper, chopped
1/2 yellow bell pepper, chopped
1/2 orange bell pepper, chopped

1 mango, chopped
1 large orange, chopped
1/4 pineapple, chopped
Juice of 1 lime and 1 lemon
1/2 cup orange juice
1 teaspoon garlic salt
1 teaspoon salt
1 teaspoon pepper

Combine the tomatoes, bell peppers, mango, orange and pineapple in a bowl and mix well with your hands, squeezing lightly to blend the flavors. Squeeze the lime and lemon juice into the bowl and mix well. Add the orange juice, garlic salt, salt and pepper and mix well. Chill, covered, for at least 24 hours to marry the flavors. Yield: 4 servings.

Kathy Schmitt, Epsilon Delta
Waukesha, Wisconsin

RED SNAPPER IN ORANGE BUTTER

2 cups flour
1 tablespoon garlic powder
1/2 teaspoon cayenne pepper
2 teaspoons paprika
Dash of salt
Dash of pepper
2 (6-ounce) red snapper fillets

1/2 onion, diced
1/2 cup white wine
2 cups orange juice
2 cups heavy cream
1 cup (2 sticks) unsalted butter, softened
1/2 teaspoon grated orange zest

Combine the flour, garlic powder, cayenne pepper, paprika, salt and pepper in a medium bowl and mix well. Dredge the fillets in the flour mixture until well coated. Brown in hot oil in a medium ovenproof sauté pan. Place the pan in a preheated 375-degree oven and bake for 8 to 12 minutes or until fish flakes easily with a fork. Sauté the onion in hot oil until translucent, but not brown. Add the wine and cook over medium-high heat until liquid evaporates. Add the orange juice and cook until liquid is reduced by half. Add the cream and cook until liquid is again reduced by half. Remove from heat. Slowly stir in the butter and orange zest. Serve with the snapper. Yield: 2 servings.

Heather Beckman, Psi Zeta
Bartlett, Illinois

SHRIMP AND CRAB CASSEROLE

1 large green bell pepper, chopped
1 small onion, chopped
1 cup chopped celery
1 pound cooked crab meat, flaked
1 pound cooked cleaned shrimp

1 cup mayonnaise
1/2 teaspoon seafood seasoning
Pepper to taste
Worcestershire sauce to taste
1 cup bread crumbs

Combine the bell pepper, onion and celery in a large bowl and mix well. Add the crab meat and shrimp and mix well. Stir in the mayonnaise, seafood seasoning, pepper and Worcestershire sauce. Place in a buttered 2-quart casserole. Cover with the bread crumbs and dot with butter. Bake, uncovered, at 350 degrees for 30 minutes. Yield: 6 to 8 servings.

Bettie J. B. Mundhenk, Laureate Alpha Chi
Merritt Island, Florida

CAJUN CRAWFISH CORN BREAD

If you want to make some of this corn bread without jalapeños, use two 8×8-inch baking dishes. Prepare half the batter with jalapeñs, half without.

2 cups yellow cornmeal
1 tablespoon salt
1 teaspoon baking soda
6 eggs, or equivalent egg substitute
2 medium onions, chopped
1/2 cup sliced jalapeño peppers

4 cups shredded Cheddar cheese
2/3 cup vegetable oil
2 (16-ounce) cans cream-style corn
2 pounds crawfish tails, lightly rinsed

Combine the cornmeal, salt and baking soda in a large bowl and mix well. Beat the eggs well in a medium bowl. Add the onions, jalapeños, cheese, oil, corn and crawfish tails to the eggs and mix well. Add the crawfish mixture to the cornmeal mixture and mix well. Pour into a greased 12×14-inch baking dish. Bake at 375 degrees for 55 minutes or until golden brown. Yield: 12 servings.

Gail J. Selent, Xi Lambda
Baton Rouge, Louisiana

SEAFOOD QUICHE

1 1/4 cups shredded Jarlsberg cheese
1 recipe quiche pastry
6 ounces cooked crab meat, flaked, or 1 cup cooked small shrimp
2 shallots, minced

1 tablespoon butter
2 tablespoons dry sherry
1/4 teaspoon crumbled tarragon
4 eggs, lightly beaten
1 1/2 cups half-and-half
Salt and pepper to taste

Spread half the cheese in a pastry-lined quiche pan. Sauté the crab meat and shallots in the butter in a skillet over medium-low heat for 2 minutes. Add the sherry and tarragon and sauté until fumes no longer rise from sherry. Remove from heat. Combine the eggs, half-and-half, salt and pepper in a large bowl and mix well. Add the crab meat mixture and the remaining cheese and mix well. Spoon over the cheese layer in the pastry shell. Bake at 375 degrees for 30 to 35 minutes or until set and golden brown. Serve warm (not hot). Yield: 6 to 8 servings.

Anna W. Gellerson, Laureate Eta
Falmouth, Maine

CURRIED SHRIMP AND MUSHROOMS

1 medium white onion,
*   chopped*
4 bay leaves
1/2 cup (1 stick) butter
2 tablespoons flour
2 cups milk
1 teaspoon curry powder
2/3 cup dry white wine

1 (4-ounce) can sliced
*   mushrooms*
3 tablespoons garlic
*   butter, softened*
1 1/2 pounds large shrimp
4 cups shredded Swiss
*   cheese*

Sauté the onion and bay leaves in the butter in a skillet over medium heat until onion is browned. Add the flour and cook until thickened, stirring constantly. Add the milk slowly, cooking and stirring until medium thick. Stir in the curry powder, wine and mushrooms. Remove from heat. Discard the bay leaves. Grease a 2-quart baking dish with the garlic butter. Layer the shrimp, curry mixture and cheese in the baking dish. Bake at 350 degrees for 20 to 25 minutes or until hot and bubbly and shrimp is cooked. Serve over rice. Yield: 8 servings.

Ruth Dalton, Eta Beta
Gainesville, Florida

SHRIMP FETTUCCINE

1/2 cup (1 stick) butter
3 to 4 garlic cloves,
*   minced*
1/2 cup chopped fresh
*   parsley, or 1*
*   tablespoon dried*
4 cups half-and-half
3 ounces cream cheese,
*   chopped*

1 cup grated Parmesan
*   cheese*
1/2 teaspoon nutmeg
Salt and pepper to taste
1 to 1 1/2 pounds peeled
*   cooked small shrimp*
1 to 1 1/2 pounds
*   fettucine, cooked,*
*   drained*

Melt the butter in a large skillet over medium-low heat. Sauté the garlic in the butter for 5 minutes. Add the parsley, half-and-half and cream cheese. Cook until cream cheese is melted, stirring constantly. Add

the Parmesan cheese. Cook for about 10 minutes, stirring occasionally. Add the nutmeg, salt, pepper and shrimp. Cook for 5 minutes longer. Combine the fettucine and shrimp mixture in a large warm bowl and toss lightly. Top with additional chopped parsley and serve. Yield: 6 to 8 servings.

Ida Senic, Xi Eta Eta
Jeannette, Pennsylvania

SHRIMP AND SAUSAGE FETTUCINE

2 tablespoons
*   butter*
3/4 pound shrimp
*   (31 to 35 count),*
*   peeled, deveined*
1/2 pound andouille
*   sausage, cut into*
*   bite-size pieces*
1 teaspoon minced
*   garlic*
1 cup chopped green
*   onions*

Dash of fresh lemon
*   juice*
1 tablespoon Seafood
*   Magic seasoning*
1 tablespoon Cajun
*   seasoning*
1 teaspoon basil
1 teaspoon thyme
4 cups cooked fettucine
1 cup half-and-half
1 cup shredded
*   provolone cheese*

Heat the butter in a large skillet over medium heat for about 5 to 7 minutes or until lightly browned. Add the shrimp, sausage, garlic and some of the green onions. Sauté until the shrimp are almost cooked through. Stir in the lemon juice, seasonings, basil and thyme. Reduce heat. Add the fettucine and half-and-half. Cook until the ingredients are heated through, tossing until well blended. Sprinkle the cheese over the pasta. Heat until the cheese is melted, tossing frequently. Add some more green onions and a dash of Seafood Magic, heating and tossing until all is well blended and piping hot. Add a little more half-and-half if sauce is too thick, a little more cheese if too thin. Serve in a warm serving bowl. Top with finely shredded provolone, a little green onion for color and a dash of Seafood Magic to enhance the presentation. Yield: 6 servings.

Heather Milliron, Alpha Alpha Phi
Milton, Florida

Gail Wurtele, Preceptor Alpha Lambda, Dunbar, Nebraska, makes a Low-Fat Cream Soup Substitute for use in many recipes. Combine 2 cups nonfat dry milk powder, 1/4 cup beef bouillon granules, 1 teaspoon each dried thyme and basil, 1/2 teaspoon pepper, and 3/4 cup cornstarch, and store in an airtight container. Blend 1/3 cup of the mixture with 1 1/2 cups cold water and cook until thickened, stirring constantly.

SHRIMP SPAGHETTI

1 onion, chopped
1 green bell pepper, chopped
1 rib celery, chopped
1 (4-ounce) can chopped green chiles
1 garlic clove, chopped
1/4 cup (1/2 stick) butter
1 (10-ounce) can cream of celery soup
1 (10-ounce) can golden mushroom soup
1 to 2 teaspoons lemon juice
1 to 2 teaspoons Worcestershire sauce
2 to 3 pounds small or medium shrimp, peeled, deveined
8 ounces spaghetti, cooked, drained

Sauté the onion, bell pepper, celery, chiles and garlic in the butter in a skillet over medium-low heat for 5 minutes. Stir in the soups, lemon juice and Worcestershire sauce. Simmer for 10 minutes. Cook the shrimp and add to the soup mixture. Add the spaghetti. Cook until heated through, tossing to combine. Garnish with chopped green onions and serve. Yield: 6 servings.

Betty Lou Wilson, Preceptor Theta
Buhl, Idaho

SEAFOOD THERMIDOR

1 1/4 cups sliced mushrooms
1/4 cup (1/2 stick) butter or margarine
2 (10-ounce) cans cream of celery soup
1/2 teaspoon dry mustard
Dash of cayenne pepper
3 cups cooked or canned seafood
2 tablespoons Parmesan cheese

Preheat the oven to 400 degrees. Sauté the mushrooms in the butter in a large skillet over medium-low heat for 5 minutes. Stir in the soup, mustard, cayenne pepper and seafood and heat the mixture, stirring frequently. Place in a buttered 1 1/2-quart casserole or divide among 6 ramekins. Sprinkle with Parmesan cheese and paprika. Bake for 15 minutes or until piping hot and bubbly. Yield: 6 to 8 servings.

Grace Roth, Psi Master
St. Petersburg, Florida

Jo Ann Smith, Laureate Epsilon Chi, Fortuna, California, layers canned green chiles, shredded Monterey Jack cheese, and shredded Cheddar cheese in a greased baking dish, pours a batter of a large can of evaporated milk, 4 eggs, and 1/4 cup flour over the layers, bakes at 350 degrees for 30 minutes, tops generously with salsa, and bakes for 15 minutes longer to make Chiles Rellenos Casserole.

BROCCOLI LASAGNA

You may use low-fat ingredients for this dish and it will still be delicious!

10 lasagna noodles
2 (8-ounce) cans tomato sauce
1 garlic clove, minced
1 teaspoon fresh oregano
1 cup shredded carrots
1 (10-ounce) package frozen chopped broccoli, thawed
2 cups ricotta cheese
1/4 cup grated Parmesan cheese
1 cup shredded mozzarella cheese

Cook the noodles using the package directions; drain. Combine the tomato sauce, garlic and oregano in a small bowl and mix well. Combine the carrots, broccoli, ricotta and Parmesan cheese in a medium bowl and mix well. Spread about 1/2 cup of the tomato sauce mixture over the bottom of a 9×13-inch baking dish sprayed with nonstick cooking spray. Layer 3 noodles over the sauce. Spread half the broccoli mixture over the noodles. Repeat the tomato sauce, noodles and broccoli layers twice. Finish with a layer of 1/2 cup tomato sauce. Sprinkle with the mozzarella cheese. Bake at 350 degrees for 45 minutes or until hot and bubbly. Let stand for 10 to 15 minutes before cutting and serving. Yield: 6 to 8 servings.

Heather Carlson, Xi Alpha Epsilon
Olympia, Washington

MACARONI RING

1 cup elbow macaroni
3/4 cup shredded Cheddar or Swiss cheese
1 small onion, finely chopped
1 small green bell pepper, minced
1 (2-ounce) jar pimentos, drained, finely chopped
1 cup milk
1 cup fine bread crumbs
1/2 cup (1 stick) margarine, softened

Cook the macaroni in boiling salted water until tender. Rinse in cold water; drain. Combine the cheese, onion, bell pepper, pimentos, milk, bread crumbs and margarine in a bowl and mix well. Pour into a ring mold sprayed with nonstick cooking spray. Place the ring in 1 inch of water in a large shallow pan. Bake at 350 degrees for 1 hour or until the surface is crisp. Invert onto a large round serving plate. Fill the center of the ring with a thick creamed sauce containing peas, carrots and leftover chicken, turkey, ham or any other cooked meat. Yield: 8 to 10 servings.

Joan D. Burkhardt, Laureate Alpha Omega
Springfield, Illinois

FRENCH TOAST CASSEROLE

1 loaf French bread	1½ teaspoons
6 eggs	cornstarch
¾ cup milk	4½ cups fresh or frozen
¼ teaspoon baking	blueberries
powder	1½ teaspoons butter
1 teaspoon vanilla	3 tablespoons melted
extract	butter
½ cup sugar	½ cup confectioners'
1 teaspoon cinnamon	sugar

Slice the bread diagonally into 1-inch-thick slices. Arrange in a 9×13-inch baking dish. Whisk together the eggs, milk, baking powder and vanilla in a medium bowl. Pour over the bread, turning to coat. Chill, covered with plastic wrap, in the refrigerator for 8 to 12 hours. Combine the sugar, cinnamon and cornstarch in a bowl and mix well. Add the blueberries, stirring gently until coated. Layer the blueberries in a separate 9×13-inch baking dish greased with the 1½ teaspoons butter. Layer the soaked bread wettest side up over the blueberries. Brush with the 3 tablespoons melted butter. Bake in the center of the oven at 450 degrees for 20 to 25 minutes or until toast is golden and blueberries are bubbling around the sides of the pan. Remove from oven. Sift confectioners' sugar over the top. Let stand for 5 minutes. Spoon the juices over the top.
Yield: 6 to 8 servings.

Julia Harris, Alpha Epsilon Master
Bethany, Missouri

ELEGANT BRUNCH FOR A CROWD

The recipe is easily halved if you are serving a smaller crowd.

1½ loaves day-old	16 eggs
French bread, sliced,	2 cups skim milk
crusts trimmed	½ cup white wine
1 cup shredded	1 tablespoon dry
Monterey Jack cheese	mustard
1 cup shredded Swiss	Pinch of cayenne pepper
cheese	¼ teaspoon black
1 cup shredded sharp	pepper
Cheddar cheese	1½ cups light sour
1 (1-pound) roll	cream
breakfast sausage,	½ cup grated Parmesan
cooked, drained	cheese
4 green onions, finely	
chopped	

Arrange the bread slices in a single layer in two 9×13-inch baking dishes sprayed with nonstick cooking spray. Layer the Monterey Jack, Swiss and Cheddar cheeses over the bread. Cut up the sausage and layer over the cheese. Sprinkle with the green onions. Combine the eggs, milk, wine, mustard, cayenne pepper and black pepper in a large bowl and beat until foamy. Pour over the ingredients in the baking dishes. Chill, covered with plastic wrap, in the refrigerator for 8 to 12 hours. Remove the dishes from the refrigerator 30 minutes before baking. Remove plastic wrap from the dishes and cover tightly with foil. Bake at 325 degrees for 1 hour. Remove the foil. Spread the sour cream over the top and sprinkle with Parmesan cheese. Bake, uncovered, for 10 minutes longer or until golden brown.
Yield: 30 or more servings.

Dorothy W. Ahonen, Laureate Eta
Portland, Maine

GREEK QUICHE

½ cup (1 stick) butter or	1 plum tomato, seeded,
margarine, softened	chopped
3 ounces light cream	1 small onion, chopped
cheese, softened	½ green bell pepper,
1 cup flour	chopped
½ cup crumbled feta	½ red bell pepper,
cheese	chopped
½ cup shredded	1 (4-ounce) can sliced
mozzarella cheese	black olives
¼ cup grated Parmesan	¼ teaspoon each thyme,
cheese	basil and oregano
4 cooked Italian	4 eggs, beaten
sausages, casings	
removed	
1 (10-ounce) package	
frozen chopped	
spinach, thawed,	
drained	

Beat the butter and cream cheese at high speed in a mixing bowl until smooth. Add the flour, stirring until a soft dough forms. Chill, covered, for 1 to 12 hours. Press into the bottom and up the side of a deep-dish pie pan. Combine the feta, mozzarella and Parmesan in a small bowl and mix well. Chop the cooked sausage. Layer the spinach, tomato, onion, bell peppers, olives, sausage and half the cheese mixture in the quiche shell. Beat the thyme, basil and oregano into the eggs in a small bowl. Pour evenly over the cheese layer. Layer the remaining cheese mixture over the top of the quiche. Bake in a preheated 375-degree oven for 45 to 60 minutes or until set and lightly browned. Yield: 6 to 8 servings.

Lori Richardson, Delta Epsilon
Penticton, British Columbia, Canada

BREAKFAST CUSTARD

1 loaf cinnamon-apple
   bread, unsliced
1/4 cup (1/2 stick) butter,
   softened
9 eggs
4 cups milk
2 cups heavy cream

1 cup sugar
1 1/2 tablespoons vanilla
   extract
2 cups frozen sweetened
   berries (boysenberries,
   blueberries or
   raspberries), thawed

Partially freeze the cinnamon-apple bread to make slicing easier. Cut the bread into 9 slices. Grease the bottom and sides of a 10×14-inch baking dish with half the butter. Layer the bread slices in the prepared baking dish. Melt the remaining butter and brush over the bread. Combine the eggs, milk, cream, sugar and vanilla in a large mixing bowl and beat at high speed until well blended. Pour the egg mixture over the bread. Let stand for 15 minutes. Place the baking dish in a larger baking pan. Add water to the larger pan to a depth of 1 inch. Bake at 375 degrees for 35 minutes. Let stand for 10 minutes before cutting into squares. Heat the berries in a microwave or in a saucepan over medium-low heat. Ladle some berries over each serving. Add a dollop of whipped cream. Yield: 12 servings.

Ardith Eleanore Ashworth, Laureate Theta Beta
Windsor, California

FORGOTTEN SOUFFLE

Serve with fresh fruit, coffee cake, juice, and coffee.

10 to 12 slices white
   bread, crusts trimmed
3 cups shredded Cheddar
   cheese
2 cups chopped cooked
   ham
2 cups broccoli florets,
   blanched

1/2 onion, chopped,
   sautéed in butter
12 eggs
3 cups milk
1/2 teaspoon salt
1/4 teaspoon pepper

Cut the bread into cubes. Cover the bottom of a greased 9×13-inch baking dish with 2/3 of the bread cubes. Sprinkle half the cheese over the bread. Layer the ham, broccoli, onion and the remaining bread cubes over the cheese layer. Layer the remaining cheese over the top. Combine the eggs, milk, salt and pepper in a large bowl and beat until well blended. Pour evenly over the mixture in the dish. Chill, covered, for 8 to 12 hours. Bake, uncovered, at 350 degrees for 40 to 45 minutes or until set; cover with foil during the last 15 minutes of baking if necessary to avoid overbrowning. Yield: 8 to 10 servings.

Susan E. Banton, Laureate Alpha Epsilon
Lewisburg, West Virginia

PEPPER, CHEESE AND PESTO STRATA

A beautiful main course for breakfast or brunch. Serve with fruit.

3/4 cup skim milk
1 (7-ounce) container
   prepared pesto
8 eggs
3/4 teaspoon salt
1/2 teaspoon pepper
1 (1-pound) loaf French
   bread

2 (7-ounce) jars roasted
   red peppers
1 cup grated Parmesan
   cheese
1 cup sliced green onions
3 cups shredded
   mozzarella cheese

Place the milk, pesto, eggs, salt and pepper in a medium bowl and whisk to combine. Cut the bread into 1/2-inch-thick slices. Arrange half the bread slices in a single layer in a buttered 9×13-inch baking dish. Layer half the roasted peppers, half the Parmesan cheese, half the green onions and half the mozzarella cheese over the bread. Repeat the bread, pepper, Parmesan, green onion and mozzarella layers. Whisk the egg mixture again to evenly distribute the ingredients. Pour evenly over the top of the strata. Chill, covered, for 8 to 10 hours. Bake, uncovered, in a preheated 375-degree oven for 30 minutes or until hot and bubbly. Yield: 15 servings.

Kay Johnston, Xi Beta Beta
Pelham, Alabama

BILL'S CAJUN-STYLE BROCCOLI

If Bill really dislikes broccoli as much as he says, this recipe achieved a near miracle. Don't miss a special treat.

1 (20-ounce) package
   frozen broccoli,
   thawed
1 onion, chopped
3/8 (3/4 stick) cup butter
   or margarine

1 (10-ounce) can cream
   of mushroom soup
1 roll garlic cheese, cut
   into chunks
Sliced or slivered
   almonds (optional)

Cook the broccoli in boiling salted water for 3 to 5 minutes; drain. Sauté the onion in the butter in a skillet over medium-low heat for 5 minutes or until tender-crisp. Stir in the soup and garlic cheese. Heat until cheese is melted, stirring constantly. Sprinkle bread crumbs over the bottom of a buttered 2-quart casserole. Place the broccoli in the casserole. Pour the cheese mixture evenly over the broccoli. Let cool slightly. Sprinkle with the almonds. Bake at 375 degrees for 25 minutes or until hot and bubbly. Yield: 8 to 12 servings.

Rose DeRouen, Gamma Delta
New Iberia, Louisiana

TANGY BROCCOLI CASSEROLE

2 (16-ounce) packages frozen chopped broccoli	3/4 cup milk
	1 teaspoon salt
2 (10-ounce) cans cream of broccoli soup	1 (9-ounce) jar horseradish sauce

Microwave 1 of the packages of broccoli on High for 5 minutes. Turn package over and microwave for 5 minutes longer. Repeat with the other package. Combine the broccoli, soup, milk, salt and horseradish sauce in a large bowl and mix well, stirring until broccoli is coated. Spoon the broccoli mixture into a 9×13-inch baking dish sprayed with nonstick cooking spray. Bake at 350 degrees for 20 minutes or until piping hot. Yield: 10 to 12 servings.

Pearl Meulemans, Preceptor Beta Phi
Englewood, Colorado

GOLDEN CABBAGE

2 1/2 pounds cabbage, trimmed, shredded	1/4 cup cornstarch
1 tablespoon sugar	2 cups milk
1 1/2 tablespoons salt	3/4 teaspoon salt
1/4 cup (1/2 stick) butter	1 cup shredded Swiss cheese

Cook the cabbage with the sugar and 1 1/2 tablespoons salt in 2 quarts of boiling water until tender-crisp; drain. Melt the butter in a saucepan over medium heat. Whisk together the cornstarch and 1/2 cup of the milk until smooth. Whisk 3/4 teaspoon salt and cornstarch mixture into the butter. Add the remaining milk slowly, cooking until thickened and bubbly, stirring constantly. Add the cheese. Cook until melted, stirring constantly. Combine the cabbage mixture and cheese mixture in a large bowl and mix well. Spoon into a buttered 9×13-inch baking dish. Top with additional shredded cheese. Bake at 375 degrees for 15 minutes or until top is browned. Yield: more than 12 servings.

Johnnie Mae Stanford, Laureate Zeta Eta
Bryan, Texas

RUMPLEDETHUMPS

A traditional Scottish baked cabbage-and-potatoes dish for Saint Patrick's Day. Serve with corned beef and applesauce and eat it while listening to cheery Irish music!

1 pound cabbage, cut up	1/4 cup (1/2 stick) margarine
1 pound potatoes, peeled	
1/4 cup minced onion	2 tablespoons margarine
2 tablespoons chopped chives	2/3 cup shredded Cheddar cheese

Boil the cabbage in salted water for 10 minutes; drain. Boil the potatoes in salted water for 20 minutes or until tender; drain. Chop the cabbage and potatoes and combine in a large bowl. Sauté the onion and chives in the 1/4 cup margarine in a skillet over medium-low heat until tender. Add the onion mixture to the cabbage mixture and toss to combine. Remove to a buttered 1 1/2-quart baking dish. Dot with the 2 tablespoons margarine. Sprinkle with the cheese. Bake at 350 degrees for 30 minutes. Yield: 6 servings.

Kathleen Meehan, Xi Beta Pi
Renton, Washington

EGGPLANT ROMANO

2 or 3 eggplants, peeled, cubed	10 ounces Italian bread crumbs
1 cup chopped onions	2 cups shredded Romano cheese
2 or 3 garlic cloves, pressed	2 eggs, beaten
2 pounds shrimp, peeled, deveined, chopped	1/2 cup chopped green olives

Simmer the eggplants in salted water until tender; drain. Sauté the onions, garlic and shrimp in hot oil until shrimp is cooked. Combine the shrimp mixture and eggplants in a large bowl. Add the bread crumbs, cheese, eggs and olives and mix well. Spoon into a buttered 9×13-inch baking pan. Dot with butter. Bake, uncovered, at 350 degrees for 1 hour. Yield: 15 servings.

Mary Greco Hill, Laureate Omega
Kirkland, Washington

CREAMY POTATOES

4 cups mashed freshly cooked potatoes	3/4 cup sour cream
	2 1/2 teaspoons salt
2/3 cup cream-style cottage cheese	1/8 teaspoon white pepper
1 1/2 tablespoons grated onion	1/2 cup chopped toasted almonds

Add no milk or butter when you mash the potatoes and mash them very well. Press the cottage cheese through a sieve or process in a blender until smooth. Combine the warm mashed potatoes and cottage cheese in a bowl and mix well. Stir in the next 4 ingredients. Spoon into a buttered shallow 2-quart baking dish. Brush the surface with melted butter. Bake, uncovered, at 350 degrees for 30 minutes. Place under the broiler for a few minutes to brown the surface. Sprinkle with the almonds. Yield: 8 servings.

Mary Brooks, Preceptor Alpha Sigma
Knoxville, Tennessee

GARDEN BAKED POTATOES

4 russet potatoes
2 tablespoons butter or
  margarine
1 small onion, chopped
1 (10-ounce) package
  frozen chopped
  broccoli, thawed,
  drained
1/2 cup ranch salad
  dressing

1 cup shredded Cheddar
  cheese
1 tablespoon
  vegetable oil
2 teaspoons dried
  parsley
Salt and pepper to taste

Pierce the potatoes and microwave on High for 12 minutes, turning several times. Bake in a preheated 425-degree oven for 15 minutes. Remove from oven. Slice off the tops of the potatoes. Scoop out the pulp, leaving 1/4-inch shells. Mash the pulp in a medium bowl. Heat a small skillet over medium heat. Add the butter. Sauté the onion for about 5 minutes or until tender. Add the sautéed onion, broccoli and salad dressing to the potato pulp and mix well. Stir in the cheese or sprinkle the cheese over the surface of the mixture. Brush the outside of the potato shells with the oil. Spoon the pulp mixture into the potato shells. Arrange on a baking sheet. Bake for about 15 minutes or until heated through. Sprinkle with parsley, salt and pepper. Yield: 4 servings.

Griff Jappé, Laureate Delta Xi
Lehigh Acres, Florida

ORIENTAL POTATO MASH

8 medium potatoes,
  peeled
3 to 4 tablespoons
  butter
1/2 to 3/4 cup milk
8 carrots, sliced or
  grated
4 ribs celery, sliced or
  chopped
1/2 to 1 red onion, sliced
  or grated

11/2 pounds lean ground
  beef
2 to 3 teaspoons pressed
  garlic
2 to 3 teaspoons grated
  gingerroot
Sesame oil
4 tablespoons oyster
  sauce
2 tablespoons soy sauce
Salt and pepper to taste

Boil the potatoes for 20 minutes or until tender. Whip the potatoes with the butter and milk. Stir-fry the carrots, celery and onion in hot oil in a skillet until tender. Brown the ground beef with the garlic and ginger in the sesame oil in a large skillet, stirring until ground beef is crumbly; drain. Stir in the oyster sauce, soy sauce, salt and pepper. Layer half the potato mixture, the ground beef mixture, the carrot mixture and the remaining potato mixture in a buttered 2-quart baking dish. Top with sliced cheese or another topping of your choice. Bake at 350 degrees for 15 to 20 minutes or until hot and lightly browned. Yield: 8 servings.

Barbara Howe, Preceptor Gamma Tau
Sacramento, California

SOUTHWEST POTATOES

2 large baking potatoes
1 cup shredded Colby
  cheese
6 slices bacon, crisp-
  cooked, crumbled

1/3 cup sliced green
  onions
1/4 cup barbecue sauce

Scrub the potatoes and cut into 1/4-inch slices. Brush both sides of each slice lightly with vegetable oil. Arrange in a single layer on a baking sheet. Bake at 450 degrees for 20 minutes or until lightly browned. Mix the cheese, bacon and green onions together in a small bowl. Brush the potato slices with the barbecue sauce. Sprinkle with the cheese mixture. Bake for 3 to 5 minutes longer or until cheese is melted. Yield: 2 to 4 servings.

Christi Bentley, Epsilon Xi
Marshall, Missouri

BAKED YELLOW SQUASH

1 pound of yellow
  summer squash
1 (10-ounce) can
  evaporated milk
1/2 cup (1 stick)
  margarine

1/4 to 1/2 teaspoon garlic
  salt
Paprika

Wash the squash, remove the stem ends and halve lengthwise. Arrange the halves side by side with cut sides up in a buttered 9-inch-square baking pan. Pour the evaporated milk evenly over the squash. Top with pats of margarine. Sprinkle with garlic salt and paprika. Bake at 325 degrees for 25 minutes or until tender. Yield: 5 or 6 servings.

Margery E. Bell, Laureate Gamma Rho
Winter Haven, Florida

VEGETABLE MEDLEY

2 cups sliced mushrooms
3 cups sliced zucchini
2 green bell peppers, cut
  into strips
1 cup sliced onions
1/2 cup sliced carrots
1 large garlic clove,
  minced

1/2 teaspoon crushed
  basil leaves
2 tablespoons vegetable
  or olive oil
1/2 teaspoon salt
1 (10-ounce) can tomato
  soup

Sauté the mushrooms, zucchini, bell peppers, onions, carrots, garlic and basil in hot oil in a large heavy skillet for 5 minutes. Stir in the salt and soup. Cook over low heat, covered, for 15 minutes, stirring occasionally. Cook, uncovered, for 3 minutes longer. Serve with Parmesan cheese. Yield: 4 servings.

June I. Phillips, Xi Delta Lambda
Houston, British Columbia, Canada

ANZAC BISCUITS

This recipe was originally used to make cookies for soldiers during World War II.

1 teaspoon baking soda	1½ cups rolled oats
2 tablespoons boiling water	1½ cups raw sugar
½ cup (1 stick) butter, melted	1½ cups flour
2 tablespoons light corn syrup	1½ cups shredded coconut

Dissolve the baking soda in the boiling water in a bowl. Stir in the butter and corn syrup. Combine the oats, sugar, flour and coconut in a separate bowl and mix well. Add to the liquid ingredients and mix well. Drop by tablespoonfuls 2 inches apart onto a greased cookie sheet. Bake at 350 degrees for 10 to 15 minutes or until edges begin to brown. Store in an airtight container. Yield: about 2 dozen.

Dianne Robinson, Preceptor Alpha Theta
Oakton, Virginia

MASHED POTATO BISCUITS

Keep extra copies of this recipe on hand, for people are sure to ask for the recipe every time.

1 cup mashed cooked potatoes	3 cups baking mix
¼ cup sugar	2 tablespoons melted butter
2 eggs	

Combine the potatoes, sugar, eggs and baking mix in a bowl and mix well. Stir in enough milk to make a soft dough. Knead 5 strokes on a floured surface. Roll into a ¼-inch-thick rectangle. Cut into squares. Fold each square over once. Brush with butter. Arrange on an ungreased cookie sheet. Bake at 375 degrees for 25 minutes or until brown. Yield: 8 servings.

Henrietta M. Martz, Preceptor Nu Omega
Sutter Creek, California

PEACHY SOUR CREAM COFFEE CAKE

2 cups chopped pecans	1½ teaspoons baking powder
⅓ cup packed brown sugar	½ teaspoon baking soda
3 tablespoons sugar	½ teaspoon salt
1 teaspoon cinnamon	1 cup sour cream
½ cup (1 stick) butter-flavored shortening	1 teaspoon vanilla extract
1 cup sugar	2 cups sliced peeled fresh peaches
2 eggs	
2 cups flour	

Combine the pecans, brown sugar, 3 tablespoons sugar and cinnamon in a bowl; mix well to make the streusel. Cream the shortening and 1 cup sugar in a mixing bowl until light and fluffy. Beat in the eggs. Combine the flour, baking powder, baking soda and salt in a bowl and mix well. Add the flour mixture alternately with a mixture of the sour cream and vanilla to the butter mixture. Beat until smooth. Pour half the batter into a buttered 9-inch springform pan. Sprinkle evenly with 1 cup of the streusel. Top with the remaining batter and ½ cup of the streusel. Bake at 350 degrees for 30 minutes. Arrange the peaches over the top. Sprinkle with the remaining streusel. Bake for 30 to 40 minutes longer or until cake tests done. Cool in the pan for 10 minutes. Remove to a wire rack to cool completely. Yield: 12 servings.

Beverly Scott, Laureate Beta Chi
Elma, Washington

FUNNEL CAKES

1¼ cups sifted flour	¾ cup milk
2 tablespoons sugar	1 egg, beaten
1 teaspoon baking powder	Vegetable oil for deep-frying
¼ teaspoon salt	

Sift the flour, sugar, baking powder and salt into a medium bowl. Make a well in the center of the ingredients. Pour in a mixture of the milk and egg. Beat with a wooden spoon until smooth. Pour ½ cup of the batter into a funnel, holding a finger over the spout; add a little more milk to the batter if necessary to make it of the proper pouring consistency. Drop the batter from the funnel into hot vegetable oil, making the funnel cake. Fry until golden brown, turning once with a slotted utensil. Lift the cakes from the oil with a slotted utensil or tongs; drain on paper towels. Sprinkle with confectioners' sugar or cinnamon sugar, or serve with warmed pie filling.
Yield: 4 to 6 servings.

Sandy McCollum, Xi Gamma Phi
Liberty, Missouri

❖ NORTHWEST PEAR BREAD WITH MAPLE BUTTER

This is a delicious moist tea bread filled with nuggets of pears. Any kind of pear may be used in this recipe, but Bosc or Anjou pears are best. Try usng apples instead of pears, or serving topped with vanilla ice cream or whipped cream.

2 eggs	1 teaspoon baking
3/4 cup canola oil	powder
1 cup sugar	1/2 teaspoon salt
1 teaspoon vanilla	1 teaspoon cinnamon
extract	3/4 cup walnuts, chopped
1 Bosc pear, cored,	1 Bosc pear, cored, sliced
grated	1/4 cup honey (optional)
2 cups flour	Maple Walnut Butter
1 teaspoon baking soda	

Beat the eggs, oil and sugar in a mixing bowl until light and fluffy. Stir in the vanilla and grated pear. Combine the flour, baking soda, baking powder, salt, cinnamon and 1/2 cup of the nuts in a small bowl and mix well. Add the flour mixture to the egg mixture, stirring just until moistened. Spoon into a greased 41/2×81/2-inch metal loaf pan. Arrange the pear slices over the surface. Sprinkle with the remaining 1/4 cup walnuts. Bake at 350 degrees for 50 to 60 minutes or until a cake tester inserted in the center comes out clean. Cool in the pan for 15 minutes. Brush with honey. Remove to a wire rack to cool completely. Serve with Maple Walnut butter.
Yield: 10 to 12 servings.

MAPLE WALNUT BUTTER

1 cup maple syrup	1/2 cup walnuts, chopped
1 cinnamon stick	
3/4 cup (11/2 sticks)	
butter, melted	

Boil the syrup with the cinnamon stick in a saucepan for 8 to 10 minutes or until the soft-ball stage; do not stir. Remove from heat. Discard the cinnamon. Add the butter, whisking until opaque and thickened. Stir in the walnuts.

Carolyn Raudabush, Xi Gamma Mu
Grinnell, Iowa

IRISH SODA BREAD

4 cups flour	3 cups seedless raisins
1/2 cup sugar	1 tablespoon caraway
2 teaspoons baking	seeds (optional)
powder	2 eggs, beaten
1 teaspoon baking soda	11/4 cups buttermilk
3/4 teaspoon salt	1 cup sour cream

Combine the flour, sugar, baking powder, baking soda, salt, raisins and caraway seeds in a large bowl and mix well. Combine the eggs, buttermilk and sour cream in a small bowl and blend well. Stir into the flour mixture to form a dough. Knead the dough in the bowl about 10 to 12 strokes; dough will be very sticky. Grease a 9-inch round cast-iron skillet or baking pan and dust with flour. Place the dough in the prepared skillet. Cut a 1/2-inch-deep slice across the top of the dough with a sharp knife. Sprinkle the surface with a little flour. Bake at 350 degrees for 65 to 75 minutes or until bread tests done.
Yield: about 24 servings.

Veronica Scrogham, Preceptor Zeta Mu
Sacramento, California

OVERNIGHT PANCAKES

Unlike regular pancakes, these will not get soggy after syrup and butter or fruit sauce is added.

1 envelope dry yeast	2 teaspoons sugar
1/4 cup warm (110 to 115	1 teaspoon salt
degrees) water	6 eggs
4 cups flour	4 cups buttermilk
2 tablespoons baking	1/4 cup vegetable oil
powder	Ruby Red Breakfast
2 teaspoons baking soda	Sauce

Dissolve the yeast in the water in a small bowl; let stand for 5 minutes. Combine the flour, baking powder, baking soda, sugar and salt in a large bowl and mix well. Beat the eggs, buttermilk and oil together in another bowl. Add to the dry ingredients and stir just until moistened. Stir in the yeast mixture. Chill, covered, for 8 to 12 hours. Pour 1/4 cup at a time onto a hot, lightly greased griddle. Cook until bubbles appear on the surface and the underside is golden brown. Turn the pancake. Cook until second side is golden brown. Serve with Ruby Red Breakfast Sauce or hot maple syrup. Yield: 21/2 dozen.

RUBY RED BREAKFAST SAUCE

The sauce is also good with ham, pork, or chicken.

1 (21-ounce) can cherry	1/4 cup maple syrup
pie filling	1/4 cup orange juice
1 (15-ounce) can	3 tablespoons butter or
cranberry sauce,	margarine
whole or jellied	

Combine the pie filling, cranberry sauce, syrup, orange juice and butter in a saucepan over medium-low heat. Heat until butter is melted and mixture is hot. Another way to heat it is to microwave on High for 3 minutes, stir, then microwave for 2 to 3 minutes longer or until butter is melted and mixture is heated through. Stir. Serve warm over pancakes or French toast. Yield: 4 cups.

Ann Sample, Preceptor Alpha Rho
Albuquerque, New Mexico

APPLE NUT HOTCAKES

1 cup flour	3/4 cup milk
2 tablespoons sugar	2 teaspoons vanilla
2 teaspoons baking	extract
powder	2 egg whites
1/2 teaspoon salt	1/2 cup chopped walnuts
1/2 teaspoon cinnamon	1/2 cup shredded peeled
3 tablespoons melted	apple
butter	Apple Syrup

Combine the flour, sugar, baking powder, salt and cinnamon in a large bowl and mix well. Combine the butter, milk and vanilla in another bowl and mix well. Add the milk mixture to the dry ingredients, stirring just until moistened. Beat the egg whites in a mixing bowl until stiff peaks form. Fold the stiffly beaten egg whites, walnuts and apple into the batter gently. Pour 1/4 cup at a time onto a hot, lightly greased griddle. Cook until bubbles appear on the surface and underside is golden brown. Turn the pancake. Cook until second side is golden brown. Serve with Apple Syrup. Yield: 10 to 12 hotcakes.

APPLE SYRUP

1/4 cup sugar	1/4 teaspoon allspice
1 1/3 tablespoons	1 1/2 cups apple juice
cornstarch	

Combine the sugar, cornstarch and allspice in a medium saucepan over medium heat. Stir in the apple juice. Cook for about 6 to 8 minutes or until thickened, stirring frequently.

Linda Gonzalez, Preceptor Gamma Kappa
Virginia Beach, Virginia

Florence Santarsieri, Xi Mu Eta, Orange Park, Florida, makes Double German Coffee Cake by preparing a chocolate or yellow mix using package directions, stirring in a can of coconut pecan frosting, baking, and frosting with a second can of frosting.

Virginia Tyler, Thomaston, Georgia, makes Coconut Toast by spreading bread slices cut as desired with a mixture of 1/2 cup melted butter, 1 cup sugar, 1 egg, 1 teaspoon vanilla, and flaked coconut and baking at 350 degrees until crisp and golden.

SUNRISE SCONES

1 3/4 cups flour	1/2 cup dried sweetened
3 tablespoons sugar	cranberries
2 1/2 teaspoons baking	1 egg, beaten
powder	Half-and-half as needed
2 teaspoons grated	1 1/2 to 3 teaspoons
orange zest	orange marmalade
1/2 teaspoon cream of	1/2 cup (1 stick) butter,
tartar	softened
1/3 cup (2/3 stick) butter,	
softened	

Combine the flour, sugar, baking powder, orange zest and cream of tartar in a medium bowl. Cut in the 1/3 cup butter with a pastry blender until the mixture resembles fine crumbs. Stir in the cranberries, egg and just enough half-and-half to make a dough that leaves the side of the bowl. Turn the dough onto a lightly floured surface. Knead lightly 10 times. Roll into a 9-inch circle. Cut into 12 wedges. Place the wedges 1 inch apart on a baking sheet. Brush with beaten egg. Sprinkle each wedge with 1/2 teaspoon sugar. Bake at 400 degrees for 10 to 12 minutes or until golden brown. Serve with orange butter made by blending the marmalade into the 1/2 cup butter. Yield: 1 dozen.

Joan Quebe, Laureate Zeta Sigma
Lubbock, Texas

NEVER-FAIL YEAST ROLLS

1 envelope dry yeast	1 (9-ounce) package
1 1/2 cups warm (110 to	yellow or white cake
115 degrees) water	mix
3 1/4 cups flour	1/2 teaspoon salt

Dissolve the yeast in the warm water in a large mixing bowl. Beat in the flour, dry cake mix and salt; do not knead. Place in a greased bowl, turning to coat the surface. Let rise, covered, in a warm place for about 1 hour or until doubled in bulk. Punch the dough down; divide in half. Roll each portion into a 12-inch circle. Cut each circle into 12 wedges. Roll up each wedge, beginning at the wide end. Place point side down on greased baking sheets. Brush with melted butter or margarine. Let rise, covered, for about 25 minutes or until doubled in bulk. Bake at 350 degrees for 12 to 15 minutes or until golden brown. Yield: 2 dozen.

Susan Mercer, Xi Beta Gamma
Overland Park, Kansas

QUICK DINNER ROLLS

This recipe appeared in my 12th-grade Home-Ec book, and I have used it ever since.

1 envelope dry yeast	2¼ cups flour
1 cup warm water	1 egg
2 tablespoons sugar	2 tablespoons
1 teaspoon salt	shortening

Dissolve the yeast in the warm water in a large mixing bowl. Stir in the sugar, salt and half the flour. Beat with a spoon until smooth. Add the egg and shortening and mix well. Add the remaining flour, beating until smooth, scraping down the sides of the bowl. Let rise, covered, in a warm place for about 30 minutes or until doubled in bulk. Butter a large 12-cup muffin tin. Stir down the dough and spoon into the muffin cups, filling them half way. Let the dough rise, covered, in a warm place for about 20 to 30 minutes or until it reaches the top of the muffin tin. Bake in a preheated 400-degree oven for 15 to 20 minutes or until golden brown. Yield: 1 dozen.

Beverley Neff, Laureate Tau
South Charleston, West Virginia

CHOCOLATE BUTTERMILK WAFFLES

You can use any kind of fruit, fresh or frozen, for the topping. Mixed berries are delicious as well.

3 cups sliced strawberries	½ teaspoon baking soda
½ cup sugar	1 cup buttermilk
1 cup flour	2 eggs, separated
⅔ cup sugar	¼ cup (½ stick) butter, melted
½ cup sifted baking cocoa	½ teaspoon vanilla extract
¾ teaspoon cinnamon	
½ teaspoon baking powder	

Combine the strawberries and ½ cup sugar in a small bowl and let stand at room temperature. Stir the flour, ⅔ cup sugar, baking cocoa, cinnamon, baking powder and baking soda together in a large bowl. Make a well in the center. Pour in a mixture of the buttermilk, egg yolks, butter and vanilla and whisk until well combined. Beat the egg whites in a separate bowl until stiff peaks form. Stir ¼ of the stiffly beaten egg whites into the batter. Fold in the remaining egg whites. Pour ⅓ cup batter onto hot waffle iron. Bake using manufacturer's directions. Top with the sugared strawberries. Yield: 10 to 12 waffles.

Suzanne Rivard
Gananoque, Ontario, Canada

SAUCY APPLE SWIRL CAKE

¼ cup sugar	1⅔ cups applesauce
2 teaspoons cinnamon	3 eggs
1 (2-layer) package yellow cake mix	

Blend the sugar and cinnamon. Butter a 10-inch tube pan or bundt pan and dust with 1 teaspoon of the cinnamon mixture. Combine the cake mix, applesauce and eggs in a large bowl and mix well. Beat as directed on the cake mix package. Pour into the prepared pan, reserving 1½ cups of the batter. Sprinkle with the cinnamon mixture. Top with the reserved batter. Swirl the cinnamon mixture through the batter with a table knife or spatula. Bake at 350 degrees for 35 to 45 minutes or until cake tests done. Cool in the pan for 15 minutes. Invert onto a serving plate. Yield: 12 servings.

Phyllis Wagner, Chi Master
Lake Havasu City, Arizona

BANANA NUT CAKE

½ cup shortening	1 teaspoon baking powder
1½ cups sugar	1 teaspoon baking soda
1 egg	1 teaspoon salt
1 egg yolk	¾ cup buttermilk
1 cup mashed very ripe banana	½ cup English walnuts
2 cups flour	

Cream the shortening and sugar in a mixing bowl until light and fluffy. Beat in the egg, egg yolk and banana. Sift the flour, baking powder, baking soda and salt together. Add alternately with the buttermilk to the banana mixture. Fold in the nuts. Pour into a 9×13-inch baking dish or two 8-inch cake pans sprayed with nonstick cooking spray. Bake at 325 degrees for 25 to 30 minutes or until cake tests done. Serve with ice cream, whipped cream or a creamy frosting. Yield: 20 to 24 servings.

Marge Shoemaker, Preceptor Epsilon Iota
Warren, Ohio

BEET CAKE

1 cup mashed cooked beets	1 teaspoon salt
1 cup drained crushed pineapple	2 teaspoons baking soda
1 cup cottage cheese	2 teaspoons cinnamon
1 cup chopped walnuts or pecans	2 teaspoons vanilla extract
2½ cups flour	1½ cups vegetable oil
	2 cups sugar
	2 eggs

Combine the beets, pineapple, cottage cheese, nuts, flour, salt, baking soda, cinnamon, vanilla, oil, sugar and eggs in a large bowl and mix well. Pour into a greased 9×13-inch baking dish. Bake at 375 degrees for 45 to 50 minutes. Cool in the pan. Frost with cream cheese frosting or dust with confectioners' sugar. Yield: 15 to 24 servings.

Carol Kubanda, Preceptor Delta Nu
Oak Park, Illinois

CHOCOLATE CAKE

3 ounces unsweetened chocolate	Pinch of salt
1/2 cup (1 stick) margarine	1 1/4 teaspoons baking soda
1 cup hot water	2 cups sugar
2 eggs	1 teaspoon vanilla extract
1 cup sour cream	Chocolate Fudge Frosting
2 cups flour	

Combine the chocolate, margarine and water in a saucepan over low heat. Heat until chocolate and margarine are melted, stirring occasionally. Remove from heat. Combine the eggs and sour cream in a small bowl and mix well. Combine the flour, salt and baking soda in another bowl. Combine the sugar, chocolate mixture, sour cream mixture, dry ingredients and vanilla in that order in a mixing bowl, mixing at medium speed after each addition; do not overbeat. Frost with Chocolate Fudge Frosting. Yield: 12 to 16 servings.

CHOCOLATE FUDGE FROSTING

3 tablespoons milk	1/3 cup semisweet chocolate chips
3 tablespoons margarine	
2/3 cup sugar	

Combine the milk, margarine and sugar in a saucepan over medium-high heat and bring to a boil. Boil gently for 30 seconds. Remove from heat. Add the chocolate chips, stirring until melted. Let cool for about 5 minutes. Beat at high speed until of spreading consistency.

Nancy Bickford, Preceptor Lambada
Arvada, Colorado

Elizabeth A. Costello, Mu Master, Council Bluffs, Iowa, makes No-Fuss Apricot Cake by mixing a lemon cake mix with 3 eggs and a can of apricot pie filling, pouring into a 9×13-inch cake pan, sprinkling with a mixture of brown sugar and coconut, and baking at 350 degrees for 35 minutes.

APPLESAUCE CHOCOLATE CAKE

3/4 cup applesauce	1/4 teaspoon salt
1 cup sugar	1 1/2 cups semisweet chocolate chips
1 teaspoon vanilla extract	1 1/2 cups chopped pecans
3 eggs	12 ounces whipped topping
1/2 cup baking cocoa	3/4 cup chocolate pudding
1/4 teaspoon baking powder	
1/2 cup flour	

Combine the applesauce, sugar and vanilla in a bowl and mix well. Beat in the eggs. Beat in the next 4 ingredients. Spread in a greased 8×8-inch baking pan. Sprinkle the chocolate chips and pecans over the top. Bake at 350 degrees for 20 to 25 minutes or until cake begins to pull away from the sides of the pan. Cool completely. Blend the whipped topping and chocolate pudding. Spread over the cooled cake. Decorate the top of the cake with chocolate syrup if desired. Yield: 16 to 20 servings.

Becky Castellari, Preceptor Delta
Centralia, Illinois

TEXAS SHEET CAKE

1 cup (2 sticks) margarine	1/4 cup (1/2 stick) margarine
1 cup water	2 tablespoons baking cocoa
1/4 cup baking cocoa	4 tablespoons milk
2 cups flour	2 cups confectioners' sugar
2 cups sugar	1/2 teaspoon vanilla extract
1/2 teaspoon salt	
2 large eggs	1/2 cup chopped walnuts or pecans (optional)
1 cup sour cream	
1 teaspoon baking soda	

Combine the 1 cup margarine, water and the 1/4 cup baking cocoa in a deep saucepan over medium heat. Bring to a boil; reduce heat. Simmer for 2 minutes, stirring occasionally. Stir in the flour, sugar and salt. Remove from heat. Beat in the next 3 ingredients until smooth. Pour into a greased and floured 10×15-inch cake pan. Bake at 375 degrees for 20 to 25 minutes or until cake tests done. Cool in the pan on a wire rack for 10 minutes. Mix the 1/4 cup margarine, the 2 tablespoons baking cocoa and milk in a saucepan over medium heat. Bring to a boil; reduce heat. Simmer for 1 minute. Remove from heat. Stir in the remaining ingredients. Spread quickly over the warm sheet cake. Yield: 10 to 30 servings.

Joy Sundin, Beta Omicron
Prince Rupert, British Columbia, Canada

DARK CHOCOLATE CAKE

A very, very moist chocolate cake, especially delicious with coconut pecan frosting.

2 cups flour
2 cups sugar
3/4 cup baking cocoa
1 teaspoon salt
2 teaspoons baking soda

1 cup liquid shortening
2 eggs, beaten
1 teaspoon vanilla
  extract
2 cups boiling water

Combine the flour, sugar, baking cocoa, salt and baking soda in a bowl and mix well. Make a well in the mixture. Pour the shortening, eggs, vanilla and boiling water into the well. Mix until smooth. Bake at 350 degrees for 35 minutes in 2 foil-lined round cake pans. Cool, frost and serve. Yield: 12 to 15 servings.

Marilyn A. Doyle, Delta Master
Rochester, New York

DEVIL'S FOOD CAKE WITH CARAMEL ICING

4 cups packed dark
  brown sugar
1 cup (2 sticks) butter,
  softened
1/2 cup buttermilk or
  sour milk
3 cups flour

1 teaspoon baking soda
1/2 cup boiling water
1/2 cup baking cocoa
1/2 cup heavy cream
1 teaspoon vanilla
  extract

Combine half the brown sugar, half the butter, the buttermilk and the flour in a large mixing bowl and mix well. Stir the baking soda into the boiling water. Stir the baking cocoa into the baking soda mixture. Stir the cocoa mixture into the flour mixture. Pour into 2 greased and floured 8- or 9-inch cake pans. Bake at 350 degrees for 25 minutes or until cakes test done. Cool on a wire rack. Combine the remaining 2 cups brown sugar, the remaining 1/2 cup butter and the cream in a heavy saucepan and bring to a boil. Cook to the soft-ball stage. Remove from heat. Stir in the vanilla. Beat with a spoon until mixture is of desired spreading consistency. Use to frost the cake. Yield: 12 servings.

Hattie Lee Frock, Laureate Alpha Beta
Colorado Springs, Colorado

Diana Embrey, Xi Epsilon Xi, Falmouth, Virginia, makes Lemon Meringue Angel Cake by splitting an angel food cake into 5 layers, spreading lemon pie filling between the layers, covering with a recipe of meringue, sprinkling with coconut, and baking at 350 degrees for 12 minutes.

MAPLE WALNUT CHIFFON CAKE

Prepare this as a little girl's birthday cake and decorate it with a doll Put a fancy top on the doll and use the cake as a skirt.

1 2/3 cups flour
1 tablespoon baking
  powder
1 teaspoon salt
1 1/2 cups sugar
1/2 cup vegetable oil
5 egg yolks
3/4 cup warm water
1 teaspoon vanilla
  extract

1/2 teaspoon maple
  flavoring
1/2 cup chopped walnuts
7 egg whites
1/2 teaspoon cream of
  tartar
Maple Frosting

Combine the flour, baking powder, salt, sugar, oil, egg yolks, water, vanilla and maple flavoring in a large bowl and mix until smooth. Stir in the walnuts. Beat the egg whites with the cream of tartar in a larger bowl until stiff peaks form. Fold the batter gently into the stiffly beaten egg whites. Bake at 350 degrees in a greased 10-inch tube pan for 1 1/2 hours. Cool in the pan for 10 minutes. Remove to a wire rack to cool completely. Invert onto a serving plate. Frost with Maple Frosting. Yield: 16 servings.

MAPLE FROSTING

1/2 cup (1 stick) butter or
  margarine, softened
2 1/2 cups confectioners'
  sugar
2 egg yolks
3 tablespoons heavy
  cream

1 teaspoon vanilla
  extract
1 teaspoon maple
  flavoring

Beat the butter at high speed in a mixing bowl until fluffy. Add 1 cup of the confectioners' sugar gradually, beating until light and fluffy. Beat in the egg yolks. Add the cream, vanilla, maple flavoring and the remaining confectioners' sugar and beat until smooth.

Beverly Lischinski, Alpha
Winnipeg, Manitoba, Canada

LEMON POUND CAKE

1 (2-layer) package
  lemon cake mix
1 small package lemon
  instant pudding mix
4 large eggs, beaten
3/4 cup vegetable oil
3/4 cup water

2 cups confectioners'
  sugar
1/3 cup orange or lemon
  juice
2 tablespoons
  vegetable oil

Combine the cake mix, pudding mix, eggs, 3/4 cup oil and the water in a mixing bowl and beat at medium speed for 2 minutes. Pour into a bundt or tube pan sprayed with nonstick cooking spray. Bake at 325 degrees for 1 hour. Cool in the pan for 5 minutes and prick all over with a fork. Pour a mixture of the confectioners' sugar, orange juice and 2 tablespoons oil over the warm cake. Let stand for at least 1/2 hour before removing from pan. Yield: 22 to 24 servings.

Beth Menefee, Xi Beta Alpha
Artesia, New Mexico

PINEAPPLE KIWI CAKE

1 (2-layer) package pudding-in-mix yellow cake mix	*1 small package vanilla instant pudding mix*
1 (20-ounce) can crushed pineapple	*1 cup milk*
2 or 3 kiwi fruit, peeled, sliced	*8 ounces whipped topping*
	1/4 cup finely chopped walnuts (optional)

Prepare and bake the cake mix using the package directions for a 9×13-inch cake pan. Cool slightly in the pan. Prick the cake all over with a fork. Pour the undrained pineapple over the cake. Arrange the kiwi slices over the pineapple. Prepare the pudding using the directions on the package, using only 1 cup milk. Fold the whipped topping into the pudding until well blended. Spread the pudding mixture evenly over the cake. Sprinkle with the chopped nuts. Chill, covered, until ready to serve. Yield: 12 servings.

Maggie Salles, Xi Mu Delta
Atwater, California

SAINT PATRICK'S DAY CAKE

1 (2-layer) yellow or white cake mix	*1 teaspoon almond extract*
2 small packages pistachio instant pudding mix	*1/3 cup vegetable oil*
1 cup club soda	*1 cup sour cream*
4 eggs, beaten	*8 ounces whipped topping*

Combine the cake mix, 1 of the packages of pudding mix, club soda, almond extract and oil in a large mixing bowl and mix well. Reserve 1 cup of the mixture for the topping. Beat in the eggs. Spread the egg mixture in a greased 9×13-inch baking pan. Bake at 325 degrees for 25 minutes or until cake tests done. Cool in the pan on a wire rack. Combine the reserved cake mixture, sour cream, the remaining package of pudding mix and whipped topping and mix well. Spread over the cooled cake. Yield: 15 servings.

Janei Kunselman, Epsilon
Spearman, Texas

IRISH CREAM BARS

1 (2-layer) moist-style yellow cake mix	*1 (16-ounce) can ready-to-use cream cheese frosting*
3 eggs	
2/3 cup Bailey's Irish cream	*1 (10-ounce) package vanilla milk chips*
1/3 cup vegetable oil	

Prepare the cake mix using the package directions, substituting the 3 eggs, Irish cream and 1/3 cup oil for the ingredients listed on the package. Pour half the batter into a greased and floured 10×15-inch cake pan. Beat the frosting and vanilla milk chips into the remaining batter. Drop large spoonfuls of the mixture over the plain batter. Swirl with a fork for a marbled effect. Bake at 350 degrees for 25 to 30 minutes or until the cake tests done. Cool in the pan. Cut into bars. Chill, covered, until ready to serve; bars will soften after chilling. Yield: 3 dozen.

Audrey Taylor, Preceptor Beta
Tempe, Arizona

BANANA BARS

1/2 cup (1 stick) butter or margarine, softened	*1 teaspoon baking soda*
1 1/2 cups sugar	*1/2 teaspoon salt*
2 eggs	*1/3 cup (2/3 stick) butter or margarine*
3/4 cup sour cream	*6 tablespoons milk*
2 mashed ripe bananas	*1 (1-pound) package confectioners' sugar*
1 teaspoon vanilla extract	*1 cup chopped walnuts or pecans*
2 scant cups flour	

Cream 1/2 cup butter and the sugar in a mixing bowl until light and fluffy. Beat in the eggs. Add the sour cream, bananas and vanilla and mix well. Add a mixture of the flour, baking soda and salt and mix well. Pour into a greased 10×15-inch cake pan. Bake at 350 degrees for 18 to 20 minutes or until cake tests done. Combine 1/3 cup butter and the milk in a heavy saucepan over medium-high heat. Bring to a boil. Remove from heat. Add the confectioners' sugar and mix well. Stir in the nuts. Spread over the warm banana cake. Cut into bars. Yield: 3 dozen.

Sue Sacco, Laureate Beta Iota
Centerville, Iowa

BLARNEY STONES

Tint the thin icing a medium green for Saint Patrick's Day.

6 eggs, separated
2 cups sugar
3 tablespoons lemon
  juice
1 teaspoon grated lemon
  zest
1/3 cup hot water
2 cups flour, sifted
2 teaspoons baking
  powder

1/4 teaspoon salt
1 (1-pound) package
  confectioners' sugar
2 teaspoons vanilla
  extract
Pinch of salt
5 to 6 tablespoons milk
1 pound salted peanuts,
  chopped

Beat the egg yolks in a mixing bowl until thick and lemon-colored. Add the sugar gradually, beating well. Beat in the lemon juice and zest. Add the hot water and beat well. Sift the flour, baking powder and salt together. Add the flour mixture to the egg mixture, beating at low speed. Beat the egg whites in a separate bowl until stiff but not dry. Fold into the batter. Pour into a greased and floured 9×13-inch baking pan. Bake at 350 degrees for 35 to 40 minutes or until cake tests done. Cool in the pan for 10 minutes. Remove to a wire rack to cool completely. Combine the confectioners' sugar, vanilla, salt and enough milk to make a thin icing and beat well. Cut the cooled cake into 48 squares. Spread the icing over all sides of each square. Roll the iced squares in the peanuts. Yield: 4 dozen.

Shelly Johnson, Laureate Eta
Klamath Falls, Oregon

CANDY BAR BROWNIES

3/4 cup melted butter
2 cups sugar
4 eggs
2 teaspoons vanilla
  extract
1 1/2 cups flour
1/3 cup baking cocoa

1/2 teaspoon baking
  powder
1/4 teaspoon salt
4 Snickers bars, chopped
3 (1 1/2-ounce) plain
  chocolate bars,
  chopped

Combine the butter, sugar, eggs and vanilla in a bowl and mix well. Combine the flour, baking cocoa, baking powder and salt in another bowl; mix well. Add the flour mixture to the egg mixture, reserving 1/4 cup of the flour mixture in a bowl, and mix well. Toss the Snickers pieces with the reserved flour mixture. Stir the Snickers mixture into the batter. Spread in a greased 9×13-inch baking dish. Sprinkle the chopped chocolate bars over the top. Bake at 350 degrees for 30 to 35 minutes or until a wooden pick inserted in the center comes out clean; do not overbake. Let cool before cutting. Yield: 3 dozen.

Irene Johnson, Preceptor Tau
Silver Bay, Massachusetts

PEANUT BUTTER FUDGE BROWNIES

1 (21-ounce) package
  brownie mix
1/2 cup very hot water
1/2 cup vegetable oil
2 eggs
2 3/4 cups sugar
1/2 cup (1 stick)
  margarine
1 (5-ounce) can
  evaporated milk

1 1/4 cups creamy peanut
  butter
1 cup semisweet
  chocolate chips
1 (7-ounce) jar
  marshmallow creme
1 teaspoon vanilla
  extract

Combine the brownie mix, water, oil and eggs in a large bowl. Beat 50 strokes by hand. Spread the batter in a greased 9×13-inch baking pan. Bake at 350 degrees for 30 minutes. Begin making the fudge immediately upon removing the brownies from the oven. Combine the sugar, margarine and evaporated milk in a 3-quart saucepan. Bring to a rolling boil, stirring constantly. Boil over medium heat for 5 minutes or to 234 degrees on a candy thermometer, stirring constantly. Remove from heat. Add the peanut butter and chocolate chips, stirring until melted. Add the marshmallow creme and vanilla and beat by hand until well blended. Pour over the warm brownies immediately, smoothing to the edges. Yield: 3 dozen.

Patti Confer, Preceptor Alpha Upsilon
Tamaqua, Pennsylvania

CHOCOLATE CREAM CHEESE COOKIES

Melt 1/4 cup of the second batch of chocolate chips to drizzle over the baked cookies.

1/2 cup (1 stick) butter,
  softened
8 ounces cream
  cheese or light
  cream cheese,
  softened
1 1/2 cups sugar
1 egg

1 3/4 cups chocolate
  raspberry chips or
  chocolate chips
2 1/4 cups flour
1 1/2 teaspoons baking
  soda
1/2 cup chopped walnuts
  or pecans (optional)

Cream the butter, cream cheese and sugar in a mixing bowl until light and fluffy. Beat in the egg. Melt 1 cup of the chocolate chips and stir into the butter mixture. Stir in the flour, baking soda, nuts and remaining chocolate chips. Drop by tablespoonfuls 2 inches apart onto ungreased cookie sheets. Bake at 350 degrees, 1 dozen at a time, for 10 to 12 minutes or until firm around the edges. Remove to a wire rack to cool. Yield: 4 dozen.

Kathleen Weich, Xi Lambda
Scarborough, Ontario, Canada

CHOCOLATE BARS IN A JAR

1/4 cup each milk chocolate chips, white chocolate chips and semisweet chocolate chips	1/2 cup packed dark brown sugar
1/2 cup chopped walnuts, toasted	1 cup baking mix
	1/2 cup packed light brown sugar
	1 cup baking mix

Layer the ingredients carefully in the order listed in a 1-quart wide-mouth glass jar: milk chocolate chips, white chocolate chips, semisweet chocolate chips, walnuts, dark brown sugar, 1 cup baking mix, light brown sugar and another cup of baking mix. If there is any space left in the jar, add more semisweet chocolate chips to fill. Place the lid on the jar. Cut an 8-inch circle of decorative fabric. Center the fabric over the lid. Hold in place with ribbon or raffia. Attach a gift card that reads: "Empty contents of jar into a medium bowl. Stir in 1/2 cup butter or margarine, melted; 1 large egg; and 1 teaspoon vanilla. Press into an 8-inch-square baking pan sprayed with nonstick cooking spray. Bake at 350 degrees for 18 to 22 minutes or until bars are light golden brown and center is almost set. Yield: 16 bars.

Judy Johnson, Alpha Sigma
St. Cloud, Florida

CARAMEL-TOPPED BROWNIES

1 (20-ounce) package fudge brownie mix	1 1/4 to 1 3/4 cups chopped Mounds Bars
3 tablespoons vegetable oil	3/4 to 1 cup chopped walnuts
1 (8-ounce) can sweetened condensed milk	Caramel ice cream topping

Prepare the brownie mix using the package directions, reducing the amount of oil to 3 tablespoons. Pour into a lightly greased 9×13-inch baking pan. Pour the condensed milk evenly over the brownie mixture. Sprinkle with the chopped Mounds Bars and walnuts. Drizzle with caramel sauce. Bake at 350 degrees for 36 to 38 minutes. Cool completely in the pan on a wire rack. Cut into bars. Yield: 2 dozen.

Nona H. Copeland, Theta Xi
Dyersburg, Tennessee

CHOCOLATE SNACK BARS

2 cups crushed vanilla wafers (60 wafers)	1 (14-ounce) can sweetened condensed milk
1/4 cup sugar	1 cup thin pretzels or pretzel sticks
1 cup baking cocoa	1 cup walnuts or pecans, coarsely chopped
1 cup (2 sticks) cold margarine, sliced	
1 cup miniature marshmallows	
1 cup sweetened flaked coconut	

Combine the wafer crumbs, sugar and half the baking cocoa in a bowl and mix well. Cut half the margarine into the mixture until it resembles coarse crumbs. Press the crumb mixture evenly over the bottom and 1/2 inch up the sides of a greased 9×13-inch baking pan. Layer the marshmallows and coconut over the crumb mixture. Combine the sweetened condensed milk, remaining 1/2 cup baking cocoa and remaining 1/2 cup margarine in a microwave-safe bowl. Microwave on High for 60 to 90 seconds or until mixture is smooth when stirred. Pour the chocolate mixture evenly over the coconut. Break the pretzels into 1/2-inch pieces. Sprinkle the pretzel pieces and nuts over the chocolate mixture. Press down firmly. Bake at 350 degrees for 25 to 30 minutes or just until bubbly on top. Cool completely. Cut into bars. Yield: 3 dozen.

Amy J. Panter, Xi Beta Gamma
Overland Park, Kansas

CINNAMON ROLL-UPS

16 to 18 slices of bread, crusts trimmed	2 tablespoons sugar
8 ounces cream cheese, softened	1/2 cup chopped pecans (optional)
1 egg yolk	1 cup (2 sticks) butter or margarine, melted
1 teaspoon vanilla extract	1 cup sugar
	1 tablespoon cinnamon

Roll the bread slices very thin. Mix the cream cheese, egg yolk, vanilla, 2 tablespoons sugar and the pecans in a bowl. Spread the cream cheese mixture over the flattened bread slices. Roll each slice tightly into a log. Dip the slices in the melted butter and roll in a mixture of the 1 cup sugar and the cinnamon. Freeze for 1 hour or until ready to bake. Slice each log horizontally into 6 or 7 disks and arrange on a cookie sheet. Bake in a preheated 250-degree oven for 15 minutes or less until bottom is lightly browned. Yield: 8 dozen.

Virginia P. Haas, Iota Master
Columbus, Ohio

DATE-FILLED OATMEAL COOKIES

1 pound dates	1 teaspoon baking soda
1 cup water	1/2 cup buttermilk
1 cup sugar	3 cups quick-cooking
1 cup (2 sticks) butter,	rolled oats
softened	2 cups flour
1 cup packed brown	1/2 teaspoon salt
sugar	

Combine the dates, water and sugar in a saucepan over medium heat. Simmer until dates are soft. Remove from heat. Cream the butter and brown sugar in a mixing bowl until light and fluffy. Stir the baking soda into the buttermilk. Add to the butter mixture alternately with the oats, mixing well after each addition. Stir in enough flour to make a workable dough. Roll into 1/8-inch thickness on a floured surface. Cut with a round cookie cutter. Place 1 teaspoon of the date mixture in the center of each cookie. Place another cookie over the top and press the edges to enclose the filling. Bake at 350 degrees on greased cookie sheets for 20 to 25 minutes or until edges begin to brown. Yield: 15 to 20 cookies.

Donna Fanshier, Theta Master
Great Bend, Kansas

HEAVENLY BANANA PIE

2 ripe bananas, mashed	1 baked (9-inch) pie
1 cup sugar	shell
2 egg whites	1 1/2 cups whipped cream
Pinch of salt	1/2 cup chopped walnuts
1/8 teaspoon almond	1/2 cup sliced cherries
extract	

Combine the bananas, sugar, unbeaten egg whites, salt and almond extract in a mixing bowl and beat until stiff. Pour the banana mixture into the pie shell. Bake at 300 degrees for 20 minutes. Spread whipped cream over the cooled pie. Decorate with walnuts and cherries. Yield: 8 servings.

Charlotte Backstedt, Xi Beta Xi
El Cajon, California

SOUR CREAM CRANBERRY PIE

1 1/2 cups dried	1/4 teaspoon ground
cranberries	cloves
3/4 cup sugar	Pinch of salt
1 1/2 tablespoons flour	1 tablespoon lemon
1 1/2 cups sour cream	juice
4 eggs, separated	1 baked 9-inch pie shell
2 whole eggs	1 tablespoon cold water
1 1/2 teaspoons cinnamon	1/2 cup sugar
1/2 teaspoon nutmeg	

Soak the cranberries in hot water for 15 minutes; drain well. Mix the 3/4 cup sugar and the flour in a saucepan. Stir in the cranberries, sour cream, 4 egg yolks, whole eggs, cinnamon, nutmeg, cloves, salt and lemon juice. Cook over medium heat until mixture boils and thickens, stirring constantly. Pour into the pie shell. Beat the 4 egg whites with the cold water in a bowl until soft peaks form. Add the 1/2 cup sugar gradually, beating until stiff peaks form. Spread over the cranberry filling, sealing to the edge. Bake at 350 degrees for 15 minutes or until light brown. Yield: 6 to 8 servings.

Mae Belle Herczeg, Lambda Master
Vancouver, British Columbia, Canada

DAIQUIRI PIE

1 (4-ounce) package	2 eggs, slightly beaten
lemon pudding mix	1/2 cup light rum
1 (3-ounce) package lime	12 ounces whipped
gelatin	topping
1/3 cup sugar	1 (9-inch) graham
2 1/2 cups water	cracker pie shell

Mix the pudding mix, gelatin and sugar in a saucepan. Blend in 1/2 cup of the water and the eggs. Stir in the remaining 2 cups water. Bring to a boil over medium heat, stirring constantly. Remove from heat. Stir in the rum. Chill, covered, for at least 1 hour. Blend the whipped topping into the chilled mixture. Spoon into the pie shell. Chill until firm. Garnish with additional whipped topping and lime slices. Yield: 6 to 8 servings.

Mary Louise Eayrs, Delta Master
Kalispell, Montana

LEMON PIES

2 small packages vanilla	2 3/4 cups low-fat or
instant sugar-free	fat-free milk
pudding mix	8 ounces fat-free
1 (1/2-ounce) package	whipped topping
sugar-free	2 (9-inch) graham
lemonade mix	cracker pie shells
4 packets sugar	1 teaspoon grated
substitute with	lemon zest
aspartame	

Mix the first 3 ingredients in a medium bowl. Add the milk gradually, beating with a wire whisk until thickened. Fold in the whipped topping gently. Spoon the mixture evenly into the pie shells. Garnish with the lemon zest. Chill, covered, in the refrigerator for at least 3 hours. Yield: 32 servings.

Joan M. Teuscher, Preceptor Eta Omicron
Sacramento, California

LIME PIE

1¼ cups graham cracker crumbs

3 tablespoons sugar

⅓ cup (⅔ stick) margarine, melted

1 (7-ounce) bottle lemon-lime soda

1 (3-ounce) package lime gelatin

1 pint vanilla ice cream

Mix the graham cracker crumbs, sugar and margarine together in a bowl. Press the mixture into a 9-inch pie pan. Bake in a preheated 350-degree oven for 8 minutes. Cool completely. Heat the lemon-lime soda to the boiling point. Combine the hot lemon-lime soda and the gelatin in a mixing bowl and mix well. Cool briefly. Add the ice cream to the warm gelatin mixture and beat at high speed until smooth. Pour quickly into the prepared pie crust. Decorate the top with whipped cream or whipped topping and lime slices, or sprinkle with crushed graham crackers. Chill until firm. Yield: 6 to 8 servings.

Betty Jane Orme, Laureate Iota
Maysville, Kentucky

MACADAMIA NUT PIE

3 egg whites

½ teaspoon baking powder

1 cup sugar

1 teaspoon vanilla extract

1 cup crushed graham crackers

½ cup grated coconut

½ cup chopped macadamia nuts

1 cup whipping cream

2 teaspoons sugar

Beat the egg whites with the baking powder until stiff peaks form. Add the 1 cup sugar and the vanilla gradually, beating until of meringue consistency. Fold in the cracker crumbs, coconut and nuts. Pour into a 9-inch pie pan sprayed with nonstick cooking spray. Bake at 350 degrees for 30 minutes. Cool completely. Beat the whipping cream and the 2 teaspoons sugar until stiff peaks form. Spread over the cooled pie. Yield: 6 to 8 servings.

Viola Stillman, Alpha Xi Gamma
San Marcos, Texas

PEANUT BUTTER PIE

1¼ cups chocolate cookie crumbs

¼ cup sugar

¼ cup (½ stick) margarine, melted

1 cup sugar

8 ounces cream cheese, softened

1 cup creamy peanut butter

1 tablespoon margarine, softened

1 teaspoon vanilla extract

1 cup whipping cream, whipped

Combine the cookie crumbs, the ¼ cup sugar and the ¼ cup margarine in a small bowl and mix well. Press into a 9-inch pie pan to form a shell. Bake in a preheated 350-degree oven for 10 minutes. Cool completely. Combine the 1 cup sugar, cream cheese, peanut butter, the 1 tablespoon margarine and the vanilla in a mixing bowl and beat until smooth. Fold in the whipped cream. Spoon gently into the cookie crust. Garnish with chocolate cookie crumbs. Chill, covered, until ready to serve. Yield: 8 to 10 servings.

Shirley Fitch, Preceptor Rho
Flagstaff, Arizona

CHOCOLATE PEANUT BUTTER PIE

1½ cups crushed chocolate sandwich cookies

1 cup peanut butter, softened

4 ounces cream cheese, softened

¾ cup confectioners' sugar

2 tablespoons whole milk

2 tablespoons chopped peanuts

3 cups whipping cream

1 to 1⅓ cups semisweet chocolate chips, chopped

Combine the cookie crumbs and ¼ cup of the peanut butter in a bowl and mix well. Press the mixture into the bottom of a 9-inch springform pan sprayed with nonstick cooking spray. Bake in a preheated 350-degree oven for 8 to 10 minutes. Combine the cream cheese and confectioners' sugar in a mixing bowl and beat at high speed until smooth. Add the remaining ¾ cup peanut butter and the milk and beat at high speed for 1 minute. Stir in the peanuts. Beat 2¼ cups of the whipping cream until stiff peaks form. Fold into the peanut butter mixture. Pour into the prepared crust. Chill, covered, for 2 to 3 hours or until firm. Combine the chocolate chips and the remaining ¾ cup cream in a saucepan over medium heat. Cook until chocolate is melted, stirring constantly. Remove from heat. Cool for 2 to 3 minutes, stirring constantly. Remove the side of the springform pan. Pour the chocolate mixture over the pie, allowing some to drip down the side. Chill for at least 2 hours before serving. Yield: 16 servings.

Lenora VanDusen, Preceptor Beta
Steady Brook, Newfoundland, Canada

Cheryl Feist, Xi Zeta, Chadron, Nebraska, makes Any-Flavor Quick Cream Pie by preparing 2 small packages of chocolate, lemon, banana, or other flavor instant pudding with 1½ cups milk, folding in 8 ounces whipped topping, and pouring into a graham cracker pie shell. Chill, covered, for 3 hours.

PINEAPPLE CHESS PIE

1½ cups sugar
3 tablespoons cornmeal
2 tablespoons flour
¼ teaspoon salt
4 large eggs, slightly
  beaten
1 teaspoon vanilla
  extract

¼ cup (½ stick) butter
  or margarine, melted
1 (3-ounce) can flaked
  coconut
1 (15-ounce) can crushed
  pineapple, drained
1 unbaked (9-inch) pie
  shell

Combine the sugar, cornmeal, flour and salt in a bowl and mix well. Add the eggs and vanilla and stir until blended. Stir in the butter, coconut and pineapple. Pour into the pie shell. Bake at 350 degrees for 1 hour or until set; cover loosely with foil after 40 minutes of baking if necessary to prevent overbrowning.
Yield: 6 to 8 servings.

Wanda Williams, Preceptor Alpha Zeta
Grand Junction, Colorado

RHUBARB CUSTARD PIE

2 cups flour
2 tablespoons sugar
1 cup (2 sticks) cold
  butter, sliced
6 cups rhubarb cut into
  ½-inch pieces
6 eggs, separated
2 cups sugar

1 tablespoon flour
½ teaspoon salt
1 cup heavy cream
1 tablespoon tapioca
¾ cup sugar
1 teaspoon vanilla
  extract

Combine the 2 cups flour and 2 tablespoons sugar in a bowl. Cut in the butter until the mixture resembles coarse crumbs. Pat into a greased 10×13-inch baking pan. Bake in a preheated 350-degree oven for 10 minutes or until crust is lightly browned; cool. Turn the oven temperature to 400 degrees. Layer the rhubarb pieces in the cooled crust. Combine the egg yolks, 2 cups sugar, 1 tablespoon flour, salt and cream in a bowl and mix until smooth and creamy. Stir in the tapioca. Pour evenly over the rhubarb. Bake for 10 minutes. Reduce the oven temperature to 325 degrees. Bake for 30 minutes or until almost set. Beat the egg whites in a mixing bowl until soft peaks form. Add the ¾ cup sugar gradually, beating until stiff peaks form. Beat in the vanilla. Remove the almost-set pie from the oven. Top with the meringue, sealing to the edge. Turn the oven temperature to 350 degrees. Bake the pie for 15 minutes or until meringue is lightly browned; watch carefully and be sure to remove before overbrowning occurs.
Yield: 12 to 15 servings.

Rose Lanctot, Xi Gamma Zeta
Tucson, Arizona

ALMOND TARTS

2 eggs
1¼ cups ground or
  puréed cooked white
  rice
1 cup (2 sticks) butter,
  or ½ cup butter plus
  ½ cup margarine,
  softened

1 cup sugar
1 teaspoon almond
  extract
¼ teaspoon salt
Fruit jam
1 recipe pie pastry

Beat the eggs in a bowl until thick and pale yellow. Stir in the ground rice. Cream the butter and sugar in a mixing bowl until light and fluffy. Stir into the egg mixture. Add the almond extract and salt and mix well. Place ½ teaspoon of jam in each of 12 to 24 pastry-lined muffin cups or tart pans. Cover with spoonfuls of the rice mixture. Bake at 375 degrees for 20 minutes or until pastry is done.
Yield: 12 to 24 tarts.

Elinor Sanderson, Laureate Alpha Lambda
Phoenix, Arizona

AMARETTO CHEESECAKE

1½ cups chocolate wafer
  crumbs
1 cup finely chopped
  toasted almonds
⅓ cup sugar
6 tablespoons butter,
  softened
24 ounces cream cheese,
  softened
1 cup sugar

4 eggs
⅓ cup heavy cream
½ cup amaretto
2 teaspoons vanilla
  extract
2 cups sour cream
1 tablespoon sugar
½ cup sliced toasted
  almonds

Combine the chocolate wafer crumbs, 1 cup chopped almonds, ⅓ cup sugar and butter in a bowl and mix well. Press into the bottom and up the side of a buttered 9½-inch springform pan. Beat the cream cheese with 1 cup sugar in a mixing bowl until smooth. Add the eggs 1 at a time, beating well after each addition. Add the cream, amaretto and half the vanilla and beat until light. Pour the mixture into the crumb-lined pan. Bake at 375 degrees for 45 minutes. Let cool for 5 minutes. Combine the sour cream, 1 tablespoon sugar and the remaining 1 teaspoon vanilla in a small bowl and mix well. Spread over the cheesecake. Bake for 5 minutes longer. Cool completely. Chill, covered, until ready to serve. Press the sliced almonds around the top edge of the cheesecake.
Yield: 12 servings.

Cathy Jackson, Xi Gamma Tau
Ft. Wayne, Indiana

AMARETTO CHOCOLATE CHEESECAKE

6 (2¹/₂-inch) chocolate
  graham cracker
  squares, crushed
2¹/₃ cups part-skim
  ricotta cheese
4 ounces nonfat cream
  cheese, softened
¹/₂ cup sugar

¹/₄ cup baking cocoa
1 egg
3 tablespoons flour
2 tablespoons amaretto
1 teaspoon vanilla
  extract
2 tablespoons semisweet
  chocolate chips

Sprinkle the graham cracker crumbs evenly over the bottom of an 8-inch springform pan sprayed with nonstick cooking spray. Combine the ricotta, cream cheese, sugar, baking cocoa, egg, flour, amaretto and vanilla in a blender or food processor container and process until smooth. Stir in the chocolate chips. Pour the cheese mixture over the chocolate crumbs. Bake at 325 degrees for 1¹/₂ hours or until a knife inserted in the center comes out clean. Cool completely in the pan on a wire rack. Chill, covered, for at least 3 hours before serving. Yield: 12 servings.

Roxanne R. Lester, Xi Xi
Fairbanks, Alaska

BANANA CREAM CHEESECAKE

1³/₄ cups graham cracker
  crumbs
¹/₄ cup sugar
¹/₂ cup (1 stick) butter,
  melted
8 ounces cream cheese,
  softened
¹/₂ cup sugar

8 ounces whipped
  topping
3 to 4 firm medium
  bananas, sliced
1 (3-ounce) package
  banana cream instant
  pudding mix
1³/₄ cups cold milk

Combine the graham cracker crumbs and ¹/₄ cup sugar in a small bowl and mix well. Stir in the butter. Reserve ¹/₂ cup of the mixture. Press the remaining crumb mixture into the bottom and up the side of a greased 9-inch springform pan or 9-inch-square baking pan. Bake in a preheated 350-degree oven for 5 to 7 minutes or until lightly browned. Cool on a wire rack. Combine the cream cheese and ¹/₂ cup sugar in a mixing bowl and beat until smooth. Fold in half the whipped topping. Arrange half the banana slices over the crust. Layer half the cream cheese mixture over the bananas. Repeat the layers. Combine the pudding mix and milk in a bowl and beat until smooth. Fold in the remaining whipped topping. Pour over the cream cheese layer. Sprinkle with the reserved crumb mixture. Chill, covered, for at least 1 to 2 hours or until set. Yield: 10 servings.

Ann B. Lucas, Laureate Lambda
Polson, Montana

CHOCOLATE MALT CHEESECAKE

¹/₃ cup (²/₃ stick)
  unsalted butter or
  margarine, melted
1 cup pretzel or graham
  cracker crumbs
¹/₄ cup sugar
24 ounces cream cheese,
  softened
1 (14-ounce) can
  sweetened condensed
  milk

1 cup semisweet
  chocolate chips,
  melted
³/₄ cup chocolate malt
  powder
4 eggs
1 teaspoon vanilla
  extract

Combine the butter, pretzel crumbs and sugar in a small bowl and mix well. Pat into the bottom of a 9-inch springform pan sprayed with nonstick cooking spray. Place the cream cheese in a large bowl and beat at high speed until fluffy. Beat in the condensed milk. Add the melted chocolate, chocolate malt powder, eggs and vanilla and beat until smooth. Pour into the prepared pan. Bake at 300 degrees for 65 minutes or until cake springs back when lightly touched. Cool completely. Chill, covered, until ready to serve. Garnish with chocolate shavings if desired. Yield: 12 to 14 servings.

Carol Berry, Xi Upsilon
Springfield, Missouri

LADYFINGER CHEESECAKE

²/₃ cup (1¹/₃ sticks)
  butter, melted
¹/₄ cup sugar
2 (11-ounce) packages
  no-bake cheesecake
  mix
1 (3-ounce) package
  ladyfingers

8 ounces cream cheese,
  softened
3 cups milk
12 ounces whipped
  topping
1 (21-ounce) can cherry
  pie filling

Combine the butter, sugar and the contents of the crust packages from the cheesecake mix in a bowl and mix well. Press into an ungreased 10-inch springform pan. Halve the ladyfingers crosswise and stand them against the side of the pan to form a ring. Beat the cream cheese and ¹/₂ cup of the milk at medium speed in a large mixing bowl until smooth. Beat in the remaining 2¹/₂ cups milk. Add the contents of the cheesecake filling packages and beat until smooth. Beat at high speed for 3 minutes longer. Fold in the whipped topping gently. Pour the mixture into the prepared pan. Chill, covered, in the refrigerator for at least 1 hour. Top with the pie filling and serve. Yield: 12 servings.

Bettie Ellis, Laureate Gamma
Seguin, Texas

PEACH BLUEBERRY COBBLER

1/2 cup (1 stick) butter or margarine	*Dash of salt*
1 cup flour	*2/3 cup milk*
1 cup sugar	*2 (29-ounce) cans sliced peaches, drained*
1 teaspoon baking powder	*1 cup frozen blueberries*

Melt the butter and pour into a 9×13-inch baking pan, tilting to coat the bottom of the pan. Stir the flour, sugar, baking powder and salt together in a bowl. Add the milk and whisk until smooth to make the batter. Pour into the prepared baking pan. Spoon the peaches over the batter. Sprinkle with the blueberries. Sprinkle a mixture of cinnamon and sugar lightly over the top if desired. Bake at 325 degrees for 35 to 45 minutes or until golden brown. Yield: 8 to 10 servings.

Jody Bruns, Theta Nu
Batesville, Indiana

ALMOND APRICOT TORTONI

An easy make-ahead recipe.

1 cup crushed vanilla wafers	*1/3 cup chopped toasted almonds*
3 tablespoons butter, melted	*3 pints vanilla ice cream, softened*
1 teaspoon vanilla extract	*12 ounces apricot preserves*

Combine the wafer crumbs, butter and vanilla in a small bowl and mix well. Reserve 1/4 cup of the mixture for the topping. Sprinkle half the remaining mixture over the bottom of an 8×8-inch baking dish sprayed with nonstick cooking spray; press down. Spoon half the ice cream evenly over the crumbs. Heat the preserves slightly in the microwave or in a saucepan over low heat. Drizzle over the ice cream layer. Repeat the crumb, ice cream and preserves layers. Sprinkle with the reserved crumb topping. Cover the pan tightly. Freeze for at least 2 hours until ready to serve. Cut into squares. Yield: 9 servings.

Patricia L. Ward, Kappa Rho
Deland, Florida

WHITE COFFEE ICE CREAM

1 quart half-and-half	*4 large egg yolks*
1 cup sugar	
4 ounces French roast whole coffee beans	

Combine the half-and-half and sugar in a large saucepan over medium heat. Bring to a boil, stirring to dissolve the sugar. Remove from heat. Stir in the coffee beans. Let stand in the refrigerator, covered, for about 3 hours. Strain into a large heavy saucepan. Discard the beans. Whisk the egg yolks in a small bowl until thick and pale yellow. Whisk the yolks into the sugar mixture. Cook over medium heat until mixture is thick enough to leave a path when a finger is run along it, stirring occasionally with a wooden spoon. Refrigerate, covered, until well chilled. Pour into an ice cream freezer container. Freeze using manufacturer's directions. Yield: 1 1/2 quarts.

Patricia R. Soard, Theta Psi
Cookeville, Tennessee

LEMON ICE DESSERT

Serve topped with sliced fresh fruit and a chocolate cookie on the side. Prepare it at the beginning of the summer and you will have a yummy dessert on hand for several weeks.

4 1/2 quarts heavy cream	*2 tablespoons almond extract*
6 cups white sugar	
2 cups slivered toasted almonds	*2 teaspoons vanilla extract*
Grated zest of 10 lemons	*2 cups lemon juice*

Place the cream in a very large bowl; a metal bowl is best. Add the sugar and stir until dissolved; it will require stirring for a long time. Stir in the almonds, lemon zest, almond extract, vanilla and lemon juice 1 ingredient at a time in the order listed. Freeze, covered, in the large bowl or in several smaller ones. Let stand for about 1 hour at room temperature before scooping into serving bowls. Yield: 1 1/2 gallons.

Maureen MacDonald, Laureate Gamma Rho
Oakville, Ontario, Canada

ELEGANT LEMON SORBET

1/2 cup fresh lemon juice	*1 tablespoon vodka, or 2 to 3 tablespoons white wine*
2 teaspoons freshly grated lemon zest	
1 1/2 cups cold water	*4 to 6 drops of yellow food coloring*
1 1/4 cups sugar	

Combine the lemon juice and zest, water, sugar and vodka in a large bowl. Let stand for 3 to 5 minutes, stirring frequently until sugar is dissolved. Chill, covered, until mixture is at 40 degrees or cooler. Pour into a small ice cream freezer container. Freeze using manufacturer's directions. Scoop into a small container, seal tightly and freeze until firm. Sorbet may be kept frozen for up to 3 days. Yield: 4 servings.

Photograph for this recipe is on the cover.

SHERBET ICE CREAM CAKE

This recipe sounds like a lot of trouble, but it really isn't, and it makes a beautiful dessert.

1½ pints raspberry
   sherbet
1½ pints orange sherbet
1½ pints pistachio ice
   cream
3 quarts vanilla ice
   cream
2 cups chopped pecans

2 cups shaved candy-
   making chocolate or
   coarsely chopped
   semisweet chocolate
   pieces
2 cups whipping cream
Green food coloring
1 pint fresh strawberries

Chill a 10-inch tube pan in the freezer. Shape 8 balls from each of the raspberry, orange and pistachio desserts with a No. 20 ice cream scoop; there will be a total of 24 balls. Place the dessert balls in a chilled 10×15-inch cake pan or on foil-covered heavy cardboard and freeze until very firm. Beat half the vanilla ice cream in a large bowl with a wooden spoon or electric mixer until it resembles a heavy batter. Stir in half the pecans and half the shaved chocolate. Spoon enough of the ice cream mixture into the chilled tube pan to make a 1-inch layer. Arrange some of the raspberry, orange and pistachio balls over the ice cream layer, alternating them against the center tube and the side of the pan. Spoon the rest of the ice cream mixture over the balls. Return to the freezer. Beat the remaining 1½ quarts ice cream in a large bowl with the spoon or mixer until softened. Stir in the remaining pecans and shaved chocolate. Continue to alternate raspberry, orange and pistachio balls over the ice cream layer and cover them with a layer of ice cream mixture until the tube pan is full. Cover with foil. Return to the freezer. Cover a 10-inch cardboard circle with foil or select a 10-inch serving plate. Remove the tube pan from the freezer. Run a knife around the outside and inside edges. Dip the pan quickly in and out of lukewarm water. Lay the foil-covered cardboard circle over the top of the pan. Invert pan; unmold ice cream. Return to the freezer. Whip the cream in a large chilled bowl with chilled beaters until stiff peaks form; beat in a few drops of food coloring to tint a delicate green. Remove the ice cream cake from the freezer. Frost quickly with the tinted whipped cream; return to the freezer until serving time. Slide the dessert from the foil-covered circle to a serving plate. Garnish the base and top center with strawberries. Yield: 10 to 12 servings.

Oleta B. Hindman, Laureate Alpha Nu
McAllen, Texas

ICE CREAM SANDWICHES

1 egg
½ cup shortening
¼ cup (½ stick) butter
   or margarine, softened
1 teaspoon vanilla
   extract

1 (2-layer) package
   chocolate cake mix
½ gallon ice cream, in a
   square (not round)
   container

Combine the egg, shortening, butter, vanilla and half the dry cake mix in a large bowl and beat until smooth. Stir in the remaining cake mix. Divide the dough into 4 equal parts. Roll each part into a 6×10-inch rectangle on a lightly floured surface. Cut each rectangle into eight 2½×3-inch rectangles. Arrange on ungreased baking sheets. Bake in a preheated 375-degree oven for 6 to 8 minutes or until edges appear set; centers will look slightly puffed. Prick the surfaces lightly with a fork. Let cool. Remove from the baking sheets. Slice the ice cream into 3/4-inch-thick slabs. Press each ice cream slab gently between 2 chocolate rectangles. Freeze, wrapped in foil or plastic wrap, for at least 24 hours. Yield: 16 servings.

Charla Parker, Beta Eta
Alva, Oklahoma

BANANA BUTTERFINGER PUDDING

1 cup cold milk
1 (3-ounce) package
   banana instant
   pudding mix
3 (2-ounce) Butterfinger
   candy bars, crushed

8 ounces whipped
   topping
3 firm medium bananas,
   sliced

Combine the milk and pudding mix in a mixing bowl and beat until smooth and thickened. Reserve 1/3 cup of the crushed candy bars for the topping. Fold the whipped topping, bananas and the remaining crushed candy bars into the pudding mixture. Spoon into serving bowls or a bowl. Chill, covered, until ready to serve. Sprinkle with the reserved candy bars just before serving. Yield: 4 to 6 servings.

Joyce Brandt, Master Alpha Beta
Augusta, Kansas

Noreen Tetz, Xi Gamma, Winnipeg, Manitoba, Canada, makes Lemon Butter to be used as a filling in tart shells or a sauce over angel food cake. She whisks 4 eggs with 2 cups sugar in a double boiler, adds ½ cup butter and the juice of 3 or 4 lemons, and cooks over hot water for 30 minutes or until thickened, stirring frequently. Cool completely and store in a covered container in the refrigerator.

OLD-FASHIONED BREAD PUDDING

2 eggs	4 cups cubed bread
3/4 cup sugar	1 teaspoon cinnamon
1 cup milk	1/4 cup (1/2 stick) butter
4 teaspoons vanilla extract	1/2 cup sugar
1/4 teaspoon nutmeg	1 1/2 cups water

Combine the eggs and the 3/4 cup sugar in a bowl and mix well. Beat in the milk, half the vanilla and the nutmeg, 1 ingredient at a time. Layer the bread cubes in a buttered 2-quart baking dish, sprinkling each layer with cinnamon. Pour the egg mixture over the bread and stir gently. Bake at 350 degrees for about 45 minutes. Let cool slightly. Combine the butter, the 1/2 cup sugar and the water in a saucepan over medium heat. Bring to a boil; remove from heat. Stir in the remaining 2 teaspoons vanilla. Serve warm over the warm bread pudding. Yield: 4 servings.

Karen Zentz, Alpha Epsilon Nu
Holden, Missouri

LEMON PUDDING

3 tablespoons flour	1 cup milk
3 tablespoons butter, softened	Juice of 1 lemon
1 cup sugar	Grated zest of 1 lemon
2 egg yolks, beaten	2 egg whites

Combine the flour, butter, 3/4 cup of the sugar, egg yolks, milk, and lemon juice and zest in a bowl and beat until well mixed. Beat the egg whites in another bowl until stiff peaks form. Beat the remaining 1/4 cup sugar into the egg whites. Fold into the lemon mixture. Pour into a buttered 6×8×2-inch baking dish. Set the pan into a larger shallow pan of hot water. Bake in the water bath at 350 degrees for 45 minutes. Chill, covered, until ready to serve, for at least 2 hours. Serve topped with whipped cream. Yield: 4 servings.

Nancy A. Sharp, Laureate Beta Gamma
Lake Alfred, Florida

Diane Bancroft-Billings, Preceptor Alpha Pi, Manchester, Tennessee, makes a Peach Surprise Dessert that couldn't be easier. She places well-drained canned peach halves in a baking dish with the hollow side up, adds a tablespoon brown sugar and a tablespoon of Virgin Islands spiced rum to each hollow, and tops each with a large marshmallow cut into quarters. Bake at 350 degrees for 15 minutes or until the marshmallows are toasted.

BAKED PERSIMMON PUDDING

2 cups flour	1 cup milk
1 tablespoon baking powder	2 eggs
2 teaspoons baking soda	2 cups chopped walnuts
1 teaspoon salt	2 cups ripe persimmon pulp
1/2 teaspoon cinnamon	2 teaspoons vanilla extract
1/4 teaspoon nutmeg	Lemon Sauce or Rum Sauce
2 cups sugar	
3 tablespoons butter, softened	

Sift together the flour, baking powder, baking soda, salt, cinnamon, nutmeg and 1 1/2 cups of the sugar. Cream the butter and the remaining 1/2 cup sugar in a mixing bowl until light and fluffy. Add the sifted dry ingredients and milk alternately, mixing well after each addition. Add the eggs 1 at a time, beating well after each addition. Add the nuts and stir well. Combine the persimmon pulp and baking soda in a bowl and mix well; mixture will foam. Add the persimmon mixture to the flour mixture and beat well. Pour into an oiled or waxed paper-lined 9×13-inch baking pan or two 9×9-inch pans. Bake at 350 degrees for 1 1/4 hours or at 325 degrees for 1 1/2 hours. Serve with Lemon Sauce or Rum Sauce.
Yield: 15 to 25 servings.

LEMON SAUCE

1 cup sugar	1 tablespoon lemon juice
2 tablespoons flour	1/4 cup butter
1 tablespoon cornstarch	
2 cups boiling water	
1 tablespoon grated lemon zest	

Combine the sugar, flour and cornstarch in a bowl and mix well. Pour the boiling water over the sugar mixture. Add the lemon zest and juice and the butter and stir well. Serve warm or chilled.

RUM SAUCE

1 cup sugar	2 teaspoons rum extract
2 tablespoons flour	3 tablespoons rum
1 tablespoon cornstarch	3 tablespoons butter
2 cups boiling water	

Combine the sugar, flour and cornstarch in a bowl and mix well. Pour the boiling water over the sugar mixture. Add the rum extract, rum and butter and stir well. Serve warm or chilled.

Billie Porter, Preceptor Iota Beta
Camarillo, California

STICKY TOFFEE PUDDING

You may substitute 2 cups regular flour mixed with 1 teaspoon baking powder for the self-rising flour.

1/2 teaspoon baking soda	2 cups self-rising flour
4 ounces dates, finely chopped	1/2 teaspoon salt
	1/2 cup (1 stick) butter
1 cup boiling water	1 cup packed light brown sugar
1/4 cup (1/2 stick) butter, softened	10 ounces heavy cream
1 cup sugar	1/4 teaspoon vanilla
1 egg	

Sprinkle the baking soda over the dates in a bowl. Pour the boiling water over the date mixture. Cream 1/4 cup butter and the sugar in a mixing bowl until light and fluffy. Beat in the egg. Add a mixture of the flour and salt gradually, beating after each addition. Beat in the date mixture. Pour into a greased 9×9-inch baking pan. Bake at 350 degrees for 45 to 50 minutes or until the cake tests done. Melt 1/2 cup butter in a heavy saucepan over medium-high heat. Stir in the brown sugar, cream and vanilla and bring to a full rolling boil. Remove from heat. Reheat when ready to serve. Place a slice of cake in each individual pudding dish. Cover with softened vanilla ice cream. Pour the warm sauce over the ice cream. Garnish with a dab of whipped cream. Yield: 9 to 16 servings.

Helen Berlando, Gamma Master
Lethbridge, Alberta, Canada

MOTHER'S DAY TRIFLE

1 large angel food cake	1 (10-ounce) can blueberries, drained
1/2 (3-ounce) package orange gelatin	
1 (11-ounce) can mandarin oranges, drained	1 (3-ounce) package strawberry gelatin
	1 (10-ounce) package frozen strawberries, thawed
1/2 gallon vanilla ice cream, slightly softened	16 ounces whipped topping
1 (3-ounce) package lemon gelatin	

Break the angel food cake into bite-size pieces. Layer 1/3 of the pieces in the bottom of a greased large bundt or tube pan. Sprinkle with the dry orange gelatin. Layer the orange slices over the gelatin layer. Spread 1/3 of the ice cream over the orange slices. Repeat the layering pattern with cake pieces, lemon gelatin, blueberries and ice cream. Repeat once again with cake pieces, strawberry gelatin, strawberries and the remaining ice cream. Freeze, covered, for at least 24 hours. Invert onto a serving plate. Frost with whipped topping. Return to the freezer until 1/2 hour before serving time. Yield: 16 to 20 servings.

Flora L. Simay, Alpha Sigma Master
Palm Desert, California

CHERRY TRIFLE

1 angel food cake mix	1 or 2 (12-ounce) cans cherry pie filling
1 white chocolate instant pudding mix	
	16 ounces whipped topping
1 French vanilla instant pudding mix	
2 tablespoons chunky peanut butter (optional)	

Prepare and bake the angel food cake using the package directions; cool. Prepare the pudding mixes according to the "pie directions" on the packages; stir the peanut butter into one of the pudding mixes. Break the angel food cake into bite-size pieces. Layer cake pieces, chocolate pudding, cake pieces, cherry pie filling, cake pieces, vanilla pudding, cake pieces and cherry pie filling in the tube pan. Top with whipped topping. Chill, covered, for at least 3 hours before serving. Yield: 10 to 15 servings.

Rita Wolfe, Kappa Master
Keytesville, Missouri

FRUIT TRIFLE

1 angel food cake	1/4 cup sugar
2 (15-ounce) cans dark Bing cherries	2 2/3 tablespoons cornstarch
2 (10-ounce) packages frozen raspberries	16 ounces whipped topping
2 (10-ounce) packages frozen strawberries	

Break the angel food cake into bite-size pieces. Drain the cherries, reserving the liquid. Thaw and drain the raspberries and strawberries, reserving the liquid. Combine the sugar and cornstarch in a saucepan and mix well. Place the saucepan over medium-high heat. Add the reserved cherry, raspberry and strawberry liquid gradually, cooking until mixture boils and thickens, stirring constantly. Remove from heat. Cool slightly. Stir in the cherries, raspberries and strawberries. Alternate layers of cake pieces, fruit mixture and whipped topping in a large transparent bowl until all ingredients are used. Chill, covered, in the refrigerator for 8 to 12 hours.
Yield: more than 25 servings.

Carolyn Martinson, Xi Alpha Beta
Birchwood, Minnesota

RASPBERRY SWIRL DESSERT

2²/₃ cups toasted flaked
  coconut
¹/₃ cup (²/₃ stick) butter
  or margarine, melted
1 (10-ounce) package
  frozen red raspberries
  in syrup, thawed
1 tablespoon cornstarch
1 envelope unflavored
  gelatin

1 (14-ounce) can
  sweetened condensed
  milk
1 cup sour cream
3 tablespoons orange
  liqueur
1 cup whipping cream,
  stiffly whipped

Combine the coconut and butter in a small bowl and mix well. Press firmly over the bottom and up the side of an 8- to 9-inch springform pan sprayed with nonstick cooking spray. Chill, covered. Process the raspberries in a blender until smooth. Combine the raspberries and cornstarch in a small saucepan over medium heat. Cook until thickened, stirring constantly. Remove from heat; let cool to room temperature. Sprinkle the gelatin over ¹/₄ cup cold water in a small saucepan; let stand for 1 minute. Place over low heat and cook, stirring until gelatin dissolves. Remove from heat. Mix the condensed milk, sour cream, liqueur and gelatin mixture in a large bowl. Fold in the whipped cream. Chill for 10 minutes, or until mixture mounds slightly. Spread half the gelatin mixture in the prepared pan. Top with dollops of half the raspberry mixture. Repeat the layering. Swirl the raspberry mixture through the gelatin mixture with a table knife or spatula. Chill, covered, for 6 hours or until set. Remove the side of the pan. Refrigerate leftovers. Yield: 10 to 12 servings.

Pauline Chilton, Laureate Lambda
West Vancouver, British Columbia

RASPBERRY NUT DELIGHT

¹/₄ cup (¹/₂ stick) butter,
  softened
20 to 22 vanilla wafers,
  crushed
¹/₂ cup finely chopped
  macadamia nuts
1 (14-ounce) can
  sweetened condensed
  milk

3 tablespoons frozen
  orange juice
  concentrate
1 cup whipping cream,
  whipped
1 (10-ounce) package
  frozen raspberries,
  thawed

Mix the first 3 ingredients in a bowl. Press the mixture into a springform pan or 8-inch pie plate sprayed with nonstick cooking spray. Bake in a preheated 325-degree oven for 10 minutes or until lightly browned; cool. Combine the condensed milk, orange juice concentrate and whipped cream in a bowl and mix well. Fold in the undrained rasp-

berries. Pour into the prepared pan. Freeze for at least 8 hours before serving. Garnish each serving with whipped cream and a berry if desired. Yield: 6 to 8 servings.

Geri Ravenhorst, Xi Phi Omega
Perris, California

RIBBON GELATIN

4 (3-ounce) packages
  lemon, orange, lime
  and strawberry
  gelatin
2 cups milk
1 cup sugar

2 envelopes unflavored
  gelatin
2 cups sour cream
1 tablespoon vanilla
  extract

Dissolve one of the flavored gelatins in ³/₄ cup hot water. Stir in ³/₄ cup cold water. Chill for about 45 minutes or until set. Combine the milk and sugar in a saucepan over medium-high heat and bring to a boil. Remove from heat. Dissolve the unflavored gelatin in ¹/₂ cup cold water in a medium bowl. Add a mixture of the sour cream and vanilla and stir well. Add the sour cream mixture to the sugar mixture and blend. Spoon 1¹/₂ cups of the sour cream mixture over the chilled gelatin. Chill for about 45 minutes or until set. Repeat the process with the other 3 gelatin flavors, alternating gelatin and sour cream mixture layers, ending with a gelatin layer on the top. Yield: about 24 servings.

Lisa Dowling, Kappa Nu
Cloyne, Ontario, Canada

STRAWBERRY TORTE

6 egg whites, at room
  temperature
1 teaspoon vanilla
  extract
¹/₂ teaspoon cream of
  tartar

¹/₂ teaspoon vinegar
1²/₃ cups sugar
Whipping cream,
  whipped
Strawberries

Butter a 9-inch springform pan; let stand in the refrigerator. Beat the egg whites in a very large mixing bowl with the vanilla, cream of tartar and vinegar for 10 to 15 minutes or until very stiff peaks form. Add the sugar gradually, beating constantly until sugar is well blended. Pour the mixture into the chilled springform pan. Place the pan in a preheated 500-degree oven; turn off the oven immediately. Let stand in the closed oven for 5 to 12 hours. Remove the side of the pan. Place the torte on a torte plate. Cover with whipped cream and strawberries. Yield: 12 to 14 servings.

F. Kay Brown, Xi Kappa Nu
Carterville, Illinois

Men's Recipes for All Occasions

Any day is a good day to celebrate the men in our lives—by letting them do the cooking! Once again, Beta Sigma Phi presents its traditional chapter of favorite recipes selected by men. Whether they prepare these delicacies themselves or simply consume them, men know what they like to eat.

What trends do we see this year in male preferences? First, it appears that men actually do have good taste—at least when it comes to food. The recipes they've picked are simply scrumptious. Second, our male friends seem to exhibit a wide range of favorites. You'll find items from soup to nuts, enough to make any occasion extra special. So turn the pages and see for yourself.

PEPPERY PEACH CHEESE BALL

Instead of shaping the mixture into a ball, you may mound it in a pie plate or other round pan and sprinkle the cheese over it.

16 ounces cream cheese, softened	2 cups shredded Monterey Jack cheese
1/3 (18-ounce) jar spicy peach preserves	1 (8-ounce) package Thin Crisp Triscuits or Wheat Thins
1 tablespoon chopped jalapeño peppers	
1 rounded tablespoon chopped onion	

Combine the cream cheese, preserves, jalapeños and onion in a large bowl and mix well. Chill, covered, in the refrigerator for about 1 hour. Shape into a ball. Roll in the Monterey Jack cheese. Serve with the crackers. May be prepared up to 48 hours before serving. Yield: 10 to 12 servings.

Robert, husband of Idell Henderson, Preceptor Theta
Virginia, Minnesota

CRAB DIP CASSEROLE

16 ounces cream cheese, softened	1 teaspoon dry mustard
1 cup sour cream	1/8 teaspoon garlic salt
4 rounded tablespoons mayonnaise	1/2 cup shredded Cheddar cheese
Juice of 1/2 lemon	1 pound cooked flaked crab meat
3 tablespoons Worcestershire sauce	Paprika

Combine the cream cheese, sour cream, mayonnaise, lemon juice, Worcestershire sauce, mustard and garlic salt in the order listed in a bowl, mixing well after each addition. Stir in half the Cheddar cheese. Fold in the crab meat. Place in a 2-quart casserole sprayed with nonstick cooking spray. Sprinkle the remaining 1/4 cup cheese over the crab mixture. Sprinkle with paprika. Bake, uncovered, at 350 degrees for 30 minutes. Serve warm with crackers. Yield: 4 cups.

Thad, husband of Margaret Ellen Kalmanowicz
Xi Alpha Theta
Kennedyville, Maryland

SALMON BALL

1 (15-ounce) can salmon, drained, flaked	Salt to taste
8 ounces cream cheese, softened	2 teaspoons finely chopped onion
1 teaspoon lemon juice	1 teaspoon smoke flavoring
1 teaspoon horseradish	Chopped parsley

Combine the salmon, cream cheese, lemon juice, horseradish, salt, onion and smoke flavoring in a bowl and mix well. Shape into a ball. Roll in the parsley. Chill, covered, in the refrigerator until serving time. Serve with crackers. May also be made in a well-greased mold and garnished as desired. Yield: 2 1/2 cups.

Dennis, husband of Velinda Burnsed, Xi Delta Beta
Savannah, Georgia

HALF-TIME MEATBALLS

The past 50 years have been filled with memories of "lip-smacking" husbands devouring these meatballs at holiday gatherings and sorority parties. The meatballs may be prepared a day before serving, or frozen to be used later.

2 cups bread cubes (about 4 slices, crusts trimmed)	Dash of Tabasco sauce
1/2 cup milk	2 tablespoons soy sauce
1 pound lean ground beef	1 tablespoon Worcestershire sauce
1 pound ground sausage	Garlic salt to taste
2 (5-ounce) cans water chestnuts	1 (10-ounce) can beef gravy, warmed

Soak the bread cubes in the milk for about 10 minutes. Drain; squeeze out all moisture possible. Combine the soaked bread cubes, ground beef, sausage, water chestnuts, Tabasco sauce, soy sauce, Worcestershire sauce and garlic salt in a large bowl and mix well. Shape into bite-size balls. Brown in a skillet over medium heat until cooked through. Serve hot, covered with the gravy. Yield: 85 meatballs.

Phil, husband of Bettie Wolpers, Preceptor Beta Xi
San Diego, California

SAVORY PORK WONTONS

1/2 pound ground pork, cooked, drained	1 bunch green onions, chopped
8 ounces cream cheese with chives and onion, softened	1 (32-count) package wonton wrappers
1 teaspoon ground ginger	2 tablespoons sesame seeds
1 teaspoon dark sesame oil	1 (16-ounce) bottle sweet-and-sour sauce

Combine the pork, cream cheese, ginger, sesame oil and green onions in a medium bowl and mix well. Place 1 tablespoon of the pork mixture in the center of each wonton wrapper. Bring the corners together over the mixture and twist. Arrange in a 10×15-inch cake pan, pressing to flatten the bottoms of the wontons. Brush lightly with water. Sprinkle with sesame seeds. Bake in a preheated 425-degree oven for 10 to 12 minutes or until golden brown. Remove from the pan and drain on paper towels. Serve with the sweet-and-sour sauce. Yield: 32 wontons.

Roger, husband of Lannie Oberg, Xi Alpha
Carson City, Nevada

PEPPERMINT PATTY COFFEE

This has become a traditional "after-Thanksgiving-dinner" drink for us. I like it best after dinner, but there is no rule that says it cannot be served any time. Stir the drink and voila! You have a delicious coffee that tastes like a peppermint patty in a cup.

Chocolate syrup   Coffee
Crème de menthe

Tilt a coffee cup at a 45-degree angle and coat the inside with chocolate syrup. Pour a half-shot of crème de menthe into the cup. Fill with hot coffee and stir gently with a spoon. Yield: varies.

Tony Michalski, boyfriend of Gina Marie Aleo, Xi Zeta Psi
Wilkes-Barre, Pennsylvania

CLAM CHOWDER

This chowder was always a family favorite for dinner when the first cold snap hit Florida, and we always looked forward to leftovers for lunch the next day.

2 (6-ounce) cans   3/4 cup (1 1/2 sticks) butter
  chopped clams   3/4 cup flour
1 cup chopped onions   1 1/2 teaspoons salt
1 cup chopped celery   1 1/2 teaspoons sugar
2 cups chopped red   1 teaspoon pepper
  potatoes   1 quart half-and-half

Drain the clams, reserving the liquid. Combine the onions, celery and potatoes in a large kettle. Pour in the reserved clam liquid and enough water to cover the vegetables. Bring to a boil; reduce heat to medium low. Cook, uncovered, for about 20 minutes or until vegetables are tender. Melt the butter in a saucepan over low heat. Whisk in the flour. Add the salt, sugar, pepper and half-and-half to the vegetable mixture and stir. Stir in the clams. Bring to a boil; reduce heat. Stir in the flour mixture. Simmer until thick, stirring occasionally. Continue to simmer for a total of about 30 to 40 minutes for best flavor. Yield: about 10 servings.

Ed, husband of Jana Johnson, Xi Mu Beta
Palm City, Florida

CALIFORNIA CHOWDER

6 to 8 slices bacon,   2 tablespoons dried
  chopped   parsley
1 large onion, diced   1 teaspoon basil
6 potatoes, peeled, diced 1 teaspoon black pepper
4 (6-ounce) cans minced   1/4 teaspoon crushed red
  clams, drained, 1 1/2   pepper flakes
  cups liquid reserved   3 garlic cloves, minced
4 (14-ounce) cans stewed   2 cups half-and-half
  tomatoes   Salt to taste
1 1/2 teaspoons thyme

Cook the bacon in a skillet until crisp. Add the onion and sauté for about 5 minutes. Combine the potatoes, reserved clam liquid and enough water to cover the potatoes in a large kettle. Simmer over medium-low heat for about 20 minutes or until potatoes are tender. Stir in the bacon mixture, including pan drippings. Stir in the tomatoes and next 6 ingredients. Bring to a boil; reduce heat. Stir in the clams and half-and-half. Cook just until heated through, stirring frequently. Yield: 12 servings.

Rudolph Rother, late father of Mary Machay
Preceptor Alpha Upsilon
Tamaqua, Pennsylvania

SEAFOOD CHOWDER

2 slices bacon, crisp-   1/2 pound peeled
  cooked, crumbled   uncooked shrimp
1 medium onion, diced   1 1/2 cups diced cooked
1 rib celery, finely   potatoes
  chopped   1 cup frozen corn kernels
2 garlic cloves,   1 (6-ounce) can crab
  minced   meat, flaked
1 tablespoon flour   2 tablespoons chopped
1 cup chicken broth   fresh dill
1 cup heavy cream   1/2 teaspoon hot pepper
1/2 pound uncooked   sauce
  scallops   Salt and pepper to taste

Drain the bacon, leaving 1 tablespoon of drippings in the skillet. Add the onion, celery and garlic to the skillet. Sauté until tender. Stir in the flour. Add the chicken broth gradually, whisking until there are no lumps in the mixture. Stir in the cream. Bring to a boil; reduce heat. Stir in the scallops and shrimp. Cook over medium-low heat until scallops are opaque and shrimp is pink. Stir in the potatoes, corn and crab meat. Cook until heated through. Stir in the dill, hot pepper sauce, salt and pepper. Sprinkle with the bacon and serve. Yield: 6 servings.

Doug, husband of Patti Rogers, Theta Psi
Uxbridge, Ontario, Canada

CHINESE NEW YEAR SOUP

1 pound boneless
  skinless chicken
  breasts
1 tablespoon
  vegetable oil
5 cups hot water
3 tablespoons chicken
  bouillon granules

1 (6-ounce) can water
  chestnuts, drained,
  chopped
4 to 6 green onions,
  chopped
4 hard-cooked eggs
2 cups cooked spaghetti
Soy sauce to taste

Rinse the chicken and pat dry. Cut into cubes. Brown in the oil in a large saucepan over medium heat. Add the water. Bring to a boil; reduce heat. Stir in the bouillon, water chestnuts and green onions. Simmer for 15 minutes. Place a sliced hard-cooked egg and 1/2 cup cooked spaghetti in each individual soup bowl. Ladle 1/4 of the soup into each bowl. Serve with soy sauce. Yield: 4 servings.

David, husband of Kimberly Mangels, Beta Delta
Havre, Montana

BURGUNDY ONION SOUP

Serve with a crisp salad and the French bread that remains after making the soup.

4 large yellow onions,
  sliced
1/2 cup (1 stick) butter
4 (16-ounce) cans beef
  consommé
1/4 teaspoon salt
1/8 teaspoon freshly
  ground pepper

1 teaspoon
  Worcestershire sauce
1 cup burgundy
12 slices Emmentaler
  cheese
1 baguette (loaf of
  French bread), thickly
  sliced

Sauté the onions in the butter in a large skillet over medium-low heat until onions are creamy but not brown. Stir in the next 4 ingredients. Bring to a boil; reduce heat to low. Stir in the burgundy. Keep hot. Use six 5-inch straight-sided ovenproof bowls. Place a slice of cheese in the bottom of each bowl. Ladle onion soup into each bowl to within 1 inch of the rim. Place a slice of bread over the surface and top with additional cheese. Place the 6 bowls on a tray in a 450-degree oven. Heat until the cheese bubbles. Yield: 6 generous servings.

Charles, husband of Janice C. Lewis, Laureate Alpha Nu
Scottsdale, Arizona

Wayne, son of Susanna T. Scott, Comox, British Columbia, Canada, loves Hot Apple Juice made by simmering 4 cups apple juice with 1/4 cup packed brown sugar, 6 each whole cloves and allspice, and 3 cinnamon sticks.

POTATO SOUP

I like to add a couple of slices of Cheddar cheese to my bowl of soup and my husband adds crackers.

1 pound lean ground
  beef
6 cups water
2 ribs celery, chopped
1 medium onion,
  chopped
5 medium potatoes,
  peeled, chopped

2 cups shredded cabbage
1 teaspoon Italian
  seasoning
1 teaspoon salt
1/2 teaspoon pepper
1/2 teaspoon celery seed
2 bay leaves
2 cups milk

Crumble the uncooked ground beef into the water in a 4-quart saucepan. Add the celery, onion, potatoes, cabbage, Italian seasoning, salt, pepper, celery seed and bay leaves. Cook over low heat for about 1 1/2 hours or until vegetables are tender and beef is cooked through. Discard the bay leaves. Stir in the milk. Cook just until heated through; do not boil. Serve piping hot. Yield: 6 servings.

Jim, husband of Sue Schrock, Xi Mu Chi
Garden City, Missouri

POTATO CHEESE SOUP

3 cups diced uncooked
  potatoes
3/4 cup diced celery
3/4 cup diced carrots
1 tablespoon minced
  onion
1 teaspoon parsley
  flakes

1 1/2 cups water
Salt and pepper to taste
1 envelope cream of
  chicken soup mix
2 cups milk
1/2 pound Velveeta
  cheese, cubed

Combine the potatoes, celery, carrots, onion, parsley flakes, water, salt and pepper in a large kettle. Bring to a boil; reduce heat. Simmer for about 20 minutes or until vegetables are tender. Stir in the soup mix, milk and cheese. Heat until cheese is melted, stirring frequently. Yield: 8 to 10 servings.

Bill, husband of Jan Hedges, Preceptor Alpha Eta
Merriam, Kansas

Jason, son of Jo Newsted, Xi Gamma Gamma, Kalamazoo, Michigan, is the bass player with Metallica as well as an accomplished cook. He prepared this Baby Spinach Delight for Jo's birthday by combining a package of baby spinach, rinsed and patted dry, with a cup of tiny grape tomatoes, 1/2 cup sliced fresh mushrooms, and 1/2 cup English walnut halves in a glass bowl. Add desired amount of Paul Newman's vinegar and oil dressing, toss lightly, and serve immediately.

SPICY SOUR SOUP

Serve with Chinese food—egg rolls and sweet-and-sour chicken.

3 medium pork medallions	8 ounces frozen peas
1 to 2 tablespoons vegetable oil	8 ounces frozen corn
	1 teaspoon white pepper
4 (10-ounce) cans chicken broth with garlic	8 ounces sliced fresh mushrooms
1 (10-ounce) can Italian chicken broth	1 small bunch green onions, trimmed, sliced
2 tablespoons soy sauce	8 ounces frozen salad shrimp
1/4 cup red wine vinegar	

Cut the pork into bite-size pieces. Sauté in hot oil in a large kettle until cooked through. Add the 5 cans of chicken broth, soy sauce, vinegar, peas, corn, pepper, mushrooms and green onions. Cook, covered, over medium-low heat for 1 hour to marry the flavors, stirring occasionally. Add the shrimp and cook for 20 minutes longer or just until the shrimp turn pink. Yield: 8 to 10 servings.

Kenny, husband of Brenda LeNoue, Alpha Delta
Lead, South Dakota

SHRIMP SOUP

The recipe makes 6 small servings or 4 large servings. If serving a group of men, double the recipe. Serve with garlic toast.

1/4 cup finely chopped onion	Salt to taste
2 tablespoons butter	Paprika to taste
1/4 cup flour	1 (4-ounce) can tiny shrimp, or 1 small bag of frozen shrimp
2 cups milk	
1 (10-ounce) can cream of shrimp soup	1/2 cup cubed Cheddar cheese
1/4 cup grated carrot	
1/4 cup finely chopped celery	

Sauté the onion in the butter in a skillet over medium-low heat until tender. Whisk in the flour until well blended with the butter. Stir in the milk and soup. Cook until thickened, stirring constantly. Add the carrot, celery, salt, paprika and shrimp, mixing well. Add the cheese and cook until melted, stirring frequently. Simmer for 15 minutes longer. Yield: 6 servings.

Frank, husband of Barbara Hess, Xi Alpha Kappa
Red Lodge, Montana

BROCCOLI CURRY SALAD

1 cup mayonnaise-type salad dressing	2 cups red seedless grapes
1/2 cup sugar	12 slices bacon, crisp-cooked, crumbled
2 tablespoons white vinegar	2/3 cup toasted slivered almonds
1/2 teaspoon curry powder	1/2 cup chopped green onions
4 cups chopped broccoli	
1 cup chopped celery	

Shake the salad dressing, sugar, vinegar and curry powder in a covered jar until well blended. Chill in the refrigerator for 8 to 12 hours. Place the broccoli, celery, grapes, bacon, almonds and green onions in a large salad bowl and toss to combine. Add the dressing just before serving and toss well.
Yield: 8 to 10 servings.

Ken Brownlee, partner of Sharon Steep
Goderich, Ontario, Canada

LAMB CHOP SALAD

A great empty-nester dinner, fast and easy.

4 lamb chops	4 large dashes of balsamic vinegar
Olive oil for frying	
4 handfuls mesclun (young greens)	4 teaspoons extra-virgin olive oil
Goat cheese	

Fry the chops in the olive oil for frying in a medium skillet over medium-low heat until to desired doneness, about 5 minutes on each side for medium rare. Spread the mesclun on a serving plate. Cover with a liberal amount of goat cheese. Arrange the chops over the cheese. Heat the vinegar and the 4 teaspoons olive oil in a small saucepan over low heat until warm. Drizzle the warm dressing over the chop salad. Yield: 2 servings.

John, husband of Penny Porter, Preceptor Alpha Gamma
Yankton, South Dakota

Bob Boe, brother of Dorrene King, Preceptor Epsilon Zeta, Atwater, California, makes his special Chief Boe's Bleu Cheese Salad Dressing for his appreciative family and friends. He blends 1 cup sour cream with 2 cups mayonnaise, adds a teaspoon of lemon juice and 2 teaspoons of Worcestershire sauce, and blends well. After mixing in 1/2 cup crumbled bleu cheese, he pours the dressing into a 1-quart jar and keeps it tightly covered in the refrigerator.

BARBECUED BEEF

1 (5- to 6-pound) beef roast	1/4 cup dry mustard
1 1/2 cups ketchup	1/4 teaspoon Worcestershire sauce
1/4 cup packed brown sugar	1/4 teaspoon cayenne pepper
1 teaspoon celery seed	1 teaspoon liquid smoke

Place the beef and enough water to cover it in a 6-quart kettle over medium heat. Simmer, covered, for 1 to 2 hours or until beef is cooked through, adding more water as necessary. Shred the beef with a fork and place in a slow cooker set on Low. Combine the ketchup, brown sugar, celery seed, mustard, Worcestershire sauce, cayenne pepper and liquid smoke in a saucepan over medium heat. Simmer for 5 minutes, stirring occasionally. Pour over the beef in the slow cooker and mix well. Serve any time after 5 minutes have passed. Serve on buns with chips on the side. Yield: more than 15 servings.

Perry, husband of Lisa M. Parkhurst, Lambda Upsilon
Pleasant Hill, Missouri

MEXICAN BARBECUE

1 (16-ounce) can refried beans	1 cup chopped onion
10 to 12 large flour tortillas	1 cup chopped tomatoes
	1 cup guacamole
1 pound brisket, cooked, chopped	Sour cream (optional)

Heat the refried beans. Warm the tortillas. Spread a tablespoon of beans over each tortilla. Layer the brisket, onion, tomatoes and guacamole over the beans. Roll up as for a burrito. Top with sour cream. Yield: 10 to 12 servings.

Jim, husband of Ruth Zinn, Laureate Zeta Beta
Canyon, Texas

✤ CRANBERRY GLAZED ROAST

1 (4-pound) boneless top sirloin roast, trimmed of fat	2 garlic cloves, minced
	1 teaspoon dry mustard
1 teaspoon vegetable oil	1/2 teaspoon marjoram
1 (10-ounce) can beef broth	1/2 teaspoon salt
	1/4 teaspoon pepper
3/4 cup whole cranberry sauce	8 medium potatoes, peeled, quartered
1/2 cup ketchup	4 large carrots, quartered
1/2 envelope dry onion soup mix	

Brown the roast on all sides in hot oil in a large skillet. Remove to a large roasting pan. Whisk together the undiluted broth, cranberry sauce, ketchup, soup mix, garlic, mustard, marjoram, salt and pepper in a medium bowl. Pour the sauce over the roast. Bake, covered, at 350 degrees for 2 hours, basting occasionally with the juices. Place the potatoes and carrots in the roasting pan. Spoon the juices over the vegetables. Bake, covered, for 1 hour longer. Cut roast into thin slices. Arrange on a serving plate surrounded by the vegetables. Serve the juices on the side. Yield: 8 servings.

Steve, husband of Paulette Willett, Preceptor Beta Mu
Kamloops, British Columbia, Canada

BEEF TENDERLOIN

1 whole beef tenderloin, well-trimmed	1/4 teaspoon salt
	1/4 cup Worcestershire sauce
1 tablespoon ground thyme	1 cup water
1 teaspoon white pepper	
1 tablespoon seasoned salt	

Place the beef on a large sheet of foil. Rub the thyme into the beef. Combine the white pepper, seasoned salt and salt and mix well. Sprinkle the pepper mixture over the beef; roll the beef to coat evenly with the spices. Wrap tightly in the foil. Chill in the refrigerator for at least 12 hours. Let stand at room temperature for 1 hour before cooking. Remove the foil. Place the beef in a roasting pan and drizzle with the Worcestershire sauce. Pour the water into the pan. Bake at 400 degrees to 140 degrees on a meat thermometer for rare, 150 degrees for medium rare. Let stand for 10 minutes before slicing. Yield: varies.

Bill, husband of J. J. Bolton, Mu Eta
Brechin, Ontario, Canada

BURGUNDY ROAST

Serve with loaded baked potatoes, creamed corn, and applesauce.

1/3 cup red wine vinegar	6 medium-size bay leaves
2 tablespoons thyme	
2 tablespoons olive oil	2 tablespoons paprika
1 (5- to 6-pound) pork roast	1/2 pound red grapes, halved

Combine the vinegar, thyme and olive oil in a small roasting pan and mix well. Place the pork in the pan and brush with the vinegar mixture. Roast in a preheated 500-degree oven for 10 minutes. Reduce the oven temperature to 300 degrees. Arrange the bay leaves over the pork and sprinkle with the paprika. Roast for 3½ hours or until cooked through, basting occasionally with the pan juices. Add the grape halves to the pan juices and roast for 15 minutes longer, basting once more. Yield: 10 to 12 servings.

Matt, son of Linda Greenwood, Preceptor Alpha
Hammond, Oregon

EAST-MEETS-WEST CHILI

1½ pounds linguiça (sausage)	1 tablespoon garlic salt
2 pounds lean ground beef	½ teaspoon pepper
	2 tablespoons cumin
2 large yellow onions, chopped	½ cup dried parsley
	½ cup chili powder
1 (12-ounce) can beer	1 cup soy sauce
2 (28-ounce) cans whole peeled tomatoes	2 (29-ounce) cans pinto beans (optional)

Cut the linguiça into ½-inch chunks. Brown the ground beef with the linguiça in a skillet for about 20 minutes, stirring until ground beef is crumbly; drain. Add the onions and beer. Bring to a boil. Stir in the undrained tomatoes, garlic salt, pepper, cumin, parsley and chili powder. Bring to a second boil; reduce heat. Simmer, uncovered, for 2 hours. Stir in the beans just before serving and heat well.
Yield: 8 to 10 servings.

Larry, husband of Judy Date, Xi Chi Eta
Turlock, California

JON-BEN-GETTY

1½ to 2 pounds lean ground beef	1 (10-ounce) can chicken gumbo soup
¼ cup chopped onion	1 (10-ounce) can tomato soup
1 tablespoon chili powder	10 ounces egg noodles, cooked, drained
1 (15-ounce) can whole kernel corn	1 pound Velveeta cheese, sliced
1 (15-ounce) can peas, drained	

Brown the ground beef with the onion and chili powder in a skillet, stirring until ground beef is crumbly; drain. Drain the corn, reserving 1 cup of the liquid. Combine the ground beef mixture, corn, reserved corn liquid, peas, soups and noodles in a large bowl and mix well. Spread in a 9×13-inch baking pan sprayed with nonstick cooking spray. Top with Velveeta slices. Bake at 325 degrees for about 20 minutes or until Velveeta is melted. Yield: 4 to 6 servings.

Mark, husband of Terri Nagel
Jackson, Missouri

SWEET CHILI

1 (15-ounce) can pork and beans	¼ cup ketchup
	⅓ cup packed brown sugar
1 (15-ounce) can barbecued beans	1 teaspoon chili powder
1 (15-ounce) can baked beans	2 large onions, coarsely chopped
1 (15-ounce) can kidney beans	1 pound bacon, crisp-cooked, crumbled
1 (15-ounce) can chili beans	2 pounds lean ground beef
2 (15-ounce) cans stewed tomatoes	

Combine all the beans, the tomatoes, ketchup, brown sugar and chili powder in a 5-quart kettle over medium heat. Sauté the onions in hot oil in a skillet until tender. Stir into the bean mixture. Stir the bacon into the bean mixture. Brown the ground beef in a skillet, stirring until crumbly; drain. Stir into the bean mixture. Reduce heat to low. Simmer for at least 1 hour. Yield: 12 to 15 servings.

Kurt Kuntz, fiancé of Cindy Frank, Alpha
Everett, Washington

DEER JERKY

½ cup Worcestershire sauce	1 teaspoon salt
	2 tablespoons curry powder
½ cup soy sauce	¼ teaspoon onion powder
2 garlic cloves, minced	
1 tablespoon brown sugar	¼ teaspoon liquid smoke
1 teaspoon black pepper	
¼ teaspoon cayenne pepper	Venison

Combine the Worcestershire sauce, soy sauce, garlic, brown sugar, black pepper, cayenne pepper, salt, curry powder, onion powder and liquid smoke in a large bowl and mix well. Remove all visible fat from the venison. Cut the venison into very thin slices and add to the marinade. Marinate the venison, covered, in the Worcestershire sauce mixture in the refrigerator for 8 to 12 hours, stirring occasionally. Remove the venison to a roasting pan and sprinkle with additional cayenne pepper. Place in a preheated 250-degree oven. Reduce the oven temperature to 175 degrees. Bake for 3 to 6 hours or until no moisture remains in the meat. Yield: varies.

James Lemmons, father of Delaina Schadler, Theta Zeta
Pocahontas, Arkansas

PASTA E FAGIOLI

Ditalini, or "little thimbles," is a small tubular pasta like a very short macaroni.

1 pound lean ground
  beef
1½ teaspoons vegetable
  oil
1 medium onion,
  chopped
4 carrots, slivered
3 ribs celery, diced
1 (24-ounce) can diced
  tomatoes
1 cup drained red kidney
  beans

6 cups beef stock
1½ teaspoons oregano
1¼ teaspoons pepper
2½ teaspoons chopped
  fresh parsley
¾ teaspoon Tabasco
  sauce
3 cups spaghetti sauce
4 ounces ditalini,
  cooked, drained

Brown the ground beef in the oil in a skillet, stirring until crumbly; drain. Stir in the onion, carrots, celery and undrained tomatoes. Simmer for 10 minutes. Rinse and drain the kidney beans and stir into the beef mixture. Stir in the stock, oregano, pepper, parsley and Tabasco sauce. Simmer for about 45 minutes or until celery and carrots are tender. Stir in the spaghetti sauce and ditalini. Serve hot.
Yield: 4½ quarts.

Tom, husband of Elaine Wilson, Laureate Beta
Warwick, Rhode Island

VEAL BIRDS

Serve with ketchup, mustard, or other dips, or serve on a platter with spaghetti or a potato casserole.

2 pounds ground veal or
  turkey
1 pound lean ground
  beef or pork
2 eggs
1 medium onion,
  chopped
1 teaspoon each garlic
  powder, parsley
  flakes, oregano, basil,
  thyme and dry
  mustard

Ketchup to moisten
  (½ to ¾ cup)
Salt and pepper to taste
Italian bread crumbs to
  bind (1 cup or more)
Milk to moisten (½ to
  ¾ cup)

Combine the veal, ground beef, eggs, onion, garlic powder, parsley flakes, oregano, basil, thyme, mustard and ketchup in a large bowl and mix well. Mix in enough bread crumbs to bind the mixture and enough milk to moisten it. Shape into "drumsticks" around kebab sticks or popsicle sticks. Roll in additional bread crumbs until coated. Arrange on a foil-lined baking sheet sprayed with nonstick cooking spray. Bake at 350 degrees for ¾ to 1 hour or until cooked through and coating is crisp, checking and turning after about 30 minutes of baking.
Yield: 12 servings.

Terry, husband of Rennie Hughes, Gamma Xi
Herrin, Illinois

MEXICAN HASH

4 baked red or yellow
  potatoes
2 tablespoons olive or
  canola oil
1 onion, diced
½ pound cooked beef,
  ham or chicken,
  chopped

1 cup salsa
¼ teaspoon garlic
  powder

Peel the baked potatoes if desired; cut into ¼-inch cubes. Heat the oil in a skillet and sauté the onion until tender. Add the potatoes and cook until heated through, stirring occasionally. Add the beef. Cook for 3 to 4 minutes. Add the salsa and garlic powder. Cook until heated through and liquid is absorbed, stirring occasionally. Yield: 4 servings.

Joe Meinert, fiancé of Cora Collins, Preceptor Zeta Sigma
Blue Springs, Missouri

HOMEMADE BARBECUE SAUCE

2 to 3 garlic cloves,
  crushed
¾ cup white vinegar
1 (6-ounce) can tomato
  paste
¼ cup dark molasses
¼ cup light molasses
¼ cup water
2 tablespoons orange
  marmalade
1½ teaspoons salt
½ teaspoon black
  pepper

½ teaspoon ground
  ginger
½ teaspoon dry mustard
¼ teaspoon allspice
¼ teaspoon celery seed
¼ teaspoon dried thyme
  leaves
⅛ teaspoon cayenne
  pepper
1 onion, diced
1 small bay leaf
1 tablespoon liquid
  smoke

Combine the garlic, vinegar, tomato paste, dark and light molasses, water, marmalade, salt, black pepper, ginger, mustard, allspice, celery seed, thyme, cayenne pepper, onion and bay leaf in a medium saucepan over medium-high heat. Bring to a boil; reduce heat. Simmer gently, uncovered, for 20 minutes, stirring occasionally. Remove from heat. Discard the bay leaf. Stir in the liquid smoke.
Yield: 2½ cups.

Johnnie, husband of Frances Sullivan, Xi Rho Theta
Ennis, Texas

SAUSAGE STEW

2 quarts water
1 to 1½ pounds Polish
   sausage, cut into
   1- to 1½-inch
   slices
1 medium onion, thinly
   sliced
1 head cabbage, cut into
   8 wedges

6 to 8 medium to large
   potatoes, peeled, cut
   into 1- to 1½-inch
   cubes
2 teaspoons chicken
   bouillon granules, or
   2 chicken bouillon
   cubes
Salt and pepper to taste

Bring the water to a simmer in a large kettle over medium heat. Add the sausage, onion, cabbage and potatoes. Stir in the bouillon, salt and pepper. Simmer slowly until potatoes and cabbage are tender; do not allow them to become mushy. Yield: 8 servings.

Ted, husband of Dianna Mueller, Beta Nu
Chester, Illinois

CURRIED BRATWURST

Some hard rolls are better than others, so experiment until you find the kind you like best. Use the Johnston's brand of bratwurst if you can find it. Eat the bratwurst with a fork and dip the rolls in the thick, gravy-like curry sauce.

6 links smoked cooked
   bratwurst, cut into
   bite-size pieces
1 small or medium
   onion, finely chopped
1 large tomato, chopped
2 tablespoons butter
Flour

3 (10-ounce) cans beef
   consommé
2 tablespoons curry
   powder, or to taste
Ketchup to taste
6 to 8 small hard rolls

Place the bratwurst in a large skillet over medium heat with enough water to cover. Simmer until bratwurst is heated through, watching to make sure it does not dry out. Sauté the onion and tomato in the butter in another large skillet. Stir in enough flour to make a paste. Stir in the consommé gradually; add enough water to make a sauce of the desired consistency. Cook for about 10 minutes, stirring constantly. Stir in the curry powder. Place individual servings of bratwurst in soup bowls and cover with the curry sauce. Serve with ketchup, additional curry powder and hard rolls. Yield: 3 to 6 servings.

Bruce Bunting, son-in-law of Betty Watson, Zeta Beta
Timberon, New Mexico

ORIENTAL SAUSAGE

We like to serve this savory dish with fried rice with almonds.

1 green bell pepper,
   chopped
1 medium onion,
   quartered
1 pound smoked
   sausage, cut into ½-
   inch pieces
1 tablespoon butter or
   margarine

1 tablespoon cornstarch
⅛ teaspoon ground
   ginger
1 tablespoon vinegar
1 tablespoon soy sauce
½ cup apricot preserves
8 ounces drained
   pineapple chunks

Sauté the bell pepper, onion and sausage in the butter for about 5 minutes. Combine the cornstarch, ginger, vinegar, soy sauce and preserves in a small bowl and mix well. Stir the cornstarch mixture into the sausage mixture. Cook over low heat until sauce thickens, stirring frequently. Stir in the pineapple and cook until heated through. Serve over rice or Chinese noodles. Yield: 6 servings.

Cameron, husband of Janet L. Myles, Xi Beta Mu
Elkins, West Virginia

STROMBOLI SANDWICHES

2 pounds lean ground
   beef
2 pounds mild Italian
   sausage
¼ cup chopped onion
1 teaspoon whole fennel
   seeds
2 cups ketchup
2 cups tomato sauce
½ cup grated Parmesan
   cheese

2 teaspoons garlic salt
2 teaspoons oregano
3 tablespoons butter,
   softened
2 teaspoons garlic
   powder
2 teaspoons paprika
8 French rolls, split
16 slices mozzarella
   cheese

Brown the ground beef with the sausage in a skillet, stirring until crumbly; drain. Stir in the onion, fennel seeds, ketchup, tomato sauce, Parmesan cheese, garlic salt and oregano. Simmer over medium-low heat for 10 minutes, stirring occasionally. Blend the butter with the garlic powder and paprika. Spread the butter mixture over the opened rolls. Layer the beef mixture and mozzarella slices over the bottom halves of the rolls. Close the sandwiches and wrap each one in foil. Bake at 350 degrees for about 30 minutes. Slice each sandwich in half diagonally. Top with bread-and-butter pickles. Yield: 8 servings.

Tem, husband of Anne Fugit, Xi Pi Rho
Napa, California

GRILLED PORK BUTT ROAST

1 (3- to 5-pound) pork
    butt or shoulder roast
15 garlic cloves
3 to 4 tablespoons
    Tony's Seasoning

2 to 4 tablespoons
    seasoned salt
1 to 2 tablespoons onion
    powder

Cut slits in the roast in many places with a sharp knife. Cut each clove of garlic into 3 pieces and insert in the slits. Sprinkle with Tony's seasoning, seasoned salt and onion powder. Score crisscross cuts through the fat on the roast until the meat below the fat can be seen. Let stand, covered, in the refrigerator for 8 to 12 hours. Turn once and let stand for 12 hours longer. Grill over white-hot coals for 4 hours, turning as necessary. Yield: 6 to 10 servings.

Brien McGlynn, employer of Sheree C. Daniel, Xi Lambda
Baton Rouge, Louisiana

CASHEW CHICKEN

2 tablespoons
    vegetable oil
2 teaspoons sugar
2 teaspoons cornstarch
2 teaspoons soy sauce
2 boneless skinless
    chicken breasts,
    cubed
2 chicken bouillon cubes
2 tablespoons
    cornstarch
1/4 cup soy sauce
1 1/2 cups water

1 tablespoon vegetable
    oil
1 cup chopped broccoli
1 (4-ounce) can
    mushrooms, drained
1/4 cup sliced red bell
    pepper
1/4 cup sliced green bell
    pepper
1/4 cup sliced green
    onions
1/2 cup cashews

Combine 2 tablespoons oil, sugar, 2 teaspoons cornstarch and 2 teaspoons soy sauce in a bowl and blend well to make the marinade. Stir in the chicken. Marinate, covered, in the refrigerator for at least 2 hours. Combine the bouillon, 2 tablespoons cornstarch, 1/4 cup soy sauce and the water in a small bowl; blend well and set aside. Drain the chicken and discard the marinade. Stir-fry the marinated chicken in 1 tablespoon hot oil in a large wok until browned. Remove the chicken from the wok. Stir-fry the broccoli, mushrooms, bell peppers and green onions in the wok until broccoli is tender-crisp. Return the chicken to the wok. Stir in the bouillon mixture. Cook until thickened, stirring constantly. Stir in the cashews. Serve over rice. Yield: 2 to 4 servings.

Corey, husband of Kelly Miller, Xi Theta Alpha
Lexington, Missouri

DEEP-FRIED TURKEY

2 (16-ounce) bottles
    zesty Italian dressing
1/2 (16-ounce) bottle
    Louisiana Hot Sauce
1 tablespoon garlic
    powder
1 tablespoon dry
    mustard

1 tablespoon salt
1 tablespoon onion
    powder
1 (12- to 15-pound)
    turkey
6 gallons (about) peanut
    oil

Strain the salad dressing and discard the solids. Combine the strained dressing, Hot Sauce, garlic powder, mustard, salt and onion powder in a bowl and blend. Inject the dressing mixture with a syringe into the meaty portions—breast, legs and thighs—of the turkey, using the entire mixture. Heat the oil in a deep-fryer to 350 degrees. Deep-fry the turkey for 4 minutes per pound (about 1 hour for a 15-pound turkey). Drain and serve. Yield: varies.

Editor's Note: To determine the amount of peanut oil more precisely, place the turkey in the container to be used for deep frying and fill with enough water to cover the turkey adequately without overflowing the container. Remove the turkey, drain and pat dry and proceed as above. Measure the water in the container to determine the amount of peanut oil required.

Terry, husband of Delaina Schadler, Theta Zeta
Pocahontas, Arkansas

BEEF PORK HAM LOAF

People of all ages rave about this moist ham loaf. It can be prepared ahead of serving time and frozen.

1 pound ground beef
1 pound ground pork
1 pound ground cooked
    ham
2 eggs
1 1/4 cups milk

2 cups crushed graham
    crackers
1 (10-ounce) can tomato
    soup
1/3 cup vinegar

Combine the beef, pork, ham, eggs, milk and cracker crumbs in a large bowl and mix well. Shape into loaves and place in two 9-inch loaf pans. Place the pans on a baking sheet or in a shallow baking pan. Bake at 325 degrees for 1 hour or until cooked through. Remove from oven. Poke holes in the top of the loaves. Pour a mixture of the soup and vinegar over the loaves. Return to the oven and bake for 1 hour longer, basting occasionally.
Yield: 8 to 10 servings.

Lloyd, husband of Marilyn A. Philipps, Zeta Kappa
Roosevelt, Arizona

PHEASANT CASSEROLE

1½ pounds pheasant breasts, cooked, chopped	1 cup milk
1½ cups shredded Swiss cheese	1 (6-ounce) package stovetop stuffing mix
1 (10-ounce) can cream of mushroom soup	½ cup chicken broth

Arrange the pheasant breasts in a greased 9×13-inch baking pan. Layer the cheese over the pheasant. Pour a mixture of the soup and milk evenly over the cheese. Pour a mixture of the stuffing mix, stuffing mix seasonings and broth over the soup mixture. Bake, covered, at 350 degrees for 45 minutes. Uncover and bake for 15 minutes longer. Yield: 8 servings.

Darron, husband of Nancy Steffen, Nu Zeta
New Liberty, Iowa

SAVORY PHEASANT

6 whole pheasant breasts	1 tablespoon prepared mustard
½ cup flour	3 tablespoons ketchup
12 medium red potatoes	1 green bell pepper, diced
2 (10-ounce) cans cream of mushroom soup	1 large onion, diced
3 cups milk	2 tablespoons Kitchen Bouquet
	1 teaspoon garlic salt

Dredge the pheasant breasts in the flour. Brown in butter in a skillet. Slice the potatoes into a 9×13-inch baking dish sprayed with nonstick cooking spray. Combine the soup, milk, mustard, ketchup, bell pepper, onion, Kitchen Bouquet and garlic salt in a bowl and mix well. Pour evenly over the potatoes. Arrange the pheasant breasts over the top. Bake at 300 degrees for 2 hours. Yield: 6 servings.

Joel, husband of Theresa Horn, Beta Xi
Huron, South Dakota

SOUTHWESTERN JAVELINA

A javelina is a collared peccary—a small wild hog.

2 to 3 pounds javelina meat, cubed	¾ cup vinegar
1 onion, chopped	⅓ cup vegetable oil
5 garlic cloves, sliced	1 tablespoon salt
1 rib celery, sliced	½ teaspoon thyme
1 tomato, diced	½ teaspoon black pepper
3 dried red chiles, crushed	

Fill a 3½-quart slow cooker ⅓ full of water. Add the javelina meat, onion, garlic, celery, tomato, chiles, vinegar, oil, salt, thyme and pepper and stir well. Fill with water to ½ inch of the rim. Cook on Low for about 12 hours. Yield: 8 servings.

Kenneth, husband of Sharon F. Hunt, Gamma Epsilon
Oracle, Arizona

VENISON LOAF

1 medium onion, chopped	2 eggs
½ small green bell pepper, chopped	1 (15-ounce) can diced tomatoes
2 garlic cloves, chopped	1 teaspoon salt
1 pound ground venison	½ teaspoon pepper
½ pound ground pork	¾ cup cracker crumbs

Combine the onion, bell pepper, garlic, venison, pork, eggs, undrained tomatoes, salt, pepper and cracker crumbs in a large bowl and mix well. Shape into 2 loaves and place in a greased 9×13-inch baking dish. Bake at 350 degrees for 1¼ hours or to 170 degrees on a meat thermometer. Yield: 8 servings.

Ronald, husband of Martha A. Newman, Xi Kappa
Kettering, Ohio

❖ BLACKENED CATFISH

4 (8-ounce) catfish fillets	1 teaspoon salt
¾ cup (½ sticks) butter, melted	1 tablespoon paprika
1 tablespoon white pepper	½ teaspoon red pepper
1 tablespoon black pepper	¼ teaspoon thyme
1 teaspoon garlic powder	¼ teaspoon oregano
	¼ teaspoon dill
	1 teaspoon chili powder

Heat a cast-iron skillet over medium heat for about 8 minutes. Dip each catfish fillet in melted butter and sprinkle both sides with a mixture of the white pepper, black pepper, garlic powder, salt, paprika, red pepper, thyme, oregano, dill and chili powder. Place the fillets in the preheated skillet. Drizzle with 2 tablespoons of the melted butter. Cook for several minutes on each side or until charred. The cooking time will vary depending on the thickness of the fillets. Yield: 4 servings.

Jerome, husband of K. K. LeBlanc, Xi Rho
Carlyss, Louisiana

HALIBUT BAKE

2½ pounds skinless
    halibut or grouper
    fillets
2 teaspoons garlic salt
¼ teaspoon white
    pepper
1 medium onion,
    chopped
4 to 6 garlic cloves,
    chopped

2 tablespoons olive oil
1½ cups regular or light
    mayonnaise
1½ cups regular or low-
    fat sour cream
¼ cup chopped green
    onion, including
    green tops
½ cup grated Parmesan
    cheese

Cut the fish into serving pieces. Sprinkle with the garlic salt and pepper. Sauté the onion and garlic in the olive oil in a skillet over medium heat until tender-crisp. Remove with a slotted spoon; drain on a paper towel. Combine the mayonnaise, sour cream, green onion and half the Parmesan cheese in a mixing bowl and mix well. Arrange half the fish fillets in a single layer in a 9×13-inch baking pan lightly sprayed with nonstick cooking spray. Spread half the sour cream mixture over the fillets. Layer half the onion mixture over the sour cream mixture. Layer the remaining fillets, sour cream mixture and onion mixture over the first layers. Sprinkle with the remaining ¼ cup Parmesan cheese. Bake in a preheated 350-degree oven for 30 to 40 minutes or until fish tests done. Yield: 6 servings.

Jim, husband of J. Ann Franklin, Preceptor Alpha Zeta
Toledo, Oregon

SMOKED SALMON

2 teaspoons sugar
1 teaspoon salt
1 teaspoon freshly
    ground black pepper

1¼ pounds fresh salmon
    fillet, center cut, skin
    left on

Combine the sugar, salt and pepper and mix well. Rub the sugar mixture into the salmon. Chill, covered, in the refrigerator for at least 1 hour. Soak 2 cups of wood chips in a bucket of water. Prepare the charcoal grill. Lay the wet wood over the red hot coals. Brush a piece of heavy aluminum foil with olive oil. Place the salmon skin side down on the foil. Set on the grill. Cover the grill. Let smoke for 10 to 15 minutes or until salmon is flaky in the center. Yield: 4 servings.

Troy, husband of Jill K. Gullett, Zeta Pi
Iowa City, Iowa

CEDAR PLANK GRILLED SALMON

Each plank of cedar should be at least 4 by 6 inches.

½ cup vegetable oil
1 tablespoon minced
    garlic
½ tablespoon thyme

½ tablespoon oregano
Salt and pepper to taste
2 (6-ounce) salmon
    fillets

Soak 2 cedar planks in water for 8 to 12 hours. Combine the oil, garlic, thyme and oregano in a small bowl and mix well. Place the fillets on the soaked planks. Brush the oregano mixture over the fillets. Place the salmon-bearing planks over hot coals. Cover the grill. Cook for 10 to 15 minutes or until fish flakes in center, checking every 5 minutes to see if fish is done. Yield: 2 servings.

Matt Leeland, significant other of Heather Beckman
Psi Zeta
Bartlett, Illinois

BAKED STUFFED SHRIMP

1 pound medium shrimp,
    cleaned, deveined
1 tablespoon lemon
    juice
8 ounces flaked crab
    meat
2 tablespoons minced
    onion
2 tablespoons
    mayonnaise
2 tablespoons dry
    vermouth
¼ cup bread crumbs

¼ teaspoon dry mustard
¼ teaspoon salt
Few grains of black
    pepper
3 tablespoons olive oil
3 garlic cloves, crushed
2 tablespoons chopped
    parsley
1 tablespoon chopped
    chives
1 teaspoon mixed dried
    herbs (chervil, basil,
    tarragon)

Sprinkle the shrimp with the lemon juice. Combine the crab meat, onion, mayonnaise, vermouth, bread crumbs, mustard, salt and pepper in a bowl and mix well. Split each shrimp down its curved side, almost through to the other side. Open to make a cavity for the stuffing. Fill each shrimp with 1 rounded tablespoon of the crab stuffing. Mix together the olive oil, garlic, parsley, chives and mixed herbs. Spread the mixture over a large baking sheet. Arrange the shrimp over the olive oil layer. Bake in a preheated 400-degree oven for 10 minutes or until shrimp turns opaque. Yield: 6 servings.

Bill, husband of Gail Giles, Xi Epsilon Beta
Edinburg, Virginia

SHRIMP KABOBS

1½ cups (3 sticks) butter or margarine	⅛ teaspoon oregano
¼ cup lemon juice	¼ teaspoon basil
¼ teaspoon cumin	⅛ teaspoon thyme
½ teaspoon garlic powder	Dash of cayenne pepper
½ teaspoon onion powder	3 dozen medium shrimp
	Mushrooms
	Bell peppers, cut up
	Onion wedges

Melt the butter. Combine the lemon juice, cumin, garlic powder, onion powder, oregano, basil, thyme and cayenne pepper in a bowl and mix well. Stir in the butter. Thread the shrimp, mushrooms, bell pepper pieces and onion wedges alternately onto 6 skewers; do not pack together. Brush with the butter mixture. Grill over medium coals for about 5 minutes or until shrimp is cooked through, turning several times and basting with the butter mixture. Yield: 6 servings.

*Keith, son of Ann Doucet, Laureate Zeta Gamma
Deer Park, Texas*

TOMATO BASIL LINGUINI

¼ cup olive oil	½ teaspoon oregano
2 medium onions	Salt and pepper to taste
1 garlic clove, minced	1 (4-ounce) can mushrooms, drained
2 (14-ounce) cans diced tomatoes with basil, garlic, oregano	1 pound linguini, cooked, drained, kept warm
2 tablespoons basil	

Heat the olive oil in a large heavy skillet over medium-low heat. Cook the onions in the hot oil until soft and transparent, about 10 minutes. Stir in the garlic and cook for 2 minutes longer. Stir in the tomatoes, basil and oregano. Bring to a boil over high heat. Cook until some of the liquid has evaporated, about 5 minutes. Add the salt and pepper. Add the pasta and toss to combine. Serve with Parmesan cheese. Yield: 4 to 6 servings.

*Chuck, husband of Monica Golson, Eta Delta
Trussville, Alabama*

Rance Prewett, son of Linda Humphrey, Xi Epsilon Upsilon, Medicine Lodge, Kansas, makes a Marinated Flank Steak that his family likes as well as Prime Rib. He marinates a 3-pound flank steak in a mixture of 1¼ cups soy sauce, 6 tablespoons honey, 2 tablespoons white vinegar, 1½ teaspoons each garlic powder and ginger, ¾ cup peanut oil, and a sliced green onion for 24 hours. Place on a very hot grill for 3 to 4 minutes on each side and slice thinly across the grain.

❖ PEPPERY PORTOBELLOS WITH PASTA

1 pound portobello mushrooms	¼ teaspoon crushed red pepper flakes
12 ounces fettucine	1 (15-ounce) can crushed tomatoes
¼ cup olive oil	1 cup chicken or vegetable broth
1 teaspoon salt	8 ounces asparagus or green beans
1 teaspoon black pepper	
1 tablespoon minced garlic	

Remove the stems from the portobellos and slice thinly. Bring a large covered kettle of water to a boil. Cook the pasta for about 10 minutes or until tender; drain. Heat half the olive oil in a large skillet over high heat. Add the mushrooms, salt and pepper and sauté for 5 minutes. Remove the mushrooms from the skillet; cover and keep warm. Add the remaining 2 tablespoons olive oil to the same skillet over medium heat. Add the garlic and red pepper flakes. Cook until garlic is golden brown. Add the undrained tomatoes and the chicken broth. Bring to a boil; reduce heat. Add the asparagus. Simmer for about 3 minutes. Stir in the mushrooms. Serve over the pasta. Yield: 6 servings.

*Lee, husband of Mary Beth Peters, Preceptor Gamma Xi
Gardner, Kansas*

TORTELLINI PRIMAVERA

½ cup (1 stick) butter	1 (4-ounce) can sliced mushrooms, drained
¾ cup grated Parmesan cheese	4 ounces thinly sliced deli ham, julienned
1½ cups half-and-half	½ teaspoon garlic powder
8 ounces frozen cheese tortellini	
8 ounces frozen peas	

Melt the butter in a medium saucepan over low heat. Stir in the cheese and half-and-half. Cook until thickened, stirring frequently. Prepare the tortellini using the package directions. Microwave the peas using the package directions. Stir the peas, mushrooms, ham and garlic powder into the cheese sauce. Cook until heated through. Place the drained tortellini on a serving platter. Pour the sauce over the tortellini. Serve immediately. Yield: 4 servings.

*Doug, husband of Sheila Range Lueking, Chi Sigma
Centralia, Illinois*

Brad, husband of Beverly Attebery, Xi Nu, Weiser, Idaho, combines 2 pounds chicken strips, a 12-ounce can of cola, and 1¼ cups hickory-flavored barbecue sauce in a Dutch oven and simmers for 1 hour to make his Sunday Night Barbecued Chicken.

BACHELOR'S SUPPER

1 pound sliced bacon,
cut into inch-long
pieces
5 large potatoes,
coarsely chopped
1 large onion, coarsely
chopped

1 (6-ounce) can sliced
mushrooms
Salt and pepper to taste
6 eggs, well beaten
(optional)

Cook the bacon in a large skillet until almost done. Remove the bacon from the skillet, leaving the drippings. Sauté the potatoes in the bacon drippings for about 5 minutes, coating well. Add the onion and sauté for 5 minutes longer. Return the bacon to the skillet and cook until potatoes and onion are tender and bacon is well cooked. Stir in the mushrooms, salt and pepper. Cook until heated through. Pour in the eggs and cook until scrambled if you want an additional food item. Yield: 4 large servings.

Jim, husband of Susan Brenner, Xi Gamma
Anchorage, Alaska

SWISS CORN OMELET

My husband Gerald can have this omelet ready from start to finish in 15 to 18 minutes. I love it when he prepares it for guests, because I always "flunk" omelets!

6 eggs
1 (8-ounce) can cream-
style corn
1/2 teaspoon tarragon
Salt and pepper to taste
2 teaspoons butter

1 medium tomato,
seeded, chopped
3/4 cup shredded Swiss
cheese
1 teaspoon chopped
fresh parsley

Whisk the eggs in a large bowl. Add the corn, tarragon, salt and pepper and beat to combine. Heat the butter in a 10- to 12-inch slope-sided skillet or omelet pan over medium heat, or spray the hot skillet with nonstick cooking spray. Pour in the egg mixture. Cook without stirring, but lifting the edges occasionally to allow uncooked egg mixture to flow to the bottom of the skillet; cook for 4 to 5 minutes or until the egg mixture is set but still moist. Spoon the tomato over half the omelet. Sprinkle with the cheese. Fold the omelet over with a spatula. Remove to a serving platter. Sprinkle with the parsley and serve immediately. Yield: 3 to 4 servings.

Gerald, husband of Hazel I. Ivey, Beta Epsilon Omicron
Brackettville, Texas

BAUNA CAUDA (VEGETABLE FONDUE)

This dish is a Christmas Eve tradition that was passed down through Italian generations. Your appetite for it will grow every time you have it!

1/3 cup vegetable oil
3 garlic cloves
2/3 cup (11/3 sticks) butter
1 (2-ounce) can
anchovies
1 head cabbage

3 green bell peppers
1 pound mushrooms
1 rib celery
1 small head
cauliflower, broken
into small florets

Heat the oil to 375 degrees in an electric frying pan. Cook the garlic in the hot oil for 1 minute. Add the butter and undrained anchovies and stir until butter is melted to make a sauce. Cut the cabbage, bell peppers, mushrooms and celery into bite-size pieces. Cook the vegetables, including the cauliflower, in the hot sauce in batches. Serve small portions in individual dishes with good French bread or other fresh bread. Yield: 4 to 6 servings.

Lou, husband of Mary Lou Girodo, Rho Master
Trinidad, Colorado

SAVORY CORN AND LIMAS

2 tablespoons butter
2 ribs celery, chopped
1 small onion, thinly
sliced
1 garlic clove, minced
2 cups fresh corn kernels
1 cup frozen lima beans
2 tablespoons chopped
parsley

1 tablespoon seasoned
rice vinegar
1/4 teaspoon salt
1/4 teaspoon coarse black
pepper
1 medium tomato,
chopped

Melt the butter in a 12-inch skillet over medium-low heat. Add the celery, onion and garlic. Cook for 10 minutes, stirring frequently. Add the corn, lima beans, parsley, vinegar, salt and pepper. Sauté for 5 minutes or until heated through. Stir in the tomatoes. Remove from heat. Serve hot or warm. Yield: 6 servings.

Jim, son of Faye Westphal, Laureate Alpha Phi
Dubuque, Iowa

Bruce, husband of Karen Berning, Preceptor Eta Theta, Robertsville, Missouri, melts 1/4 cup butter in a saucepan, blends in 1/4 cup flour, stirs in 2 cups milk and a dash of Worcestershire sauce, and cooks until thickened, stirring constantly. Add 10 chopped hard-cooked eggs, heat to serving temperature, and serve on toast for Creamed Eggs on Toast.

SEASONED EGGPLANT

1 small eggplant, peeled, chopped	Dash of Everglades Fire seasoning or cayenne pepper
1 medium onion, halved, thinly sliced	Garlic salt to taste
2 tablespoons olive oil	2 tablespoons grated Parmesan cheese
4 to 6 small to medium tomatoes, peeled, chopped	1 to 2 cups shredded Monterey Jack or mozzarella cheese
1 teaspoon Italian seasoning	

Sauté the eggplant and onion in the olive oil in a large skillet until eggplant is tender and onion is translucent. Stir in the tomatoes, Italian seasoning, Everglades Fire seasoning and garlic salt. Simmer, covered, for about 5 to 10 minutes or until most of liquid is gone. Add the Parmesan cheese at the end of the cooking time. Remove the vegetables to a microwave-safe serving dish. Sprinkle with the Monterey Jack cheese. Microwave on High for 30 seconds if the cheese does not melt completely. Serve with nacho chips, or serve as a sauce over rice or pasta. Yield: 2 to 3 cups.

Christopher, son of Wanda Walters, Omega Lambda
Wellborn, Florida

STUFFED ONION ROUNDS

Serve with a green salad and grilled fresh corn.

1 pound lean ground beef	1/2 teaspoon dry mustard
2 tablespoons minced onion	1 tablespoon ketchup
1 teaspoon minced garlic	2 tablespoons seasoned dry bread crumbs
2 tablespoons minced parsley	1 teaspoon Worcestershire sauce
1 egg	3 large Spanish onions, peeled, cut into 1 1/4-inch rings

Combine the ground beef, onion, garlic, parsley, egg, mustard, ketchup, bread crumbs and Worcestershire sauce in a bowl and mix well. Shape the mixture into twelve 2-inch meatballs. Cut a slit down the side of each onion ring. Wrap an onion ring around each meatball. Secure with wooden picks, or thread several onto a skewer. Grill over hot coals or on an electric grill for 10 minutes or until to desired doneness, turning occasionally. Yield: 2 to 3 servings.

Canyoun Williams, dance partner of Lorraine L. Kirkpatrick
Preceptor Gamma Delta
Barstow, California

GARLIC POTATOES

2 pounds red potatoes	2 teaspoons dillweed
1/3 cup (2/3 stick) butter, melted	1 teaspoon seasoned salt
1/4 cup crushed garlic	1 teaspoon paprika

Wash the unpeeled potatoes. Cut into 1-inch cubes. Combine the potatoes and a mixture of the butter and garlic in a bowl and mix well. Spread the mixture in a 9×9-inch baking dish. Sprinkle the dillweed, seasoned salt and paprika over the potatoes and stir until well coated. Bake at 425 degrees for 45 to 60 minutes or until golden brown, stirring every 10 to 15 minutes. Yield: 3 to 4 servings.

Doug, son of Eileen Sanders, Preceptor Iota
Eugene, Oregon

BROILED ROMAS

1 tablespoon seasoned rice vinegar	8 firm Roma tomatoes, halved
1 tablespoon olive oil	1/2 cup grated Parmesan cheese
1 teaspoon sweet basil	Chopped fresh parsley
1 teaspoon cumin	
Salt to taste	
Chili powder to taste (optional)	

Combine the vinegar, olive oil, basil, cumin, salt and chili powder in a bowl and mix well to make the marinade. Stir in the tomatoes. Marinate the tomatoes, covered, in the refrigerator for 1 hour, turning often. Arrange the tomatoes cut side up in a large shallow baking dish. Sprinkle with the Parmesan cheese. Bake in a preheated 350-degree oven for 10 minutes. Broil for about 3 to 5 minutes or just until Parmesan cheese is slightly toasted. Sprinkle with parsley and serve immediately. Yield: 4 to 6 servings.

Neil, husband of Marilee H. King, Xi Mu
Jerome, Idaho

Pat, husband of Mary Lou McGee, Beta Master, Springfield, Massachusetts, belongs to a gourmet group whose male members developed a menu using alcohol in every course. Drunken Carrots is a specialty. Combine 1/4 cup each butter, packed brown sugar, and apricot brandy in a saucepan and bring to a boil. Steam a 10-ounce package of baby carrots to desired tenderness, drain well, and top with the brandy sauce.

PICKLED GARLIC

2 cups garlic cloves
    (6 bulbs)
1¼ cups white vinegar
¼ cup sugar
½ teaspoon whole black
    peppercorns
½ teaspoon mustard
    seeds, or 1 teaspoon
    picking spice
1 bay leaf
½ teaspoon coarse
    picking salt

Peel the garlic cloves; cut any extra-thick cloves in half lengthwise. Combine the vinegar, sugar, peppercorns, mustard seeds, bay leaf and pickling salt in a medium saucepan over high heat. Bring to a boil, stirring until the sugar dissolves. Stir in the garlic. Return to a boil. Cook, uncovered, for 1 minute, stirring occasionally. Remove from heat. Pour the garlic mixture into a sterilized 2-cup jar with a canning lid. Chill, sealed, in the refrigerator for 24 hours or longer. Keep refrigerated. Yield: 2 cups.

*Three men in the family of a dear friend of Lynn Lineham
Xi Gamma Sigma
Brentwood Bay, British Columbia, Canada*

OLD-FASHIONED CORN BREAD DRESSING

When I prepare the skillets of corn bread I use 2 cups of cornmeal, 1 cup of flour, and enough buttermilk to moisten the batter.

2 skillets of corn bread
1 small loaf white bread
1 rib celery, cut into
    pieces
2 medium onions, cut
    into pieces
5 (15-ounce) cans
    chicken broth
8 eggs
3 to 4 tablespoons sage
Salt and pepper to taste
1 cooked turkey breast,
    cooled

Break apart the cooled corn bread and grate it into a large roasting pan. Grate the white bread into the pan and mix well. Purée the celery and onions in a blender or food processor. Pour the celery purée over the bread mixture. Beat the chicken broth into the bread mixture with an electric mixer. Add the eggs 1 at a time, beating well after each addition. Beat in the sage, salt, pepper and any drippings from roasting the turkey breast. The mixture should be smooth and pourable; add water if necessary. Pull and cut small pieces from the turkey breast. Fold into the bread mixture. Bake, covered, at 350 degrees for 45 to 50 minutes. Bake, uncovered, for 15 to 20 minutes longer or until browned and cooked through. Yield: 24 servings.

*Jerry, husband of Becky S. Baggett, Xi Delta Omicron
Smyrna, Tennessee*

ORANGE BREAD

1 cup orange juice
¼ cup hot water
1 tablespoon butter
1 egg
¼ cup sugar
2 tablespoons grated
    orange zest
3 cups bread flour
2 teaspoons yeast

Add precise amounts of the orange juice, water, butter, egg, sugar, orange zest, bread flour and yeast to a bread machine pan in the order listed. Set the machine on the basic white bread cycle with medium to normal color setting. Yield: 1 (1½-pound) loaf.

*Dave, husband of Joyce Bladorn, Laureate Beta Upsilon
Chico, California*

MORNING GLORY MUFFINS

2 cups flour
1¼ cups sugar
2 teaspoons baking soda
2 teaspoons cinnamon
½ teaspoon salt
2 cups grated carrots
½ cup raisins
½ cup crushed walnuts
½ cup rolled oats
1 apple, peeled, grated
3 eggs
1 cup vegetable oil
2 teaspoons vanilla
    extract

Mix the flour, sugar, baking soda, cinnamon and salt in a large bowl. Stir in the next 5 ingredients. Beat the eggs in a medium bowl; add the oil and vanilla and beat for 2 minutes longer. Stir into the flour mixture just until moistened. Spoon into well-greased or paper-lined muffin cups. Bake at 350 degrees for 20 minutes. Yield: 14 large or 18 small muffins.

*Gregory, husband of Laura Lee Flett, Alpha
Winnipeg, Manitoba, Canada*

GERMAN NEW YEAR'S CAKES

1½ cups sugar
1 cup dark corn syrup
¾ tablespoon anise seed
1 cup raisins
1 cup hot water
½ teaspoon baking soda
½ teaspoon salt
2 eggs
3 cups rye flour
3 cups flour
1 pound sliced bacon,
    crisp-cooked

Combine the first 5 ingredients in a bowl and stir until sugar is dissolved. Let cool. Stir in the baking soda and salt. Stir in the eggs. Add the flours ½ cup at a time, stirring well. Place a bacon slice on a griddle preheated to 350 degrees. Ladle ½ cup of the batter over the bacon to make a circle. Place a second bacon slice over the circle of batter. Cook until brown on both sides, turning once as for a pancake. Serve warm or cold. Yield: 15 to 20 cakes.

*Glenn, husband of Jan Meints, Laureate Alpha Omega
Belmond, Iowa*

SAUSAGE BREAD

2 (1-pound) loaves
  frozen bread dough,
  thawed
1 pound Italian sausage
2 eggs
2 cups shredded
  mozzarella cheese
1/4 cup grated Parmesan
  cheese
1/2 teaspoon garlic
  powder

Flatten each loaf of bread dough to 1/2-inch thickness. Brown the sausage in a skillet until cooked through, stirring until crumbly; drain. Let cool. Combine the sausage, eggs, cheeses and garlic powder in a bowl and mix well. Spread half the sausage mixture over each rectangle of bread dough; press into the dough. Fold a third of the dough to the center. Fold over the remaining third and pinch to seal. Place on a well-greased baking sheet. Bake at 375 degrees for 20 to 30 minutes or until golden. Slice and serve.
Yield: 12 to 24 servings.

James Sr., husband of Esther Adkins, Preceptor Gamma Sigma
Hartford City, Indiana

BELGIAN WAFFLES

Well worth the effort to make them, these are the best waffles ever, especially for a romantic breakfast in bed.

2 teaspoons fast-rising
  yeast
2 cups lukewarm milk
4 eggs, separated
1/2 cup melted butter
1 teaspoon vanilla
  extract
2 1/2 cups flour
1/2 teaspoon salt
1 tablespoon sugar
Sliced fresh strawberries
  or peaches
Whipped cream

Sprinkle the yeast over the milk in a bowl. Beat the egg yolks and stir into the yeast mixture. Stir in the butter and vanilla. Combine the flour, salt and sugar and mix well. Stir the dry ingredients into the yeast mixture. Beat the egg whites in a bowl until stiff peaks form. Fold carefully into the batter. Let stand, covered, in a warm place for 45 minutes or until doubled in bulk. Pour 3/4 to 1 cup batter onto a hot waffle iron. Bake until golden brown. Yield: 5 or 6 waffles.

Dave, husband of Cathy Janes, Alpha Omega
Port Alberni, British Columbia, Canada

Chuck, husband of Sally Goss, Preceptor Psi, Little Rock, Arkansas, cooks 1 1/2 cups sugar and 1/2 cup orange juice to the soft-ball stage, stirs in 3 cups pecan halves until cloudy, and separates the pecans on waxed paper to make Orange Pecans.

DECADENT CHOCOLATE CUPCAKES

7 1/2 cups flour
1/4 cup baking powder
2 teaspoons salt
2 cups sugar
1/2 cup baking cocoa
8 large eggs, lightly
  beaten
4 cups skim milk
1 cup melted margarine
4 cups semisweet
  chocolate chips
3 ounces cream cheese,
  softened
3 cups confectioners'
  sugar

Sift the flour, baking powder, salt, sugar and baking cocoa into a large bowl. Add a mixture of the eggs, milk and margarine to the dry ingredients, stirring just until moistened. Stir in the chocolate chips. Cream the cream cheese and confectioners' sugar in a mixing bowl until light and fluffy. Fill well-greased muffin cups 1/3 full with the cocoa mixture. Place 1/2 teaspoon of the cream cheese mixture over the center of each. Add more cocoa mixture until muffin cups are 2/3 full. Bake in the center of a 400-degree oven for 18 minutes. Cool in the pans for 20 minutes. Remove to a wire rack to cool completely.
Yield: 4 to 4 1/2 dozen.

Robert Erskine, significant other of Brenda Best
Preceptor Alpha Delta
Maple Ridge, British Columbia, Canada

JAM JAMS

1 cup shortening or
  margarine
1 cup packed brown
  sugar
6 tablespoons corn
  syrup
2 eggs, well beaten
1 teaspoon lemon or
  vanilla extract
3 1/2 cups (about) flour
2 teaspoons baking soda
Jam or dates

Cream the shortening and brown sugar in a mixing bowl until light and fluffy. Stir in the corn syrup and eggs. Add the vanilla. Combine the flour and baking soda in a separate bowl, then stir into the egg mixture. Chill, wrapped in plastic wrap, in the refrigerator for 2 to 3 hours, or longer if desired. Divide the chilled dough into 3 or 4 balls. Roll out flat, then use cookie cutters to cut into desired shapes. Arrange on a greased cookie sheet. Bake at 375 degrees for 6 to 8 minutes. Press a spoonful of jam or a piece of date into each while warm. Cool the cookies on the cookie sheet for 1 to 2 minutes and remove to wire racks to cool completely.
Yield: 4 dozen.

Al, husband of Charlotte M. Leader, Xi Master
Langley, British Columbia, Canada

KRUMKAKE

Do not use oil as a substitute for the margarine. Bake on an electric krumkake iron, which should be plugged into a 110- to 120-volt wall outlet and pre-heated for 7 to 8 minutes with grids closed.

4 eggs, lightly beaten
1 cup sugar
1/2 cup (1 stick) margarine, melted, cooled

1/2 teaspoon cardamom seed
1 1/2 cups flour
2 tablespoons cornstarch

Combine the eggs and sugar and beat lightly; do not overbeat. Add the margarine and cardamom. Sift the flour and cornstarch together; add to the egg mixture. Dough will be sticky enough to be dropped by teaspoonfuls onto a krumkake iron. Bake until golden brown. Gently remove from the iron; roll around cone roller and hold until cool. Cookies will retain cone shape. Serve plain or filled with whipped cream. Yield: 40 cookies.

*Jim, husband, and Jason, son of JeAnne Selby
Laureate Theta
Bismarck, North Dakota*

OATMEAL COOKIES

2 cups flour
2 teaspoons baking powder
1 teaspoon baking soda
1 teaspoon cinnamon
1 cup (2 sticks) butter, softened

1 1/2 cups sugar
1/2 teaspoon salt
2 eggs
2 cups broken-up pecans
1 cup raisins
2 cups rolled oats
6 tablespoons sweet milk

Sift together the first 4 ingredients and set aside. Cream the butter, sugar and salt in a mixing bowl until light and fluffy. Beat in the eggs. Stir in the pecans, raisins and rolled oats. Add the sifted dry ingredients and milk alternately, mixing well after each addition. Drop by tablespoonfuls 2 inches apart onto an ungreased cookie sheet. Bake at 350 degrees for 8 to 10 minutes or until edges begin to brown. Yield: 4 dozen.

*Don, husband of Carol Carpenter, Preceptor Theta Iota
Pampa, Texas*

David, husband of Becky Linn, Xi Delta Mu, Abilene, Kansas, makes Peanut Delights by melting 2 cups peanut butter chips with a can of sweetened condensed milk and 2 tablespoons margarine, stirring in 8 ounces miniature marshmallows, and pouring over half of a 24-ounce jar dry-roasted peanuts in a 9×13-inch dish, pressing the remaining peanuts on top and cutting into squares when cool.

A-BREAK-FOR-MOM COOKIES

When Mom needed a little down time or some time to work on a deadline, Dad often hustled us into the kitchen to bake cookies. We always laughed and enjoyed our cookie-baking time with him.

1 cup (2 sticks) butter, softened
1/2 cup sugar
1/2 cup packed light brown sugar
1 large egg
2 cups flour
1 teaspoon cream of tartar

1/2 teaspoon baking soda
1/4 teaspoon salt
1/2 cup rolled oats
1 cup crisp rice cereal
1/2 cup shredded coconut
1/2 cup chopped pecans
1 cup slivered almonds

Cream the butter and sugars in a large mixing bowl until light and fluffy. Add the egg and beat until well blended. Combine the flour, cream of tartar, baking soda, salt and oats in a bowl and mix well. Add the flour mixture to the butter mixture and mix well. Stir in the rice cereal, coconut, pecans and almonds. Drop by rounded tablespoonfuls about 2 inches apart onto ungreased cookie sheets. Bake in a preheated 350-degree oven for 10 to 12 minutes or until lightly browned. Cool on the cookie sheet for 1 to 2 minutes and remove to a wire rack to cool completely. Store in an airtight container. Yield: 4 dozen.

*Robert, father of Sarah Carter
Paragould, Arkansas*

SCOTCHEROOS

1 cup corn syrup
1 1/2 cups crunchy peanut butter
1 cup sugar
6 cups crisp rice cereal

2 cups semisweet chocolate chips
2 cups butterscotch chips

Combine the syrup, peanut butter and sugar in a large saucepan over medium heat. Bring to a boil, stirring frequently until the sugar dissolves completely and the mixture is smooth and well blended. Remove from heat. Stir in the rice cereal. Pour over a greased cookie sheet. Pat gently to make an even layer. Melt the chocolate chips and butterscotch chips in a saucepan over low heat or in the microwave, stirring frequently. Spread the melted chocolate mixture evenly over the rice cereal layer. Let stand in the refrigerator for 20 to 30 minutes or until firm. Cut into squares. Yield: 20 to 30 squares.

*Reeves, husband, and Chuck, Harry and Rick, sons of
Neva C. Taylor, Preceptor Alpha Epsilon
Keyser, West Virginia*

GRAPE PIE

My mother baked fabulous cookies. When I asked for a recipe, the answer was always "whatever was in the refrigerator at the time." When I heard of a pie contest, I looked in the refrigerator and pantry. The result was this recipe . . . which I have been told is fabulous.

24 ounces graham
   crackers, crushed
6 ounces hazelnuts,
   ground
1/2 cup (1 stick) butter,
   melted
1/4 teaspoon vanilla
   extract
1/3 cup beer
1/3 cup packed brown
   sugar
2 cups seedless mixed
   grapes

1/2 cup raisins
8 ounces cream cheese,
   softened
1 cup sour cream
1 cup packed brown
   sugar
2 cups whipping cream
1/4 cup sugar
1 teaspoon vanilla
   extract

Process the graham crackers and hazelnuts to a semi-fine texture in a blender. Stir in the butter, 1/4 teaspoon vanilla, beer and 1/3 cup brown sugar to make a workable dough. Press thickly into the bottoms and up the sides of two 8-inch pie plates. Bake at 375 degrees for about 10 minutes. Let cool. Chop the grapes, reserving 10 whole grapes. Combine the chopped grapes and raisins in a large bowl and mix well. Combine the cream cheese, sour cream and brown sugar in a blender and process until smooth. Fold into the grape mixture. Spread into the cooled graham cracker crust. Whip the cream with 1/4 cup sugar and 1 teaspoon vanilla until stiff peaks form. Spread evenly over the pies. Top with the reserved grapes. Chill, covered, in the refrigerator for 1 to 2 hours. Serve with ice cream. Yield: 10 to 12 servings.

*Russ, husband of Pat Crawford, Preceptor Psi
Battle Ground, Washington*

RHUBARB CUSTARD PIE

Enough rhubarb to fill
   pie shell when cut up
1 unbaked (9-inch) pie
   shell
2 eggs

2 tablespoons flour
Pinch of salt
1 1/2 cups sugar
1 tablespoon butter,
   softened

Wash the rhubarb and cut into 1-inch pieces. Fill the pie shell with the rhubarb. Combine the eggs, flour, salt, sugar and butter in a mixing bowl and beat until smooth. Pour evenly over the rhubarb. Bake at 400 degrees for 1 hour. Yield: 6 to 8 servings.

*Dave, son of Muriel Mullins, Eta Zeta
Simcoe, Ontario, Canada*

BAKED CHOCOLATE PUDDING CAKE

1 cup flour
3/4 cup sugar
2 teaspoons baking
   powder
1/4 teaspoon salt
2 tablespoons baking
   cocoa
1/2 cup milk
2 tablespoons melted
   butter

1 teaspoon vanilla
   extract
1/2 cup chopped pecans
   or walnuts
1/2 cup sugar
1/2 cup packed brown
   sugar
1/4 cup (heaping) baking
   cocoa
1 cup water

Sift the first 5 ingredients into a bowl. Add the milk, butter and vanilla; mix well. Stir in the pecans. Pour into an 8×8-inch baking dish sprayed with nonstick cooking spray. Sprinkle with a mixture of 1/2 cup sugar, 1/2 cup brown sugar and the 1/4 cup baking cocoa. Drizzle the water over the top. Bake at 350 degrees for 15 to 20 minutes or until cake tests done. Yield: 6 servings.

*John, husband of Sheila Turner, Xi Gamma Lambda
Ogallala, Nebraska*

CHOCOLATE HAZELNUT
BREAD PUDDING

To toast hazelnuts, spread in a baking pan and bake at 350 degrees for 10 to 12 minutes or until they are fragrant and the papery skins begin to flake. Cool, then rub between fingers to remove the skins.

6 slices firm white bread
1 cup heavy cream
2 cups 1% milk
1 cup semisweet
   chocolate chips
2 tablespoons sugar

4 teaspoons instant
   coffee granules
3 large eggs
1/2 cup hazelnuts,
   toasted, chopped

Cut each bread slice into 4 triangles. Arrange in a greased 2-quart shallow baking dish, triangles overlapping. Bring the cream and half the milk to a simmer in a 1-quart saucepan over medium heat; remove from heat. Stir in the chocolate chips, sugar and coffee granules. Let stand for 2 minutes. Whisk until blended. Whisk the remaining 1 cup milk and the eggs in a large bowl until well blended. Whisk in the chocolate mixture. Pour evenly over the bread. Sprinkle with hazelnuts. Place the baking dish in a water bath. Bake at 350 degrees for 55 to 60 minutes or until a knife inserted near the center comes out clean. Remove the dish to a wire rack. Serve warm, cold or at room temperature. Yield: 12 servings.

*Johnnie, husband of Connie E. Jennings
Xi Alpha Gamma Zeta
Baytown, Texas*

Metric Equivalents

A*lthough the United States has opted to postpone converting to metric measurements, most other countries, including England and Canada, use the metric system. The following chart provides convenient approximate equivalents for allowing use of regular kitchen measures when cooking from foreign recipes.*

Volume

These metric measures are approximate benchmarks for purposes of home food preparation.
1 milliliter = 1 cubic centimeter = 1 gram

Liquid	Dry
1 teaspoon = 5 milliliters	1 quart = 1 liter
1 tablespoon = 15 milliliters	1 ounce = 30 grams
1 fluid ounce = 30 milliliters	1 pound = 450 grams
1 cup = 250 milliliters	2.2 pounds = 1 kilogram
1 pint = 500 milliliters	

Weight	Length
1 ounce = 28 grams	1 inch = $2^1/_2$ centimeters
1 pound = 450 grams	$^1/_{16}$ inch = 1 millimeter

Formulas Using Conversion Factors

When approximate conversions are not accurate enough, use these formulas to convert measures from one system to another.

Measurements	Formulas
ounces to grams:	# ounces x 28.3 = # grams
grams to ounces:	# grams x 0.035 = # ounces
pounds to grams:	# pounds x 453.6 = # grams
pounds to kilograms	# pounds x 0.45 = # kilograms
ounces to milliliters:	# ounces x 30 = # milliliters
cups to liters:	# cups x 0.24 = # liters
inches to centimeters	# inches x 2.54 = # centimeters
centimeters to inches:	# centimeters x 0.39 = # inches

Approximate Weight to Volume

*Some ingredients which we commonly measure by volume are measured
by weight in foreign recipes. Here are a few examples for easy reference.*

flour, all-purpose, unsifted	1 pound = 450 grams = $3^1/_2$ cups
flour, all-purpose, sifted	1 pound = 450 grams = 4 cups
sugar, granulated	1 pound = 450 grams = 2 cups
sugar, brown, packed	1 pound = 450 grams = $2^1/_4$ cups
sugar, confectioners'	1 pound = 450 grams = 4 cups
sugar, confectioners', sifted	1 pound = 450 grams = $4^1/_2$ cups
butter	1 pound = 450 grams = 2 cups

Temperature

*Remember that foreign recipes frequently express temperatures
in Centigrade rather than Fahrenheit.*

Temperatures	Fahrenheit	Centigrade
room temperature	68°	20°
water boils	212°	100°
baking temperature	350°	177°
baking temperature	375°	190.5°
baking temperature	400°	204.4°
baking temperature	425°	218.3°
baking temperature	450°	232°

Use the following formulas when temperature conversions are necessary.

Centigrade degrees x $9/_5$ + 32 = Fahrenheit degrees
Fahrenheit degrees - 32 x $5/_9$ = Centigrade degrees

American Measurement Equivalents

1 tablespoon = 3 teaspoons	12 tablespoons = $3/_4$ cup
2 tablespoons = 1 ounce	16 tablespoons = 1 cup
4 tablespoons = $1/_4$ cup	1 cup = 8 ounces
5 tablespoons + 1 teaspoon	2 cups = 1 pint
= $1/_3$ cup	4 cups = 1 quart
8 tablespoons = $1/_2$ cup	4 quarts = 1 gallon

Merit Winners

THANKSGIVING
First Place
Toler, Teresa L., page 112
Second Place
Kellerman, Natasha,
page 115
Third Place
Pidd, Jo An, page 100
Honorable Mention
Allred, Jan, page 101
Ayers, Eileen, page 112
Beck, Marie, page 109
Bertsch, Marsha, page 116
Bottyan, Valerie, page 99
Bouvier, Karen A., page 102
Cape, Carol, page 106
Jazdzewski, Sandy, page 102
Krause, Phyllis M., page 103
Mathis, Cindy, page 114
McLoud, Mary, page 105
Nygren, Connie R.,
page 108
Patton, Dolores, page 103
Reed, Virginia, page 101
Rohlfs, Nina, page 100
Stroh, Linda L., page 106
Tucker, Linda M., page 111
Umbriac, Marie, page 104

CHRISTMAS
First Place
Kelarek, Margie, page 125
Second Place
Simpson, Shirley, page 126
Third Place
Dawson, Katrina, page 146
Honorable Mention
Bleick, Pat, page 129
Bogan, Mary, page 137
Bradshaw, Karen, page 123
Brewer, Robyn, page 130
Brushaber, Lucy K.,
page 126
Chartvant, Jackie, page 128
Devillier, Denise, page 138
Dull, Beverly Christian,
page 137
Easingwood, Joy, page 144
Franklin, Sandy, page 140
Gillmore, Patricia A.,
page 135

Henry, Dianne, page 134
Johnson-Clark, Barbara,
page 124
Kubic, Marian, page 128
Laser, Alma D., page 129
Lee, Sonya, page 123
Luus, Donna, page 128
McGuire, Jean, page 126
Missildine, Liz, page 121
Rosequist, Greer, page 131
Tubbs, Cynthia, page 133
Wallace, Eugenia, page 146
Weems, Gladys, page 122
Welsh, Cecelia, page 121
Wilburn, Margaret,
page 124

SPECIAL OCCASIONS
First Place
McCoy, Merline, page 150
Second Place
Raudabush, Carolyn,
page 176
Third Place
Casson, Karen, page 156
Honorable Mention
Ashworth, Ardith Eleanore,
page 172
Bedford, George Anne,
page 166
Berry, Carol, page 187
Burd, Joni L., page 151
Carlson, Heather, page 170
Chase, Janis, page 157
Clark, Georgia R., page 158
Coe, Jan, page 157
Cooper, Roxanna E., page 166
DiBeneditto, Janice, page 165
Harris, Julia, page 171
Herczeg, Mae Belle, page 184
Hill, Mary Greco, page 173
Hindman, Oleta B.,
page 189
Holt, Sandy, page 153
Horn, Sharon, page 152
Jackson, Cathy, page 186
Johnston, Kay, page 172
Kubanda, Carol, page 178
Lewis, Linda, page 153
Lucas, Ann B., page 187
Mawer, Anita J., page 152

Meulemans, Pearl, page 173
Milliron, Heather, page 169
Ravenhorst, Geri, page 192
Richardt, Jean, page 155
Ritchie, Marion, page 154
Rivard, Suzanne, page 178
Salles, Maggie, page 181
Sample, Ann, page 176
Selent, Gail J., page 168
Spangenberg, Julie,
page 160
Tetz, Noreen, page 189
Wagner, Phyllis, page 178

MEN'S RECIPES FOR ALL OCCASIONS
First Place
Steve, husband of Paulette
Willett, page 198
Second Place
Jerome, husband of
K. K. LeBlanc, page 203
Third Place
Lee, husband of Mary Beth
Peters, page 205
Honorable Mention
Larry, husband of Judy Date,
page 199
Tem, husband of Anne Fugit,
page 201
Matt, son of Linda
Greenwood, page 198
Gerald, husband of Hazel I.
Ivey, page 206
Dave, husband of Cathy
Janes, page 209
Canyoun Williams, dance
partner of Lorraine L.
Kirkpatrick, page 207
Charles, husband of Janice C.
Lewis, page 196
Corey, husband of Kelly
Miller, page 202
Bill, husband of Gail Giles,
page 204
John, husband of Penny
Porter, page 197
Doug, husband of Patti
Rogers, page 195
Christopher, son of Wanda
Walters, page 207

Index

Beta Sigma Phi Cookbooks

available from *Favorite Recipes® Press* are chock-full of
home-tested recipes from Beta Sigma Phi members that earn you
the best compliment of all… "More Please!"

Every cookbook includes:

☆ delicious, family-
   pleasing recipes

☆ lay-flat binding

☆ wipe-clean color covers

☆ easy-to-read format

☆ comprehensive index

☆ almost 1,000 recipes

To place your order,
call our toll-free number
1-800-251-1520
or clip and mail the
convenient form below.

BETA SIGMA PHI COOKBOOKS	Item #	Qty.	U.S. Retail Price	Canadian Retail Price	Total
Simple Celebrations	68255		$9.95	$12.95	
The Millennium Cookbook	70150		$9.95	$12.95	
Shipping and Handling		1	$1.95	$ 2.95	
TOTAL AMOUNT					

☐ Payment Enclosed
☐ Please Charge My   ☐ American Express
                       ☐ Discover
                       ☐ MasterCard
                       ☐ Visa

Canadian orders: checks or money orders only

Signature _____

Account Number _____

Name _____

Address _____

City _____ State ____ Zip _____

No COD orders please.

Call our toll-free number for
faster ordering.

Please allow 30 days for delivery.

Mail completed order form to:

Favorite Recipes® Press
P.O. Box 305147
Nashville, TN 37230